Understanding Autobiographical

The field of autobiographical memory has made dramatic advances since the first collection of papers in the area was published in 1986. Now, over 25 years on, this book reviews and integrates the many theories, perspectives, and approaches that have evolved over the last decades. A truly eminent collection of editors and contributors appraise the basic neural systems of autobiographical memory; its underlying cognitive structures and retrieval processes; how it develops in infancy and childhood, and then breaks down in aging; its social and cultural aspects; and its relation to personality and the self.

Autobiographical memory has demonstrated a strong ability to establish clear empirical generalizations, and has shown its practical relevance by deepening our understanding of several clinical disorders – as well as the induction of false memories in the legal system. It has also become an important topic for brain studies, and helped to enlarge our general understanding of the brain.

Dorthe Berntsen is a Professor in the Department of Psychology and Behavioural Sciences at Aarhus University, where she was awarded a Center of Excellence grant from the Danish National Research Foundation to establish the Center on Autobiographical Memory Research. She is the author of *Involuntary Autobiographical Memories: An Introduction to the Unbidden Past* (Cambridge, 2009).

David C. Rubin is Juanita M. Kreps Professor of Psychology and Neuroscience at Duke University and is affiliated with the Center on Autobiographical Memory at Aarhus University. He is a leading researcher in the field of autobiographical memory and the editor of *Remembering Our Past: Studies in Autobiographical Memory* (Cambridge, 1996) and *Autobiographical Memory* (Cambridge, 1986), among other books.

Understanding Autobiographical Memory

Theories and approaches

Edited by

Dorthe Berntsen

and

David C. Rubin

CAMBRIDGE
UNIVERSITY PRESS

CAMBRIDGE UNIVERSITY PRESS
Cambridge, New York, Melbourne, Madrid, Cape Town,
Singapore, São Paulo, Delhi, Mexico City

Cambridge University Press
The Edinburgh Building, Cambridge CB2 8RU, UK

Published in the United States of America by
Cambridge University Press, New York

www.cambridge.org
Information on this title: www.cambridge.org/9780521189330

First published 2012

A catalogue record for this publication is available from the British Library

Library of Congress Cataloguing in Publication data
Understanding autobiographical memory : theories and approaches / Dorthe
Berntsen, David C. Rubin, eds.
    p.   cm
ISBN 978-0-521-18933-0 (pbk.)
1. Autobiographical memory.   I. Berntsen, Dorthe, 1962–
II. Rubin, David C.
BF378.A87U53 2012
153.1'3–dc23
                                                          2012013330
ISBN 978-1-107-00730-7 Hardback
ISBN 978-0-521-18933-0 Paperback

In memory of Ulric Neisser

Contents

Figures

Tables

Contributors

ALAN BADDELEY,
University of York, UK

PATRICIA J. BAUER,
Emory University, USA

DORTHE BERNTSEN,
Aarhus University, Denmark

CARISSA L. BROADBRIDGE,
Wayne State University, USA

NORMAN R. BROWN,
University of Alberta, Canada

FREDRICK G. CONRAD,
University of Michigan, USA

MARTIN A. CONWAY,
City University, London, UK

ALEXANDRU CUC,
Nova Southeastern University, USA

ARNAUD D'ARGEMBEAU,
University of Liège, Belgium

MERLIN DONALD,
Queen's University, Canada

JOSEPH M. FITZGERALD,
Wayne State University, USA

ROBYN FIVUSH,
Emory University, USA

TILMANN HABERMAS,
Frankfurt University, Germany

TIA G. B. HANSEN,
Aalborg University, Denmark

WILLIAM HIRST,
New School for Social Research, USA

LAURA JOBSON,
Medical Research Council Cognition and Brain Sciences Unit,
Cambridge, and University of East Anglia, UK

KIE J. KUWABARA,
University of New Hampshire, USA

PETER J. LEE,
University of Alberta, Canada

MORRIS MOSCOVITCH,
University of Toronto and Rotman Research Institute, Canada

DAVID B. PILLEMER,
University of New Hampshire, USA

DAVID C. RUBIN,
Duke University, USA

PEGGY L. ST. JACQUES,
Harvard University, USA

SARAH A. VANDERVEEN,
University of Calgary, Canada

DANA WOHL,
New School for Social Research, USA

Preface

The chapters included in this book were given as invited addresses at the conference "Theoretical Perspectives on Autobiographical Memory," which was held in Aarhus, Denmark, June 13–15, 2010. It was the first open-call conference dedicated to the study of autobiographical memories. The conference involved more than 150 participants from more than 15 different countries, testifying to the internal scope of the field. The conference brought together some of the most outstanding researchers on autobiographical memory. Each of them presented their key findings and particular theoretical perspective on the field. The conference marked the opening of the Center on Autobiographical Memory Research (CON AMORE) at Aarhus University funded by the Danish National Research Foundation's Center of Excellence Program.

Acknowledgements

The editors thank the Danish National Research Foundation for funding. We also thank center administrator Jette Odgaard Villemoes and Cambridge University Press editors Hetty Marx and Josephine Lane for valuable assistance.

1 Introduction

Dorthe Berntsen and David C. Rubin

The ability to remember personal events is at the heart of what defines an individual as a person with obligations, roles, and commitments in a given society. It enables us to draw lessons from our past and plan our personal future. It helps us to orientate and participate in complex social communities. Autobiographical memory is therefore crucial for a sense of identity, continuity, and direction in life.

In spite of this significance, concerted and systematic psychological research on autobiographical memory only began to emerge in the 1980s, roughly a hundred years after the publication of the first book launching experimental research on memory (Ebbinghaus, 1885/1964). Until then, experimental memory research had been focused on testing learning and memory for verbal material.

Research on autobiographical memory broke away from the existing field of memory research by introducing new methodological, theoretical, and philosophical challenges (e.g., Brewer, 1986; Crovitz and Schiffman, 1974; Neisser, 1982). For that reason, autobiographical memory researchers often had difficulty in getting their work published in existing psychology journals. Instead, edited books became an important medium for scientific exchange during the first decade.

The first edited book on autobiographical memory was published in the middle of the 1980s (Rubin, 1986). At this time, the autobiographical memory field was small and exotic. A total of roughly 20 journal articles had been published on this topic (according to a literature search using *autobiographical memory* as a keyword in the database PsycINFO, July 2011). A decade later, when a sequel was published (Rubin, 1996), there were about 200 published journal articles. In 2011, when this introduction was written, a similar literature search revealed a total of 1,900 published journal articles (see Figure 1.1). Thus, about 25 years after the publication of the first book launching research on autobiographical memory, the field has grown dramatically.

A number of factors have contributed to this success. One is the introduction of two important journals. The journal *Applied Cognitive*

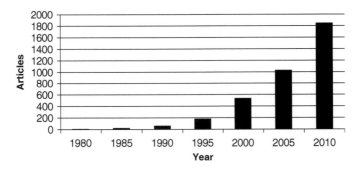

Figure 1.1. Accumulative number of peer reviewed articles with autobiographical memory as a keyword from 1980 to 2010.

Psychology was started by Graham Davies in 1987, and served as the official journal for the Society of Applied Research on Memory and Cognition (SARMAC). The journal *Memory* was started in 1995 by Susan E. Gathercole and Martin A. Conway. Both journals were open to studies conducted outside the traditional laboratory paradigms and very quickly became important outlets for the growing field of autobiographical memory research. Other important factors were the existence of a few vibrant research communities pursuing research on autobiographical memory and serving as important meeting places for more isolated autobiographical memory researchers around the world. Two key centers were the Emory Cognition Project, headed by Ulrich Neisser, and the MRC: Applied Cognition Unit at Cambridge University, directed by Alan Baddeley.

It is beyond the scope of this introduction to provide an exhaustive review of the progress that the autobiographical memory field has made over the years. The following only serves as a few key examples, illustrating that autobiographical memory research has yielded novel, robust, and replicable findings that could not have been discovered through more traditional memory studies in laboratory settings with verbal material.

Developmental research conducted in the 1980s showed that the ability to remember past personal events is present much earlier in life than had originally been thought. Systematic studies showed that children as young as 2.5 years of age were able to remember unique personal events that had taken place several months earlier (Fivush, Gray, and Fromhoff, 1987). Such observations forced researchers to radically reconsider young children's memory abilities and to revise the prevalent understanding of childhood amnesia as reflecting lack of encoding and retention of experiences experienced in early life.

Other researchers demonstrated that the long-term retention of auto-biographical memories deviated from Ebbinghaus' (1885) standard forgetting curve by showing a marked increase of memories deriving from young adulthood (Rubin, Wetzler, and Nebes, 1986). This reminiscence bump has been replicated many times for many different kinds of self-related memory material and has spurred a variety of related research.

Studies of autobiographical memory in clinical disorders similarly have led to robust and important findings. Notably, using the Crovitz and Schiffman (1974) cue-word technique, Williams and colleagues demonstrated that people suffering from depression have difficulty in retrieving autobiographical memories of unique events. Instead of specific episodes, depressed individuals tend to retrieve script-like summary representations of many similar occurrences. This overgeneral memory effect may reflect reduced executive control processes in depression, as well as avoidance and rumination (Williams, Barnhofer, Crane, et al., 2007).

One particular problem that autobiographical memory researchers had to address was the problem of measuring accuracy. This was handled by the use of diary studies in which participants recorded personal events, for which their memory was later tested. Among other things, such diary studies yielded novel findings on the accuracy of dating of personal events, and how dating errors are systematically shaped by different levels of temporal schemata. Diary studies generally testified to the reconstructive nature of autobiographical remembering (e.g., Thompson, Skowronski, Larsen, et al., 1996).

People can have subjectively vivid representations of personal events which they believe are memories, but which turn out to be purely imagined events. The demonstration that it is possible to induce such false memories by simply having people imagine events that were described to them as real events from their own childhood (Hyman, Husband, and Billings, 1995; Loftus and Pickrell, 1995) highlighted the constructive nature of autobiographical remembering and had substantial effects on the forensic system. The practical significance of these findings was not limited to the USA (where most of this research was conducted). The false-memory research led to changes in the legal practices in many other countries as well and also made psychotherapists more alert to the risk of inducing memory illusions during psychotherapy (see McNally, 2003, for review and discussion).

Many other characteristics of memories than their accuracy are important for understanding autobiographical memory. Research on autobio-graphical memory has spurred the development of reliable measures of conscious experience during remembering, including qualities of reliving, emotion, and mental imagery (Johnson, 1988; Rubin, Schrauf, and

Greenberg, 2003). Such subjective measures have been found to agree well with measures of underlying brain activity as obtained through brain-scanning experiments (Daselaar, Rice, Greenberg, *et al.*, 2008). Such converging evidence demonstrates the validity of subjective reports of conscious experience.

Autobiographical remembering has been the subject of many neuro-psychological and brain-imaging studies, showing how the construction of personal memories recruits different subsystems of the brain. Studies of autobiographical remembering have thereby informed our understanding of how neural activity relates to conscious experience.

We also know considerably more about the contents and functions of autobiographical remembering than we did 25 years ago. Researchers have found reliable ways of conceptualizing and measuring the adaptive functions of autobiographical remembering (Pillemer, 2003). We know that autobiographical events vary with regard to their complexities and the amount of episodic details included. Increasingly sophisticated ways of conceptualizing and measuring specificity have been developed and have shown the consistent effects of aging (Levine, Svoboda, Hay, *et al.*, 2002). Cultural background also has documented effects on the content and onset of autobiographical remembering (Wang, 2006).

In short, over the last three decades, research on autobiographical memory has demonstrated its potential in numerous ways. It has shown a strong ability to establish clear empirical generalizations, which could not have been established through traditional laboratory experiments. It has shown its practical relevance, among other things, by deepening our understanding of several clinical disorders, and by demonstrating the induction of false memories in the legal system. It has become an important topic for brain studies, and thus helped to enlarge our general understanding of the brain.

The central goal of the present book is to help to provide an overview and integration of the many theories, perspectives, and approaches that have evolved over the last three decades. We omit two important areas, simply because it is beyond the scope of the present book to include everything of relevance to autobiographical memory. One omitted area is research on false memories and other issues directly related to eyewitness psychology. The other omitted area is clinical aspects of autobiographical memory, which we believe should have its own volume at a later point in time, due to the specific questions characterizing this particular and very rapidly developing research domain.

All chapters in the book offer a review and theoretical integration of findings in a particular area of autobiographical memory research. The book consists of fifteen chapters and a discussion chapter. The fifteen chapters are grouped in five parts, each with its own overarching topic. The five parts are as follows: (1) Approaches to the study of autobiographical memory, (2) Neural studies of autobiographical memory, (3) Social and cultural aspects of autobiographical memory, (4) Development of autobiographical memory from infancy to old age, and (5) Evolution and basic processes of autobiographical memory. The following serves as a brief description of the contents of these parts.

Approaches to the study of autobiographical memory

The four chapters in this section describe different approaches to the study of autobiographical memory. The chapter by Rubin examines the neural and biological bases of autobiographical information. In his theoretical model, the processing of autobiographical information and construction of memories are based on the interplay of functionally distinct subsystems of the mind and brain. The chapter by Conway and Jobson emphasizes the central role of the self, its goals, and its social and cultural context in the processing of autobiographical information and construction of memories. It thus combines and integrates a motivational approach with a more standard, information-processing account. Autobiographical remembering and motivated forgetting were studied by psychoanalysts through case observations long before the cognitively oriented examination of autobiographical memory began. The chapter by Habermas offers a rare review of such early psychoanalytic and psychodynamic theories of autobiographical memory, and discusses their differences and similarities with modern cognitive approaches. The section ends with a chapter by Baddeley. As one of the early pioneers of autobiographical memory research, Baddeley now returns to the field and critically evaluates different approaches to the study of autobiographical memory from a historical perspective.

Neural studies of autobiographical memory

The two chapters in this section review and evaluate how autobiographical memory research has helped to enlarge our understanding of brain processes as well as how studies of the neural underpinnings of autobiographical memory have added significantly to our understanding of its basic behavioral characteristics. The chapter by Moscovitch addresses how neuropsychological studies of autobiographical memory have informed our broader understanding of how memories are retained at the neural level on a long-term basis. The chapter by St. Jacques reviews the rapidly growing field of functional neuroimaging studies of autobiographical memory, and describes how such studies have been useful for the understanding of the neural basis of memory processes more broadly.

Social and cultural aspects of autobiographical memory

Often cognitive psychologists treat memories and remembering as processes that take place entirely within each individual, without considering how one individual's memory is embedded in a larger social, cultural, and historical context. The three chapters in this section each helps to correct this limitation by discussing how such larger contexts help to structure the organization and content of autobiographical memories as well as their retrieval and forgetting. The chapter by Brown and colleagues examines the effects of historical events on the organization of autobiographical memories. On the basis of a series of recently published large-scale studies, they argue that only events that "change the fabric of everyday life" will have lasting effects on memory organization. Hirst and colleagues discuss the notion of collective memory and review studies showing how the social context affects retrieval and forgetting and thereby makes autobiographical memories within a social group more collective and uniform. The chapter by Pillemer and Kuwabara addresses the directive functions of autobiographical remembering and thus how our memories help to set the course for our behavior and goals. By discussing the functional aspects of remembering, Pillemer and Kuwabara address how autobiographical memories become adaptive in a larger social and cultural context.

Development of autobiographical memory from infancy to old age

The three chapters in this section address the development of autobiographical memory from infancy to old age. The chapters offer different perspectives on this topic and focus on different parts of the life span. The chapter by Bauer reviews research on memory in infancy and early childhood and discusses what these findings add to the understanding of infantile amnesia – that is, the finding that older children and adults generally are unable to remember experiences from the first three years of life. The chapter by Fivush reviews and discusses how conversations with caregivers shape the development of autobiographical memory in the preschool years, and thus how sociocultural factors affect autobiographical memory development. The chapter by Fitzgerald and Broadbridge is concerned with autobiographical memory development from adolescence to old age. Among other things, the chapter discusses the reminiscence bump – that is, the increase of memories from young adulthood relative to the surrounding periods that is observed in middle-aged and older adults across a variety of autobiographical memory tasks.

Evolution and basic processes of autobiographical memory

The three chapters in this section all deal with relatively novel areas of autobiographical memory research. All three chapters attempt to make theoretical and empirical connections between autobiographical memory – as this topic is most frequently studied – and other basic mental processes, thereby extending the concept of autobiographical remembering. Donald's chapter discusses the functions and developments of autobiographical memory in an evolutionary perspective. Among other things, he discusses whether the memory of personally experienced events is a uniquely human phenomenon or whether more primitive forms of autobiographical (episodic) remembering may be found among other species. Donald argues that many nonhuman species are capable of episodic remembering when prompted by concrete cues in the environment, but are unable to initiate the recall process in a decontextualized and controlled fashion. Berntsen addresses the phenomenon of involuntary (spontaneous) autobiographical remembering and argues that it is a basic mode of autobiographical memory that may be evolutionarily earlier than the more cognitively demanding (and much more studied) voluntary retrieval mode. D'Argembeau reviews an accumulating amount of findings suggesting that the ability to remember the personal past and imagine the personal future is supported by the same cognitive and neural processes. He discusses the underlying knowledge structures and the central role of motivational factors.

Discussion

This section includes only one chapter, in which the editors attempt to integrate the main points of the preceding chapters into a coherent ecological theory of autobiographical memory.

References

Brewer, W. (1986). What is autobiographical memory? In Rubin (ed.), *Autobiographical memory* (pp. 25–49).

Crovitz, H. F. and Schiffman, H. (1974). Frequency of episodic memories as a function of their age. *Bulletin of the Psychonomic Society*, **4**, 517–518.

Daselaar, S. M., Rice, H. J., Greenberg, D. L., Cabeza, R., LaBar, K. S., and Rubin, D. C. (2008). The spatiotemporal dynamics of autobiographical memory: neural correlates of recall, emotional intensity, and reliving. *Cerebral Cortex*, **18**(1), 217–229.

Ebbinghaus, H. (1885/1964). *Memory: a contribution to experimental psychology.* New York: Dover Publications.

Fivush, R., Gray, J. T., and Fromhoff, F. A. (1987). Two year olds talk about the past. *Cognitive Development*, **2**, 393–410.

Hyman, I. E., Husband, T. H., and Billings, F. J. (1995). False memories of childhood experiences. *Applied Cognitive Psychology*, **9**, 181–197.

Johnson, M. K. (1988). Reality monitoring: an experimental phenomenological approach. *Journal of Experimental Psychology: General*, **117**, 390–394.

Levine, B., Svoboda, E., Hay, J. F., Winocur, G., and Moscovitch, M. (2002). Aging and autobiographical memory: dissociating episodic from semantic retrieval. *Psychology & Aging*, **17**(4), 677–689.

Loftus, E. F. and Pickrell, J. E. (1995). The formation of false memories. *Psychiatric Annals*, **25**, 720–725.

McNally, R. J. (2003). *Remembering trauma.* Cambridge, MA: Harvard University Press.

Neisser, U. (ed.) (1982). *Memory observed: remembering in natural contexts.* San Francisco: Freeman.

Pillemer, D. B. (2003). Directive functions of autobiographical memory: the guiding power of the specific episode. *Memory*, **11**, 193–202.

Rubin, D. C. (ed.) (1986). *Autobiographical memory.* New York: Cambridge University Press.

  (ed.) (1996). *Remembering our past: studies in autobiographical memory.* New York: Cambridge University Press.

Rubin, D. C., Schrauf, R. W., and Greenberg, D. L. (2003). Belief and recollection of autobiographical memories. *Memory Cognition*, **31**(6), 887–901.

Rubin, D. C., Wetzler, S. E., and Nebes, R. D. (1986). Autobiographical memory across the adult lifespan. In Rubin (ed.), *Autobiographical memory* (pp. 202–221).

Thompson, C. V., Skowronski, J. S., Larsen, S. F., and Betz, A. L. (1996). *Autobiographical memory: remembering what and remembering when.* New York: Lawrence Erlbaum.

Wang, Q. (2006). Earliest recollections of self and others in European American and Taiwanese young adults. *Psychological Science*, **17**, 708–714.

Williams, J. M. G., Barnhofer, T., Crane, C., Hermans, D., Raes. F., Watkins, E., and Dalgleish, T. (2007). Autobiographical memory specificity and emotional disorder. *Psychological Bulletin*, **113**(1), 122–148.

Part I

Approaches to the study of autobiographical memory

How should studies on autobiographical memory be approached? The four chapters in this section address this question from different perspectives. The chapter by Rubin examines the neural and biological bases of autobiographical information. Rubin describes the construction of autobiographical memories as an interaction between functionally distinct subsystems of the mind and brain. He also discusses the implications of this view for our broader understanding of memory. The chapter by Habermas links modern research on autobiographical memory to the earlier psychoanalytic approach to the same phenomenon. Habermas offers a unique introduction to psychodynamic theories of autobiographical memory, and discusses the differences and similarities between these early approaches and modern ones. The chapter by Conway and Jobson addresses the role of the self, its goals, and its social and cultural context in the processing of autobiographical information and construction of memories. This chapter thus emphasizes the cultural, social, and motivational aspects of autobiographical remembering. The section ends with a chapter by Baddeley. As one of the early pioneers of autobiographical memory research, Baddeley takes a historical perspective and evaluates a number of different empirical approaches that have emerged over the years. He concludes by a call for more theoretical integration.

2   The basic systems model of autobiographical memory

David C. Rubin

I outline the basic systems model, a theory that can account for the encoding and retrieval of autobiographical memories (Rubin, 1998, 2005, 2006). Next I demonstrate that the model adapts easily for other related tasks in order to address what aspects of autobiographical memory the basic systems model is trying to explain, and how varying the activity of the basic systems can produce different classes of memories. Finally, in order to contrast the model most starkly to current cognitive theory and major alternative accounts of autobiographical memory based on it, I consider four central assumptions that lead to three fundamental claims, which are all counter to the basic systems model but which are central to other accounts of cognition and autobiographical memory. The clearer and stronger my discussion of these claims, the easier it will be to see if I am misguided. I may be wrong, but I will try not to be boring.

The model applied to an autobiographical event

The prototypical autobiographical event whose memory I wish to explain is a single ride on a merry-go-round at an amusement park. This chapter is about a model that could describe an autobiographical memory of this event if it were based on our most basic, solid, current understanding of the mind and the brain, instead of trying to modify models initially based on a 1960s computer. The model needs to account for or include the phenomenological, metacognitive judgments of reliving the ride and believing that it really happened to you, the various emotions from boredom to joy that might accompany this particular event, a general knowledge of the physical ride that would allow you to choose a seat with or without vertical motion, the script for paying for and taking such a ride, and a narrative context in which this event is embedded and which helps you understand and share with others the significance of the ride. Components should include rich visual imagery for the brightly colored animals, auditory imagery for the imitation calliope, spatial imagery for the ride and its surrounds, olfactory imagery for odors from nearby food stands, kinesthetic imagery of motion, and even an account of why the visual and spatial images are stronger than the olfactory and kinesthetic ones.

Introductory perception, cognition, and neuroscience textbooks have long divided the mind and brain into basic systems including separate systems for each of the senses, language, emotion, and motor output (Rubin, 2006). Moreover, we know that each system has its own functions, processes, structures, kinds of schemata, and types of errors, which have been studied individually. The scientists who study the mind and the brain divide their journals and societies along these lines. However, modern cognitive theory is slow to return to these divisions from its 50-year-old computer metaphor and the accompanying concept that I termed *homogenized information*: information that is the same for the whole mind, that is abstract and propositional, and that does not depend on the unique functions and properties of each basic system (Rubin, 2006).

My colleagues and I have developed as simple a model as we could that accounts for the behavioral data, using such a neurally based set of systems. We have integrated the behavioral data based on people's rating of the activity in each system (Rubin, Burt, and Fifield, 2003; Rubin, Schrauf, and Greenberg, 2003), as well as findings from neuropsychology (Greenberg and Rubin, 2003; Greenberg, Eacott, Brechin, *et al.*, 2005) and neuroimaging (Daselaar, Rice, Greenberg, *et al.*, 2008; St. Jacques, Botzung, Miles, *et al.*, 2011). As shown in Figure 2.1, the basic systems included in the model are event memory, search and retrieval, vision, audition, tactile sense, olfaction, gustation, spatial imagery, language,

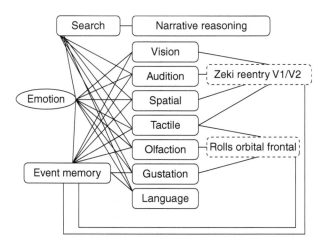

Figure 2.1. A schematic of the basic systems model.

emotion, narrative, and others not shown, including kinesthesis, pain, vestibular function, and motor output. In earlier work (Rubin, 2006), I called the hippocampus-based, event-memory system the explicit memory system, but event memory is more accurate.

Each component system in the basic systems model has a long intellectual and experimental history. Most of the components date back as far as the recorded history of speculation about the mind (e.g., the five senses, narrative, and emotion as separate entities). Three exceptions are the separate components for language and narrative, a division which is based on current behavioral and neuropsychological data (Rubin and Greenberg, 2003); the event-memory system, which has been a subject of study at least since the amnesic patient H.M. (see Moscovitch, this volume); and the search-and-retrieval system, a construct that in memory research dates back at least to the control processes of Atkinson and Shiffrin (1971) and Baddeley's (1986) central executive. It would be exceedingly difficult to deny that any of the basic systems are useful scientific concepts that describe components of the mind and brain. Each can be supported by results from (1) neuroanatomy, (2) neuropsychology, (3) neuroimaging, (4) cognitive-experimental psychology, and (5) individual differences research. Knowledge from all five sources sharpens and constrains predictions regarding memory functions of all the basic systems. Moreover, each system, with the possible exception of the event-memory system, is used for tasks other than memory. Thus, each system is the only system of its kind in a model that could be extended to explain cognition in general, and so the considerable amount already known about each system from its non-mnemonic functions further constrains its functioning as a component system of memory. What is novel is that the differences among the systems and the implications of these differences for memory are taken seriously (but see Barsalou, 1999, for a similar approach to semantic memory).

According to the model, all autobiographical memories are constructed through the interaction of the basic systems. Stability and change in memories are due to the schemata of each system (e.g., narrative schemata, visual schemata, auditory schemata) as well as to how the various systems interact. Properties of autobiographical memories that are centered in a single system can be measured by self-report and other behavior and neural activity in that system. Properties that depend on multiple systems, such as metacognitive judgments of reliving and belief, can be predicted by the degree of activity in these systems. Autobiographical memories are not constructed from a general, abstract, propositional cognitive structure of homogenized information, but rather from sensory, language, emotion, and other systems, each of which uses fundamentally different structures and processes for fundamentally different kinds of information.

Missing from Figure 2.1 is a self-system, but the model is not self-less. As noted earlier (Rubin, 2006), the self as an enduring essence and a set of goals often does the work in psychology that the soul once did in earlier attempts to understand human nature. We know more about autobiographical memory than we do about such a self, and so it would appear to be backwards to explain autobiographical memory using the self. However, we do know a considerable amount about the various schemata in the basic systems that can account for aspects of the self and that can be used to help us understand autobiographical memory. Thus, in the basic systems model, thoughts and behaviors often attributed to the self as a unitary concept are distributed among the existing systems much in the spirit of Neisser (1988a), who postulated various aspects of the self including a narrative self and an ecological self that would keep track of spatial location.

The coordination among and development of the systems

Coordination   Separating cognition into basic systems immediately raises novel theoretical questions. The first and most obvious is how to put cognition back together; that is, how to coordinate the systems. One solution not used because it lacks any behavioral or neural support and needlessly adds homogenized information back into the model is to have a language of the mind used by a centralized coordinating system (Fodor, 1983). Instead, three basic systems provide different kinds of *general coordination*. The hippocampus-based, event-memory system provides a "dumb" coordination that binds together in an automatic, modular fashion everything that occurs at the same time into one event that could later be retrieved as an autobiographical memory (Moscovitch, 1992, this volume). This is useful because we often do not know until later which events will need to be recalled. The emotion system is important for "smart" coordination based on the discrepancy between what was expected and what occurred, surprise, interest, and emotional arousal. The frontal search and retrieval system provides a "smarter" system that finds components of a memory when cued by other components, while using inhibitory mechanisms to suppress dominant responses that do not fit all the criteria set by the known cues (Moscovitch and Melo, 1997; St. Jacques, this volume). Substantial evidence indicates that we have all three kinds of general coordination systems and that they are subject to damage independently. Depending on the situation, the three types of coordination are involved to differing degrees, resulting in differing memory strengths for differing retrieval cues and motivational states. The basic systems model points to areas of ignorance that need study, such as specifying how such coordination would actually function in specific situations (see Rubin, 2006, for details).

We also have forms of *specific coordination* that are local in that they involve only a few systems or subsystems. Two are shown in dotted-line boxes in Figure 2.1. One is for the aspects of the visual, gustatory, olfactory, tactile, and emotion systems that integrate in orbital frontal cortex to produce taste and regulate intake of nutrients relatively independently of other systems (Rolls, 2004). Another specific coordination extends Zeki's (1993) idea of reentry from visual to multisensory coordination by suggesting that primary visual cortex can serve as a general spatial mapping area, a claim consistent with evidence that it has and uses inputs from touch and audition. Thus, the ventral (as well as the dorsal) visual pathway may be better viewed as a multisensory pathway. For instance, the ventral pathway includes areas that are active during both visual and haptic presentation of objects. Other sensory modalities that do not code for location in the world, such as olfaction and gustation, do not appear to send information to the visual cortex or to take part in such spatial mapping (see Rubin, 2006, for details).

Two final points on coordination among systems should be made. First, although some autobiographical memory retrieval occurs quickly, presumably involving the medial-temporal event memory and emotion systems for coordination, other retrieval involving the frontal search and retrieval system is slower, often taking about 10 seconds. Functional magnetic resonance imaging (fMRI) typically scans the entire brain every 1.5 to 2 seconds. Therefore, as shown in Figure 2.2, the construction process is slow enough to observe with fMRI. Participants pressed a button when they had retrieved an autobiographical memory to a word cue, and we used the fMRI signature of that button press in the motor cortex, as shown in the middle panel, as a marker for timing in the brain. Before the button press, areas involved in the event memory and the search and retrieval system are more involved; after the button press, visual areas are involved in maintaining and elaborating the memory. Memories rated as more emotional *after* elaboration activate the amygdala in the period *before* the button press, emphasizing the role of the emotion system in coordinating the retrieval process (Daselaar *et al.*, 2008).

The second point is that coordination can be extremely powerful because, unlike laboratory-designed material, outside the laboratory coordination among systems can severely limit the choice of the to-be-remembered material. Consider the following example of the power of interactions among systems (Rubin and Wallace, 1989). The language system category cue of "building material" produced the word *steel* as a category exemplar with a probability (p) of .00, and the auditory cue "rhymes with *eel*" also produced *steel* with a probability of .00. Thus, the expected probability of these cues combined producing *steel*, if they were independent, would be $p_a + p_b - (p_a \times p_b)$ or .00. However, the combined cue "a building material rhyming with *eel*" produced *steel* with a probability of 1.00, because there is no alternative. In general, cues from different systems can combine to produce extremely strong effects by providing extremely likely responses for a given situation.

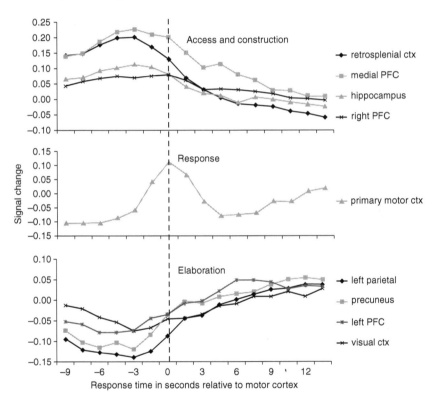

Figure 2.2. fMRI response-related activity in the motor cortex resulting from the button press indicating that a memory was accessed is shown in the middle panel. It provides a reference for the timing of other activity. Brain regions shown in the top panel showed greater activity during the access and construction of word-cued autobiographical memories and a descending slope at and after the time the memory was accessed. Brain regions shown in the bottom panel showed greater activity during elaboration and an ascending slope at and after the memory was accessed. Ctx = cortex, PFC = prefrontal cortex.

Development   A second obvious theoretical question involves development (see Bauer, this volume; Fivush, this volume). In isolating the basic systems, the question of their individual life-span development naturally arises. From this perspective, some strengths and many weaknesses of our current knowledge appear. By making assumptions and using what data are available, various systems can be shown to differ in their relative effectiveness over the life span; some increase monotonically, others decrease monotonically, and still others have inverted U-shaped curves (Rubin, 2002). However, the data needed for a serious analysis often do not exist. Nonetheless, as shown in Figure 2.3, we know sensory systems generally tend to decline with aging, and we can approximate the search and retrieval system by using measures of fluid intelligence. Language as measured by vocabulary and mean length of utterance develops earlier than the ability to tell a narrative of life story (Fivush, this volume; Habermas and Bluck, 2000). Accordingly, changes in the systems' roles in autobiographical memory should be dynamic at the behavioral and neural levels of analysis. An analysis of how the developmental changes contribute to autobiographical memory and how the interactions among the systems develop is still lacking. This will not be an easy task, but viewing issues of development in this way may prove useful.

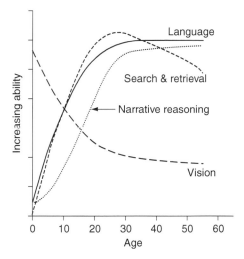

Figure 2.3. A hypothetical set of developmental trajectories for some systems where reasonable plots can be drawn.

The basic systems model applied to related tasks

Having provided an account of what is needed to describe the encoding and retrieval of a prototypical autobiographical event, I would like to ask what else the theory can do in order to show how the basic systems needed to construct an autobiographical memory can be used for other tasks and kinds of memories, and thereby where autobiographical memory fits into a theory of memory and cognition in general. A variant of the basic systems model was first developed to account for oral traditions (Rubin, 1995). The singing of a ballad or epic seems to require all the components of an autobiographical memory once a suspension of disbelief is allowed and a fantasy or historical world is entered. But what kind of memory is a ballad or epic of a hero sung as if the singer were a witness to the event? It is certainly not episodic or autobiographical memory according to their normal definitions. It is not sung as if it were semantic memory; there is a clear setting and narrative, imagery, emotion, and often a kind of belief and reliving. Moreover, the same construction processes are at work (Rubin, 1995, 2006).

Given such similar explanations for different domains, I branch out from the prototypical encoding and retrieval of an autobiographical event to related tasks and to-be-remembered items. A main advantage of having individual systems is that the degree to which they are active can be measured behaviorally and neurally, and it can account for seemingly different kinds of cognitive products.

- Consider the prototypical event, a unique ride on a merry-go-round, except that it is for one you routinely rode. This might lead to a less recollected memory because it would rely on more general and less event-specific knowledge (see Brewer, 1986; Levine, Svoboda, Hay, et al., 2002) and it might come with less hippocampal involvement and less specific visual imagery (Rubin, Schrauf, Greenberg, 2003).

- Consider the prototypical event but for a future or past imagined ride with space aliens on a flying saucer after they abduct you. As with actual events, this construction is based on general knowledge, your ability to construct plausible events, and, according to Bartlett (1932, p. 213), "a little outstanding detail which commonly appears in image or in language form." Recollection and physiological reaction indicating emotion activity (McNally, Lasco, Clancy, et al., 2004) would require enhanced imagery and perhaps stong narrative ties to one's life (Berntsen and Rubin, 2006).

- Consider the prototypical event except that a life-threatening accident on the ride leaves you with a diagnosis of post-traumatic stress disorder and extremely vivid, highly recollected voluntary memories and involuntary memories that could be described as "flashbacks." Changes in the activity of the basic systems that increase availability, especially the emotion system, can account for such memories (Rubin, Berntsen, and Bohni, 2008; Rubin, Boals, and Berntsen, 2008; Rubin, Dennis, and Beckham, 2011).

- Consider the prototypical event that produces a detailed memory about your life that is accurate and that you believe to be accurate, but that comes as a fact with no sense of recollection (Brewer, 1986, 1996). We know a good deal from studies measuring the metacognitive judgments of belief and reliving and the basic systems of the model about how this could occur (Rubin, Schrauf, and Greenberg, 2003; Rubin and Siegler, 2004).
- Consider a memory for the prototypical event that you believe and recollect, but that turns out to be completely fabricated. Again we know a good deal about how the basic systems operate in such situations (Sheen, Kemp, and Rubin, 2001).
- Consider a memory for the prototypical event but one purposely altered for any of a number of purposes such as enhancing the role you played for personal, political, or therapeutic reasons through retellings (Marsh, 2007; Neisser, 1981) or through psychotherapy. Here the narrative reasoning function of the search and retrieval system plays an increased role.
- Consider the prototypical event, but incorporating it with modifications suitable for an entertaining play, story, or ballad you are composing in which the event is portrayed as believable and one the narrator is recollecting (Rubin, 1995; Rubin, Wallace, and Houston, 1993). Not much change is needed in the activity of the systems, just a suspension of disbelief.
- Consider providing the description of the prototypical merry-go-round ride with all related scripted material for a newcomer to our culture; that is, a request for knowledge (i.e., a semantic memory) rather than a request for an event (i.e., an episodic memory). Here a decrease in the event memory system is needed.

Thus, changes in the level of activity in the basic systems can account for a wide range of nominally different tasks. Here these changes are presented in a casual fashion, but most are supported by published data on behavioral ratings or neural activity. Autobiographical memory for a single prototypical event shares most processes with the examples listed including past and future imagined events, "accurate" and "false" memories, everyday and traumatic memories, and episodic and semantic memories. Thus, it would be efficient and parsimonious if such tasks could be accounted for by the same theory with specific, principled, and fairly minor modifications. For future events (see D'Argembeau, this volume) and false memories, but not for all of the contrasts, this is what psychologists usually do. For all these tasks, working out the details is a goal of the basic systems model, and for many we have made progress. In general, the basic systems are involved in varying degrees in all of cognition, including perception, attention, language, problem solving, and decision making.

The model contrasted with our current approaches

Four flawed assumptions from cognitive psychology

As I see it, there are four unstated assumptions that are common in cognitive psychology and that become serious flaws when they are used to formulate a neurally plausible account of autobiographical memory. The first flaw is using the computer metaphor of memory instead of starting with more current understanding of neural functions. Early cognitive theories of memory based on the hardware of 1960s computers came with many assumptions that turned out to be advances at the time, but are no longer useful. These include homogenized information, digital rather than analog processing, and a distinction between short-term and long-term memory, each with its own location and properties reflecting the active short-term central processor whose memory was overwritten and the passive, relatively permanent, long-term storage of the computer (see Rubin, 2006, for an extended discussion).

The second flaw is extending theories devised to explain laboratory tasks to real-world situations, especially when it is done in an incremental fashion. The laboratory is an ideal place to test theories, but extending theories developed for laboratory tasks beyond the laboratory is generally a bad idea (Hintzman, 2011). Theories made for experimental paradigms can be less well specified than is needed when applied to general situations, and factors minimized to obtain experimental control cannot be easily added back. People adjust in flexible, intelligent ways that prohibit this strategy.

The third flaw is making a process into a thing that exists over time in a specific neural location. This is a reification of the process of *remembering*, as in Bartlett's (1932) title, into an object called a *memory*, as in Ebbinghaus' (1885/1964) title. Students of oral traditions often say that a ballad or epic comes into existence as a performance and then disappears (Rubin, 1995). Its recording, which is a physical process that makes it into a fixed, authored variant should not be confused with the act of performing, which is a psychological process that depends on the audience and context. The same is true of autobiographical memory.

The fourth flaw is a tendency to make opposing alternatives, especially dichotomies, when graded distinctions are more appropriate. Newell's (1973) paper, "You can't play 20 questions with nature and win," convincingly argues that binary theoretical and empirical distinctions, such as semantic versus episodic memory and short-term versus long-term memory, never endure in cognition. One alternative approach Newell offered was to take "a genuine slab of human behavior" (p. 303), which for him was chess and for me is autobiographical memory, and to try to build a model of it.

Three fundamental challenges to cognitive psychology

Each of these four flawed assumptions helps maintain three commonly held, theoretically central concepts of theories that are counter to the basic systems model. They are separate episodic and semantic memory systems, separate short- and long-term memory systems, and fixed, hierarchical, computer-like representations as a way of understanding autobiographical memory. You may have noted their absence in Figure 2.1. These three concepts remain useful descriptions of behavior, but they cannot remain as neural systems in their current form. Semantic and episodic memories describe two different kinds of knowledge, not two neurally based memory systems each duplicating information needed by the other. Short- and long-term memories become different degrees of activity in the same neural systems, and other aspects of working memory are distributed among the systems of Figure 2.1. Hierarchical, computer-like representations used to describe autobiographical memory are neither flexible enough nor supported at the neural level.

If we wish to build a model of memory that is based on what we now know about both behavior and its neural basis, we have to negotiate concepts between these two levels (Rubin, 1995). Such a radical break is needed to truly integrate our understanding of brain and behavior. Skinner (1974) could forcefully argue that neural explanations in cognition are based on a "conceptual nervous system," one devised specifically and circularly to account for the behaviors needing explanation. Today we can do better. However, it requires simultaneous consideration of brain and behavior. For instance, based on earlier reviews, St. Jacques (this volume, Figure 7.1) uses "recollection" where I use "event memory" and uses "control processes" and "self-referential process" where I use "search and retrieval." These are close enough only for a start. Progress will occur by simultaneously contrasting the differences in concepts and neural activation to uncover the best account of cognition. Similarly, networks empirically observed during autobiographical memory construction and elaboration need to be related to our existing knowledge of neural systems (St. Jacques, Kragel, and Rubin, 2011).

Separate semantic and episodic memory systems

The existence of separate semantic and episodic memory systems in autobiographical memory is not supported. Episodic memories are about events that occurred at a single time and place to a person. Reliving, recollecting, traveling back in time, believing they really happened, recalling them from a first-person (or field) versus a third-person (or observer) perspective, and a whole host of other phenomenological and philosophical properties listed by Tulving (1983, p. 35, Table 3.1) and Brewer (1996) can be supported by such memories. Moreover, as Tulving notes, one can testify by using episodic memories in court without being an expert witness, and test their veridicality by personal belief rather than social consensus. One simply cannot make these judgments for the semantic memory that merry-go-rounds usually have brightly colored statues of animals on them or that canaries are yellow. The differences are in the kinds of things being remembered. Knowledge and events are different ontological categories. One can say different things about them, but it is not necessary to have separate memory systems for each.

The distinction between episodic and semantic memories has occurred in various forms throughout the history of philosophy (Herrmann, 1982; also see Brewer, 1996), and is needed for the study of autobiographical memory. If we do not have different memory systems to account for this observation, we have to say how we remember these different classes of material. Tulving's (1972, 1983, 2002) distinction between episodic and semantic memory systems changed over time, producing strong debates along the way (see Ratcliff and McKoon, 1986; Ratcliff, McKoon, and Dell, 1986; Tulving, 1986, 2002). The easiest assumption, and the one I have made in the past in an attempt to integrate laboratory and autobiographical memory (Cabeza, Prince, Daselaar, *et al.*, 2004; Rubin, 2005, 2006), is that autobiographical memory is episodic, and therefore not semantic, memory. Alternatively, if autobiographical memory organizes all of one's memories, episodic memory must be a part of autobiographical memory (Conway, 2005; Conway and Jobson, this volume). However, on reflection, both alternatives are wrong. Episodic and semantic memories need not be products of fundamentally different memory systems called episodic and semantic memory.

A separate issue makes this much more than a debate about definitions. The issue is the extent to which a particular memory is composed of general knowledge versus information that is unique to the event itself (Levine *et al.*, 2002; Rubin, Burt, and Fifield, 2003; Williams, 1996). If one takes a constructivist approach, this will have no easy answer. Schemata will be used both to find information that turns out to be accurate and the information that is filled in. It will not be a case of finding details in the storehouse of memory and filling in blanks from a storehouse of defaults. As the earlier merry-go-round examples show, separating the semantic knowledge from the event-specific information used in constructing the memory will not be an easy task, though we have many laboratory and real-world examples of how such construction works and what errors it tends to produce.

The basic systems model constructs autobiographical memories by using the systems shown in Figure 2.1. Each system has knowledge in it that may be of a general schematic form or may be of a more detailed form that could tie to a unique event depending on the cues available. Behaviorally, we cannot tell whether instances or schema-like prototypes are stored (Hintzman, 1986). Compared to semantic memories, episodic memories are recalled with increased activity in the event-memory system that bound the aspects of an event that occurred at a particular time and place but are stored in individual systems. The search and retrieval system helps to further select the relevant event according to the cues given and to find or reject details that do not fit the specific memory wanted.

The episodic–semantic memory distinction accounts for many findings. We account for the same findings without two separate neural memory systems. Most storage is in the relevant neural systems of the basic systems model, including the individual senses and emotion. If a memory for an event that could have occurred at a single time and place is constructed, the event-memory system is centrally involved, and the search and retrieval systems attempts to restrict the memory to the most plausible solution. This is in general agreement with neural accounts of normal functioning, development, and acquired neural damage. Where it is not, the details of the basic system model will need modification, but it is difficult to imagine new findings that will lead to information stored in neurally distinct episodic and semantic memory systems.

In summary, the distinction between semantic and episodic memories as products rather than as memory systems is real. They have different contents that support different inferences and phenomenological reports. Nonetheless, autobiographical memories consist of both general semantic knowledge and details that are unique to a given time and place. There is no process-pure episodic or semantic memory content in autobiographical memory and no separate episodic or semantic memory systems to store it.

A separate short-term memory system

The existence of a separate short-term or working memory system with an episodic buffer used in constructing autobiographical memories is not supported. The division between short- and long-term memory has a venerable tradition. There is a clear phenomenological distinction between memories which are and are not in the "conscious now" (James, 1890). However, we can have a conscious now for memories without there being a short-term memory where they temporarily reside. The conscious *now* for past events may be no more than the part of our memory that behaviorally is the focus of attention, or neurally is the most active (for related views, see Cowan, 1995; Jonides, Lewis, Nee, *et al.*, 2008; Oberauer, 2009; Öztekin, Davachi, and McElree, 2010; Postle, 2006), or has the most activity in a neural network model of memory. The reified, short-term memory alternative became dominant when the hardware of the 1960s mainframe computer became *the* model for memory (Atkinson and Shiffrin, 1971). Short-term memory was a thing that did what the central processor did. It held information temporarily in a very limited store while it was being manipulated, but it provided no permanent storage. If the computer crashed, everything in the central processor was lost. Permanent storage was in an unchanging (except for possible deterioration), passive, extremely large long-term memory that survived even power failures. Studies of short-term memory concentrated on isolated items of verbal material and how they could be rehearsed and organized for efficient storage in and later retrieval from long-term memory.

Baddeley (1986, 2007) significantly broadened the concept of short-term memory into the concept of working memory. Working memory has an executive control that was expanded from control processes in short-term memory, and that does many things that others might attribute to the concept of attention. It originally had two short-term storage systems, one for visual-spatial information and one for linguistic sounds, and it later added a third storage system, an episodic buffer. The working memory model does not include such storage systems for other basic systems or even for nonlinguistic sounds.

Empirical support for this model is limited. If short-term memory is a memory, it should have a *capacity*, a *duration*, and a *location* in the brain that supports its behavior. Decades of research have not been encouraging. The *capacity* ranges from 7 ± 2 chunks (Atkinson and Shiffrin, 1971), to four items, to one item (see Jonides *et al.*, 2008, for a review). Its *duration* for lists of isolated words has varied from 1.9 seconds (Baddeley, 1986) to 30 seconds (Atkinson and Shiffrin, 1971), and possibly much longer (Ericsson and Kintsch, 1995). (For an insiders' review, see Miyake and Shah, 1999.) Studies based on physiological manipulations in rodents and brain injury in humans, including closed head injury, produced an extreme range of estimates of durations of memory loss that were initially considered as a measure of transfer from short- to long-term memory. However, the biological processes supporting the transfer of information from temporary to more permanent storage is a cascade of processes of various durations (see Dudai, 2004). Behavioral studies of retention functions have not provided a clear break that would indicate two different memory stores with different decay functions or parameters (Rubin and Wenzel, 1996; Wickelgren, 1973). The *location* of short-term memory was once specific enough that local neurological damage was used to argue for its existence. As with the capacity and duration estimates, the data became messy. The conceptual change from short-term to working memory did not help. In fMRI studies, the visual-spatial sketchpad is distributed throughout most of the cortical visual and spatial systems and executive control has been found in much of frontal cortex (Jonides *et al.*, 2008; Smith and Jonides, 1999). Parallel distributed processing models that attempt biological plausibility often include a quickly changing short-term measure of activity and a more stable measure of long-term strength that both operate on a unitary memory structure rather than two distinct stores.

In the basic systems model, functions of the central executive are taken over by the search and retrieval system. The function of the episodic buffer is taken by activity in the individual systems that contain the information the episodic buffer was supposed to integrate. But what about the classic storage systems for which there is the most evidence, the phonological loop and the visual-spatial sketchpad? My view is that they are really special and not just the current activity in the visual, spatial, and language system as I had previously proposed for the basic systems model (Rubin, 2006). Given the chapters in this volume by Donald, by Fivush, and by Hirst, Cuc, and Wohl, combined with the empirical support for these two storage systems compared to ones for all other systems (Baddeley, 1986, 2007, personal communication), it is reasonable to assume that these two storage buffers are more developed, more important, and easier to demonstrate as functioning behavioral memory systems because they hold information needed for communication with ourselves and others, information that must be maintained in the conscious now to be communicated easily. They support the consciousness of the conscious now. The phonological loop is for language, not sound; it allows us to hear, restructure, and rehearse our linguistic thoughts and others' language. Of all the components of working memory, it is the best specified quantitatively in terms of behavior.

The visual-spatial sketchpad may be more than a visual and a spatial sketchpad. It may offer a way for us to be conscious of the spatial layout of objects in the world so we can think about them and draw them out for others. The inputs from distal senses, in addition to vision, to the reentry box in Figure 2.1 may enrich this image. Such a skill is important for individuals, but it is also important for groups that are to travel, act, and construct things together. It is not equally easy to image all senses. The nonspatial senses of olfaction and taste seem much harder than language and visual-spatial information, though quantitative studies are few (see Rubin, 2006, for a review and discussion of this issue in olfaction). Thus, the visual-spatial sketchpad may make use of the reentry coordination in Figure 2.1 as well as storage in the visual and spatial systems. In summary, in the basic systems model, many of the functions of working memory, especially those that distinguish it from the earlier short-term memory model, survive, not as their own system of memory but rather as processes incorporated into broader systems. The contents of the conscious now are increased activation in the various systems that are coordinated primarily by frontal areas and by event memory if an event is being remembered. As with the review of the episodic–semantic memory distinction, this view is in general agreement with existing findings.

Hierarchically based temporal organization

The use of a hierarchically based temporal organization as the basis for autobiographical memory is not supported. Devising a memory representation, by which I mean a specific account of how the content of memories is organized in a computer model (or the mind in quasi-computer model) can be, and often is, done in cognitive psychology. Such representations have heuristic value; they are easy to present on a piece of paper. However, at a minimum, one has to carefully define the representation and processes working on it and what they are intended to account for if the representation is to be a testable model (Rumelhart and Norman, 1986). In addition, it is hard (if not impossible) to find cases where one of two representations, each of which was favored by a researcher, was ever demonstrated to be the right one by behavioral experiments. Cognition textbooks still recount the unsuccessful attempts at sorting out where specific information about the color of canaries is stored in a representation of content for semantic domains. It also is extremely difficult to show that one class of representations is better (e.g., parallel distributed processing networks versus rules stated as propositions in language, or instances versus prototypes in categorization) (Hintzman, 1986). The legacy of such representations is part of the first three flawed assumptions and of the fourth one when specific choices have to be made in specifying the representation. No one believes that upon dissection, or even with futuristic neuroimaging techniques, such representations will be found in the brain. At best what one might find is connections that would be consistent with aspects of a representation that could allow the temporary construction of a memory.

The obvious representation to propose for autobiographical memory is some form of a temporally organized hierarchical arrangement. After all, a lifetime has periods that can be divided and subdivided in several ways that preserve the temporal order. Moreover, when you ask someone to tell you about their life, they often will go in temporal order or at least preserve temporal order for large sequences of events. Thus, when Neisser (1986, 1988b) wanted to describe the structure of autobiographical memory, he suggested an ecologically based, flexible temporal nesting. I (Rubin, 1988) objected that if such hierarchical nesting was taken as the primary form of organization and made into the representation of autobiographical memory as opposed to a guide for search processes, several problems followed, often problems that Neisser had pointed out himself in other contexts. There are multiple atemporal organizational schemes. Consider the merry-go-round ride. For me, that event is nested in many hierarchies including events with particular visitors, events at fairs, visits to Paragon Park, and events to use as examples in writing chapters. They even may include merged, repeated autobiographical memories – "repisodic memories," in Neisser's terms – which, when remembered as specific events rather than as general events, violate the fundamental idea of temporal organization. The flexibility of multiple possible retrieval strategies, each of which could be drawn as an organization, is necessary for the efficient, intelligent use of autobiographical memory. Formulating a process-model alternative to a nested representation is extremely difficult, even though it is desirable, but the integration of neural and behavioral levels of analysis makes it easier.

What is problematic for Neisser's biologically motivated, process-based proposal holds more strongly for current models (Conway, 2005; Conway and Pleydell-Pearce, 2000) in which the representation postulates specific properties for specific levels of a hierarchy based mostly on temporal organization. Such models have heuristic value as one possible representation that is useful in some circumstances, but they cannot serve as an overall representation of the highly flexible system of autobiographical memory. By specifying the representations that they do, such models make assumptions about *the* form of organization that are not fully explained or even stated.

Discussion

I have succeeded if you are questioning the basic assumptions of both the basic systems model and cognition as it is usually studied. If you are also questioning details or devising counterarguments to the basic systems model, consider examining the more detailed expositions and studies cited that have used or have led to that model, especially Rubin (2006). There is probably much to find fault with in my presentation, in the more detailed claims, and some theoretical positions, but examine the scope of what is being accounted for here and the potential to develop a detailed theory of autobiographical memory (and other complex, real-world memory). Try to find an existing alternative theory or create a new one. I humbly submit that the observations from brain and behavior that we already have will constrain you to create a theory very much like mine, or to make microtheories of domains more limited than autobiographical memory. I do not intend to subtitle this chapter "The bankruptcy of theories of laboratory memory research," but to avoid such a bankruptcy, we need serious theoretical integration of research from the laboratory and research from cognition in the wild at both the neural and behavioral levels.

Acknowledgements

This chapter owes much to the conference participants who spent time in arguing about, sharpening, and correcting my ideas. I owe special thanks to Alan Baddeley, Dorthe Berntsen, Merlin Donald, and Bill Hirst, though this in no way means that Alan and I arrived at a common theoretical understanding. I wish to thank the National Institute of Mental Health (Grant Number R01 MH066079) and the Danish National Research Foundation for funding, and Beth Marsh and our laboratories, Roberto Cabeza, and Tobias Egner for helpful discussions and comments.

References

Atkinson, R. C. and Shiffrin R. M. (1971). The control of short-term memory. *Scientific American*, **225**, 82–90.

Baddeley, A. D. (1986). *Working memory*. Oxford University Press.

(2007). *Working memory, thought and action*. Oxford University Press.

Barsalou, L. W. (1999). Perceptual symbol systems. *Behavioral and Brain Sciences*, **22**, 577–660.

Bartlett, F. C. (1932). *Remembering: a study in experimental and social psychology*. London: Cambridge University Press.

Berntsen, D. and Rubin, D. C. (2006). The centrality of event scale: a measure of integrating a trauma into one's identity and its relation to post-traumatic stress disorder symptoms. *Behaviour Research and Therapy*, **44**, 219–231.

Brewer, W. F. (1986). What is autobiographical memory? In D. C. Rubin (ed.), *Autobiographical memory* (pp. 25–49). Cambridge University Press.

(1996). What is recollective memory? In D. C. Rubin (ed.), *Remembering our past: studies in autobiographical memory* (pp. 19–66). Cambridge University Press.

Cabeza, R., Prince, S. E., Daselaar, S. M., Greenberg, D. L., Budde, M., Dolcos, F., LaBar, K. S., and Rubin, D. C. (2004). Brain activity during episodic retrieval of autobiographical and laboratory events: an fMRI study using a novel photo paradigm. *Journal of Cognitive Neuroscience*, **16**, 1583–1594.

Conway, M. (2005). Memory and the self. *Journal of Memory and Language*, **53**, 594–628.

Conway, M. A. and Pleydell-Pearce, C. W. (2000). The construction of autobiographical memories in the self-memory system. *Psychological Review*, **107**, 261–288.

Cowan, N, (1995). *Attention and memory: an integrated framework*. New York: Oxford University Press.

Daselaar, S. M., Rice, H. J., Greenberg, D. L., Cabeza, R., LaBar, K. S., and Rubin, D. C. (2008). The spatiotemporal dynamics of autobiographical memory: neural correlates of recall, emotional intensity, and reliving. *Cerebral Cortex*, **18**, 217–229.

Dudai, Y. (2004). The neurobiology of consolidation, or how stable is the engram? *Annual Review of Psychology*, **55**, 51–86.

Ebbinghaus, H. (1885/1964). *Memory: a contribution to experimental psychology*. H. A. Ruger and C. E. Bussenius (trans.). New York: Dover.

Ericsson, K. A. and Kintsch, W. (1995). Long-term working memory. *Psychological Review*, **102**, 211–245.

Fodor, J. (1983). *The modularity of mind: an essay on faculty psychology*. Cambridge, MA: MIT Press.

Greenberg, D. L., Eacott, M. J., Brechin, D., and Rubin, D. C. (2005). Visual memory loss and autobiographical amnesia: a case study. *Neuropsychologia*, **43**, 1493–1502.

Greenberg, D. L. and Rubin, D. C. (2003). The neuropsychology of autobiographical memory. *Cortex*, **39**, 687–728.

Habermas, T. and Bluck, S. (2000). Getting a life: the emergence of the life story in adolescence. *Psychological Bulletin*, **126**, 748–769.

Herrmann, D. J. (1982). The semantic-episodic distinction and the history of long-term memory typologies. *Bulletin of the Psychonomic Society*, **20**, 207–210.

Hintzman, D. L. (1986). "Schema abstraction" in a multiple-trace memory model. *Psychological Review*, **93**, 411–428.

(2011). Research strategy in the study of memory: fads, fallacies, and the search for the "coordinates of truth." *Perspectives on Psychological Science*, **6**, 253–271.

James, W. (1890). *The principles of psychology*, 2 vols. New York: Henry Holt and Co.

Jonides, J., Lewis, R. L., Nee, D. E., Lustig, C. A., Berman, M. G., and Moore, K. S. (2008). The mind and brain of short-term memory. *Annual Review of Psychology*, **59**, 193–224.

Levine, B., Svoboda, E., Hay, J. F., Winocur, G., and Moscovitch, M. (2002). Aging and autobiographical memory: dissociating episodic from semantic retrieval. *Psychology and Aging*, **17**, 677–689.

Marsh, E. J. (2007). Retelling is not the same as recalling: implications for memory. *Current Directions in Psychological Science*, **16**, 16–20.

McKoon, G., Ratcliff, R., and Dell, G. (1986). A critical evaluation of the semantic/episodic distinction. *Journal of Experimental Psychology: Learning, Memory, and Cognition*, **12**, 295–306.

McNally, R. J., Lasko, N. B., Clancy, S. A., Macklin, M. L., Pitman, R. K., and Orr, S. P. (2004). Psychophysiological responding during script-driven imagery in people reporting abduction by space aliens. *Psychological Science*, **15**, 493–497.

Miyake, A. and Shah, P. (eds.) (1999). *Models of working memory: mechanisms of active maintenance and executive control*. New York: Cambridge University Press.

Moscovitch, M. (1992). Memory and working-with-memory: a component process model based on modules and central systems. *Journal of Cognitive Neuroscience*, **4**, 257–267.

Moscovitch, M. and Melo, B. (1997). Strategic retrieval and the frontal lobes: evidence from confabulation and amnesia. *Neuropsychologia*, **35**, 1017–1034.

Neisser, U. (1981). John Dean's memory. *Cognition*, **9**, 1–22.

(1986). Nested structure in autobiographical memory? In D. C. Rubin (ed.), *Autobiographical memory* (pp. 71–81). Cambridge University Press.

(1988a). Five kinds of self-knowledge. *Philosophical Psychology*, **1**, 35–59.

(1988b). What is ordinary memory the memory of? In U. Neisser and E. Winograd (eds.), *Remembering reconsidered: ecological and traditional approaches to the study of memory* (pp. 356–373). Cambridge University Press.

Newell, A. (1973). You can't play 20 questions with nature and win: projective comments on the papers of this symposium. In W. G. Chase (ed.), *Visual information processing* (pp. 283–308). New York: Academic Press.

Oberauer, K. (2009). Design for a working memory. *Psychology of Learning and Motivation*, **51**, 45–100.

Öztekin, I., Davachi, L., and McElree, B. (2010). Are representations in working memory distinct from representations in long-term memory? Neural evidence in support of a single store. *Psychological Science*, **21**, 1123–1133.

Postle, B. R. (2006). Working memory as an emergent property of the mind and brain. *Neuroscience*, **139**, 23–38.

Ratcliff, R. and McKoon, G. (1986). More on the distinction between episodic and semantic memories. *Journal of Experimental Psychology: Learning, Memory, and Cognition*, **12**, 312–313.

Ratcliff, R., McKoon, G., and Dell, G. (1986). A critical evaluation of the semantic-episodic distinction. *Journal of Experimental Psychology: Learning, Memory, and Cognition*, **12**, 295–306.

Rolls, E. T. (2004). Multisensory neuronal convergence of taste, somatosensory, visual, olfactory, and auditory inputs. In G. Calvert, C. Spence, and B. E. Stein (eds.), *The handbook of multisensory processes* (pp. 311–331). Cambridge, MA: MIT Press.

Rubin, D. C. (1988). Go for the skill. In U. Neisser and E. Winograd (eds.), *Remembering reconsidered: ecological and traditional approaches to the study of memory* (pp. 374–382). Cambridge University Press.

(1995). *Memory in oral traditions: the cognitive psychology of epic, ballads, and counting-out rhymes.* New York: Oxford University Press.

(1998). Beginnings of a theory of autobiographical remembering. In C. P. Thompson, D. J. Herrmann, D. Bruce, J. D. Reed, D. G. Payne, and M. P. Toglia (eds.), *Autobiographical memory: theoretical and applied perspectives* (pp. 47–67). Mahwah, NJ: Lawrence Erlbaum Associates.

(2002). Autobiographical memory across the lifespan. In P. Graf and N. Ohta (eds.), *Lifespan development of human memory* (pp. 159–184). Cambridge, MA: MIT Press.

(2005). A basic systems approach to autobiographical memory. *Current Directions in Psychological Science,* **14**, 79–83.

(2006). The basic-systems model of episodic memory. *Perspectives on Psychological Science,* **1**, 277–311.

Rubin, D. C., Berntsen, D., and Bohni, M. K. (2008). A memory-based model of posttraumatic stress disorder: evaluating basic assumptions underlying the PTSD diagnosis. *Psychological Review,* **115**, 985–1011.

Rubin, D. C., Boals, A., and Berntsen, D. (2008). Memory in posttraumatic stress disorder: properties of voluntary and involuntary, traumatic and non-traumatic autobiographical memories in people with and without PTSD symptoms. *Journal of Experimental Psychology: General,* **137**, 591–614.

Rubin, D. C., Burt, C. D., and Fifield, S. J. (2003). Experimental manipulation of the phenomenology of memory. *Memory & Cognition,* **31**, 877–886.

Rubin, D. C., Dennis, M. F., and Beckham. J. C. (2011). Autobiographical memory for stressful events: the role of autobiographical memory in posttraumatic stress disorder. *Consciousness and Cognition,* **20**, 840–856.

Rubin, D. C. and Greenberg, D. L. (2003). The role of narrative in recollection: a view from cognitive and neuropsychology. In G. Fireman, T. McVay, and O. Flanagan (eds.), *Narrative and consciousness: literature, psychology, and the brain* (pp. 53–85). New York: Oxford University Press.

Rubin, D. C., Schrauf, R. W., and Greenberg, D. L. (2003). Belief and recollection of autobiographical memories. *Memory & Cognition,* **31**, 887–901.

Rubin, D. C. and Siegler, I. C. (2004). Facets of personality and the phenomenology of autobiographical memory. *Applied Cognitive Psychology,* **18**, 913–930.

Rubin, D. C. and Wallace, W. T. (1989). Rhyme and reason: analyses of dual retrieval cues. *Journal of Experimental Psychology: Learning, Memory, and Cognition,* **15**, 698–709.

Rubin, D. C., Wallace, W. T., and Houston, B. C. (1993). The beginnings of expertise for ballads. *Cognitive Science,* **17**, 435–462.

Rubin, D. C. and Wenzel, A. E. (1996). One hundred years of forgetting: a quantitative description of retention. *Psychological Review,* **103**, 734–760.

Rumelhart, D. E. and Norman, D. A. (1986). Representation in memory. In R. C. Atkinson, R. J. Herrnstein, G. Lindzey, and R. D. Luce (eds.), *Steven's handbook of experimental psychology* (2nd edn.), vol. 2: *Learning and cognition* (pp. 511–587). New York: Wiley.

Sheen, M., Kemp, S., and Rubin, D. C. (2001). Twins dispute memory ownership: a new false memory phenomenon. *Memory & Cognition*, **29**, 779–788.

Skinner, B. F. (1974). *About behaviorism*. New York: Alfred A. Knopf.

Smith, E. E. and Jonides, J. (1997). Working memory: a view from neuroimaging. *Cognitive Psychology*, **33**, 5–42.

(1999). Neuroscience – storage and executive processes in the frontal lobes. *Science*, **283**, 1657–1661.

St. Jacques, P. L., Botzung, A., Miles, A., and Rubin, D. C. (2011). Functional neuroimaging of emotionally intense autobiographical memories in post-traumatic stress disorder. *Journal of Psychiatric Research*, **45**, 630–637.

St. Jacques, P. L., Kragel, P. A., and Rubin, D. C. (2011). Dynamic neural networks supporting memory retrieval. *NeuroImage*, **57**, 608–616.

Tulving, E. (1972). Episodic and semantic memory. In E. Tulving and W. Donaldson (eds.), *Organization of memory*. New York: Academic Press.

(1983). *Elements of episodic memory*. New York: Oxford University Press.

(1986). What kind of a hypothesis is the distinction between episodic and semantic memory? *Journal of Experimental Psychology: Learning, Memory, and Cognition*, **12**, 307–311.

(2002). Episodic memory: from mind to brain. *Annual Review of Psychology*, **53**, 1–25.

Wickelgren, W. A. (1973). The long and the short of memory. *Psychological Bulletin*, **80**, 425–438.

Williams, M. J. G. (1996). Depression and the specificity of autobiographical memory. In D. C. Rubin (ed.), *Remembering our past: studies in autobiographical remembering* (pp. 244–267). Cambridge University Press.

Zeki, S. (1993). *A vision of the brain*. Oxford: Blackwell.

3 Identity, emotion, and the social matrix of autobiographical memory: a psychoanalytic narrative view

Tilmann Habermas

Psychoanalysis is over a hundred years old, and the cognitive revolution in psychology dates back over half a century. Psychoanalysis no longer focuses on sexual drives and the Oedipus complex, and cognitive psychology has long transcended the computer metaphor. Still, theoretical traditions leave a strong, often implicit imprint on later generations by passing on basic assumptions and taken-for-granted methods. Consequently I was more than happy to follow the editors' suggestion to compare psychoanalytic and cognitive concepts of autobiographical memory. When I came across Martin Conway's 2006 paper, "Reading Freud," my heart sank, because on three pages he shows how central insights of Freud have been taken up by and have become ingrained in current cognitive research, foremost in his own work. On the basis of these commonalities, this chapter will highlight three differences in the general approach to autobiographical memory between current psychoanalytic and cognitive theories. These are (1) the relevance of identity to memory; (2) the hierarchical nature of memory modalities, ranging from action to emotion to words and narrative; and (3) the intrinsically interpersonal and social nature of remembering. Because psychoanalytic theories are not based on experimental, but on clinical evidence, my approach weds psychoanalytic theory with narrative methods. Therefore points will be illustrated with examples from narrative research and clinical vignettes.

Motivation, identity, and narrative: the life story

Cognitive models of normal autobiographical memory

For over a century, memory psychology followed Ebbinghaus' (1880) model of memorizing minimal isolated elements and measuring their reproducibility over time. Tulving (1972) originally coined the terms

Thanks to Anna Kenney for editorial help.

semantic memory for knowledge of interrelated, atemporal items versus *episodic memory* for more accidental, unintegrated items related only to the situation in which they were first learned, the prime example being lists of meaningless words introduced by Ebbinghaus. Semantic memory opened the path for cognitive psychology to build models of the organization of knowledge and its influence on the learning and retaining of new information.

Although the concept of episodic memory was later transformed and expanded to finally include any remembering of experiences (Tulving, 1983, 2002), it was rather the concept of semantic memory that inspired giving up experimental control over learning conditions and shifting the focus from learning to remembering, and thereby opening the perspective to everyday experiences. Both David Rubin's observation of the reminiscence bump in late adolescence (Rubin, Wetzler, and Nebes, 1986) and Martin Conway's model of the autobiographical knowledge base with three levels of abstraction (Conway and Pleydell-Pearce, 2000) belong to this phase of memory psychology. Rubin's observation was a major advance because it showed that the traditional forgetting curve and its mathematical formulation could be applied to memories, the encoding of which had not been controlled, and that transforming abstract time into the time of a human life reveals additional regularities of forgetting. Conway's model was also a major advance because it integrated autobiographical memories with autobiographical knowledge and provided a theoretical rationale for the differential accessibility of material for intentional and unintentional remembering.

Psychoanalytic models of motivated distortions of autobiographical memory: narrative versus historical truth

Compared to this advanced cognitive model of autobiographical memory, psychoanalytic theory is less interested in the normal workings of memory than in the effects of personality-related motivation on memory. Motivation influences autobiographical memory at two levels, that of single memories and that of the life story.

First, specific memories are distorted to protect the self. Defense mechanisms are activated to exclude or modify information that threatens to an unbearable degree individuals' sense of self-consistency with their wished-for ideal self (embarrassment), with their sense of moral self (guilt feelings; S. Freud, 1923), or with their sense of security (anxiety; A. Freud, 1966/1936). These conceptions have entered the psychological discourse as *self-serving biases* (Greenwald, 1980), deemphasizing the often aggressive and sexual motives that necessitate self-serving distortions.

In addition, not only may memories be distorted or repressed, but also several memories that share a common conflictual theme may be condensed into a *nuclear scene* (Tomkins, 1992). Specific memories may also be bent in the direction of unconscious fantasies, such as being excluded by two others (primary scene, Oedipal scene). Childhood memories are especially open to be changed to condense a variety of conflictual biographical references into one innocent scene; this is termed *screen memory* by Freud (1899). These condensed memories not only distort historical facts but may also, at the same time, reveal central concerns and conflicts of the individual (Langs, 1965). Similarly, Jefferson Singer's concept of *self-defining memories* (Singer and Salovey, 1993) links these to central themes and unresolved conflict within the individual. A more organized version of screen memories is the *personal myth* (Kris, 1956), an elaborated, starkly idealized version of one's childhood that is constructed by some individuals with a narcissistic personality disorder (Kernberg, 1992).

Second, Erik Erikson (1968) enlarged the view on possible motives for distorting memories by elaborating the concept of ego into that of ego identity, which is defined by major childhood identifications with parental values that may be consciously reworked in adolescence to form an individualized life story. An integrated life story binds past and present identifications and values guiding the future into one story by putting them in a temporal succession with reasoned transitions that provide both a sense of personal continuity and a sense of reasonable attempts to give life a direction. The integration and directedness of a life story are reflected in a healthy subjective sense of identity, such as in perceived personal continuity, a sense of self-consistency across situations, of being in charge of one's life and of feeling at home in one's body. Schafer (1983) elaborated Erikson's view by reinterpreting psychoanalytic psychotherapy as the process of renarrating the patient's life in a way that restores their agency and responsibility, thereby creating a sense of continuity and direction.

The requirements of the two truth criteria for memories, historical truth or correspondence to fact and narrative truth or coherence (Spence, 1982), have somewhat opposite effects on memories. Thus, especially negative, overwhelming, morally compromising, and embarrassing events as well as atypical or contradictory past events and actions create, if reported truthfully, a problem for the coherence of the life story, which tends to be constructed so as to transport a positive, moral image of the narrator. Such elements need to be neutralized or integrated with additional interpretative efforts. These normatively tend to bend events in a way so that they fit into the life story.

Vice versa, the truth criterion of correspondence requires some deviations from a coherent life story to account for what actually happened (Conway, Singer, and Tagini, 2004). Other deviations from a coherent life story may be more neurotic. For example, attributing the course of life mostly to circumstance and powerful others probably reflects a denial of one's motives and responsibility (Schafer, 1983). And incoherence of a life story often is a symptom of a severe disorder of identity, such as severe personality disorders (Kernberg, 1984) and insecure adult attachment (Main, Kaplan, and Cassidy, 1985). Incoherence results from the use of primitive defense mechanisms, such as splitting others or the self into only good and only bad.

These psychoanalytic concepts focus on a different aspect of memory than do cognitve theories – namely on the effects of personality-related motivation. A series of studies does confirm some of the psychoanalytic observations, especially self-serving biases in memory (Greenberg, 1980) and the influence of dominant motives (Woike, 2008), but also the tendency to change memories so as to increase personal continuity, except when there is an explicit conception that one has changed (Ross, 1989). Rubin and colleagues' (1986) finding of the reminiscence bump, a preferred recall from late adolescence and early adulthood, was interpreted by Fitzgerald (1988; Fitzgerald and Broadbridge, this volume) as reflecting adolescent identity formation. This was confirmed by findings that memories in the adolescent bump are linked to central self-reported characteristics of the self (Rathbone, Moulin, and Conway, 2008), to normative role transitions which amass during adolescence (Berntsen and Rubin, 2004), and to events that are deemed consequential for the life story (Glück and Bluck, 2007). At a theoretical level, Conway and colleagues (Conway and Pleydell-Pearce, 2000; Conway, Singer, and Tagini, 2004) have included cognitive versions of the self and motivation in their model of the autobiographical memory base in a fairly extensive way, covering many of the psychoanalytic observations of the influence of personality-related motivation on memory.

The life story

The two traditions thus differ in focus, which lies in general rules and normal functioning in cognitive psychology, and in the single case and the dysfunctional in psychoanalysis. This may explain why cognitive psychology has shied away from the large format of autobiographical memory, the life story. In addition, its clearest manifestation is a complex text, a life narrative, which is not easily transformed into numbers, and therefore does not easily fit the methodological frame of cognitive psychology. The life story, however, is closest to the core meaning of "autobiography" (Bluck and Habermas, 2001). Erikson's concept of the life story was elaborated in personality psychology by McAdams (e.g., McAdams and Olson, 2010). Some exemplary aspects of life story theory and studies shall demonstrate that also quantitative research into the life story is possible and that it transcends both a narrow concept of cognitive psychology and its methodology.

The distinctive aspect of the life story is its global coherence. We defined four central aspects of global coherence (Habermas and Bluck, 2000). Every culture has a concept of what a biography looks like, in terms of both form and content; for example, how it begins and ends, or which life events are normatively included. The latter has been conceived of as a *life script* by Rubin and Berntsen (2003). If a life narrative coheres with the cultural concept of biography, this creates global coherence for a listener. Second, global temporal coherence implies a basically chronological order and a temporal orientation as to when in the life specific events took place. Causal-motivational coherence is created by cause-effect-sequence links and, more importantly, by motive – consequence links that give a sense of agency and direction to a life and help bridge change and development in the individual. Finally, thematic coherence is created by showing similarities between distant parts of a life, often with the help of metaphors such as "I've always been a fighter."

The ability to create global coherence in oral life narratives was studied in a sample of 8-, 12-, 16-, and 20-year-olds. We asked participants to tell us their life, from the beginning to the end, in about 15 minutes, and to include the most important memories, so that the listener would understand how the participant had become the person she or he is at present. Life narratives were not coherent at age 8 and began to be globally coherent at age 12, increasing further across adolescence (Habermas and de Silveira, 2008; Habermas, Ehlert-Lerche, and de Silveira, 2009). This was confirmed in a study with written life narratives of 9-, 12-, and 15-year-olds by Bohn and Berntsen (2008). One way we measured global coherence was by local semantic and syntactic indicators, such as autobiographical arguments, causal links between specific events and personality traits, and exemplifications (Habermas and Paha, 2001). Another measure of coherence was the degree to which narratives were embedded by beginnings that contextualize the individual with socio-historical context (cf. Brown, Hansen, Lee, *et al.*, this volume) and start with birth, and by endings that provide a retrospective evaluation and a reasoned prospect into the future (Habermas, 2006b). Also ratings of aspects of global coherence (Habermas and de Silveira, 2008) and of the global narrative structure (Bohn and Berntsen, 2008) were used. Biographical knowledge that contributes to the cultural concept of biography, namely knowledge of age norms and of biographical salience of life events (does an event belong in a life narrative or not?), was already present to some degree at age 8, but increased across the ages of 12 and 16 (Habermas, 2007). In a similar vein, the explicit integration of single-turning-point narratives into the life story was more frequent at age 18 than at age 14 (Grysman and Hudson, 2010).

The cross-sectional findings still await longitudinal confirmation. In a first examination of the stability of life narratives, in a small subsample four years later, we found an increase with age of the number of events that were again included in the narrative (Negele and Habermas, 2010). As global coherence also increases with age, this finding suggests that life story stability is predicted by the global coherence of life narratives.

These exemplary findings show that the life story is a cognitive-linguistic format that both structures remembering and defines identity by selecting from the rich treasure of autobiographical memories some biographically salient events, and by arranging them in a specific way. Clinical observation suggests that deviations from normative forms of the life narrative may indicate psychopathological variations, such as when narratives are incoherent (Jørgensen, 2010; Kernberg, 1984; Main, Kaplan, and Cassidy, 1985) or deviate in length and speed (Daniel, 2011), or when a life is presented as happening due to chance or the influence of others, but not one's own values and decisions (Schafer, 1983). Thus, life narratives of clinically depressed patients are less temporally coherent than those of a control group; that is, they deviated more from a linear temporal order and contained more statements that something was still the same, thus conveying a sense that time stands still and that there is no development (Habermas, Ott, Schubert, *et al.*, 2008).

Thus, psychoanalysis not only emphasizes motivated distortions of single memories but also motivates distortions of the organization of autobiographical memories into a life story. This does not explicitly contradict basic assumptions of cognitive memory psychology, but does question the validity of focusing exclusively on single memories. Rubin's extension of the temporal axis of the forgetting curve to a human life should be taken a step further by extending the perspective from memories of single events to the life story (see Thomsen, 2009).

From action to perception to narrative of a past experience: the role of emotion

The aim of psychoanalytic psychotherapy is to help patients make sense of seemingly senseless symptoms, experiences, and behaviors and thereby to reappropriate and transform them into potentially intentional expressions of the self (Schafer, 1983). Psychoanalytic theories conceptualize the therapeutic process as an interpersonal one (discussed in the next section) and as a process of transforming action tendencies and perceptual elements into language and narratives, which is the topic of this section. First I will summarize this basic conception and point out implications for theories of autobiographical memory, and then I will illustrate the final part of this process, the transformation of initially cryptic to more fully understandable narrative accounts of events in the course of therapy or coping.

Reconstructing memories in psychoanalytic therapy

Although psychoanalysis aims at embedding neurotic symptoms and experiences in a biographical context, thereby establishing the life story as the most complex effective format of memory, the therapeutic process usually proceeds more bottom-up, starting from elementary building blocks of memory. The general idea is to break down distorted higher-level representations into elementary action memories and then to retranslate them into images, feelings, words, and narrative. The idea of a hierarchy of memory modalities has continued in some cognitive theories of memory, such as in the distinction between preverbal and verbal memory (Singer and Conway, 2011; White and Pillemer, 1979) and between perceptual and reflexive memory systems (Johnson and Hirst, 1993; cf. Granzow, 1994).

Freud thought that repressed memories were actively excluded from verbal representation, leaving only perceptual memory traces (Freud, 1915). At other times he thought that shut-off memories, despite being encoded linguistically, were separated from those contexts that made them significant to the self (Freud, 1914). Translating repressing and shutting-off memories into terms of Conway and Pleydell-Pearce's model (2000), some parts of repressed or barred memories could even remain verbally encoded, if only their links to higher levels of the knowledge system, including self-representations, were totally or partially blocked. Then their intentional, top-down retrieval becomes impossible, or at least their full significance remains obscured. Because these memories' links to higher levels are blocked, they can be retrieved more easily laterally by associations with other specific memories or by specific situational cues, what Berntsen (this volume) calls *involuntary remembering*.

The method of free association asks patients not to focus their attention but to put themselves into a trance-like state and to report anything that passes in their minds. This state of unfocused attention is facilitated by the suspension of action, such as when sitting or when lying on the couch, and by not being able to see the analyst. Such a position is ideal for day-dreaming (J. L. Singer, 1975) and involuntary remembering (Berntsen, 2009). Relations of contiguity or formal similarity, of displacement and condensation, of metonymies and metaphors, relate situational perceptions to memories.

Which cues are activated by free association? Freud thought that a deactivation of the censoring self would automatically facilitate repressed wishes in becoming conscious, and Klinger (1990) confirmed that current concerns color daydreams and involuntary memories, as do unfinished business and recent stirring events (Berntsen, 2009). Furthermore, the analytic setting puts the patient in an infantile, dependent position, being in psychic pain, lying on a couch, and not being able to see the other. This emotional and bodily position strongly reminds the patient of a baby in a crib or a child going to bed, cuing memories of childhood and dependency.

Free association was deemed to be an indirect path to repressed or barred memories and wishes, circumventing the censorship effected by how one wishes to see oneself. This is represented in Conway's model by the association of the self-concept with the abstract, higher levels of memory, from which intentional retrieval starts. Intentional retrieval is thus influenced more strongly by views of the real and ideal self than are involuntary memories. This is evident, for instance, in the stronger reminiscence bump in intentional retrieval of vivid or self-defining memories than when responding to cue words (cf. Rubin and Schulkind, 1997). A lateral access by way of situational cuing is therefore especially helpful for activating memories that have been partially disconnected from the self-concept and the highest-level schema of the life story (Bluck and Habermas, 2000).

One might object that also the process of narrating one's life is an activity that undercuts normal controls, because any unproblematic life event that is narrated may itself be associated with problematic memories triggered by the process of narrating. This sequential triggering of memories is typical of songs and stories (Rubin, 1995) and also applies to individual lives. Furthermore, the communicative situation engenders constraints to summarize events, to exemplify claims, and to follow a time line from the beginning to the present without leaving out biographically salient events (Schütze, 1984).

Still, facilitating loose associations evokes even fewer restrained memories than does narrating an entire life. However, this is not enough to identify core unresolved issues in patients. The concept of transference posits that important conflict-laden autobiographical memories are encoded as action tendencies, not necessarily as perceptual or verbal memories. These action tendencies relate to significant others, are exemplified by typical memories, and are reactivated with current important others such as the therapist. Thus, in therapy, situational cues do not primarily evoke memories, but first of all action tendencies directed toward the other, such as to jump up and run away, to cling to the pillow, or to hug or hit the therapist. Modern theories of emotion (Frijda, 1986) conceive emotions to be exactly such action tendencies that are elicited by the automatic assessment of a situation as corresponding to a prototypical emotion-eliciting situation. These universal emotion-eliciting schemata (such as danger eliciting fear) are idiosyncratically colored by individual life experiences that mark specific situations, for example, as dangerous (Tomkins, 1992). The following is an example from my own practice:

When a young female patient was speaking about her father, she suddenly shivered. She spontaneously commented that when as a child she had felt left alone by her father she used to feel cold. Indeed this happened when I had not been listening to her attentively. Here the action tendency is an expressive bodily reaction, signaling maybe sadness and the wish to be cuddled. According to her memories, her father had never really accepted her needs, as she failed his exceedingly high expectations.

In a first interview, a middle-aged male patient with a problem of chronic anger complained with subdued aggressiveness that people did not take their jobs as seriously as he did. I had the impression that he was also ventilating his frustration that I was mostly listening, but not actively doing something, in a way challenging my professional abilities. I had to think of a raging bull, looking for a fight with another bull, which at first made me more reticent and cautious, and this in turn must have reinforced his impression of me. He briefly hesitated, and then with a mixture of anger and humor provided the example that when he had first tried to call me I had failed to include information about a temporary absence on the answering machine. This feeling of being let down by an irresponsible, powerful other, which was typical of his chronic conflicts with superiors, later in the interview led to a memory from a phase in his life when his father had drifted off into alcoholism, leaving him alone at a young age. Narrating this memory shifted his mood from subdued anger into a more melancholic note.

Psychoanalysis theorizes that conflicting memories are retrieved first in the form of action tendencies that are elicited by the automatic appraisal of the present interpersonal situation, which may show in minimal initial action sequences, in expressive bodily movements (shivering) or mimicking (angry face), or in physiological reactions (accelerated pulse). These expressions of an action tendency may be accompanied by or lead to a conscious feeling state or a perceptual imagination, such as an image (of a bull), a smell, or a sensation (feeling cold). These in turn may then be interpreted by naming them as feeling left alone or feeling enraged. This may finally lead to an entire memory narrative, such as the answering machine story or the drinking father story (e.g., Bucci, 1990; Ferro, 1992).

In contrast to some cognitive theories of memory (e.g., Rubin, this volume), psychoanalytic theories point to a strong hierarchy in the modalities in which memories are recalled, basing autobiographical memories on traces of action tendencies which are associated with specific situational cues, especially corporal, emotional, and social cues. This conception also suggests that theories of autobiographical memory should not just categorize the evaluative component of memories as positive or negative, but that they should also conceptualize specific emotional and motivational qualities. Finally, the motivational qualities of memories cannot always be defined as being purposefully directed by goals (Conway and Pleydell-Pearce, 2000). Rather they may also be related to more open-ended, reactive action tendencies or emotions, which do move the individual, but only roughly define the direction of actions.

Coping and the transformation of narrative form

Systematic studies of the transformation of memories from action tendencies to images and feelings to narratives are difficult to design as they require interpretation of minute expressive movements and access to subjective impressions. One approach might involve the analysis of mimic reactions that precede the emergence of images and memory narratives. It is easier to study the process of how memories merge once they are communicated verbally. Stiles, Honos-Webb, and Lani (1999), as well as Bucci (1990), propose models of how narratives change in the course of psychotherapy, or, in analogy, in the course of coping. They suggest that severely problematic, defended-against experiences are first narrated only briefly and incompletely, lacking necessary contextual information, evaluations, and interpretations, therefore leaving listeners somewhat puzzled. In the course of retellings and re-elaborations of the event, narratives become longer to increasingly include evaluations and then also interpretations. In this phase the event is narrated in detail, strong emotions are aroused, and the meaning of the event is elaborated. Once the event is emotionally and cognitively processed, narratives become shorter again, but are more plausible than at the beginning of this process. This process is nicely illustrated in a case study by Nye (1996) and systematically studied by Mergenthaler (1996); see Figure 3.1.

The following narratives were elicited two and again eight weeks after the event (in the context of a seminar exercise) and exemplify the initial

action memories
sensory memories (perceptions, feelings)
naming of sensory memory
decontextualized episodic memories
autobiographically contextualized memories
rudimentary emotional narrative
elaborated, evaluated narrative
condensed, distanced, closed narrative

Figure 3.1. Phases of remembering problematic experiences.

and middle phases of the model (rudimentary and elaborated narrative).
Irene (27 years old) was asked for a memory of an angering event:

(1) Last time I got angry
(2) was two weeks ago.
(3) It may have been, well, due to my physical condition.
(4) I was very drunk,
(5) and my ex,
(6) who left me after 5 years
(7) because of his "need for freedom,"
(8) how he was standing with another girl outside during a party.
(9) And the two got along very well and embraced each other
(10) and, well, then I somehow lost control
(11) and slapped him in the face.
(12) After that I was much more angry at *myself* than at him,
(13) that I am capable of such a thing.
(14) I wouldn't really have believed it
(15) and, well, let's say
(16) I am still fighting with myself over it.

Relevant information is missing for the listener to understand what
actually happened, such as why she was attending the same party, whether
she had followed him, or whether he knew she was present. Six weeks later
she renarrated the event in more detail:

(1) My ex-boyfriend had just left me after 5 years.
(2) He no longer had "enough feelings" for me.
(3) Then came an evening
(4) when all our friends came together to have a good time.
(5) I had withdrawn from my ex,
(6) didn't talk to him anymore,
(7) ignored him.
(8) Late in the evening I saw him sitting,
(9) a girlie in front of him on the floor,
(10) leaning on him.

(11) She had been following him from early evening on.
(12) That had already been annoying me for the whole evening.
(13) And then they went outside.
(14) What a coincidence:
(15) Right then I needed to fetch some fresh air.
(16) I sat down in a safe distance and watched
(17) how the situation would develop.
(18) The girl seemed to be freezing.
(19) He took off his jacket and wrapped it around her.
(20) Deep inside I was already boiling like a volcano before the outbreak.
(21) Then I saw
(22) how she leaned on him
(23) and he held her in his arms.
(24) I only asked myself
(25) "Why on earth does he do such a thing?"
(26) because he knew I was also still there,
(27) and that the danger was, was quite big,
(28) that I would notice it.
(29) And what did she want?
(30) She already had a boyfriend of her own!
(31) I couldn't bear this image anymore,
(32) how the two were standing there,
(33) holding each other in their arms.
(34) The volcano had broken out.
(35) I jumped up,
(36) went to the two of them,
(37) and slapped my ex in the face,
(38) and then again,
(39) and again.
(40) I yelled at him,
(41) how on earth he could do this to me!
(42) I was so angry at him!
(43) And not a second later had I understood
(44) that I had just hit the one person in the face,
(45) who meant most to me.
(46) I was so sorry for everything.
(47) That was not what I had wanted.
(48) I was so mad at myself,
(49) at him,
(50) at the whole situation.
(51) But above all I asked myself
(52) how things could have gotten that far,

(53) how I could be so full of hate,
(54) and how I could hit him.
(55) I would have never believed
(56) that I was capable of such a thing.
(57) Never would I have expected this from myself.
(58) I had lost control before,
(59) but never had the – result – been so bad
(60) as it was in that moment.

This narrative is longer, there is background information (lines 1–7), the action sequence is more detailed and interspersed with evaluations and naming of emotions (lines 8–42), and it is followed by a global evaluation. There is still relatively little explanation of her motives and of how her actions might fit her self-concept.

Habermas and Berger (2011) studied how narratives of everyday hassles changed over the course of three months. As the memories became emotionally less charging, the narratives became condensed, more distanced, and more closed. Given the moderate emotionality of events, these narratives skip the first phase of Stiles' model, the changes reflecting the transition from the middle to the final phase (from elaborated to closed narratives).

Another way to characterize the effect of defensiveness and coping on narrative form is to analyze the degree to which multiple temporal and personal perspectives are represented in the text (cf. Fivush, this volume). My basic thesis is that the fewer perspectives are represented, the more defense processes have distorted and impeded remembering, whereas the more diverse temporal and personal perspectives are represented, the more successful coping has been (Habermas, 2006b). For example, Irene represents in her second narrative her own past and present perspectives as well as the ex-boyfriend's and the other girl's past perspectives. Also, the diversity of subjective perspectives included in memory narratives influences the emotions elicited in listeners (Habermas and Diel, 2010). Listeners (therapists) in turn influence the (patient's) narrative by adding perspectives, helping to integrate isolated memories into a coherent sense of self (Beran and Unoka, 2004).

However, there are limits to the correlation of the variety of narrative perspectives and degree of coping. One is that the event has to be emotional enough to justify a detailed narration and evaluation. Another limit is that under specific conditions the inclusion of additional perspectives may have traumatic effects. In a study of the life narratives of Jewish children who had survived the Holocaust hidden in other families, the psychoanalytic concept of *Nachträglichkeit*, or *deferred action*, is confirmed by many stories of how the separation from the biological family and the later separation from the host family had become traumatic not immediately but only when they were viewed retrospectively in a new and wider context (Fohn and Heenen-Wolff, 2011).

Thus, my second contention is that psychoanalysis adds to the cognitive psychology of autobiographical memory a process view that traces the gradual elaboration, narrativization, and evaluation from multiple perspectives of problematic memories for the coping process.

The social matrix of autobiographical memory

A third contribution of psychoanalysis to the knowledge of autobiographical memory is to include in the concept of memory the social situation and relationship in which remembering is embedded. The social situation and relationship are important to remembering at three different times in life: the attachment relationship(s) formed during the first year of life, the present therapeutic relationship, and those relationships which in the past have contributed to shaping memories.

Infantile attachment patterns

According to modern psychoanalysis, defensive maneuvers are embedded in typical ways of relating to others and experiencing relationships. These are formed in interactions with significant others during the first year of life (Winnicott, 1958). A rough categorization of basic ways of relating is achieved by the attachment status (Ainsworth, Blehar, Waters, et al., 1978). These individual ways of interpreting social situations, of relating, and of defending against expected negative experiences remain fairly stable across life. Relationship patterns also structure the therapeutic relationship, especially in its conflictual aspects. In Freud's (1914) original conception, this transference relationship enables the patient to remember conflictual experiences which are at the root of unresolved conflicts.

Attempting to link psychoanalytic to cognitive concepts of memory, Fonagy (1999) suggested that relationship patterns are encoded as implicit or procedural memories, inaccessible to explicit memory because they were formed before the development of verbal memory. Therefore, the aim of clinical psychoanalysis was no longer to render repressed memories conscious, but to describe the relationship patterns for the first time without any conscious remembering being involved. Psychoanalysis, in his view, has thus little to say about explicit, autobiographical memory.

Fonagy's attempt to bridge psychoanalysis and cognitive psychology is merely terminological. Also, the cognitive terms do not describe well what is theorized by psychoanalysis, because the concept of implicit memory applies to formerly explicit knowledge which has been forgotten, and the concept of procedural memory is limited to circumscribed motor abilities. Individual ways of relating to others, in contrast, have mostly never been explicated, and they are not merely cognitive or behavioral, but deeply emotional and social (Singer and Conway, 2011). Therefore, Stern and colleagues prefer to speak of *typical ways of being with a significant other* that are ingrained in implicit relational knowing (Boston Change Process Study Group, 2008; Stern, 2004). Furthermore, Fonagy's contention of the irrelevance of autobiographical memory to psychoanalytic psychotherapy can be disputed on several grounds. For example, attachment security influences the quality of autobiographical remembering, which is impeded by defense mechanisms in insecurely attached adults (Main, Kaplan, and Cassidy, 1985).

The present relationship

Even more importantly, the formation and experience of the therapeutic relationship not only reflects the patient's typical ways of relating, as the traditional concept of transference implies, but is also influenced by the individual therapist, who contributes unconsciously to the emotional bi-personal field (Ferro, 1992). Whereas, according to Fonagy, remembering has no therapeutic value, Ferro attributes to memory narratives an important role similar to that of dream or fantasy narratives. As discussed in the preceding section, they serve to fully symbolize raw action tendencies in the here and now. The co-creation of an emotional field by patient and therapist shows that both participants may have matching or complementary associations (such as my image of a bull in the second clinical vignette), which are the basis for the therapeutic use of countertransference. Thus, the raw material from which memory narratives are formed in therapy emerges from the bi-personal emotional field which is created by the present relationship. Consequently, remembering is influenced by the present matrix of the patient–therapist relationship that cannot be reduced to a mere transference of an internalized attachment relationship pattern.

Also everyday life remembering in a social situation is strongly colored by the action tendencies and emotions aroused by narrator and listener. Whereas psychoanalysis focuses on the unconscious influences of social situations on memories, psychological and linguistic studies focus on manifest communication and its influence on memory. Often remembering with another is a process of co-narration in which the listener validates or questions memories and evaluations or asks for more detail (e.g., Fiehler, 1990). Listeners may also help fill in details or co-construct a memory (Bielli, 2010; Staudinger, 1996). In some situations of shared storytelling, memories are actually co-constructed by several speakers (Deppermann, 2007).

Past social rememberings

A third social matrix which influences memories is past instances of social remembering (Bartlett, 1932; Pasupathi, 2001). Bill Hirst (Hirst, Cuc, and Wohl, this volume) has studied speaker effects on the speaker's and listener's later memory experimentally (cf. Pasupathi, 2001). Fivush, Haden, and Reese (2006) demonstrated the socializing effects of shared remembering of mothers with their young children on the children's ability to remember. The everyday importance of the formative role of past social rememberings is underlined by the high frequency with which autobiographical memories tend to be shared with others (Rimé, 2009).

We have studied the co-narrations of mothers and their adolescent offspring of the adolescent's life. Mothers scaffolded those aspects of global coherence that the child was just about to acquire, suggesting that the acquisition of the ability to narrate a whole life in a coherent fashion is also socially mediated. In addition, mothers told stories, especially from their child's early years, which only they could know about to define lasting characteristics of the adolescent. Mothers also confirmed or disputed memories that were provided by the adolescents (Habermas, Negele, and Mayer, 2010). These are discursive strategies which most probably influence the way the adolescents will later tell their life stories.

Conclusion

Three aspects of autobiographical remembering have been highlighted as central to psychoanalytic understanding of autobiographical memory as it arises from the treatment of psychologically troubled individuals. Motivated distortions of memories are driven by the implications of autobiographical remembering for the sense of who one is. This is most evident in life narratives, in which memories are included to support identity claims.

Another aspect of remembering that is central to psychoanalytic therapy is the process of constructing a memory from scratch, parting from conative urges, and leading to affective perceptions, which may then be named and understood. The fullest elaboration of basic memory traces is provided by autobiographical narratives, the form of which is both an indicator of the quality of remembering and a means to integrate a memory into one's life story.

Finally, remembering is an intrinsically social endeavor. It is originally learned with parents, influencing both the style of remembering, the typical kind of defensiveness, and the content of early self-defining memories. Also past and present social situations of remembering influence the memory, unconsciously through the emotions elicited reciprocally by the participants, as well as by more explicit communicative and co-narrative processes.

Some aspects of psychoanalytic theorizing about memory have been neglected in this chapter. For example, fantasy and imagination, which are driven by present desires and past experiences, may both distort memories and are a precondition for them, given the reconstructive nature of remembering, in which certain probable and possible memories are complemented by imagination. Beyond imagining concrete scenes, inferential and reasoning processes are also involved in remembering; they aim to explain apparently unmotivated elements and to integrate them into one's life (Habermas, 2011). Finally, memory processes may be specific for certain clinical disorders, such as post-traumatic stress disorder or depression.

References

Ainsworth, M., Blehar, M., Waters, E., and Wall, S. (1978). *Patterns of attachment.* Hillsdale, NJ: Lawrence Erlbaum Associates.

Bartlett, F. W. (1932). *Remembering: a study in experimental and social psychology.* London: Cambridge University Press.

Beran, E. and Unoka, Z. (2004). Construction of self-narrative in psychotherapeutic setting: an analysis of the mutual determination of narrative perspective taken by patient and therapist. In U. M. Quasthoff and T. Becker (eds.), *Narrative interaction* (pp. 151–169). Amsterdam: Benjamins.

Berntsen, D. (2009). *Involuntary autobiographical memories.* Oxford University Press.

Berntsen, D. and Rubin, D. (2004). Cultural life scripts structure recall from autobiographical memory. *Memory & Cognition,* **32,** 4217–4247.

Bluck, S. and Habermas, T. (2000). The life story schema. *Motivation & Emotion,* **24,** 121–147.

  (2001). Extending the study of autobiographical memory. *Review of General Psychology,* **5,** 135–147.

Bohn, A. and Berntsen, D. (2008). Life story development in childhood. *Developmental Psychology,* **44,** 1135–1147.

Boston Change Process Study Group (2008). Forms of relational meaning: issues in the relations between the implicit and reflective-verbal domains. *Psychoanalytic Dialogues,* **18,** 125–148.

Bucci, W. (1990). *Psychoanalysis and cognitive science: a multiple code theory*. New York: Guilford Press.

Conway, M. A. (2006). Memory and desire: reading Freud. *The Psychologist*, **19**, 548–550.

Conway, M. A. and Pleydell-Pearce, C. W. (2000). The construction of autobiographical memories in the self-memory system. *Psychological Review*, **107**, 261–288.

Conway, M. A., Singer, J. A., and Tagini, A. (2004). The self and autobiographical memory: correspondence and coherence. *Social Cognition*, **22**, 491–529.

Daniel, S. I. F. (2011). Adult attachment insecurity and narrative processes in psychotherapy. *Clinical Psychology and Psychotherapy*, **18**, 498–511.

De Silveira, C. and Habermas, T. (2011). Narrative means to manage responsibility in life narratives across adolescence. *Journal of Genetic Psychology*, **172**, 1–20.

Deppermann, A. (2007). Using the other for oneself: conversational practices of presenting out-group members amomg adolescents. In M. Bamberg, A. DeFina, and D. Schiffrin (eds.), *Selves and identities in narrative and discourse* (pp. 273–301). Amsterdam: John Benjamins.

Ebbinghaus, H. (1880). *Urmansukript "Über das Gedächtniß" [Original manuscript "On memory"]*. Passau: Passavia Universitätsverlag, 1983.

Erikson, E. H. (1968). *Identity, youth, and crisis*. New York: Norton.

Ferro, A. (1992). *The bi-personal field: experiences in child analysis*. London: Routledge.

Fiehler, R. (1990). *Kommunikation und Emotion*. Berlin: de Gruyter.

Fitzgerald, J. M. (1988). Vivid memories and the reminiscence phenomenon: the role of a self narrative. *Human Development*, **31**, 261–273.

Fivush, R., Haden, C. A., and Reese, E. (2006). Elaborating on elaborations: role of maternal reminiscing style in cognitive and socioemotional development. *Child Development*, **77**, 1568–1588.

Fohn, A. and Heenen-Wolff, S. (2011). The destiny of an unacknowledged trauma: the deferred retroactive effect of *après-coup* in the hidden Jewish children of wartime Belgium. *International Journal of Psychoanalysis*, **92**, 5–20.

Fonagy, P. (1999). Memory and therapeutic action. *International Journal of Psychoanalysis*, **80**, 215–223.

Freud, A. (1966/1936). *The ego and the mechanisms of defense*. London: Hogarth.

Freud, S. (1899). On screen memories. In J. Strachey (ed.), *The standard edition of the works of Sigmund Freud*, vol. III (pp. 303–323). London: Hogarth.

(1914). Remembering, repeating, and working through. In J. Strachey (ed.), *The standard edition of the works of Sigmund Freud*, vol. XII (pp. 147–156). London: Hogarth.

(1915). The unconscious. In J. Strachey (ed.), *The standard edition of the works of Sigmund Freud*, vol. XIV (pp. 166–204). London: Hogarth.

(1923). The ego and the id. In J. Strachey (ed.), *The standard edition of the works of Sigmund Freud*, vol. XIX (pp. 12–59). London: Hogarth.

Frijda, N. H. (1986). *The emotions*. New York: Cambridge University Press.

Glück, J. and Bluck, S. (2007). Looking back across the life span: a life story account of the reminiscence bump. *Memory & Cognition*, **35**, 1928–1939.

Granzow, S. (1994). *Das autobiographische Gedächtnis*. Berlin: Quintessenz.
Greenwald, A. (1980). The totalitarian ego: fabrication and revision of personal history. *American Psychologist*, **35**, 603–618.
Grysman, A. and Hudson, J. A. (2010). Abstracting and extracting: causal coherence and the development of the life story. *Memory*, **18**, 565–580.
Habermas, T. (2006a). Wie Jugendliche lernen, Lebenserzählungen zu eröffnen und beenden. In H. Welzer and H. J. Markowitsch (eds.), *Warum Menschen sich erinnern* (pp. 256–275). Stuttgart: Klett-Cotta.
(2006b). Who speaks? Who looks? Who feels? Point of view in autobiographical narratives. *International journal of Psychoanalysis*, **87**, 497–518.
(2007). How to tell a life: the development of the cultural concept of biography across the lifespan. *Journal of Cognition and Development*, **8**, 1–31.
(2011). Autobiographical reasoning: mechanisms and functions. In T. Habermas (ed.), *The development of autobiographical reasoning in adolescence and beyond* (pp. 1–17). New Directions in Child and Adolescent Development, 131. San Francisco, CA: Jossey-Bass.
Habermas, T. and Berger, N. (2011). Retelling everyday emotional events: condensation, distancing, and closure. *Cognition & Emotion*, **25**, 206–219.
Habermas, T. and Bluck, S. (2000). Getting a life: the development of the life story in adolescence. *Psychological Bulletin*, **126**, 748–769.
Habermas, T. and de Silveira, C. (2008). The development of global coherence in life narratives across adolescence: temporal, causal, and thematic aspects. *Developmental Psychology*, **44**, 707–721.
Habermas, T. and Diel, V. (2010). The emotional impact of loss narratives: event severity and narrative perspectives. *Emotion*, **10**, 312–323.
Habermas, T., Ehlert-Lerche, S., and de Silveira, C. (2009). The development of the temporal macrostructure of life narratives across adolescence: beginnings, linear narrative form, and endings. *Journal of Personality*, **77**, 527–560.
Habermas, T., Meier, M., and Mukhtar, B. (2009). Are specific emotions narrated differently? *Emotion*, **9**, 751–762.
Habermas, T., Negele, A., and Mayer, F. B. (2010). "Honey, you're jumping about" – Mothers' scaffolding of their children's and adolescents' life narration. *Cognitive Development*, **25**, 339–351.
Habermas, T., Ott, L. M., Schubert, M., Schneider, B., and Pate, A. (2008). Stuck in the past: negative bias, explanatory style, temporal order, and evaluative perspectives in life narratives of clinically depressed individuals. *Depression and Anxiety*, **25**, E121–E132.
Habermas, T. and Paha, C. (2001). The development of coherence in adolescents' life narratives. *Narrative Inquiry*, **11**, 35–54.
Haden, C. A., Haine, R. A., and Fivush, R. (1997). Developing narrative structure in parent-child reminiscing across the preschool years. *Developmental Psychology*, **33**, 295–307.
Johnson, M. K. and Hirst, W. (1993). MEM: memory subsystems as processes. In A. F. Collins, S. E. Gathercole, M. A. Conway, and P. E, Morris (eds.), *Theories of memory* (pp. 241–285). Hillsdale, NJ: Lawrence Erlbaum Associates.

Jørgensen, C. R. (2010). Identity and borderline personality disorder. *Journal of Personality Disorders*, **24**, 344–364.

Kernberg, O. F. (1984). *Severe personality disorders*. New Haven, CT: Yale University Press.

(1992). "Mythological encounters" in the psychoanalytic situation. In P. Hartocollis and I. D. Graham (eds.), *The personal myth in psychoanalytic theory* (pp. 37–48). Madison, CT: International Universities Press.

Klinger, E. (1990). *Daydreaming: using waking fantasy and imagery for self-knowledge and creativity*. New York: St. Martin's Press.

Kris, E. (1956). The personal myth. *Journal of the American Psychoanalytic Association*, **4**, 653–681.

Langs, R. J. (1965). Earliest memories and personality. *Archives of General Psychiatry*, **12**, 379–390.

Main, M., Kaplan, N., and Cassidy, J. (1985). Security in infancy, childhood, and adulthood: a move to the level of representation. *Monographs of the Society for Research in Child Development*, **50**(1–2), 66–104.

McAdams, D. P. and Olson, B. D. (2010). Personality development: continuity and change over the life course. *Annual Review of Psychology*, **61**, 517–542.

Mergenthaler, E. (1996). Emotion-abstraction patterns in verbatim protocols. *Journal of Consulting and Clinical Psychology*, **64**, 1306–1315.

Negele, A. and Habermas, T. (2010). Self-continuity across developmental change in and of repeated life narratives. In K. McLean and M. Pasupathi (eds.), *Narrative development in adolescence* (pp. 1–22). New York: Springer.

Nye, C. H. (1996). Narrative retelling in clinical treatment: a single case study. In J. R. Brandell (eds.), *Narration and therapeutic action* (pp. 113–136). New York: Haworth.

Pasupathi, M. (2001). The social construction of the personal past and its implications for adult development. *Psychological Bulletin*, **127**, 651–672.

Person, E. S. (2006). Revising our life stories: the role of memory and imagination in the psychoanalytic process. *Psychoanalytic Review*, **93**, 655–674.

Rathbone, C. J., Moulin, C. J. A., and Conway, M. A. (2008). Self-centered memories: the reminiscence bump and the self. *Memory & Cognition*, **36**, 1403–1414.

Reese, E., Chen, Y., Jack, F., and Hayne, H. (2010). Emerging identities: narrative and self in early adolescence. In K. McLean and M. Pasupathi (eds.), *Narrative development in adolescence* (pp. 23–44). New York: Springer.

Rimé, B. (2009). Emotion elicits the social sharing of emotion: theory and empirical review. *Emotion Review*, **1**, 60–85.

Ross, M. (1989). Relation of implicit theories to the construction of personal histories. *Psychological Review*, **96**, 341–357.

Rubin, D. C. (1995). *Memory in oral traditions*. Oxford University Press.

Rubin, D. C. and Berntsen, D. (2003). Life scripts help to maintain autobiographical memories of highly positive, but not highly negative events. *Memory & Cognition*, **31**, 1–14.

Rubin, D. C. and Schulkind, M. D. (1997). Distribution of important and word-cued autobiographical memories in 20, 35, and 70 year-old adults. *Psychology and Aging*, **12**, 524–535.

Rubin, D. C., Wetzler, S. E., and Nebes, D. (1986). Autobiographical memory across the lifespan. In D. C. Rubin (ed.), *Autobiographical memory* (pp. 202–221). New York: Cambridge University Press.

Schafer, R. (1983). *The analytic attitude.* New York: Basic Books.

Schütze, F. (1984). Kognitive Figuren des autobiographisches Stegreiferzählen [Cognitive figures of autobiographical narrating]. In M. Kohli and G. Robert (eds.), *Biographie und soziale Wirklichkeit* (pp. 78–118). Stuttgart: Metzler.

Singer, J. A. and Conway, M. (2011). Reconsidering therapeutic action: Loewald's cognitive neuroscience and the integration of memory's duality. *International Journal of Psychoanalysis,* **92**, 1183–1207.

Singer, J. A. and Salovey, P. (1993). *The remembered self: emotion and memory in personality.* New York: Free Press.

Singer, J. L. (1975). *The inner world of daydreaming.* New York: Harper & Row.

Spence, D. P. (1982). *Narrative truth and historical truth.* New York: Norton.

Staudinger, U. (1996). Wisdom and the social-interactive foundation of the mind. In P. Baltes and U. Staudinger (eds.), *Interactive minds* (pp. 276–316). Cambridge University Press.

Stern, D. N. (2004). *The present moment in psychotherapy and everyday life.* New York: Norton.

Stiles, W. B., Honos-Webb, L., and Lani, J. A. (1999). Some functions of narrative in the assimilation of problematic experiences. *Journal of Clinical Psychology,* **55**, 1213–1226.

Thomsen, D. (2009). There is more to life stories than memories. *Memory,* **17**, 445–457.

Tomkins, S. S. (1992). *Affect, imagery, and consciousness.* Vol. IV: *Cognition: duplication and transformations of informations.* New York: Springer.

Tulving, E. (1972). Episodic and semantic memory. In E. Tulving and W. Donaldson (eds.), *Organization of memory* (pp. 381–402). New York: Academic Press.

(1983). *Elements of episodic memory.* Oxford: Clarendon.

(2002). Episodic memory. *Annual Review of Psychology,* **53**, 1–25.

White, S. H. and Pillemer, D. B. (1979). Childhood amnesia and the development of a socially accessible memory system. In J. F. Kihlstrom and F. J. Evans (eds.), *Functional disorders of memory* (pp. 29–73). Hillsdale, NJ: Lawrence Erlbaum Associates.

Winnicott, D. W. (1958). *Through pediatrics to psychoanalysis.* London: Tavistock.

Woike, B. A. (2008). A functional framework for the influence of implicit and explicit motives on autobiographical memory. *Personality and Social Psychology Review,* **12**, 99–117.

4   On the nature of autobiographical memory

Martin A. Conway and Laura Jobson

The nature of an individual, of a self, is defined by autobiographical memories unique to that person. Memories, however, may also be shared across individuals who have experienced the same or similar events. Moreover, personal knowledge abstracted from experience, *autobiographical knowledge*, may be unique to an individual or may generalize more widely within social groups, societies, and cultures – for example, in life scripts (e.g., Berntsen and Bohn, 2009; Berntsen and Rubin, 2004) and representations of lived history (e.g., Brown, Lee, Krslak, *et al.*, 2009; Brown and Lee, 2010; Brown, Hansen, Lee, *et al.*, this volume). Autobiographical memories and knowledge are conjoined in acts of remembering (Conway, 2009) and form mental constructions that the individual experiences as memories – that is, for which they have conscious recollective experience. We conceive of this complex form of cognition as occurring in what we have termed the *self-memory system* (SMS). The SMS contains conceptual representations of the self, goal structures, autobiographical conceptual knowledge, and highly event-specific episodic memories (Conway, 2005, 2009; Conway and Pleydell-Pearce, 2000). In this chapter we briefly review the SMS and link it to more recent developments in understanding conceptual autobiographical knowledge and especially to cross-cultural aspects of autobiographical remembering.

Nature of autobiographical memory

The SMS was introduced as a conceptual framework for autobiographical memory, and, uniquely for a model of memory, it emphasizes the role of the self and goals in remembering. It is a superordinate memory system consisting of a working self, operating in conjunction with a conceptual self, to generate patterns of activation in an autobiographical knowledge base: it is these transitory patterns that are, briefly, memories. The working self comprises a motivational hierarchy of goals and sub-goals that operate to constrain cognition, and ultimately behavior, into effective ways of operating in the world. The autobiographical knowledge base comprises a hierarchy knowledge from event-specific episodic memories through to temporal linked events, and finally to abstract self-conceptual knowledge. More recently, the conceptual self was introduced, and it, alongside the working self, regulates autobiographical remembering. The conceptual self integrates the SMS model more fully with current social-cognitive theorizing about the self. It recognizes and realizes "social constructed schema and categories that define the self, other people, and typical interactions with the surrounding world ... drawn from the influences of familiar and peer socialisation, schooling and religion, as well as stories, fairy tales, myths and media influences that are constitutive of an individual's culture" (Conway, 2005, p. 597; see also Conway, Singer, and Tagini, 2004). The conceptual self consists of the life story alongside specified self-structures that exist independently of specific episodes such as personal scripts, self-with-other units relational schema, life scripts, possible selves, self-guides, representations of lived history, attitudes, values, and beliefs. While the conceptual self contains abstracted knowledge structures that exist independently of specific temporally defined incidents (episodic memories and autobiographical knowledge), the conceptual self is connected to autobiographical knowledge and the episodic memory system as it is used to activate specific instances that exemplify, contextualize, and ground the underlying themes or concepts of the conceptual self (Conway, 2005).

Figure 4.1 illustrates this organization of autobiographical memory and also includes some new developments of the framework. Importantly, the *life story* (Bluck, Alea, Habermas, *et al.*, 2005), a structure of the conceptual self representing a narrative-like account of a person's life, is considered to also contain representations of culturally generated knowledge such as *life scripts*. Life scripts are conceived of as expectations about probable activities that individuals will likely undertake or become involved with during the course of their life, such as school, university, first job, marriage, and children (see Berntsen and Rubin, 2004; Rubin and Berntsen, 2003). We also consider that representations of lived history, termed "historical defined autobiographical periods" by Brown and colleagues (Brown *et al.*, 2009; Brown *et al.*, this volume) are represented as part of the life-story narrative. These are considered further below. Such structures can be used to access the autobiographical memory knowledge base and trigger the construction of specific memories.

A further development in the SMS has been to elaborate what was initially termed *event-specific knowledge* (ESK). The term "ESK" was deliberately chosen to be relatively theory-neutral and to refer to any highly specific knowledge unique to a single or extended representation

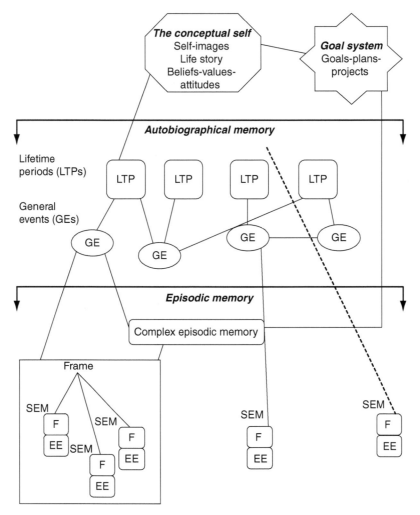

Figure 4.1. The embedding of episodic memories in autobiographical memory knowledge structures.

of experience(s). However, we now consider that there may be more complicated organization at this level in the SMS (see Conway, 2009, for a full account). The most basic unit of representation of experience is termed the *episodic element* (EE). EEs are interesting representations not least because they are *experience near*. However, they are not representations that somehow replay or allow the literal reliving of experience. Instead they are derived from more transitory representations of (conscious) experience (see Moscovitch, 1995, this volume). Note that a philosophical principle of the SMS is that experience can never be relived – it can only remembered (one cannot step in the same river twice, as the Greek philosopher Heraclitis so perceptively pointed out over 2,000 years ago). In general, EEs are not representations that can be consciously retrieved; instead they can only ever be retrieved by the process of *direct retrieval*. The notion of direct retrieval simply embodies Tulving's concept of encoding specificity (see Tulving, 1983), which in itself embodies the notion of *content-addressable memory*, an idea which simply states that in order to access an EE an effective cue must be present during retrieval. The cue must correspond in some more or less direct way to the content of an EE; otherwise, it will not be effective.

It is proposed that EEs are a species-general form of fragmentary and summary representation of recent experience and are accessible for some relatively short period of time after formation, measured in hours, and become rapidly inaccessible following a sleep cycle. In human memory, EEs become attached to more enduring conceptual knowledge which forms a "frame" for an EE. EEs in autobiographical memory are generally conceived as being in the form of images, and very often visual images. Thus, an image, held by one of us, of Jimi Hendrix saying, "This isn't my song, man" when about to play "Purple Haze" on a BBC television program (*Top of the Pops*) in the 1960s when an error was made and another song was played ("Simon Smith and His Amazing Dancing Bear" by Alan Price) constitutes an example of an EE-plus-conceptual frame, termed in the SMS framework, a *simple episodic memory* (SEM). Obviously there can be *complex episodic memories* (CEM) too (see Figure 4.1), in which a conceptual frame comes to organize several SEMs into a more complicated but still experience-near, event-specific knowledge structure. This particular development of the SMS is useful in thinking about forgetting and various types of amnesia – see Conway (2009) for further details.

Here we note, in closing this section, the critically important role of visual imagery in SEMs and CEMs. Recent neuroimaging studies from our group (e.g., St. Jacques, Conway, Lowder, *et al.*, 2011) have established that visual images when they enter into an autobiographical construction have an unusual property in that they are associated with an increase in the integration of widely distributed memory networks in the cortex and midbrain. EEs then drive generation of conceptual frames. Thus, it might be that the image of Hendrix drives the activation of (Conway's) knowledge about the music of the 1960s and that part of that knowledge might be a general event (watching *Top of the Pops*), part of a lifetime period (when I was a hippie), and part of a historically defined autobiographical period, the 1960s. As the visual and auditory images come to mind, these more conceptual, personal, and cultural knowledge structures become activated and the complicated representation shown in Figure 4.1 is now reflected in this over 40-year-old autobiographical memory of Hendrix. Interestingly, and as Schank (1982) originally pointed out, the memory also serves to solve a problem: finding a way to illustrate the workings of the SMS. That is why the SMS is considered to be so closely enmeshed with the goal system – memories solve problems, make problems, and drive motivation.

Autobiographical memory and culture

In the SMS, while the conceptual self links autobiographical remembering with one's sociocultural world, it has primarily located autobiographical remembering within the individual and in doing so somewhat separated the sociocultural world and self. The study of culture and self has resulted in the "realization that people and their sociocultural worlds are not separate from one another. Instead they require each other and complete one another. In an ongoing cycle of mutual constitution, people are socioculturally shaped shapers of their environments; they make each other up and are most productively analyzed together" (Markus and Kitayama, 2010, p. 421). The self that the SMS emphasizes in autobiographical remembering is a psychological reality that is rooted not only in the brain and the body (e.g., Cabeza and St. Jacques, this volume; LeDoux, 1996; Moscovitch, this volume; Northoff, Heinzel, de Greck, et al., 2006; Park and Huang, 2010; Rubin, this volume) but also in the sociocultural context (Markus and Kitayama, 1991, 2010); thereby the self is always situated in and reflects its context, and both the self and the context continually constitute one another (Markus and Kitayama, 2010). Consequently, autobiographical remembering both is shaped by culture and is a shaper of culture – an individual's autobiographical memories of Hendrix are shaped by the culture of the 1960s, and in turn the culture of the 1960s and the image of Hendrix are continually shaped by individuals' autobiographical memories and autobiographical knowledge. As a result of this cycle, both culture and self, and thus autobiographical remembering, are dynamic (Kashima, 2000; Kitayama, Duffy, and Uchida, 2007).

Given the self and the sociocultural world are mutually constituted, autobiographical memories not only express, develop, and maintain the self (Wang and Conway, 2004) but also in turn express, develop, and maintain culture. For example, autobiographical memory is important in developing, maintaining, and nurturing social bonds (Bluck et al., 2005) and provides material for conversation, allowing for the enrichment of social interaction (Cohen, 1998). Therefore, autobiographical remembering that reflects particular social and cultural practices will maintain and shape local habits and general rules of social interaction (Han, Leichtman, and Wang, 1998). Autobiographical memory is also used to guide present thought, feeling, and behavior (Bluck et al., 2005), in problem-solving, in the development of opinions and attitudes (Cohen, 1989, 1998), and in anchoring personal values and guiding life directions (Bluck et al., 2005). Thus, autobiographical remembering will influence culture by shaping practices, opinions, values, attitudes, societal factors, and pervasive ideas. Figure 4.2 locates the SMS (Figure 4.1) in the sociocultural context. It shows that autobiographical remembering and culture constantly comprise each other and are not separate from each other (hence the dotted line around the SMS). Figure 4.2 shows that the sociocultural world – through societal factors and pervasive ideas (e.g., economic, historical, environmental, religious, scientific, what is good? what is normal? what is moral? what is self?), institutions and products (e.g., education, health, politics, media, language), and daily situations and practices (e.g., home, work) (Markus and Kitayama, 2010) – influences the conceptual self and, hence, autobiographical remembering. As culture changes, the conceptual self changes, and in turn, autobiographical remembering changes. Consequently autobiographical remembering and the conceptual self reinforce, and occasionally alter, the sociocultural factors that shape people's lives; a "cycle of mutual constitution" (Markus and Kitayama, 2010, p. 423).

One especially influential set of sociocultural patterns which stipulate the normatively appropriate relations between the self and others is the independent/interdependent dimension (Markus and Kitayama, 1991, 2010; Triandis, 1995). Different cultures hold remarkably divergent construals of the self, others, and the interdependence between the two (e.g., Markus and Kitayama, 1991, 1994). In individualistic cultures (typically Western), the self is conceived as a unique, independent, self-contained, autonomous individual comprising a particular arrangement of internal attributes (e.g., traits, abilities, motives and values). The self behaves in a way that is consistent with these internal attributes. The goals of the independent self are to be unique, express the self, realize internal attributes, and promote its own goals. In collectivistic cultures (typically non-Western), the self is perceived as an interdependent entity attending to and fitting in with others. The self is perceived as interdependent with the surrounding context (social), and it is the other, or "self-in-relation-to-other," that is the focus of the person's experience. The goals of the interdependent self are to belong, fit in, occupy one's proper place, and

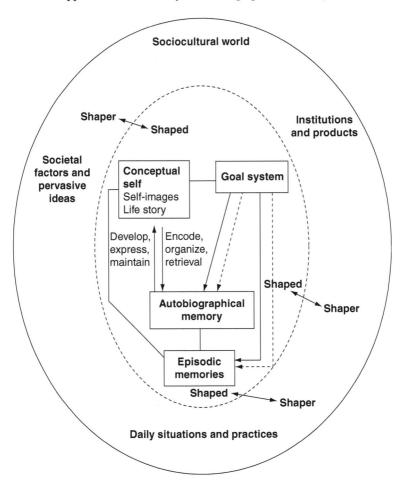

Figure 4.2. Further locating the SMS in the sociocultural world. Figure adopted from Markus and Kitayama (1994, 2010).

engage in appropriate action (see Markus and Kitayama, 1991). Such representations of self are most elaborated in memory and have been called core conceptions, salient identities, self-schema (e.g., Gergen, 1968; Markus, 1977; Stryker, 1986), or the conceptual self (see Jobson, 2009). Such representations govern cognition and behavior, enabling them to be culturally appropriate. Thus, whenever a task, event, or situation is self-relevant, cognition, emotion, and behavior are thought to be influenced, and in some cases governed, by this aspect of the conceptual self (Markus and Kitayama, 1991, 1994). While people have aspects of both an independent and an interdependent self, one self is dominant depending on the culture a person is raised in. The dominance emerges in response to various cultural factors such as language (see Marian and Kaushanskaya, 2004; Ross, Xun, and Wilson, 2002); discussions with peers (see Nelson and Fivush, 2004; Rogoff, Morelli, and Chavajay, 2010); parental/family reminiscing style (see Choi, 1992; Fivush, this volume; Han *et al.*, 1998; Mullen and Yi, 1995; Nelson and Fivush, 2004; Wang and Fivush, 2005); traditions of thought and practice (see Weber and Morris, 2010); the actions of local heroes and role models (see Markus, Uchida, Omoregie, *et al.*, 2006); and art, stories, myths, and so forth, which all highlight the "normal," the "good," and the "right way to be" (Markus and Kitayama, 2010).

The conceptual self, among other roles, is used to encode, organize, and retrieve autobiographical memories. In a unique, complex, symbiotic relationship with the conceptual self, autobiographical memories are in turn used to develop, express, and maintain the self – see Figure 4.2 (Wang and Conway, 2004). Given that episodic memory is about goals and these memories "preserve information that is highly relevant to goal processing" (Conway, 2009, p. 2306), episodic memories are motivated by goals of the conceptual self. As goals of the independent and interdependent instantiations of self differ, Jobson (2009) proposes that the working self comprises both an autonomous and relatedness hierarchy of goals and sub-goals that function to shape cognition and behavior into culturally appropriate, expected, and functional ways of operating in the world. Individuals have both autonomous and relatedness goals. In situations some types of relations, such as business transactions, will be guided relatively more by autonomous goals, while other social relations, such as family activities, will be guided relatively more by communal and relatedness concerns (Markus and Kitayama, 2010). Additionally, each individual also emphasizes independence and interdependence to varying degrees (Fiske, Kitayama, Markus, *et al.*, 1998; Greenfield, 2009; Markus and Kitayama, 2010; Triandis, 1995). Despite this, normative differences between individualistic and collectivistic cultures are marked regarding the emphasis on autonomous or relatedness goals (e.g., Fiske *et al.*, 1998; Kagitcibasi, 1996; Markus and Kitayama, 1991). Thus, while all people hold both a relatedness and an autonomous aspect of the working self, one orientation is typically dominant depending on one's culture.

Figure 4.3 illustrates that, while all people possess both a relatedness and an autonomous aspect of the working self, one orientation is dominant. This dominance is suggested to be culturally determined and aligned with the conceptual self. Hence, when an everyday event occurs, for those from collectivistic/interdependent cultures (see left-hand side of

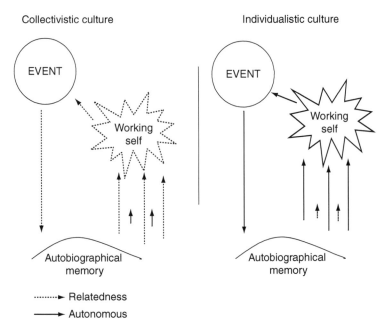

Figure 4.3. The role of autonomous and relatedness goals in autobiographical remembering.

Figure 4.3), the dominant working self, as a hierarchy of predominately relatedness goals, is activated, and used to encode and integrate the memory into the autobiographical knowledge base – this allows everyday memory to establish connections to other lifetime periods and general events that foreground relatedness, resulting in culturally appropriate elaboration. This process aligns with the conceptual self. In contrast, for those from individualistic/independent cultures (see right-hand side of Figure 4.3), the dominant working self, as a hierarchy of autonomous goals, is activated, and used to encode and integrate the memory into the autobiographical knowledge base, allowing for the elaboration of everyday memory with an emphasis on autonomy. Again, this process aligns with the conceptual self – allowing for the development, expression, and maintenance of the conceptual self and, in turn, culture (Jobson, 2009).

Accumulating findings support the influence of cultural differences in self-construal on autobiographical remembering. Research has demonstrated that children and adults from individualistic cultures provide more lengthy, autonomous, detailed, specific, and self-focused autobiographical memories that focus on individual experiences, roles, and emotions, and contain more references to internal states and own roles, preferences, and feelings than those from collectivistic cultures. In contrast, those from collectivistic cultures provide relatively skeletal accounts of past experiences that focus on collective activities, general routines, emotionally neutral events, social interactions, and daily routines. They tend to recall memories of social interactions and significant others, and focus more on the roles of other people than those from individualistic cultures (e.g., Gur-Yaish and Wang, 2006; Han et al., 1998; Jobson and O'Kearney, 2008; Wang, 2001, 2004, 2008; Wang and Conway, 2004; Wang, Conway, and Hou, 2004; Wang, Leichtman, and Davies, 2000). Those from individualistic cultures also think or talk about their memories more frequently, perceive their memories as more important, and provide more elaborate autonomous (i.e., work, achievements, school) memories (Fiske and Pillemer, 2006; Jobson and O'Kearney, 2008; Wang and Conway, 2004) than those from collectivistic cultures. Those from collectivistic cultures tend to provide more elaborate relatedness (i.e., family, community, social interactions, etc.) memories than those from individualistic cultures (Jobson and O'Kearney, 2008).

Research also supports the notion that individuals do have both autonomous and relatedness aspects of the working self, as these cultural differences can be manipulated. Wang (2008) primed Asian-American participants to focus on either their American or Asian self prior to recalling autobiographical events. She found that those who focused on their American self recalled more self-focused and less socially oriented memories than those who focused on their Asian self. Marian and Kaushanskaya (2004) investigated autobiographical memories retrieved by bicultural Russian-English bilinguals. They found that when speaking a language associated with an individualistic culture (English), participants produced more individualistic narratives, and that when retrieving a memory in a language associated with a more collectivistic culture (Russian), participants produced more collectivistic narratives, regardless of the language of encoding. They suggest that memories and self-narratives in bilinguals are mediated by the language spoken at any given time and that language functions as a vehicle for culture.

Another social-cultural factor (i.e., societal factors and pervasive ideas; Figure 4.2) that has a reciprocal relationship with the conceptual self, and thus autobiographical remembering, is the cultural life script (e.g., Berntsen and Bohn, 2009; Berntsen and Rubin, 2004). The SMS suggests that the most abstract level of autobiographical knowledge is the life story, which contains general factual and evaluative knowledge about the individual (Conway, 2005). However, the life story belongs to a specific individual, is personal, is part of autobiographical knowledge, and is the process through which an individual attempts to maintain a sense of identity and continuity through the understanding of personal meaning (Berntsen and Bohn, 2009). Nevertheless, this focus on the life story generally assumes that the organization of autobiographical memory originates in the life course of the individual and gives less focus to the way the life course is normatively described by the individual's sociocultural world (Berntsen and Bohn, 2009). Berntsen and Rubin (2004) therefore propose a cultural life script which is a mental representation of culturally expected life events that are associated with certain culturally sanctioned age norms.

A life script suggests that life events occur in a specific order and characterize a prototypical life course within a particular culture. They contain culturally important transition events and mark culturally approved transitions from one social role to another (such as coming of age, getting married, having a child, and first job). Cultures often observe certain ceremonies to acknowledge these transition events (such as for coming of age – bar mitzvah, sweet sixteen birthday party, initiation ceremonies, twenty-first birthday party). Life scripts are passed down from older generations, from observing the behavior of others (typically older) in the same culture, and from stories and cultural practices (Berntsen and Bohn, 2009; Berntsen and Rubin, 2004). We propose that just as the independent/interdependent dimension influences the conceptual self, so does the social/cultural life script. The life script is reflected in the hierarchy of goals and sub-goals of the working self. The life script provides scaffolding for the organization and retrieval of autobiographical memories. There is evidence for this from the reminiscence bump, suggesting that a cultural script forms an overarching organizational principle for autobiographical memories and future representations across the life span (see Berntsen and Bohn, 2009; Berntsen and Rubin, 2004; Bohn and Bernsten 2011; Rubin and Berntsen, 2003). It is important to note that autobiographical remembering also influences and modifies the cultural life script and thus again shapes the sociocultural world.

Social/historical periods can also influence the conceptual self and thus autobiographical remembering. Brown and colleagues (Brown and Lee, 2010; Brown et al., 2009, this volume) have suggested that historically significant periods (such as conflict and natural disasters) can sometimes organize autobiographical memory, act as landmarks, and provide thematic content which defines the lifetime period. That is, autobiographical memories and historical events can become intertwined. Brown and colleagues suggest this occurs only when these events alter the fabric of daily life in society (such as daily situations and practices; Figure 4.2) for these individuals. These events terminate most of an individual's interactions with the local, social, and material environment and signal an end to most of the individual's activities associated with elements specific to these environments. Thus, autobiographical memory and historical memory can become interrelated when public events alter the fabric of daily life (or expected cultural and societal patterns and routines). We propose that these events significantly influence the conceptual self, as they are events that have resulted in people "living in history" and have direct and pervasive effects on people's lives, and thus are represented in the conceptual self and as part of the life story narrative (Brown *et al.*, this volume). These events then provide scaffolding for the organization of autobiographical memories. Again it also seems likely that the way people recall these historical periods will also influence culture and the way culture records these events.

Episodic memories and culture

As a final point, we propose that culture also influences the properties of episodic memories. For example, once an episodic memory is formed, episodic information (details) within the memory is differentially accessible. While the activation/inhibition levels of details in an episodic memory are determined by many factors, it is likely that the goal structure of an experience is essential, as it drives attention, action, and affect, and must thereby influence encoding processes. Indeed, one of the main functions of episodic memories might be to keep a highly specific record of aspects of experience relevant to recent goal processing (see Conway, 2009). Thus, even highly specific aspects of experience will be aligned with the goals of the conceptual self, which are socially and culturally influenced. One function of episodic memories is to offer a way to accurately check on recent progress with current goals, as in the proceeding few minutes, hours, or days, or the last few days (see Conway, 2009). Episodic memories thus allow a process whereby the self can continually assess how well sociocultural expectations and goals are being achieved. This then guides future goals and plan implementation. As stated above, EEs become attached to more enduring conceptual knowledge, which forms a "frame" for an EE. That is, knowledge is gradually abstracted from episodic memories and becomes part of a more general, long-term conceptual self. Therefore, the knowledge from these instances (e.g., specific memories, earliest memories, and self-defining memories where cultural differences in self-construal have been repeatedly found) is used to develop the long-term conceptual self (e.g., which when assessed by self-concept measures is predominately either an independent or interdependent self). SEMs provide visual images that are the basis of a self-image, images of the self in the past and future, and serve to provide specific content to the goals of self (Conway, 2009). Therefore, the SEMs become directly associated with a self-image that reflects cultural and social expectations, and represents complex and fundamental goals of the self.

Summary

In this chapter, we have briefly reviewed the SMS and discussed the new developments of the framework; specifically, the elaboration of what was initially termed *event-specific knowledge*. We now consider that there may be a more complicated organization at this level in the SMS, the most basic unit of representation of experience being the *episodic element* (EE). An EE is the fragmentary and summary representation of recent experience and is accessible for a relatively short period of time after formation. EEs are generally conceived as being in the form of images (often visual images). EEs become attached to more enduring conceptual knowledge which forms a "frame" for an EE. An EE-plus-conceptual frame is termed a *simple episodic memory* (SEM). There can also be *complex episodic memories* in which a conceptual frame comes to organize several SEMs. We then briefly discussed how these developments are useful in thinking about forgetting and various types of amnesia.

Following this, we attempted to better locate the SMS within culture; autobiographical remembering both is shaped by culture and is a shaper of culture often mediated by the conceptual self. We highlighted this relationship, using the influence of the independent/interdependent dimension on the conceptual self (Jobson, 2009). The conceptual self, among other roles, is used to encode, organize, and retrieve autobiographical memories. We suggested that the working self comprises both an autonomous and a relatedness hierarchy of goals and sub-goals that function to shape cognition and behavior into culturally appropriate, expected, and functional ways of operating in the world. While individuals have both autonomous and relatedness goals, one orientation is proposed to be dominant depending on an individual's culture. This process allows for elaboration of the memories in culturally sanctioned ways, and these memories in turn develop, express, and maintain the culturally expected conceptual self (Jobson, 2009). We also went a step further to highlight that autobiographical remembering and the conceptual self reinforce, and occasionally alter, the sociocultural factors that shape people's lives; a "cycle of mutual constitution" (Markus and Kitayama, 2010). Third, we considered another two sociocultural factors that have a reciprocal relationship with the conceptual self, and thus autobiographical remembering; the cultural life script (Berntsen and Bohn, 2009; Berntsen and Rubin, 2004) and social/historical periods

(Brown *et al.*, 2010). Therefore, in this chapter, we have further developed both extremes of the SMS (Figure 4.1); the most basic unit (episodic events) and the most abstract unit (the conceptual self).

References

Berntsen, D. and Bohn, A. (2009). Cultural life scripts and individual life stories in memory. In P. Boyer and J. Wertsch (eds.), *Memory in mind and culture* (pp. 62–82). Cambridge University Press.

Berntsen, D. and Rubin, D. C. (2004). Cultural life scripts structure recall from autobiographical memory. *Memory and Cognition*, **32**, 427–442.

Bluck, S., Alea, N., Habermas, T., and Rubin, D. (2005). A tale of three functions: the self-reported uses of autobiographical memory. *Social Cognition*, **23**, 91–117.

Bohn, A. and Berntsen, D. (2011). The reminiscence bump reconsidered: children's perspective life stories show a bump in young adulthood. *Psychological Science*, **22**, 197–202.

Brown, N. R. and Lee, P. J. (2010). Public events and the organisation of autobiographical memory: an overview of the living-history project. *Behavioral Sciences of Terrorism and Political Aggression*, **2**, 133–149.

Brown, N. R., Lee, P. J., Krslak, M., Conrad, F. G., Hansen, T., Havelka, J., and Reddon, J. (2009). Living in history: how war, terrorism, and natural disaster affect the organization of autobiographical memory. *Psychological Science*, **20**, 399–405.

Choi, S. H. (1992). Communicative socialization processes: Korea and Canada. In S. Iwasaki, Y. Kashima, and K. Leung (eds.), *Innovations in cross-cultural psychology* (pp. 103–122). Amsterdam: Swets and Zeitlinger.

Cohen, G. (1989). *Memory in the real world*. Hove: Erlbaum.
  (1998). The effects of aging on autobiographical memory. In C. P. Thompson, D. J. Herrmann, D. Bruce, D. J. Read, D. G. Payne, and M. P. Toglia (eds.), *Autobiographical memory: theoretical and applied perspectives* (pp. 105–123). Hillsdale, NJ: Lawrence Erlbaum Associates.

Conway, M. A. (2005). Memory and the self. *Journal of Memory and Language*, **53**, 594–628.
  (2009). Episodic memories. *Neuropsychologia*, **47**, 2305–2313.

Conway, M. A. and Pleydell-Pearce, C. W. (2000). The construction of autobiographical memories in the self-memory system. *Psychological Review*, **107**, 261–288.

Conway, M. A., Singer, J. A., and Tagini, A. (2004). The self and autobiographical memory: correspondence and coherence. *Social Cognition*, **22**, 495–537.

Fiske, A. P., Kitayama, S., Markus, H. R., and Nisbett, R. E. (1998). The cultural matrix of social psychology. In D. T. Gilbert, S. T. Fiske, and G. Lindsey (eds.), *The handbook of social psychology*, vol. IV (pp. 915–981). Boston, MA: McGraw-Hill.

Fiske, K. E. and Pillemer, D. B. (2006). Adult recollections of earliest childhood dreams: a cross cultural study. *Memory*, **14**(1), 57–67.

Gergen, K. J. (1968). Personal consistency and the presentation of self. In C. Gordon and K. J. Gergen (eds.), *The self in social interaction: classic and contemporary perspectives* (vol. I, pp. 299–308). New York: Wiley.

Greenfield, P. M. (2009). Linking social change and developmental change: shifting pathways of human development. *Developmental Psychology*, **45**, 401–448.

Gur-Yaish, N. and Wang, Q. (2006). Self-knowledge in cultural contexts: the case of two Western cultures. In A. P. Precott (ed.), *The concept of self in psychology* (pp. 129–143). Hauppauge, NY: Nova Science Publishers.

Han, J. J., Leichtman, M. D., and Wang, Q. (1998). Autobiographical memory in Korean, Chinese, and American children. *Developmental Psychology*, **34**, 701–713.

Jobson, L. (2009). Drawing current posttraumatic stress disorder models into the cultural sphere: the development of the 'threat to the conceptual self' model. *Clinical Psychology Review*, **29**, 368–381.

Jobson, L. and O'Kearney, R. T. (2008). Cultural differences in retrieval of self-defining memories. *Journal of Cross-Cultural Psychology*, **39**, 75–80.

Kagitcibasi, C. (1996). *Family and human development across cultures: a view from the other side*. Hillsdale, NJ: Lawrence Erlbaum Associates.

Kashima, Y. (2000). Conceptions of culture and person for psychology. *Journal of Cross-Cultural Psychology*, **31**, 14–32.

Kitayama, S., Duffy, S., and Uchida, Y. (2007). Self as cultural mode of being. In S. Kitayma and D. Cohen (eds.), *Handbook of cultural psychology* (pp. 136–173). New York: Guilford Press.

LeDoux, J. E. (1996). *The emotional brain: the mysterious underpinnings of emotional life*. New York: Simon & Schuster.

Marian, V. and Kaushanskaya, M. (2004). Self-construal and emotion in bicultural bilinguals. *Journal of Memory and Language*, **51**, 190–201.

Markus, H. R. (1977). Self-schemata and processing information about the self. *Journal of Personality and Social Psychology*, **35**, 63–78.

Markus, H. R. and Kitayama, S. (1991). Culture and the self: implications for cognition, emotion, and motivation. *Psychological Review*, **98**, 224–253.

(1994). A collective fear of the collective: implications for selves and theories of selves. *Personality and Social Psychology Bulletin*, **20**, 568–579.

(2010). Cultures and selves: a cycle of mutual constitution. *Perspectives on Psychological Science*, **5**, 420–430.

Markus, H. R., Uchida, Y., Omoregie, H., Townsend, S., and Kitayama, S. (2006). Going for gold: models of agency in Japanese and American contexts. *Psychological Science*, **17**, 103–112.

Moscovitch, M. (1995). Recovered consciousness: a hypothesis concerning modularity and episodic memory. *Journal of Clinical and Experimental Neuropsychology*, **17**, 276–291.

Mullen, M. K. and Yi, S. (1995). The cultural context of talk about the past: implications for the development of autobiographical memory. *Cognitive Development*, **10**, 407–419.

Nelson, K. and Fivush, R. (2004). The emergence of autobiographical memory: a social cultural developmental theory. *Psychological Review*, **111**, 486–511.

Northoff, G., Heinzel, A., de Greck, M., Bermpohl, F., Dobrowolny, H., and Panksepp, J. (2006). Self-referential processing in our brain: a meta-analysis of imaging studies on self. *NeuroImage*, **1**, 440–457.

Park, D. C. and Huang, C.-M. (2010). Culture wires the brain: a cognitive neuroscience perspective. *Perspectives on Psychological Science*, **5**, 391–400.

Rogoff, B., Morelli, G. A., and Chavajay, P. (2010). Children's integration in communities and segregation from people of differing ages. *Perspectives on Psychological Science*, **5**, 431–440.

Ross, M., Xun, E., and Wilson, A. E. (2002). Language and the bicultural self. *Personality and Social Psychology Bulletin*, **28**, 1040–1050.

Rubin, D. C. and Berntsen, D. (2003). Life scripts help to maintain autobiographical memories of highly positive, but not highly negative, events. *Memory & Cognition*, **31**, 1–14.

Schank, R. C. (1982). *Dynamic memory*. New York: Cambridge University Press.

St. Jacques, P. L., Conway, M. A., Lowder, M. W., and Cabeza, R. (2011). Watching my mind unfold versus yours: an fMRI study using a novel camera technology to examine neural differences in self-projection of self versus other perspectives. *Journal of Cognitive Neuroscience*, **23**, 1275–1284.

Stryker, S. (1986). Identity theory: developments and extensions. In K. Yardley and T. Honess (eds.), *Self and identity* (pp. 89–104). New York: Wiley.

Triandis, H. (1995). *Individualism and collectivism*. Boulder, CO: Westview Press.

Tulving, E. (1983). *Elements of episodic memory*. New York: Oxford University Press.

Wang, Q. (2001). Culture effects on adults' earliest childhood recollection and self-description: implications for the relation between memory and the self. *Journal of Personality and Social Psychology*, **81**, 220–233.

(2004). The emergence of cultural self-construct: autobiographical memory and self description in American and Chinese children. *Developmental Psychology*, **40**(1), 3–15.

(2008). Emotion knowledge and autobiographical memory across the preschool years: a cross-cultural longitudinal investigation. *Cognition*, **108**, 117–135.

Wang, Q. and Conway, M. A. (2004). The stories we keep: autobiographical Memory in American and Chinese middle-aged adults. *Journal of Personality*, **72**, 911–938.

Wang, Q., Conway, M. A., and Hou, Y. (2004). Infantile amnesia: a cross-cultural investigation. *Cognitive Sciences*, **1**(1), 123–135.

Wang, Q. and Fivush, R. (2005). Mother–child conversations of emotionally salient events: exploring the functions of emotional reminiscing in European-American and Chinese families. *Social Development*, **14**, 473–495.

Wang, Q., Leichtman, M. D., and Davies, K. I. (2000). Sharing memories and telling stories: American and Chinese mothers and their 3-year-olds. *Memory*, **8**, 159–178.

Weber, E. U. and Morris, M. W. (2010). Culture and judgment and decision making: the constructivist turn. *Perspectives on Psychological Science*, **5**, 410–419.

5   Reflections on autobiographical memory

Alan Baddeley

I was very pleased to be invited to contribute to this book marking the foundation of a center for the study of autobiographical memory in Aarhus, but somewhat daunted, given that I have not worked in the area for a number of years. I have, however, just written a chapter on the topic in a recent textbook (Baddeley, Eysenck, and Anderson, 2009), but had emerged from my review feeling that the field still seemed somewhat fragmented and atheoretical. This seemed a good opportunity to help celebrate the foundation of a center that explicitly aims to change that perception.

Labels and definitions

I do not subscribe to the view that concepts and theories require precise definition before they can be fruitfully applied. On the contrary, my view of precise definitions is that they are possible only when one has a good understanding of the broad area, and, in the case of autobiographical memory, this is not yet. However, I think that the way in which a concept is labeled can have a major effect on its acceptance and subsequent popularity, an effect that can be positive, but may also lead to confusion if different people use the same labels in different ways. I think this is the case in the study of autobiographical memory.

In the area of long-term memory, the most influential theoretical distinctions in the last half-century have been made by Endel Tulving. His early empirical work comprised a series of elegant demonstrations of the importance of retrieval, leading to the concept of *encoding specificity* whereby remembering depends upon reinstating the cues experienced during learning. This was followed by the hugely influential distinction between *semantic* and *episodic* memory – generic knowledge of the world on one hand and memory for specific events on the other (Tulving, 1972). Tulving later placed a further constraint on episodic memory, restricting it to situations in which the rememberer is consciously aware of the prior learning experience, referring to this state as depending upon *autonoetic consciousness* (Tulving, 1989).

Despite relying on the sort of phenomenological evidence that would have seemed shocking some 20 years earlier, the distinction between "remembering," accompanied by recollection of the learning experience, and simply "knowing" that you have encountered an event, has proved to be both robust and fruitful (Gardiner, 2002). For example, the decline in performance on standard laboratory-based memory tasks with age has been shown to reflect a decline in the number of "remembered" responses while the number of correct "know" responses remains constant (Parkin and Walter, 1992). Hence, although the theoretical question of whether two phenomenological states necessarily reflect different underlying memory systems remains controversial (Shanks and St. John, 1994), at an empirical level at least, the distinction has been a fruitful one.

Tulving's terminological distinctions have been, and continue to be, important in the area of autobiographical memory, but have not been problem-free. First of all, the term "autobiographical memory" has sometimes been regarded as synonymous with episodic memory, in either its initial, more general, or its later, more specific, phenomenological sense. This can lead to confusion of two kinds. The first concerns the question of whether phenomenological experience is necessary for a memory to be regarded as autobiographical, and if so, how we conceive of memories of personally experienced events for which this recollective component has been lost. This in turn leads to the second question of whether it is useful to postulate a semantic form of autobiographical memory. In my own view the answer is clearly yes. Kopelman, Wilson, and Baddeley (1990) assumed such a distinction in creating their Autobiographical Memory Inventory (AMI), a decision that has subsequently been supported by a number of single-case, neuropsychological studies in which patients may have either preserved episodic but impaired semantic autobiographical memory (De Renzi, Liotti, and Nichelli, 1987) or the reverse (Dalla Barba, Cipolotti, and Denes, 1990). Finally, while on the topic of Tulving's conceptual contribution to the field, I should mention the concept of *mental time travel* that other chapters in this volume, as well as many recent articles in the field, suggest is becoming increasingly influential within autobiographical memory. I shall return to this later.

Figure 5.1 illustrates the way in which I myself propose to use the concepts developed by Tulving, not because I think that my view is correct and others are not, but simply to avoid misunderstanding. First of all, I use the term "episodic memory" in Tulving's earlier sense, as involving memory of a specific event, regardless of whether the details of the encoding of that event can be recollected. My own research in this area

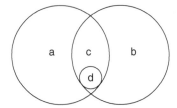

Figure 5.1. Terminology can be confusing. My own use of terms is shown above.

a. Semantic memory, e.g., "Paris is the capital of France."

b. Episodic memory, e.g., "The word France has just been mentioned."

c. Autobiographical memory: "I myself have visited France," which may or may not have:

d. A recollective component: "I remember the gale during my last visit to Paris."

has come principally through the study of amnesic patients, and I tend to think of episodic memory as the sort of thing that pure amnesic patients cannot do. I assume that it is a system that differs from other memories in allowing us to remember specific events or episodes, and that to do so it requires the event to be attached to a specific temporal or locational context. I also assume that the classic amnesic syndrome, as well as, indeed, the memory deficit shown in aging and Alzheimer's disease, reflects a deficit in this process of attaching an experience to a context, probably reflecting some kind of failure of consolidation. In order to make clear that I am not competent to be specific about the specific mechanism of consolidation, I tend to refer to this rather loosely as the *mnemonic glue hypothesis*. I assume that this process and its outcome are separate from, but related to, semantic memory, generic knowledge about the world. The two are, however, related, with patients who have gross impairments in episodic memory finding it difficult to build up new representations in semantic memory. They are, however, still capable of implicit learning, which I assume depends upon a whole series of systems in which learning is gradual, incremental, and demonstrated by performance rather than intentional recall or recognition.

Finally I would like to make a distinction between three levels of theorization. The first is natural history, based on the careful observation of phenomena within a research field. The second involves the development of micromodels that attempt to systematize such observations in a form that aims to stimulate further questions, leading to the creation of the third level of exploration in terms of theories. I regard theories as overarching frameworks that attempt to combine such micromodels into a coherent structure that will have empirically testable implications. These three approaches will tend to develop in parallel, beginning with natural history, and eventually leading to a mature science in which a series of micromodels fit within the broad theoretical framework, which can then be linked to neighboring fields of study. The view expressed in my earlier chapter (Baddeley *et al.*, 2009) was that the field of autobiographical memory had perhaps focused too much on a limited number of observational or experimental paradigms that were still closer to the natural history end of the continuum, with too little attention paid to the development of broader theoretical prospectives. That is not to say that experimenters in this area do not consider theory, but rather that they may have become too locked onto testing rather specific micromodels. A good example of this is offered by the phenomenon of flashbulb memory.

Flashbulb memory

In a highly influential paper, Brown and Kulick (1977) asked people to remember where and when they had first heard of the assassination of J. F. Kennedy. They found that people reported remarkably vivid and precise memories, just as if they were able to re-experience that event. They suggested that the current view of memory as reconstructive was wrong in this case, proposing a totally different mechanism evoked under conditions of high emotion, which they termed the "now print hypothesis." This was assumed to leave a literal representation of that particular moment that could subsequently be recalled with great precision, just as if a photograph had been taken at the time. Over the ensuing years, a very large number of studies on this topic have been carried out, principally concerned with the question of whether the representation is truly as accurate as suggested, and with the related question of why such recall is so vivid and apparently so good (Luminet and Curci, 2009).

There is no doubt that people do have very vivid recollections of the situation in which they encounter such dramatic news, although there is now considerable doubt as to whether such memories are fundamentally different from any other vivid memory (Curci and Luminet, 2009). Furthermore, there are many features of such a situation that would be likely to lead to a clear and vivid memory. In addition to their emotional impact, such events are likely to be high in social importance, to lead to subsequent discussion with friends, and to result in repeated reminders in the press both immediately and over subsequent years. Furthermore, such events are distinctive and stand out from surrounding memories, and in addition are unlikely to be overwritten by similar experiences. Flashbulb memory is, in short, a phenomenon with many explanations, which tend to be correlated and hence hard to tease apart. My general conclusion from the literature is that thirty years of work by many different groups has simply told us that the now-print hypothesis is probably unnecessary. Flashbulb memory is, however, an intrinsically intriguing phenomenon, and I have no doubt that when the next catastrophe strikes, some cognitive psychologists somewhere will, alas, be busily producing a flashbulb questionnaire. I have considerable doubts, however, as to how scientifically fruitful such future studies will prove.

Eyewitness testimony

Perhaps the most widely investigated topic within the broad remit of autobiographical memory concerns the validity of the testimony of eyewitnesses to a crime. There is no doubt that this is an important question both practically and theoretically, and that the work by Beth Loftus in particular has made a major contribution to the realization that this is a real problem that needs to be addressed by legal systems everywhere (Loftus, 1993). In understanding the problem, it was, of course, important to study those factors that are likely to have an influence on the eyewitness, with a view either to avoid misleading testimony or evoke more accurate memories. Relevant factors include the potential impact of misleading interrogation procedures, the fallibility of face recognition, how to set up an appropriate line-up of potential suspects, the effects of emotion on testimony, and the question of whether stress leads to a narrowing of attention and weapon focus. All of these can be coupled with the study of individual differences between witnesses on a basis of such factors as age, gender, and suggestibility.

Such research has certainly been useful in identifying potential sources of error in eyewitness testimony. However, the fact that the vast bulk of such work is based on simulated minor crimes, using student participants, leaves it open to the objection from a prosecuting lawyer that such conclusions are unrealistic and should be discounted. Furthermore, in an adversarial system such as that operating in the UK at least, both defense and prosecution can call expert witnesses, and given the number of variables that might influence eyewitness recall, each lawyer is likely to be able to present an interpretation based on published evidence, but with very different conclusions. This has led the judiciary in the UK to rule that the jury does not need guidance from experts on the operation of human memory, not a happy outcome of so much careful work.

One example of practical progress that has resulted from psychological research in this area is the creation of the cognitive interview, in which the psychology of memory was used to optimize the retrieval of accurate information by the witness (Geiselman, Fisher, MacKinnon, *et al.*, 1985). This has been shown to enhance recall, and has been adapted by a number of police departments worldwide. However, the interview requires special training, is lengthy, and, apparently, in practice is often truncated or omitted (Kebbell and Wagstaff, 1999; Milne and Bull, 2002).

I would suggest in general that, while research on eyewitness testimony has indeed been productive, there is a need to focus less on laboratory-based simulations and more on the much more difficult issue of applicability to genuine crime, and that this should include methods of improving the cognitive interview so as to make it briefer and more user-friendly without reducing its efficacy.

False memory

This is the area that has evoked the fiercest controversies in the field, resulting in the so called "memory wars." The problem stems from the widely held belief among some psychotherapists that many of the emotional problems experienced by their patients resulted from childhood abuse, which had then been repressed, causing a whole range of emotional problems (Bass and Davis, 1988). This encouraged such therapists to attempt to uncover memories of childhood abuse, using whatever methods seemed appropriate. This frequently led to major family disruption with the patient blaming the parent and in some cases seeking legal redress. Evidence for the veracity of such memories was often extremely weak, and in some cases they were bizarre and entirely implausible. In an attempt to tackle this problem, Loftus (1993) began to investigate the circumstances in which false memories might be induced, resulting in a substantial literature demonstrating that this was possible (Loftus and Davis, 2006; Wade and Garry, 2005). The interaction between an emotionally disturbed patient and a zealous and committed therapist is likely to prove particularly open to the creation of such false memories. This situation led, in the USA at least, to an extreme polarization between a subsection of the clinical community and cognitive psychologists working in the area.

There is no doubt that research in this area has had a positive influence on the legal process, and has led to a justified skepticism about claims of recovered memories. However, no one denies that child abuse exists, and can on occasion be forgotten, leaving the much more difficult task of finding methods of deciding whether or not abuse has occurred, and, if so, what to do about it therapeutically (Andrews, Brewin, Ochera, *et al.*,

1999; Geraerts, Arnold, Lindsay, *et al.*, 2006; Geraerts, Schooler, Merckelbach, *et al.*, 2007).

However, alongside this important but complex issue, there seems to have developed a minor industry of laboratory-based studies operating under the general banner of "false memory." The most prominent of these in recent years has been the Deese–Roediger–MacDermott (DRM) effect (Roediger and McDermott, 1995). This reflects a revival of interest in a phenomenon first observed by James Deese in 1959 of an association-based memory illusion. Participants are shown a list of words all of which are close associates to a single kernel word. Hence the word *sleep* might evoke *dream, snore, rest, bed,* etc. The kernel word is always omitted from the presentation list, for which recall or recognition is then tested. Under these circumstances, there is a marked tendency to "remember" or "recognize" the omitted kernel word, typically with some confidence. This does indeed constitute a false memory. What is in doubt, however, is the relationship, if any, to the false memories that have caused so much distress in claims of child abuse. The problem is not that such patients have a whole web of experience that focuses on abuse, but rather that they have succumbed to the belief of their therapist that this is the case. I suggest that had this phenomenon been more accurately labeled as "the associative-intrusion effect," the number of minor variations on an admittedly interesting phenomenon would have been vastly less.

Of the huge amount of research on this paradigm, very little has gone into demonstrating any link between this and the legal process. I should emphasize at this point that I do not regard the study of memory errors as unimportant. They have in the past and can in the future prove very illuminating, providing their study does not become too paradigm-bound.

Mental time travel

I shall conclude the grumpy part of my reflections with a phenomenon that is in danger of becoming the DRM of the future, in that an interesting and important phenomenon appears to have become popular largely as a result of an ingenious name. In the past, some of Endel Tulving's most interesting and innovative ideas have been, in my opinion, handicapped by his fondness for classically based neologisms. Examples include *synergistic ecphory* (Tulving, 1983) and *antonoetic consciousness*. This is not the case in his most recent – and I think perhaps most ingenious – description of episodic memory as allowing "mental time travel," whereby the rememberer is able to travel, not only into the past but also into the future, when using episodic memory to plan ahead. The term appears to have been stimulated by a densely amnesic patient who was unable to say anything about where he would be in the future, an observation that could be regarded as unsurprising. The cardinal feature of severe amnesia is disorientation in time and place: if you do not know where you are now, how can you tell where you will be in the future? What Tulving's ingenious label highlighted, however, was the role of memory in planning our future actions and guiding our behavior, an insight that has been supported by neuroimaging evidence implicating brain areas responsible for recollecting the past in projecting the future (Addis and Schacter, 2008a; Schacter, Addis, and Buckner, 2008; see also D'Argembeau, this volume).

Thinking about our future actions is not, of course, dependent entirely on episodic memory. Without semantic memory, our future projections would make little sense, and without working memory it would be difficult to set up and manipulate such future projections. No doubt, in due course, neuroimaging studies will report the activation of many relevant brain areas. Tulving has thus delivered a timely reminder that we use our memory for future planning as well as for recollection in tranquillity. We now need to move on from simply demonstrating the involvement of episodic memory to investigating it in more detail – perhaps, for example, linking it to other components of "time travel" such as working memory, semantic memory, and perhaps Johnson-Laird's concept of mental models (Johnson-Laird, 1983).

Theory

The areas I have discussed so far are all worth studying, but have largely resulted in clusters of research, producing a somewhat more detailed account of one or two striking phenomena, with little evidence of development of an overall theory of autobiographical memory. In my own view, what studies of autobiographical memory have in common is their crucial link to the observer, to the *self*. As Neisser observed in convening a series of symposia on the self, this is a topic that has been approached from a wide number of directions, philosophical, social, psychological, and neuropsychological (Neisser and Fivush, 1994). That makes it a much broader and more difficult area to capture than the study of the specific phenomena described earlier. If the philosophical, social, and cognitive approaches are to influence each other, it is necessary to have common ground, and I suspect that there has so far been too little of this to lead to the cross-fertilization for which Neisser hoped. There has, however, in my own opinion, been subsequent progress in linking autobiographical memory with concepts of the self initially based on the study of specific phenomena. One of these is the reminiscence bump.

Reminiscence bump

Rubin, Wetzler, and Nebes (1986) combined and reanalyzed data from several studies in which participants were given a series of cue words and asked for autobiographical memories. The studies involved people across a range of ages, and the reanalysis showed that for participants over 40, there was a marked tendency for memories to come from the period roughly between 20 and 30 years of age. This has now been replicated many times, and across many cultures (Conway, Wang, Hanyu, *et al.*, 2005). Why should it occur? The most plausible explanation appears to be in terms of a person's *life story*, an autobiographical record of their lives that people develop, using a series of crucial memories to structure their life and to create and maintain a self-image. The period between 20 and 30 is one in which many important changes occur, first job, college, first love, marriage, etc. These are assumed to form part of the life script that you recall when you are thinking about your past or planning your future. Interestingly, when positive, negative, and neutral memories are plotted separately, only the positive show the reminiscence bump (Berntsen and Rubin, 2002; Glück and Bluck, 2007), consistent with the evidence that memory is one of a range of mechanisms with which we maintain our self-esteem.

Memory and emotion

The study of memory more generally has benefited from the analysis of cases in which memory was impaired, ranging from the classic amnesic syndrome to patients with defective executive or phonological components of working memory (Baddeley, 2007). The same is beginning to occur in the case of autobiographical memory, with emotional factors proving an intriguing, and practically important area of study. Confabulation, the topic of my contribution to the first of David Rubin's symposia (Baddeley and Wilson, 1986), is now evoking considerable interest in neuropsychology, coupled with the development of competing theories (Gilboa and Moscovitch, 2002), while multiple-person syndrome and amnesia for focal events such as violent crime, although difficult to study, offer some intriguing questions.

A rather more common phenomenon, particularly at times of war is post-traumatic stress disorder (PTSD), which is typically accompanied by vivid and disturbing "flashback" memories of the traumatic event at the core of the disorder. This has raised similar problems to those discussed under flashbulb memory, namely the question of whether a completely different kind of memory is involved. Once again, the evidence seems, on balance, to be against the idea that it is a photograph-like reappearance of the original experience (Berntsen and Rubin, 2008). Furthermore, the very thorough series of experiments by Berntsen (this volume) suggests that, despite the link with extreme emotions, the memories evoked in PTSD are not qualitatively different from the sort of uncued memories that pop up from time to time for most people. Interestingly, such memories also tend to show a reminiscence bump (Berntsen and Rubin, 2008). So, the concept of a life script appears to be a useful one, but what else?

One of the few attempts to place the life story in a broader context is that provided by Martin Conway (2005). His model assumes a hierarchical knowledge structure in which the life story connects with a number of themes, such as work and relationships. Each of these reflects a range of life time periods – for example, working in a particular university or relating to a particular friend. These in turn are connected to more general events – individuals within the university, for example – which then may evoke specific episodic memories of particular incidents. An autobiographical memory occurs when this database is accessed by the *working self*, a complex array of active goals and self-images that plays a similar role in autobiographical memory to that played by working memory in the operation of long-term memory more generally. The working self encodes information about *what is*, *what has been*, and *what can be*, attempting to keep this knowledge base both coherent and linked with outside reality. A loss of this link can lead to confabulation or delusion.

Conway's model, which is discussed in more detail in Chapter 4 (this volume), is offered as a broad theoretical framework that attempts to provide a coherent overview of autobiographical memory, while at the same time suggesting new developments and elaborations. Apart from the new and as yet undeveloped model proposed by Rubin (this volume), it appears to be the only broad account of the relationship between autobiographical memory and self, and is used by a number of participants in the present volume.

Conway himself stresses that it is not so much a specific theory as a theoretical framework, within which more detailed subtheories and models can be embedded. I myself find this framework useful, and the appearance of Conway's model in hundreds of articles on autobiographical memory suggests that others agree.

Some new directions

When I accepted an invitation to contribute to this book, I had not worked on autobiographical memory for several years, but then in the year between the invitation and now, I have become involved in three separate approaches to the area. My work is not sufficiently developed in any of these to present in detail, but it does, I think, illustrate some areas of potential development. The first of these concerns the effects of epilepsy on memory, the second reports someone with a remarkable autobiographical memory, while the third concerns my own autobiographical memory.

Accelerated long-term forgetting

It is a widely accepted feature of memory disorders ranging from pure amnesia to Alzheimer's disease that, although the capacity to acquire new episodic information may be grossly impaired, once that information is acquired, the rate of forgetting is normal (Kopelman, 1985). In recent years, however, an increasing number of cases have been reported of patients whose initial acquisition and retention of material over a matter of hours may be normal, but who subsequently show very substantial forgetting. Consider, for example, the case of Professor X, aged 54, who reported, on returning from a conference, "I remember almost nothing that went on at the meeting ... I don't remember any of the talks! I am also completely unable to remember anything about the conference banquet even though there must have been a conference banquet somewhere at some point." When this was mentioned to his wife, she reported that he had described a very elegant restaurant with grape vines as a roof over the outdoor terrace (Butler and Zeman, 2008).

This research area is reviewed by Butler, Muhlert, and Zeman (2010), who identify three forms of epileptic amnesia, one in which recurrent episodes disrupt the memory of the immediate preceding periods; a second in which the epilepsy results in the impairment of remote memory, while leaving the capacity for new learning apparently normal; and a third which again involves normal learning but is characterized by accelerated long-term forgetting (ALF).

One of the reasons that it seems to have taken so long for these phenomena to become established is that neuropsychologists typically do not test retention over periods longer than an hour or so, on the grounds that if forgetting is likely to occur it should be detectable by this time. My own involvement is as part of a group designing much longer-term measures of forgetting that can be presented over the telephone. In order to control learning, we use an episodic memory paradigm in which we present material which is then learned and tested after various delays. We test prose passages and complex visual scenes, rather than autobiographical memory, but it would clearly be valuable if this type of memory deficit, which reveals itself clinically in terms of lacunae in autobiographical memory, could be tested autobiographically.

Temporal lobe epileptic patients are all too common, and this is an area that is likely to see considerably more research in the next few years. It seems likely that the deficit is the result of seizures of some kind in which the electrical activity in the brain interrupts consolidation. At a theoretical level, as the chapter by Moscovitch (this volume) illustrates, this is an area of considerable current activity and theoretical controversy, and I suspect the study of ALF will feature strongly over the next few years.

A remarkable memory

My second area of recent interest stems indirectly from the report by Parker, Cahill, and McGaugh (2006) of an individual with an unusually detailed and vivid autobiographical memory. The memories are very detailed and accompanied by considerable negative emotion, resembling a continuous form of flashback, with the authors suggesting an important contribution from the amygdala. This case was reported in a British newspaper, resulting in a call from the wife of someone I will call R.M. (for remarkable memory), who suggested that her husband represented a somewhat similar case. With some skepticism, I agreed to visit and test R.M. To my surprise, he did appear to have an extremely detailed access to quite remote memories. These appear to be related to specific dates. You can ask him, for example, what he was doing on March 3, 1991. He will first tell you the day of the week and then, typically, tell you what he had done on that day. Unlike those in the Parker *et al.* study, his accounts were not strongly emotional nor full of great perceptual detail, but rather resembled the account that you or I might give if asked what we had done last Wednesday. R.M. did not, however, have particularly good episodic memory, performing a free recall test and recalling a short story at about the same level as his wife, within the good normal range. His capacity for unusually good recall appears to be limited to issues that interest him, but, within this, his performance can be quite remarkable. For example, he is a fan of a not particularly successful soccer club, Bradford City, who, within their lengthy history, have had many managers. Given a particular year, providing it was after he began following the club, R.M. could correctly recall the manager, the date on which he had started, and when he had resigned or been sacked, often describing exactly where he himself was when he had heard this news.

As R.M. pointed out, it is difficult to be sure whether he is genuinely remembering or not. In order to get some idea of this, in collaboration with Martin Conway, we set up a booklet including some 96 dates, of which approximately half had some relatively striking public event, asking R.M. to go through the booklet and report the day of the week and any public event that he remembered on that day, together with information on its vividness, importance, and whether he has discussed this with other people. He virtually never got the day of the week wrong, was successful with a high proportion of the public events, and usually, but not always, had some autobiographical memory for the particular day.

How should we explain R.M.'s remarkable autobiographical memory? Unlike the patient described by Parker *et al.* (2006) whose autobiographical memories are "nonstop, uncontrollable, and automatic," R.M. does not appear to have any emotional difficulties, and the effects of his remarkable memory seem to be entirely benign. He is a man in his forties who works in an administrative capacity for the local authority and lives in a very nice house with a very pleasant wife and family. He is, however, very interested in dates and is a very adept calendrical calculator who can tell you, for any date in the relatively immediate past or future, what day of the week it was or will be. He appears to use this to structure his autobiographical memory, and mentions that sometimes, while shaving, he will think about what happened on some date in the past. I suspect he uses this as a retrieval scheme.

It seems likely that most of us access our autobiographical memories hierarchally, using a structure somewhat similar to that outlined in Conway's theoretical framework. As Bower, Clark, Lesgold, *et al.* (1969) showed, hierarchical retrieval structures can be very effective, provided the material can be readily structured as a hierarchy. However, Broadbent, Cooper, and Broadbent (1978) showed that a matrix organization could be equally efficient. I suspect that R.M. uses the date structure as a matrix that allows him to access specific days without going through a hierarchical search. Just how we test this remains to be seen.

R.M.'s amazingly good autobiographical memory provides an opportunity to revisit the question of what important function is served by autobiographical memory (Baddeley, 1988; see also Pillemer and Kuwabara, this volume). When asked what advantage he gained from his remarkably talent, R.M. thought and replied that in addition to amazing his friends, and occasionally boring his wife, it made him a sought-after member of the pub quiz team. So perhaps the capacity to carry our old diaries in our heads is not necessarily so very helpful after all.

Letters from the past

My final example concerns my own autobiographical memory. A few years ago when my mother died, I discovered that she had kept the letters that I had written to her during a year spent in the USA, immediately after

Table 5.1. *Frequency of remembered, known, and forgotten episodes and how many (in percentages) were rated as nontrivial, specific, and retold*

Remember episodes	N	Nontrivial	Specific	Retold
Vivid	10	26	8	10
Intermediate	4	1	3	3
Vague	9	2	3	?
Known	13	7	6	6
Forgotten	26	5	26	?

I graduated in 1956. Beginning to read them, I was surprised to discover in the first letter two episodes, one of which I appeared to remember very clearly and the other which I had completely forgotten. I resisted going on to read the rest and asked my then colleague, Martin Conway, if it might be interesting to do something systematic with them.

Martin subsequently developed a questionnaire, which I found a little frustrating because a good deal of it asked for the sort of detail that you would expect from a recent memory, but most of which I had forgotten, while inevitably failing to probe other things that I felt I remembered in detail. As the time for writing this chapter drew near, I decided that perhaps I would read the letters and see what I could make of them myself. I thought I knew where they were, but when I took them out I discovered a completely different set, also written from America but some 10 years later. I went through this new set, first of all identifying episodes that I had described to my mother, and subsequently going through and categorizing each as to whether I *remembered* it – categorizing three degrees of vividness of recollection – whether I *knew* it was the case but had no recollective experience, or whether it was completely forgotten.

Table 5.1 shows the result of this preliminary analysis. First of all, there were a reasonable number of events that I felt I remembered with some clarity, and a substantial number that I felt I had completely forgotten. As Table 5.1 suggests, clear memories are typically nontrivial and relatively specific in the sense that they occurred only once at a particular time and place, and they invariably were memories that I had subsequently told people about, in many cases quite often. Memories that I "knew" to be true were equally nontrivial, but tended to be less specific and less frequently redescribed. Finally, about half of the incidents were completely forgotten, most of them were trivial, all were specific, and I do not remember retelling any of them.

Are these preliminary results of any potential theoretical interest? I believe they do reflect the construction of my own life story. They also concur with the diary study carried out by Linton (1975), who found that the probability of remembering an incident from her diary was powerfully influenced by how often that incident had been probed and recalled previously. However, some of the more interesting implications come from the detail, where it was often the case that the information included in the letter was not remembered, but abundant related memories sprang to mind. Whether these are valid memories is, of course, questionable and at least one is a clear confabulation. We left for a year in America, leaving our front door wide open. I have a clear "memory" image of this viewed from the direction of our neighbors, who kindly shut it and later told us about it. I myself, however, could not have seen the open door since we left in a different direction from that seen in my recollection.

More generally, reading my past letters has changed my view of my own autobiographical memory from that of a slightly misty landscape to a construction based on a limited number of retold stories. Not peaks of memory jutting above a mist that can be penetrated with a little effort, but rather islands of recollection in a sea of forgetting.

Conclusions

There is no doubt that the field of autobiographical memory has developed and expanded greatly in recent years, built upon solid foundations on a range of important and replicable phenomena. While it seems less exciting than it was in the early days (a false memory?), it remains an extremely intriguing research area that continues to offer two important challenges. The first is to break away from the relatively safe confines of the cognitive laboratory and ensure that we expose our results to the rigors of the world outside. The second challenge is to move beyond the focus on individual, relatively isolated domains and to pull the various strands of research together within a broader theoretical framework, an enterprise that will need both cross-cultural and cross-discipline collaboration.

References

Addis, D. R. and Schacter, D. L. (2008). Constructive episodic simulation: temporal distance and detail of past and future events modulate hippocampal engagement. *Hippocampus*, **18**, 227–237.

Andrews, B., Brewin, C. R., Ochera, J., Morton, J., Bekerian, D. A., Davies, G. M., and Mollon, P. (1999). Characteristics, context and consequences of memory recovery among adults in therapy. *British Journal of Psychiatry*, **175**, 141–146.

Baddeley, A. D. (1988). But what the hell is it for? In M. M. Grunberg, P. E. Morris, and R. N. Sykes (eds.), *Practical aspects of memory: current research and issues*. Vol. I: *Memory in everyday life* (pp. 3–18). Chichester: John Wiley.

  (2007). *Working memory, thought and action*. Oxford University Press.

Baddeley, A. D., Eysenck, M., and Anderson, M. C. (2009). *Essentials of human memory*. Hove: Psychology Press.

Baddeley, A. D. and Wilson, B. (1986). Amnesia, autobiographical memory and confabulation. In D. Rubin (ed.), *Autobiographical memory* (pp. 225–252). New York: Cambridge University Press.

Bass, E. and Davis, L. (1988). *The courage to heal*. New York: Harper & Row.

Berntsen, D. and Rubin, D. C. (2002). Emotionally charged autobiographical memories across the lifespan: the recall of happy, sad, traumatic, and involuntary memories. *Psychology and Aging*, **17**, 636–652.

  (2008). The reappearence hypothesis revisited: recurrent involuntary memories after traumatic events and in everyday life. *Memory & Cognition*, **36**, 449–460.

Bower, G. H., Clark, M. C., Lesgold, A. M., and Winzenz, D. (1969). Hierarchical retrieval schemes in recall of categorised word lists. *Journal of Verbal Learning and Verbal Behavior*, **8**, 323–343.

Broadbent, D. E., Cooper, P. J., and Broadbent, M. H. (1978). A comparison of hierarchical retrieval schemes in recall. *Journal of Experimental Psychology: Human Learning and Memory*, **4**, 486–497.

Brown, R. and Kulik, J. (1977). Flashbulb memories. *Cognition*, **5**, 73–99.

Butler, C. R., Muhlert, N., and Zeman, A. Z. (2010). Accelerated long-term forgetting. In S. Della Sala (ed.), *Forgetting* (pp. 211–238). Hove: Psychology Press.

Butler, C. R. and Zeman, A. Z. (2008). Recent insights into the impairment of memory in epilepsy: transient epileptic amnesia, accelerated long-term forgetting, and remote memory impairment. *Brain*, **131**, 2243–2263.

Conway, M. A. (2005). Memory and the self. *Journal of Memory and Language*, **53**, 594–628.

Conway, M. A., Wang, Q., Hanyu, K., and Haque, S. (2005). A cross-cultural investigation of autobiographical memory. *Journal of Cross-Cultural Psychology*, **36**, 739–749.

Curci, A. and Luminet, O. (2009). General conclusions. In O. Luminet and A. Curci (eds.), *Flashbulb memories: new issues and new perspectives* (pp. 269–276). Hove: Psychology Press.

Dalla Barba, G., Cipolotti, L., and Denes, G. (1990). Autobiographical memory loss and confabulation in Korsakoff's syndrome: a case report. *Cortex*, **26**, 525–534.

Deese, J. (1959). Influence of inter-item associative strength upon immediate free recall. *Psychological Reports*, **5**, 305–312.

De Renzi, E., Liotti, M., and Nichelli, P. (1987). Semantic amnesia with preservation of autobiographical memory: a case report. *Cortex*, **23**, 575–597.

Gardiner, J. M. (2002). Episodic memory and autonoetic consciousness: a first-person approach. In A. Baddeley, J. P. Aggleton, and M. A. Conway (eds.), *Episodic memory* (pp. 11–30). Oxford University Press.

Geiselman, R. E., Fisher, R. P., MacKinnon, D. P., and Holland, H. L. (1985). Eyewitness memory enhancement in the police interview: cognitive retrieval, mnemonics versus hypnosis. *Journal of Applied Psychology*, 70, 401–412.

Geraerts, E., Arnold, M. M., Lindsay, D. S., Merckelbach, H., Jelicic, M., and Hauer, B. (2006). Forgetting of prior remembering in persons reporting recovered memories of childhood sexual abuse. *Psychological Science*, 17, 1002–1008.

Geraerts, E., Schooler, J., Merckelbach, H., Jelicic, M., Hauer, B. J. A., and Ambadar, Z. (2007). The reality of recovered memories: corroborating continuous and discontinuous memories of childhood sexual abuse. *Psychological Science*, 18, 564–568.

Gilboa, A. and Moscovitch, M. (2002). The cognitive neuroscience of confabulation: a review and a model. In A. D. Baddeley, M. D. Kopelman, and B. A. Wilson (eds.), *The handbook of memory disorders* (2nd edn., pp. 315–342). Chichester: Wiley.

Glück, J. and Bluck, S. (2007). Looking back across the life span: a life story account of the reminiscence bump. *Memory & Cognition*, 35, 1928–1939.

Johnson-Laird, P. N. (1983). *Mental models*. Cambridge University Press.

Kebbell, M. R. and Wagstaff, G. F. (1999). The effectiveness of the cognitive interview. In D. Canter and L. Allison (eds.), *Interviewing and deception* (pp. 25–39). Aldershot: Ashgate.

Kopelman, M. D. (1985). Rates of forgetting in Alzheimer-type dementia and Korsakoff's syndrome. *Neuropsychologia*, 23, 623–628.

Kopelman, M. D., Wilson, B. A., and Baddeley, A. D. (1989). The autobiographical memory interview: a new assessment of autobiographical and personal semantic memory in amnesic patients. *Journal of Clinical and Experimental Neuropsychology*, 11, 724–744.

(1990). *The Autobiographical Memory Interview*. Bury St Edmunds: Thames Valley Test Company.

Linton, M. (1975). Memory for real-world events. In D. A. Norman and D. E. Rumelhart (eds.), *Explorations in cognition* (pp. 376–404). San Francisco, CA: Freeman.

Loftus, E. F. (1993). The reality of repressed memories. *American Psychologist*, 48, 518–537.

Loftus, E. F. and Davis, D. (2006). Recovered memories. *Annual Review of Clinical Psychology*, 2, 469–498.

Luminet, O. and Curci, A. (2009). *Flashbulb memories: new issues and new perspectives*. Hove: Psychology Press.

Milne, R. and Bull, R. (2002). Back to basics: a componential analysis of the original cognitive interview mnemonics with three age groups. *Applied Cognitive Psychology*, 16, 1–11.

Neisser, U. and Fivush, R. (1994). *The remembering self: construction and accuracy in the self-narrative*. Cambridge University Press.

Parker, E. S., Cahill, L., and McGaugh, J. L. (2006). A case of unusual autobiographical remembering. *Neurocase*, **12**, 35–49.

Parkin, A. J. and Walter, B. M. (1992). Recollective experience, normal aging and frontal dysfunction. *Psychology and Aging*, **7**, 290–298.

Roediger, H. L. and McDermott, K. B. (1995). Creating false memories: remembering words not presented in lists. *Journal of Experimental Psychology: Learning, Memory, and Cognition*, **21**, 803–814.

Rubin, D. (ed.) (1986). *Autobiographical memory*. New York: Cambridge University Press.

Rubin, D. C., Wetzler, S. E., and Nebes, R. D. (1986). Autobiographical memory across the adult lifespan. In Rubin (ed.), *Autobiographical memory* (pp. 202–221).

Schacter, D. L., Addis, D. R., and Buckner, R. L. (2008). Episodic simulation of future events: concepts, data, and application. *Annals of the New York Academy of Sciences, Special Issue: The Year in Cognitive Neuroscience*, **1124**, 39–60.

Shanks, D. R. and St. John, M. F. (1994). Characteristics of dissociable human learning systems. *Behavioral and Brain Sciences*, **17**, 367–447.

Tulving, E. (1972). Episodic and semantic memory. In E. Tulving and W. Donaldson (eds.), *Organization of memory* (pp. 381–403). New York: Academic Press.

(1983). *Elements of episodic memory*. New York: Oxford University Press.

(1989). Memory: performance, knowledge and experience. *European Journal of Cognitive Psychology*, **1**, 3–26.

Wade, K. A. and Garry, M. (2005). Strategies for verifying false autobiographical memories. *American Journal of Psychology*, **118**, 587–602.

Part II

Neural studies of autobiographical memory

The two chapters in this part address the neural basis of autobiographical memory. The chapter by Moscovitch discusses how neuropsychological studies of autobiographical memory have informed our broader understanding of how memories are retained at the neural level across large time intervals. In making his arguments, Moscovitch provides a historical review of neuropsychological studies on autobiographical memory in brain-damaged patients as well as a review of more recent brain-imaging studies. The chapter by St. Jacques reviews the rapidly growing field of functional neuroimaging studies of autobiographical memory, and discusses how such studies have informed behavioral research of autobiographical memory as well as their broader relevance to the understanding of the neural basis of memory.

6 The contribution of research on autobiographical memory to past and present theories of memory consolidation

Morris Moscovitch

The past isn't dead; it isn't even past.   – William Faulkner

How memories are consolidated is a problem that is at the core of memory research. Without consolidation, memories are fleeting; distraction, interference, noxious agents, drugs, brain damage, or the mere passage of time will disrupt and eliminate them. Consolidation is the time and experience-dependent process by which newly acquired memories become stabilized so that they are relatively immune to disruption by all these influences. Not surprisingly, therefore, consolidation has been a topic of investigation since the beginning of the scientific study of memory. In this chapter, I will focus on the role that autobiographical memory has played in our understanding of the neural mechanisms implicated in consolidation.

The turn of the twentieth century

Autobiographical memory played a significant role in establishing that brain damage or trauma can disrupt consolidation, and continues to play this role during bedside investigations of memory loss. Patients are asked routinely if they know where they are, what brought them to this location, what they did recently, and what they remember about their more remote past, such as the schools they attended, the friends they had, the jobs they held, and so on. They also are asked questions regarding general knowledge, such as who is the current mayor or head of the country, and about news events from the recent and remote past. Based on such anecdotal evidence, investigators dating back to the end of the nineteenth century concluded that recent memories are more vulnerable to disruption than remote memories, presumably because the latter had an opportunity to

I thank Nick Hoang with help on this paper, the preparation of which was supported by a CIHR grant to M.M. and Gordon Winocur.

become consolidated whereas the former did not (Ribot, 1882). The term "consolidation" was coined by Müller and Pilzecker (1900) to account for the results of their behavioral, laboratory-based experiments in which they measured the time it took newly learned memories to become resistant to disruption by a subsequent, to-be-remembered event. By 1904, Burnham concluded:

The fixing [consolidation] of an impression depends on a physiological process. It takes time for an impression to become so fixed that it can be reproduced after a long interval; for it to become part of the permanent store of memory considerable time may be necessary. This we may suppose is not merely a process of making a permanent impression upon the nerve cells, but also a process of association, of organization of the new impressions with the old ones.

Thus, consolidation, though a physiological process, is determined not only by what we would now consider neurochemical or molecular mechanisms, but also by psychological operations associated with assimilating new information to existing knowledge. Conversely, once consolidated, memories are altered from their initial state, either in their content and form, or in their relation to other memories. Though investigators acknowledged the importance of psychological operations and their effects on memory, Barlett (1932) being most notable in this regard, until recently most neuropsychological theories of consolidation tended to overlook these considerations (see reviews by Dudai, 2004; Moscovitch and Winocur, 2011; Winocur, Moscovitch, and Bontempi, 2010). The theories were meant to apply across all organisms for all tasks, despite the warning note that the estimated time of consolidation, even in a single organism, such as in humans, could vary from minutes to decades. Before these matters could be addressed adequately, one needed to have a good psychological theory of memory and a good idea of the neural substrates that are implicated.

Mid-twentieth century: the discovery of the medial temporal lobe's role in memory

Until the mid-twentieth century, memory was considered to be widely distributed in the brain, in the very structures involved in apprehending events and acting on them, with no single structure being crucial (Lashley, 1950). Although there were indications, dating back to observations by Bekhterev (1907), that damage to the medial temporal lobes and related structures in the diencephalon was associated with severe memory loss, the evidence for the importance of these structures was weak. All of that changed with the publication of two seminal papers by Scoville and

Milner (1957) and Penfield and Milner (1958) showing that bilateral temporal lobectomy can lead to a profound amnesia for newly experienced events despite relatively well-preserved perceptual, motor, and cognitive functions, including short-term memory. Their analysis of the lesions leading to this deficit led them to conclude that the medial portion of the temporal lobes was especially crucial, particularly the posterior part of the hippocampus beyond the uncus.

Their finding also had implications for our understanding of memory consolidation, as most of their patients seemed to have retained memories they acquired before the surgery. Penfield and Milner's observations were based not only on systematic investigation using standard or experimental tests, though these played an important part, but also on patients' reports of their experiences, which often described autobiographical memories.

In discussing their findings regarding the role of the hippocampus and mechanisms of consolidation, Penfield and Milner (1958) speculated that

The record of the stream of consciousness, which, we believe, depends upon the integrity of the hippocampal structures, cannot be called into activity voluntarily except for a relatively short period of time [after acquisition] ... Later on, a person deals with what may be called generalizations, and can summon them to his purposes. For example, one remembers a song or a poem that been heard repeatedly, but forgets each hearing or reading, but remembers the generalization. (p. 494)

In short, the

man who has lost the bilateral hippocampal mechanism cannot form a new record of his current experience. This may be because the place where the record is laid down has been removed, or it may be that the hippocampal zone is normally utilized to lay down the record in some other area. The patient carries on, however, with the help of those things that have been learned, preserving the concepts that have been generalized from his daily experiences. He remembers words, rules of behaviour, even oft-recollected scenes from childhood, and retains his former skills. (p. 495)

Thus, Penfield and Milner linked the process of consolidation to the medial temporal lobes, and the hippocampus in particular. Although memories are still considered to be widely distributed in the brain, the hippocampus is needed initially to help represent and recover these memories, and to aid in their consolidation in extra-hippocampal sites so that, in due course, they can be used independently of the hippocampus. In the celebrated patient H.M., the period of retrograde amnesia, estimated primarily from loss of autobiographical memories, extended for about three years, which was presumably the time it took memories to become consolidated elsewhere in the brain. Based on subsequent, more controlled studies, the extent of H.M.'s retrograde amnesia, and the consolidation period, was lengthened to about eleven years (Corkin, 1984).

Another important point Penfield and Milner made concerns the type of memory representations that the hippocampus supports. The hippocampus is needed to represent "a record of the stream of consciousness," what we would now call a detailed, *episodic memory* or *recollection* of an autobiographical event. Afterwards, the memory that the person uses is based on generalizations; that is, on "concepts that have been generalized from his daily experiences," what we would now call *semantic memories*. The latter are relatively preserved after hippocampal damage.

After H.M., the very definition of consolidation also changed from one which referred to the stabilization of any memory in any structure, to one that also referred to a process of establishing memories in structures that are different from the one(s) in which the autobiographical memory was first represented. In short, the concept of *systems consolidation* arose.

The turn of the twenty-first century

That the medial temporal lobes are crucial for memory formation and for promoting consolidation was acknowledged relatively quickly. It took longer to incorporate the representational aspects of memory into models of memory consolidation, because they require the acknowledgement that there are different kinds of consolidation processes, and that hippocampally dependent memories are fundamentally different from memories consolidated in neocortex. Indeed, the last point, which is not unrelated to the first, is still the object of vigorous debate.

The literature on consolidation now distinguishes between *cohesion* or *synaptic consolidation*, and *long-term* or *systems consolidation* (Dudai, 2004; Moscovitch, 1995). Synaptic consolidation refers to neuromolecular processes that occur at the neuronal level to bring about relatively permanent synaptic changes in response to stimulation. These consolidation processes, common to all neurons capable of being modified by "experience," take minutes to hours, or at most days, to complete, though dynamic molecular events may continue over a lifetime to maintain them. By contrast, systems consolidation refers to a process of neural reorganization across different populations of neurons, or neural networks, a process which can last from hours to decades. It is with the process of systems consolidation, and its relation to changes in memory representation, that the rest of this chapter is concerned (see Bauer, this volume, for a developmental perspective).

The nature of hippocampal and extra-hippocampal representations

Developments in memory research and theory since the 1970s have proven Penfield and Milner's prescient speculations generally correct, both about how memory representations change with time, and about the role of the hippocampus and neocortex in memory representation and consolidation. There is general agreement that the medial temporal lobe (MTL)/hippocampus is crucial for declarative or explicit memory, namely memory with conscious awareness, as Penfield and Milner (1958) surmised, and is not needed for most types of implicit, or non-declarative memory such as acquisition, retention, and retrieval of perceptual and motor skills and priming (Tulving and Schacter, 1990; see Schacter, Wig, and Stevens, 2007, and Wixted and Squire, 2011, for updates).

With respect to declarative memory, Tulving (1972) distinguished two types: *episodic*, which refers to memory for a particular episode or event in one's life, and *semantic*, which refers to our knowledge about the world and facts about ourselves. In a further refinement, Tulving (1985) wished to capture the phenomenal awareness that accompanies the recovery of episodic memories, the reliving of past events, a process that he termed *recollection* and that is associated with autonoetic consciousness. That is, episodic memory is embedded with consciousness of the self as the one who experienced the event and possesses the memory. He contrasted this to a process of "knowing" in which an event or stimulus is regarded as *familiar*, such as seeing a familiar face without being able to place the person, and is associated with noetic consciousness that is akin to semantic memory. Tulving's distinction between recollection and familiarity had its antecedent in William James (1890, p. 658), who used similar concepts and identical terms. Tulving's formulation of episodic memory and the process of recollection are essentially what laypeople would call the stuff and operations of a crucial aspect of autobiographical memory. Indeed, one could make the case that this is exactly what Tulving meant to capture in a laboratory setting.

Building on Tulving's idea, and the acknowledged role of the hippocampus in episodic memory, Moscovitch (1995) proposed that the hippocampus binds together in memory those neural elements that gave rise to the multi-modal, multi-domain representations that constitute an experience, including the phenomenological awareness that is part of that experience, an idea that is not far removed from Penfield and Milner's proposal that the hippocampus is the repository of the record of the stream of consciousness. According to this view, the hippocampus enables the re-experiencing of an autobiographical event or, in Suddendorf and

Corballis's (1997) terms, it enables "mental time travel" so that we can relive the past and, as we shall see, also imagine the future. Unlike recollection, familiarity is presumed to be mediated by peri-hippocampal structures in the MTL (Aggleton and Brown, 1999; Eichenbaum, Yonelinas, and Ranganath, 2007).

The idea that the hippocampus is necessary for recollection (of autobiographical episodes) and that familiarity is dependent on other medial temporal lobe structures has gained many adherents. These ideas, however, are not universally accepted as either the only way of conceptualizing the role of these structures, or even the correct way. The hippocampus is viewed by many as being especially implicated in supporting allocentric spatial representations used for creating cognitive maps (Bird and Burgess, 2008; O'Keefe and Nadel, 1978) and for constructing scenes (Hassabis and Maguire, 2009). Squire and Wixted (2011) argue that high memory strength is a hallmark of hippocampal representations, whether they are based on recollection or familiarity, whereas extra-hippocampal structures code weaker memories.

I do not intend to adjudicate among these views. They all, however, have one idea in common: they hold hippocampal representations to be distinctly different from neocortical representations. In the next section, I consider the implication of this idea for theories of systems consolidation.

Implications of the nature of hippocampal representations for theories of systems consolidation

At the heart of standard or traditional models of systems consolidation is the proposition that the same memory that was initially represented in the hippocampus is now represented in the neocortex and possibly in other structures (Winocur *et al.*, 2010). According to such models of systems consolidation, the memory trace initially consists of an ensemble of neocortical neurons bound together by the hippocampus, but with time (and practice?) the connections among the neocortical neurons are strengthened so that the *identical* memory trace can now be retained and retrieved without hippocampal involvement. That proposition implies that pre- and post-consolidation memories are identical; they differ only in the structures that support them. How can this be possible if the nature of representations in the hippocampus is fundamentally different from that in the neocortex? Either (1) the standard model is correct and hippocampal representations are not fundamentally different from neocortical ones, at least not after consolidation; or (2) a basic premise of the standard model is wrong: the process of consolidation does not simply involve the establishment of an identical representation in the neocortex, but entails a transformation of the initial trace so that it is compatible with the types of representations that the neocortex can support. Insofar as the initial, detailed representation is retained, it continues to be dependent on the hippocampus no matter how long ago it was acquired. The second alternative bears a family resemblance to Penfield and Milner's proposal that, whereas the hippocampus stores a record of the stream of consciousness, memories represented outside the hippocampus are concerned with generalizations or concepts derived from that stream. How do studies of autobiographical memory inform this debate?

The contribution of studies on autobiographical memory to theories of systems consolidation

Although rich, episodic memories can be created in the laboratory, one would need to conduct longitudinal experiments that last years to determine which of the two alternatives is correct since that is the estimated time it takes for some memories to become consolidated. Even then, one could only study these memories by functional imaging techniques in healthy individuals. However, to know whether or not the hippocampus is necessary for representing these remote episodic memories, we have to study patients with hippocampal lesions; it would be a highly impractical strategy to conduct longitudinal studies in the morbid hope that some of the participants would be afflicted with such damage. Though fraught with problems of its own, the only solution is to study autobiographical memories acquired long before the individual is tested. It is useful to compare such memories with semantic memories, some of which may be encoded initially as part of an autobiographical episode, but with time may acquire an independent existence as semantic memories. It should be noted that it is also possible that semantic memories are encoded independently from episodic memories at initial learning (Sharon, Moscovitch, and Gilboa, 2011; Vargha-Khadem, Gadian, Watkins, *et al.*, 1997).

Research on autobiographical memory has evolved alongside laboratory research on memory, borrowing many concepts and methodological refinements from it, while retaining its distinctiveness. Autobiographical memories are not merely a catalog of episodes as if they were the real-life equivalent of what passes for events in the laboratory, namely the presentation of words, pictures, or scenes. Laboratory "events" bear little or no relation to one another, except that they all occurred in a particular experiment, and hardly any relation to the self, personal goals, and so on. These qualities, however, are integral to autobiographical episodes (Conway and Jobson, this volume; Conway, Rubin, Spinnler, and Wagenaar, 1992; Pillemer and Kuwabara, this volume; Rubin, this volume). A common view, illustrated in Figure 4.1 in Conway and Jobson (this volume), is that autobiographical memories consist of a nested hierarchy of memories, related to the self-memory system, that increase in abstraction or generality (or inclusiveness) as one moves up the hierarchy, from the detailed experience-near, sensory-perceptual-affective-conceptual (SPAC) *episodic elements* at the bottom of the hierarchy, to more *complex episodes*, to more conceptual, *general events* and *lifetime periods* (Conway, 2009; Conway and Jobson, this volume) both of which confer autobiographical meaning on the lower levels; all are related to higher conceptions of the self, which includes self-image, beliefs, and life stories, and to goals and plans. It is not surprising, therefore, that although there is overlap in the regions of the brain that are implicated in memory for laboratory events and autobiographical episodes, especially in the medial temporal lobe, there also are important discrepancies, particularly with respect to regions of the prefrontal cortex associated with the self, planning, etc. (see Cabeza and St. Jacques, 2007; Gilboa, 2004; St. Jacques, this volume; Svoboda, McKinnon, and Levine, 2006). For an illustration of the embedding of episodic memories in autobiographical memory knowledge structures, see Figure 4.1 in Conway and Jobson (this volume)

Given such models of autobiographical memory, a number of questions arise. Does systems consolidation apply equally to autobiographical memories and semantic memories related to general knowledge? Does it apply equally to the hierarchical components or aspects of autobiographical memory? Are some more likely to be dependent for a longer time on the hippocampus than others? In short, does the fractionation of autobiographical memory after brain damage honor the hierarchical divisions in models of autobiographical memory? It is unlikely that a one-to-one correspondence exists between levels in the model and their neural instantiation, but it is important to determine if there is even a rough correspondence, as this lies at the heart of the debate regarding which of the two alternatives mentioned earlier (p. 96) best captures the data.

In reviewing the literature on consolidation, Nadel and Moscovitch (1997) noted that retrograde amnesia (RA) for detailed memories of autobiographical events, what passes for simple episodic memories and episodic elements in the model, was severe and extensive, sometimes encompassing an entire lifetime, whereas RA for semantic memory related to public events and personalities was much more limited. This evidence formed the basis of our *multiple trace theory* (MTT), in which we proposed that the medial temporal lobes, particularly the hippocampi, were needed to retain and retrieve detailed memories of autobiographical episodes no matter how long ago they were acquired. By comparison, the same structures contributed to the retention and retrieval of semantic memories only until they were consolidated in the neocortex, from where they could be recovered without hippocampal involvement.

Building on MTT and extending it, Winocur and his collaborators (Winocur and Moscovitch, 2011; Winocur et al., 2010) proposed the *transformation hypothesis*, which states, in accord with Penfield and Milner (1958), that the initial hippocampal memory supports the development in the neocortex of a less detailed, schematic version that retains the gist of the initial memory, but not its contextual details. As memories undergo a process of transformation from context-specific, detailed memories (Conway's *episodic elements*) to more context-general semantic memories (Conway's *complex episodic memories* or *general events* and levels higher in the hierarchy), they lose their dependence on the hippocampus and become represented primarily in the neocortex. The time course of this process is determined by the content of the memory, task demands, and the ease with which recent memories, acquired in an autobiographical episode, can be transformed and assimilated to an existing body of knowledge and modified by it. The two types of memory can also coexist, and there can continue to be a dynamic interplay between them such that one or the other may be dominant at the time of retrieval, and that one can influence the extent to which the other is acquired, retained, or transformed.

The literature on consolidation of semantic memory as it reflects knowledge of people and public events, and even of vocabulary, is consistent in showing that there is a temporally graded retrograde amnesia, lasting on the order of 10 years, following even extensive damage to the medial temporal lobes (for recent reviews, see Winocur and Moscovitch, 2011; Winocur et al., 2010). The extent and severity of the retrograde component increases as posterior, lateral, and anterior neocortical structures become affected (Bright, Buckman, Fradera, et al., 2006; Fujii, Moscovitch, and Nadel, 2000; Kapur, 1999; Kopelman and Kapur, 2001; Squire and Wixted, 2011; Westmacott, Freedman, Black, et al., 2004b).

These latter findings suggest that the same would apply for those aspects of autobiographical memory that resemble semantic memory, such as facts about oneself, one's self-image, and even what one did during certain lifetime periods. In short, those aspects of autobiographical memory that are at the top of the hierarchy should be relatively spared.

Here, too, the evidence is fairly consistent. Amnesia following medial temporal or diencephalic lesions hardly, if at all, affects one's sense of self or one's self-image (Conway, 2009; Fujii et al., 2000; Klein, Loftus, and Kihlstrom, 1996). These aspects are perturbed, however, when the damage extends to cortical structures in the anterior temporal and pre-frontal cortex.

The story is still consistent, though somewhat different, for general events and lifetime periods. For these there is a temporally graded retro-grade amnesia that resembles knowledge about public personalities and events (Bright et al., 2006; Fujii et al., 2000; Kopelman and Kapur, 2001; Moscovitch et al., 2010; Squire and Wixted, 2011; Winocur and Moscovitch, 2011).

The inconsistencies in the literature on the effects of medial temporal lobe lesions appear when one considers elements at the lower levels of the hierarchy, namely the autobiographical episodes themselves. It was gen-erally believed that memory for even these episodes became independent of the hippocampus with time, and could be retained and retrieved directly from the neocortex (Squire and Wixted, 2011). There were, however, dissenters from this view who claimed all truly episodic memo-ries, including autobiographical ones that were acquired in the remote past, were lost or damaged following lesions of the medial temporal lobes and related diencephalic structures (Kinsbourne and Wood, 1975; Sanders and Warrington, 1971).

What accounts for this discrepancy? Although a number of factors could be contributing, two stand out. The first is that the size and location of the lesion determines the temporal extent and severity of retrograde amnesia (Squire and Wixted, 2011), and the second factor is that the tests of autobiographical memory often conflate episodic and semantic infor-mation (Winocur et al., 2010; Winocur and Moscovitch, 2011). When recounting an episode, there are often semantic elements in it which are preserved, yet may be mistaken for episodic details (Levine, Svoboda, Hay, et al., 2002).

To address both of these issues, investigators, using volumetric analyses of structural MRI images, have taken great care to delineate the size and location of the lesion. They also have developed assessment tools and scoring procedures that distinguish more clearly than had been done previously between episodic and more semantic aspects of autobiograph-ical memory. Thus, Kopelman, Wilson, and Baddeley (1989) divide their Autbiographical Memory Inventory (AMI) into two portions, Personal Semantics and Autobiographical Episodes, and the subject is requested to provide information about each from three different life periods, child-hood, young adulthood, and the last five years. By comparison, Levine et al. (2002) used the Autobiographical Interview (AI) to ask individuals to describe in detail an autobiographical event from five different life peri-ods, from childhood to the recent past. They then classified each unit of the description as internal (namely, specific to that episode and likely to tap episodic memory) and external (related to the episode but not specific to it, and, therefore, likely to engage semantic memory). Within each category, the units are classified even more finely by categorizing memories as perceptual, spatial, thoughts, etc. (see below). Piolino, Desgranges, and Eustache (2009) created an "episodicity" index, using similar measures pertaining to the specificity of episodic memory, as well as judgments of conscious recollection (autonoetic consciousness). A fourth approach used by some investigators is to test memory not by free recall, but by recognition of sentences depicting autobiographical events at an episodic, generic, or semantic level (Gilboa, Winocur, Rosenbaum, *et al.*, 2006).

Even with these new procedures in place, the discrepancies have not been resolved. The majority of investigations, including those in which H.M. was retested (Steinvorth, Levine, and Corkin, 2005), show temporally extensive and severe retrograde amnesia for autobiographical episodes, especially when using Levine *et al.*'s AI and tests of recognition. Other studies, however, show that such remote memories tend to be spared, no matter how episodic they are. By contrast, all investigators agree that nonepisodic memories, such as are gauged by personal semantics and external details, show a temporal gradient, with remote memories being relatively spared. This literature has been reviewed extensively, and the reader is referred to the more recent publications, for details of this controversy, and the arguments and evidence on both sides (see Piolino *et al.*, 2009; Squire and Wixted, 2011; Winocur *et al.*, 2010; Winocur and Moscovitch, 2011).

Because a possible source of the controversy is the variable nature of the lesions and the effects they produce, functional neuroimaging studies of neurologically intact people provide a possible resolution to the debate. If the hippocampus is implicated in retention and retrieval of detailed autobiogrpahical memories, then it should be equally activated during retrieval of such memories, no matter how old they are, whereas if its involvement is temporally limited, then its activation will diminish with the age of the memory that is retrieved. Here, with few exceptions, the evidence favors the view that the hippocampus continues to be involved in retention and retrieval of detailed, vivid autobiographical memories, no matter how long ago they were acquired. By contrast, less vivid or detailed memories and semantic memories show a time-limited dependence on the hippocampus, with less activation for remote than recent memories. (Here, too, the reader is referred to the same recent reviews on this topic, as above.)

Microanalysis of autobiographical memory

When co-varying for age, and for recollective aspects of autobiographical memory such as detail, emotionality, personal significance, and episodicity, investigators found that hippocampal involvement is not modulated by age at all. Instead, the extent of hippocampal involvement is related to the recollective aspects, both in functional neuroimaging studies and in studies of patients with focal lesions or degenerative disorders such as Alzheimer's disease (Addis, Moscovitch, Crawley, et al., 2004; Gilboa, Winocur, Grady, et al., 2004; Piolino et al., 2009).

These findings led St-Laurent, Moscovitch, Levine, et al. (2009) to examine more carefully what aspects of autobiographical memories acquired within the last ten years are especially vulnerable to disruption by unilateral MTL epilepsy or lobectomy. Using the AI, they found little difference between patients and controls with respect to retrieval of external details, consistent with previous observations. Retention of internal (episodic) details was impaired, as expected, but most revealing was that not all internal details were equally affected. Retention and retrieval of event details, what corresponds roughly to what Conway (2009) and Conway and Jobson (this volume, see Figure 4.1) would call simple or complex episodic memories that capture the gist of an event, were relatively spared, whereas temporal and thought/emotion details, but especially perceptual details, were much reduced. Thus, what are most dependent on the MTL, and the hippocampus in particular, are the episodic elements at the lowest level of Conway's hierarchy that code for near-sensory experiences.

This was confirmed in another analysis in which St-Laurent, Moscovitch, Tau, et al. (2011) segmented each narrative according to the subevents that constitute it. For example, going to a restaurant may have a number of subevents: entering the restaurant, being seated, ordering food, discussion during the meal, etc. To assess the temporal resolution of the memories, St-Laurent et al. (2011) tallied the number of actions taking place within each subevent, as well as the temporal order of both, thus providing a sense of the temporal resolution of episodic memory. They found that the number of subevents and their temporal order were intact in patients, compared to controls, but the number of actions in each subevent was reduced in patients indicating that memory for the minute by minute replay of the episode was impaired.

One should note that the patients all had unilateral damage and were not amnesic but simply memory-impaired. Whether the effects would be similarly circumscribed in patients with bilateral lesions, or whether they would extend to higher levels in the autobiographical memory hierarchy, remains to be determined.

The immediacy of autobiographical memory and its dependence on the MTL

When recollections of past events are perceptually detailed, they impart a sense of immediacy to memory, making one feel that one truly is reliving past events in the present moment. This impression is reflected even in the language people use to describe these events. Park, St-Laurent, McAndrews, *et al.* (2011) documented this by comparing the use of the *historical present* in the narratives of MTL patients and controls.

The historical present is a literary and rhetorical device for both oral and written narratives, common to several different languages, including English (Pillemer, 2003; Pillemer and Kuwabara, this volume). The historical present tense appears as a present tense form, but clearly refers to a past event. For example, as recorded in *The New York Times* 9/11 oral history project, *The Sept. 11 Records*, Jody Bell, an emergency medical technician who was at the scene, describes the event from his perspective:

We *jumped* out of the car. We *turned* around, and we *see* the building on fire. We *see* the smoke coming out of the building and automatically assumed that we were bombed again, that another bomb went off in the World Trade Center [italics added].

Although all these actions took place in the past, Bell switches from using the past tense (*jumped, turned*) to the historical present tense (*see*), rather than the past tense *saw*, to describe his memory of the events. The traditional interpretation of the historical present tense is that it indexes the narrator's reliving of the moment while describing the event (Pillemer, 2003).

If this is so, Park *et al.* (2011) predicted that the MTL patients would use the historical present proportionately less often than controls. Indeed, this was the case – the ratio of the historical present to past tense was lower by a factor greater than 1 to 3 in patients than in controls. Most interestingly, this difference was found only for the internal details of the narrative, and, in controls, it correlated significantly with those aspects of the narrative that St-Laurent *et al.* (2009, 2011) found to distinguish patients from controls, namely the number of perceptual details, and the number of actions within a subevent.

The MTL patients' loss of memory specificity is reflected in other aspects of language, such as their diminished use of the definite article (see Duff, Gupta, Hengst, *et al.*, 2011), probably because they did not have a precise memory of the referent item, whether a word, event, person, or place, which the article indicates.

The dynamic interaction of episodic and semantic components of autobiographical memory and general knowledge

The evidence we reviewed so far favors the second of the two alternatives considered at the beginning of this section. Consistent with MTT and the transformation hypothesis, memories that lose their hippocampal dependence during systems consolidation are transformed versions of the original: those memories lose the experiential richness of the original while retaining its gist. Experientially rich memories of autobiographical episodes, the episodic elements of autobiographical memories (Conway, 2009), remain perpetually linked to the hippocampus, much as Penfield and Milner (1958) proposed.

This raises two questions:

(1) Would the perceptually rich, autobiographical components of any memory also be dependent on the hippocampus?

(2) If the hippocampus enables mental time travel, can one travel as easily forward in time as backwards?

Based on MTT, the transformation hypothesis, and the evidence we summarize briefly below, the short answer to both questions is "yes." According to the transformation hypothesis, both types of memory can coexist and interact, with the rich perceptual component continually dependent on the hippocampus even though the schematic, general component can be recovered without it.

To address the first question, we asked participants to recall, in rich detail, autobiographical events that were repeated many times, such as a birthday party or holiday dinner, which assume a generic quality, and would be considered as part of semantic memory. Participants were required either to imagine such events while in the scanner (Addis *et al.*, 2004) or to provide a verbal description outside it (St-Laurent *et al.*, 2009, 2011). The results, in both cases, were essentially indistinguishable from those obtained when participants were imagining and describing a unique event. The hippocampus, along with other regions of the cortex that comprise an autobiographical network, was activated in the scanner, and MTL lesions both altered the network (Addis, Moscovitch, and McAndrews, 2007) and reduced the amount of perceptual, but not event, details. We concluded that retention and/or retrieval of richly detailed aspects of memories, whether pertaining to unique or generic memories, and whether referring to events in the recent or remote past, depended on an autobiographical memory network of which the hippocampus is the hub.

We reached the same conclusion based on another series of studies in which we asked participants to rate famous names (Westmacott, Black, Freedman, *et al.*, 2004a) and public events (Petrican, Gopie, Leach, *et al.*, 2010) according to their semantic attributes (what knowledge they have of the individual or event) and episodic attributes (what recollections they elicit). In all cases, we found that although these items and tasks are considered to tap semantic memory, there also is a recollective component associated with many of them. For example, you may not only know a great deal about Princess Diana, but you may also have a clear recollection of the circumstances of her death and what you were doing when you heard about it. This recollective component benefited performance, as gauged by accuracy and speed, on semantic tests related to those items, such as in naming faces and in reading, classifying, and recalling famous names. In all cases, control participants responded more quickly and more accurately to items that were high in recollection than those that were not, even when the semantic component was equivalent. Most interestingly, the performance advantage associated with the recollective component was lost in patients with MTL lesions no matter how long ago the famous personality (Westmacott *et al.*, 2004a) or public event (Petrican *et al.*, 2010) first became prominent. The semantic component, however, remained relatively unaffected, as indicated by the fact that the patients were still capable of performing the tasks based only on their semantic knowledge. In a functional neuroimaging analog of Westmacott *et al.*'s study, Park, McAndrews, Westmacott, *et al.* (2007) found that the hippocampus was activated more when judging the occupation of names that had a recollective component than for those that were merely familiar.

Beyond consolidation of old memories

Addressing the second question takes us away from memory consolidation, though the findings may have some implications for it. If all remote memories were represented in the neocortex, as the standard consolidation model predicts, the hippocampus should not be any more implicated in imagining new situations or creating new scenes than it would be in recovering old memories; in both cases, individuals could draw on their old neocortical memories and recombine them to suit the demands of the task. If the hippocampus is implicated, such results call the standard theory into question as does its involvement in recovering old, detailed memories. This is why such studies also have become a bone of contention among consolidation theorists.

The state of the literature on future thinking and imagining closely resembles that on autobiographical memory. The evidence from functional neuroimaging overwhelmingly shows activation of the hippo-campus, along with most, but not all, of the structures comprising the autobiographical memory network (D'Argembeau, this volume; Szpunar, 2010). The evidence from patients with MTL damage, whether sustained early (Kwan, Caarson, Addis, et al., 2010; Maguire, Vargha-Khadem, and Hassabis, 2010) or late in life, or resulting from trauma or degeneration, is more variable, though, on the whole, it, too, argues against the standard consolidation model (see Maguire and Hassabis, 2011; Race, Keane, and Verfaellie, 2011; Squire, McDuff, and Fascino, 2011).

Even among investigators who agree that the hippocampus is needed to support such functions, it is not clear what aspect of the representation and the underlying process is crucial. Is the critical factor the spatial component that is involved in scene construction (Hassabis and Maguire, 2009) or is it the perceptual and emotional representation involved in episodic simulation (Addis, Pan, and Vu, et al., 2009; Schacter and Addis, 2007)? Also, it is not known whether the hippo-campus is important because it draws on fragments of old spatial or perceptual memories, which flexibly recombine other regions to form new ones, or because the combinatorial process itself is dependent on the hippocampus. The latter is unlikely to account fully for its persistent role in remote memory and imagination, because patients can construct narratives normally when presented with pictures (Race et al., 2011), and because patients are impaired not only on recall but also on tests of recognition where such combinatorial processes play a minimal role (Gilboa et al., 2006). Finally, there is suggestive evidence of regional specialization within the hippocampus such that recovery of remote, old memories depends more on the posterior hippocampus, and recovery of more recent memories and the formation of future "memories," more on the anterior hippocampus, along with the different cortical networks to which each of these regions is functionally connected (Addis et al., 2009; Gilboa et al., 2004; Poppenk, McIntosh, Craik, et al., 2010).

Why do we need such detailed autobiographical memories?

It has been noted by many people that, outside the laboratory, memories are rarely invoked for their own sake, but are used to prepare for the future, solve problems in the present (Pillemer, 2003; Pillemer and Kuwabara, current volume), and promote social interactions. Even when autobiographical memories are recovered unintentionally, some-thing that occurs often daily (Berntsen, 2009; Hintzman, 2011), they are likely to serve a function related to the current goals of the individual (Berntsen, 2009, this volume).

But why must memories be so detailed? Would not schematic representations of autobiographical events do as well? Pillemer (2003) and Schacter and his collaborators have noted that such details are necessary in order to simulate personal goal-directed scenarios, especially when we are confronted with open-ended problems for which no rule or algorithm is available to reach a solution (Gerlach, Spreng, Gilmore, et al., 2011). Here, rich autobiographical memories provide a template to which elements of the current problem situation can be matched, and evoke those aspects of the memory which may be used to derive a solution. The more detailed the simulation, the better.

Sheldon, McAndrews, and Moscovitch (2011) tested this idea by administering the Means-Ends-Problem-Solving Test (MEPS) (Platt and Spivack, 1975) to healthy young and older controls, and patients with MTL epilepsy or unilateral MTL lesions. The MEPS is a standardized social problem-solving task in which the person is given the beginning of a scenario which states the problem (e.g., You move into a new neighborhood and want to make friends) and its resolution (You now have friends). The person is required to provide the middle portion to indicate how one arrived at that resolution. Relevant solutions are those that bring one closer to the end state.

Overall, older adults performed worse than young adults on the MEPS, because hippocampal deterioration with age leads to diminished autobiographical memories. Patients with MTL lesions performed worst of all. Using a modified version of the AI to score the participants' narratives, Sheldon et al. (2011) also found that, across all subjects, the number of internal (episodic) details correlated very highly with the number of relevant solutions the individual provided. There was no correlation with external (semantic) details. In a separate session, they asked older adults also to provide narratives of autobiographical events unrelated to the problems. The correlation of the number of relevant solutions with internal details of this narrative was equally robust, confirming that common processes underlie the individual's ability to recall autobiographical episodes and create plausible simulations which aid problem-solving.

Conclusion

The theories and findings reviewed in this chapter highlight the important role that studies of autobiographical memory played in developing and testing theories of memory and its consolidation since the turn of the twentieth century. Theoretical, methodological, and technological advances enabled the confirmation of some of the early ideas, such as James' (1890) distinction between recollection and familiarity, while challenging others, such as Ribot's dictum that after brain injury all old memories are less vulnerable to disruption or loss than recent memories. The evidence we reviewed, I believe, challenges the model of systems consolidation and favors MTT and the transformation hypothesis, which can be considered an updated and modified version of Penfield and Milner's (1958) proposals. The hippocampus is needed perpetually for retention and retrieval of perceptually and temporally detailed memories of unique or repeated autobiographical events, which correspond to the lower levels in the autobiographical memory hierarchy. Most memories do not retain such perceptually rich information, but are transformed and assimilated into higher-order autobiographical representations, so that they become more schematic and semantic with time. In accord with the transformation hypothesis, these memories, which represent higher levels in the autobiographical memory hierarchy, become independent of the hippocampus and are represented in the neocortex and other structures. Though we believe the evidence supports our model, we have also indicated where the points of contention lie with other models.

As we noted throughout the chapter, the hippocampus is merely the hub of a larger, autobiographical network. Less is known about how the hippocampus interacts with these other structures, what they contribute to different aspects of autobiographical memory, whether and how they aid the transformation process, and whether the information they represent and the operations they perform are affected by systems consolidation and reconsolidation. Exciting developments are taking place on these fronts, but it is too early to draw any definitive conclusions (see McKenzie and Eichenbaum, 2011; Nieuwenhuis and Takashima, 2011; St. Jacques, this volume; van Kesteren, Fernandez, Norris, *et al.*, 2010; Wang and Morris, 2010). It seems certain, however, that studies of autobiographical memory will continue to play an important role in addressing these issues.

References

Addis, D. R., Moscovitch, M., Crawley, A. P., and McAndrews, M. P. (2004). Recollective qualities modulate hippocampal activation during autobiographical memory retrieval. *Hippocampus*, **18**, 752–762.

Addis, D. R., Moscovitch, M., and McAndrews, M. P. (2007). Consequences of hippocampal damage across the autobiographical memory network in left temporal lobe epilepsy. *Brain*, **130**(Pt 9), 2327–2342.

Addis, D. R., Pan, L., Vu, M. A., Laiser, N., and Schacter, D. L. (2009). Constructive episodic simulation of the future and the past: distinct subsystems of a core brain network mediate imagining and remembering. *Neuropsychologia*, **47**(11), 2222–2238.

Aggleton, J. P. and Brown, M. W. (1999). Episodic memory, amnesia, and the hippocampal-anterior thalamic axis. *Behavioral and Brain Sciences*, **22**, 425–444.

Bartlett, F. C. (1932). *Remembering: a study in experimental and social psychology.* Cambridge University Press.

Bekhterev, V. M. (1907). Essentials of the study of brain functions. *Transactions of the Clinic for Mental and Nervous Diseases* (No. 6). St. Petersburg.

Berntsen, D. (2009). *Involuntary autobiographical memories: an introduction to the unbidden past.* Cambridge University Press.

Bird, C. M. and Burgess, N. (2008). The hippocampus and memory: insights from spatial processing. *Nature Reviews Neuroscience*, **9**(3), 182–194.

Bright, P., Buckman, J., Fradera, A., Yoshimasu, H., Colchester, A. C., and Kopelman, M. D. (2006). Retrograde amnesia in patients with hippocampal, medial temporal, temporal lobe, or frontal pathology. *Learning Memory*, **13**(5), 545–557.

Burnham, W. H. (1904). Retroactive amnesia: illustrative cases and a tentative explanation. *American Journal of Psychology*, **14**, 382–396.

Cabeza, R. and St. Jacques, P. (2007). Functional neuroimaging of autobiographical memory. *Trends in Cognitive Science*, **11**(5), 219–227.

Conway, M. A. (2009). Episodic memories. *Neuropsychologia*, **47**(11), 2305–2313.

Conway, M. A., Rubin, D. C., Spinnler, H., and Wagenaar, W. A. (eds.) (1992). *Theoretical perspectives on autobiographical memory* (pp. 167–194). Dordrecht: Kluwer Academic.

Corkin, S. (1984). Lasting consequences of bilateral medial temporal lobectomy: clinical course and experimental findings in H.M. *Neurology*, **4**, 249–259.

Dudai, Y. (2004). The neurobiology of consolidations, or, how stable is the engram? *Annual Review of Psychology*, **55**, 51–86.

Duff, M. C., Gupta, R., Hengst, J. A., Tranel, D., and Cohen, N. J. (2011). The use of definite references signals declarative memory: evidence from patients with hippocampal amnesia. *Psychological Science*, **22**(5), 666–673.

Eichenbaum, H., Yonelinas, A. P., and Ranganath, C. (2007). The medial temporal lobe and recognition memory. *Annual Review of Neuroscience*, **30**, 123–152.

Fujii, T., Moscovitch, M., and Nadel, L. (2000). Consolidation, retrograde amnesia, and the temporal lobe. In F. Boller and J. Grafman (eds.), *The handbook of neuropsychology* (2nd edn.), vol. II (pp. 233 250). Amsterdam: Elsevier.

Gerlach, K. D., Spreng, R. N., Gilmore, A. W., and Schacter, D. L. (2011). Solving future problems: default network and executive activity associated with goal-directed mental simulations. *NeuroImage*, **55**, 1816–1824.

Gilboa, A. (2004). Autobiographical and episodic memory – one and the same? Evidence from prefrontal activation in neuroimaging studies. *Neuropsychologia*, **42**(10), 1336–1349.

Gilboa, A., Winocur, G., Grady, C. L., Hevenor, S. J., and Moscovitch, M. (2004). Remembering out past: functional neuroanatomy of recollection of recent and very remote personal events. *Cerebral Cortex*, **14**(10), 1214–1225.

Gilboa, A., Winocur, G., Rosenbaum, R. S., Poreh, A., Gao, F., Black, S. E., and Moscovitch, M. (2006). Hippocampal contributions to recollection in retrograde and anterograde amnesia. *Hippocampus*, **16**(11), 966–980.

Hassabis, D. and Maguire, E. A. (2009). Patients with hippocampal amnesia cannot imagine new experiences. *Proceedings of the National Academy of Sciences of the United States of America*, **104**(5), 1726–1731.

Hintzman, D. L. (2011). Research strategy in the study of memory: fads, fallacies, and the search for the "coordiantes of truth." *Perspectives on Pshychological Science*, **6**, 253–271.

James, W. (1890). *Principles of psychology*, vol. I. New York: Henry Holt and Co.

Kapur, N. (1999). Syndromes of retrograde amnesia: a conceptual and empirical synthesis. *Psychological Bulletin*, **125**(6), 800–825.

Kinsbourne, M. and Wood, F. (1975). Short-term memory processes and the amnesic syndrome. In D. Deutsch, and J. A. Deutsch (eds.), *Short-term memory* (pp. 258–291). New York: Academic Press.

Klein, S. B., Loftus, J., and Kihlstrom, J. F. (1996). Self-knowledge of an amnesic patient: toward a neuropsychology of personality and social psychology. *Journal of Experimental Psychology General*, **125**(3), 250–260.

Kopelman, M. D. and Kapur, N. (2001). The loss of episodic memories in retrograde amnesia: single-case and group studies. *Philosophical Transactions of the Royal Society of London. Series B, Biolgical Sciences*, **356**(1413), 1409–1421.

Kopelman, M. D., Wilson, B. A., and Baddeley, A. D. (1989). The autobiographical memory interview: a new assessment of autobiographical and personal semantic memory in amnesic patients. *Journal of Clinical and Experimental Neuropsychology*, **11**, 724–744.

Kwan, D., Caarson, N., Addis, D. R., and Rosebaum, R. S. (2010). Deficits in past remembering extend to future imagining in a case of developmental amnesia. *Neuropsychologia*, **48**, 3179–3186.

Lashley, K. S. (1950). In search of the engram. *Sympisa for the Society of Experimental Biology*, **4**, 454–482.

Levine, B., Svoboda, E., Hay, J. F., and Winocur, G. (2002). Aging and autobiographical memory: dissociating episodic from semantic retrieval. *Psychology and Aging*, **17**, 677–689.

Maguire, E. A. (2001). Neuroimaging studies of autiobiographical event memory. *Philosophical Transactions of the Royal Society of London. Series B, Biological Sciences*, **356**, 1441–1451.

Maguire, E. A. and Hassabis, D. (2011). Role of the hippocampus in imagination and future thinking. *Proceedings of the National Academy of Sciences of the United States of America*, **108**(11), E39.

Maguire, E. A., Vargha-Khadem, F., and Hassabis, D. (2010). Imagining fictitious and future experiences: evidence from developmental amnesia. *Neuropsychologia*, **48**, 3187–3192.

McKenzie, S. and Eichenbaum, H. (2011). Consolidation and reconsolidation: two lives of memories? *Neuron*, **71**(2), 224–233.

Moscovitch, M. (1995). Recovered consciousness: a hypothesis concerning modularity and episodic memory. *Journal of Clinical and Experimetnal Neuropsychology*, **17**(2), 276–290.

Moscovitch, M., Vriezen, E., and Goshen-Gottstein, Y. (1993). Implicit tests of memory in patients with focal lesions or degenerative brain disorders. In F. Boller and J. Grafman (eds.), *The handbook of neuropsychology*, vol. VIII (pp. 133–173). Amsterdam: Elsevier Science.

Müller, G. E. and Pilzecker, A. (1900). Experimentelle Beiträge zur Lehre vom Gedächtnis. *Zeitschrift für Psychologie und Physiologie der Sinnesorgane*, **S1**, 1–288.

Nadel, L. and Moscovitch, M. (1997). Memory consolidation, retrograde amnesia and the hippocampal complex. *Current Opinion in Neurobiology*, 7, 217–227.

Nieuwenhuis, I. L. C. and Takashima, A. (2011). The role of the ventromedial prefrontal cortex in memory consolidation. *Behavioural Brain Research*, **218**, 325–334.

O'Keefe, J. and Nadel, L. (1978). *The hippocampus as a cognitive map*. Oxford University Press.

Park, L., McAndrews, M. P., Westmacott, R., and Moscovitch, M. (2007). Recollection in semantic decisions: contribution of personal memories to semantic judgements as revealed by behavior and functional neuroimaging. Paper presented at meeting of the Psychonomics Society, Long Beach, CA, November.

Park, L., St-Laurent, M., McAndrews, M. P., and Moscovitch, M. (2011). The immediacy of recollection: the use of the historical present in narratives of autobiographical episodes by patients with unilateral temporal lobe epilepsy. *Neuropsychologia*, 49(5), 1171–1176.

Penfield, W. and Milner, B. (1958). Memory deficit produced by bilateral lesions in the hippocampal zone. *A.M.A. Archives of Neurology and Psychiatry*, 79(5), 475–497.

Petrican, R., Gopie, N., Leach, L., Chow, T. W., Richards, B., and Moscovitch, M. (2010). Recollection and familiarity for public events in neurologically intact older adults and two brain-damaged patients. *Neuropsychologia*, 48(4), 945–960.

Pillemer, D. B. (2003). Directive functions of autobiographical memory: the guiding power of the specific episode. *Memory*, 11(2), 193–202.

Piolino, P., Desgranges, B., and Eustache, F. (2009). Episodic autobiographical memories over the course of time: cognitive, neuropsychological and neuro-imaging findings. *Neuropsychologia*, 47(11), 2314–2329.

Platt, J. and Spivack, G. (1975). *Manual for the Means-Ends Problem-Solving Test (MEPS): a measure of interpersonal problem-solving skill.* Philadelphia: Hahnemann Medical College and Hospital.

Poppenk, J., McIntosh, A. R., Craik, F. I., and Moscovitch, M. (2010). Prior experience modulates the neural mechanisms of episodic memory formation. *Journal of Neuroscience*, 30, 4707–4716.

Race, E., Keane, M. M., and Verfaellie, M. (2011). Medial temporal lobe damage causes deficits in episodic memory and episodic future thinking not attribut-able to deficits in narrative construction. *Journal of Neuroscience*, 31(28), 10262–10269.

Ribot, R. (1882). *Diseases of memory*. New York: Appleton.

Sanders, H. I. and Warrington, E. K. (1971). Memory for remote events in amnesic patients. *Brain*, **94**, 661–668.

Schacter, D. L. and Addis, D. R. (2007). The cognitive neuroscience of constructive memory: remembering the past and imagining the future. *Philosophical Transactions of the Royal Society of London. Series B, Biological Sciences*, **362** (1481), 773–786.

Schacter, D. L., Wig, G. S., and Stevens, W. D. (2007). Reduction in cortical activity during priming. *Current Opinion in Neurobiology*, **17**, 171–176.

Sheldon, S., McAndrews, M. P., and Moscovitch, M. (2011). Episodic memory processes mediated by the medial temporal lobes contribute to open-ended problem-solving. *Neuropsychologia*, **49**, 2439–2447.

Scoville, W. and Milner, B. (1957). Loss of recent memory after bilateral hippocampal lesions. *Journal of Neurology Neurosurgery, and Psychiatry*, **20**, 11–21.

Sharon, T., Moscovitch, M., and Gilboa, A. (2011). Rapid neocortical acquisition of long-term arbitrary associations independent of the hippocampus. *Proceedings of the National Academy of Sciences of the United States of America*, **108**(3), 1146–1151.

Squire, L. R., McDuff, S. G., and Frascino, J. C. (2011). Reply to Maguire and Hassabis: autobiographical memory and future imagining. *Proceedings of the National Academy of Sciences of the United States of America*, **108**(11), E40.

Squire, L. R., van der Horst, A. S., McDuff, S. G., Frascino, J. C., Hopkins, R. O., and Mauldin, K. N. (2010). Role of the hippocampus in remembering the past and imagining the future. *Proceedings of the National Academy of Sciences of the United States of America*, **107**(44), 19044–19048.

Squire, L. R. and Wixted, J. T. (2011). The cognitive neuroscience of human memory since H.M. *Annual Review Neuroscience*, **34**, 259–288.

St-Laurent, M., Moscovitch, M., Levine, B., and McAndrews, M. P. (2009). Determinants of autobiographical memory in patients with unilateral temporal lobe epilepsy or excisions. *Neuropsychologia*, **47**(11), 2211–2221.

St-Laurent, M., Moscovitch, M., Tau, M., and McAndrews, M. P. (2011). The temporal unraveling of autobiographical memory narratives in patients with temporal lobe epilepsy or excisions. *Hippocampus*, **21**(4), 409–421.

Steinvorth, S., Levine, B., and Corkin, S. (2005). Medial temporal lobe structures are needed to re-experience remote autobiographical memories: evidence from H.M. and W.R. *Neuropsychologia*, **43**(4), 479–496.

Suddendorf, T. and Corballis, M. C. (1997). Mental time travel and the evolution of the human mind. *Genetic Social, and General Psychology Monographs*, **123**(2), 133–167.

Svoboda, E., McKinnon, M. C., and Levine, B. (2006). The functional neuroanatomy of autobiographical memory: a meta-analysis. *Neuropsychologia*, **44**(12), 2189–2208.

Szpunar, K. K. (2010). Episodic future thought: an emerging concept. *Perspectives on Psycholgical Science*, **5**, 142–162.

Tulving, E. (1972). Episodic and semantic memory. In E. Tulving and W. Donaldson (eds.), *Organization of memory* (pp. 381–403). New York: Academic Press.

  (1985). Memory and consciousness. *Canadian Psychology*, **26**(1), 1–12.

Tulving, E. and Schacter, D. L. (1990). Priming and human memory systems. *Science*, **247**(4940), 301–306.

van Kesteren, M. T., Fernandez, G., Norris, D. G., and Hermans, E. J. (2010). Persistent schema-dependent hippocampal-neocortical connectivity during memory encoding and postencoding rest in humans. *Proceedings of the National Academy of Sciences of the United States of America*, **107**, 7550–7555.

Vargha-Khadem, F., Gadian, D. G., Watkins, K. E., Connelly, A., Van Paesschen, W., and Mishkin, M. (1997). Differential effects of early hippocampal pathology on episodic and semantic memory. *Science*, **277**(5324), 376–380.

Wang, S. H. and Morris, R. G. (2010). Hippocampal-neocortical interactions in memory formation, consolidation, and reconsolidation. *Annual Review of Psychology*, **61**, 49–79.

Westmacott, R., Black, S. E., Freedman, M., and Moscovitch, M. (2004a). The contribution of autobiographical significance to semantic memory: evidence from Alzheimer's disease, semantic dementia, and amnesia. *Neuropsychologia*, **31**, 25–48.

Westmacott, R., Freedman, M., Black, S. E., Stokes, K. A., and Moscovitch, M. (2004b). Temporally graded semantic memory loss in Alzheimer's disease: cross-sectional and longitudinal studies. *Cognitive Neuropsychology*, **21**(2), 353–378.

Winocur, G. and Moscovitch, M. (2011). Memory transformation and systems consolidation. *Journal of the International Neuropsychological Society*, **17**, 766–780.

Winocur, G., Moscovitch, M., and Bontempi, B. (2010). Memory formation and long-term retention in humans and animals: convergence towards a transformation account of hippocampal-neocortical interactions. *Neuropsychologia*, **48**(8), 2339–2356.

7 Functional neuroimaging of autobiographical memory

Peggy L. St. Jacques

Autobiographical memory (AM) refers to memory for events from our own personal past. In the last decade there has been an explosion in the number of functional neuroimaging studies of AM, which is best exemplified in the number of reviews on this topic, varying from those focusing on the core regions involved in AM retrieval and methodological challenges (Maguire, 2001; Svoboda, McKinnon, and Levine, 2006), to emphasizing task-related differences in AM versus laboratory memory studies (Gilboa, 2004; McDermott, Szpunar, and Christ, 2009) or highlighting task-invariant patterns of activations common to AM and other similar tasks, such as imagining the future (e.g., Buckner and Carroll, 2007; Hassabis and Maguire, 2007; Schacter, Addis, and Buckner, 2007; Spreng and Grady, 2010). Functional neuroimaging studies of AM are important because they can investigate the neural correlates of processes that are difficult to study in laboratory stimuli (Cabeza and St. Jacques, 2007; St. Jacques and Cabeza, 2012). An AM researcher, however, may still question what exactly such studies contribute to our theoretical understanding of personal memory. The present chapter considers three integral aspects of AM where functional neuroimaging data provide us with important insights. First, functional neuroimaging studies can inform our understanding of the *complex retrieval processes* in AM by allowing the examination of separable phases of memory retrieval. Second, such studies can distinguish the specific role of *self-reference* in AM and how it potentially directs memory construction. Third, functional neuroimaging studies of AM offer compelling ideas regarding the role of *recollection* in the timing and interaction of multiple component processes during retrieval, as well as the potential contribution of *familiarity processes* in recognizing autobiographical experiences. Before turning to these aspects, I first briefly review the main functional neuroimaging methods for investigating AM and the core brain regions typically involved in AM retrieval, which will be relevant to the studies discussed here.

Overview of functional neuroimaging of AM

Eliciting AMs in the scanning environment

Several methods have been used to investigate AM with functional neuroimaging (for review, see Cabeza and St. Jacques, 2007). The primary challenge of these methods is balancing the ability to exert control over the phenomenological properties of memory retrieval while also maintaining ecological validity (for review, see Cabeza and St. Jacques, 2007; Maguire, 2001; Svoboda *et al.*, 2006). For example, it is particularly difficult to determine the retrieval cues that will be effective in eliciting AMs without also interfering with the properties of the retrieved memory during scanning and subsequent interpretations of brain activation (Cabeza and St. Jacques, 2007). Here I discuss two of the main methods, relevant to the studies reviewed below, which represent the extremes of control.

In the *generic cues method* (e.g., Daselaar, Rice, Greenberg, *et al.*, 2008; St. Jacques, Botzung, Miles, *et al.*, 2011) AMs are generated from novel retrieval cues (e.g., *table*; Crovitz and Schiffman, 1974) and there is less experimental control over the type and properties of the retrieved memories. Memories elicited by generic cues are not necessarily emotional or significant, but they are unrehearsed such that retrieval in the scanner tends to be protracted and is not contaminated by recent retrieval attempts. These aspects result in two primary advantages for interpreting functional neuroimaging data. First, online ratings of *reliving*, the senses of re-experiencing, and other phenomenological properties associated with memory retrieval during scanning are more accurate. This is important because phenomenological ratings and other properties of the retrieved memory can be used to examine trial-to-trial fluctuations in behavior as a function of brain activity by parametric analysis. Second, memory construction processes can be investigated more easily. Combined with a self-paced design, the protracted construction processes associated with the generic cue method make it possible to disentangle the functional activations associated with separable retrieval phases by using functional magnetic resonance imaging (fMRI). In these studies, participants search for a memory, press a button once a memory is formed, and then maintain and elaborate upon the memory. The self-paced button press is then used to segregate the search and maintenance/elaboration phases (see also Rubin, this volume, Figure 2.2).

In the *prospective method*, participants are asked to keep a record of events in their lives to be used as retrieval cues in the scanner (e.g., Cabeza, Prince, Daselaar, *et al.*, 2004; St. Jacques, Rubin, Labar, *et al.*, 2008). One of the main advantages of the prospective method is that it allows the greatest amount of control over the properties of retrieved memories. For example, it allows accuracy to be assessed, and this is important given that brain activity tends to vary as a function of retrieval accuracy (e.g., Daselaar, Fleck, Prince, *et al.*, 2006). Until recently, however, the main disadvantage of the prospective method was that it interfered with the natural encoding of AMs. With innovative camera technologies that employ sensors and timers to automatically capture hundreds of photographs when worn, it is now possible to prospectively generate idiosyncratic and visually rich retrieval cues, which may be more effective in eliciting autobiographical memories in the laboratory (e.g., St. Jacques, Conway, and Cabeza, 2010; St. Jacques, Conway, Lowder, *et al.*, 2011a). For example, SenseCam (also known as ViconRevue) is a small wearable digital camera that has electronic sensors (e.g., light, heat) that can automatically trigger thousands of photographs in a single day. This differs considerably from typical use of a digital camera to generate retrieval cues to elicit AMs during scanning (e.g., Cabeza *et al.*, 2004; St. Jacques *et al.*, 2008), because it does not disrupt the experience of events through the act of taking a photograph. Also, several photographs from a particular event (e.g., eating ice cream) can be consecutively viewed to create a dynamic retrieval cue (www.youtube.com/watch?v=sr1i-sICafs). The SenseCam lens also maximizes the field of view to better capture the perspective of the wearer by incorporating a wide-angle (fish-eye) lens. An additional advantage of these sensor-based camera technologies is that they are easier to implement in special populations (e.g., Berry, Kapur, Williams, *et al.*, 2007; Pauly-Takacs, Moulin, and Estlin, 2010) because they require minimal input from the user.

Core regions involved in AM

Recalling memories from our personal past involves a distributed set of primarily left-lateralized brain regions (Maguire, 2001), although not all studies show this pattern (for review, see Svoboda *et al.*, 2006), which has been referred to as the AM retrieval network (see Figure 7.1). AM retrieval depends upon control processes mediated by the lateral prefrontal cortex (PFC) (Petrides, 2005; also see Miller and Cohen, 2001) and top-down attention mediated by the dorsal parietal cortex (DPC) (for reviews, see Cabeza, 2008; Cabeza, Ciaramelli, Olson, *et al.*, 2008), which guide the search and construction of spatiotemporally specific AMs supported by semantic information about oneself and the world. Because the

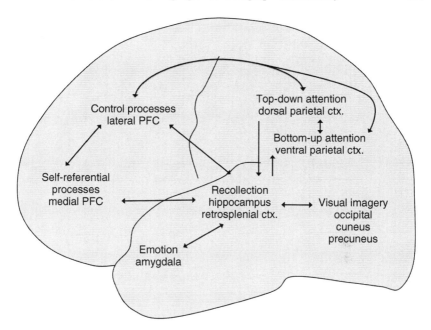

Figure 7.1. Schematic of the brain regions typically involved in autobiographical memory retrieval. Ctx = cortex, PFC = prefrontal cortex.

final target of AM construction is a personal memory, it is critically dependent on self-referential processing involving the recruitment of the medial PFC (e.g., Craik, Moroz, Moscovitch, *et al.*, 1999; Kelley, Macrae, Wyland, *et al.*, 2002; Macrae, Moran, Heatherton, *et al.*, 2004). The ability to retrieve a rich episodic AM also depends upon recollection processes, mediated by the hippocampus and retrosplenial cortex (for review, see Diana, Yonelinas, and Ranganath, 2007; e.g., Valenstein, Bowers, VerFaellie, *et al.*, 1987) and is enhanced by emotional processing in the amygdala (for review, see LaBar and Cabeza, 2006) and visual imagery in occipital and cuneus/precuneus regions (Greenberg and Rubin, 2003). As memory details are retrieved, there is greater bottom-up attention mediated by the ventral parietal cortex (e.g., Berryhill, Phuong, Picasso, *et al.*, 2007; for reviews, see Cabeza, 2008; Cabeza *et al.*, 2008). There is interaction among these and other brain regions during AM retrieval, but for simplicity I discuss in isolation only the most important regions relevant to the present discussion.

Contribution of functional neuroimaging to theoretical perspectives of AM

Below I consider how functional neuroimaging studies have provided insight into three integral components of AM: (1) complex retrieval, (2) self-reference, and (3) recollection.

Complex retrieval

Previous functional neuroimaging studies have emphasized that AM retrieval involves controlled search processes associated with the recruitment of the PFC. The link between memory search and controlled retrieval processes in AM was first detected by an early positron emission tomography study that found activation in lateral PFC regions when comparing AM to semantic memory (Conway, Turk, Miller, et al., 1999). Although activation differences between these tasks may reflect many different factors (e.g., Cabeza et al., 2004) the link between AM and activations in the lateral PFC and other brain regions was supported by subsequent reviews (Maguire, 2001; Svoboda et al., 2006). The lateral PFC activity elicited by AM retrieval is predominantly left-lateralized (Maguire, 2001; Svoboda et al., 2006), and this is thought to reflect the contribution of semantic information to AM. Consistent with this suggestion, the left-lateralized pattern of activation in the PFC during AM is observed irrespective of the nature of the eliciting cue (Denkova, Botzung, Scheiber, et al., 2006). These findings provide empirical support for the model proposed by Conway and colleagues (Conway, 2001, 2005; Conway and Pleydell-Pearce, 2000), which suggests that AM construction typically involves generative retrieval associated with effortful and protracted search processes supported by semantic knowledge.

The protracted retrieval length of AMs combined with the generic cue method and a self-paced design during fMRI scanning enables the segregation of brain regions involved in different phases of memory retrieval (Daselaar et al., 2008; St. Jacques, Botzung, et al., 2011; St. Jacques, Kragel, and Rubin, 2011; St. Jacques, Rubin, and Cabeza, 2010). For example, Daselaar et al. (2008) compared activity related to the search period of AM with the maintenance/elaboration period. The initial search period was found to engage frontal regions involved in retrieval effort (right lateral PFC) and self-referential processes (medial PFC) but also posterior regions involved in accessing the memory trace (hippocampus, retrosplenial cortex), whereas the later period recruited posterior regions involved in the retrieval of contextual details (visual cortex, precuneus) and frontal regions linked to working memory (left lateral PFC). By segregating the search and elaboration phases of memory construction, the fMRI results show that AM retrieval relies upon separable component processes that come online at different points in time. Other research groups using different methods have largely found consistent results (e.g., Botzung, Denkova, Ciuciu, *et al.*, 2008; Conway, Pleydell-Pearce, Whitecross, *et al.*, 2003; Steinvorth, Corkin, and Halgren, 2006). The engagement of multiple frontal and posterior regions across the separable phases of retrieval demonstrates additional complexity regarding the generative nature of AM retrieval. These findings inform current models of AM (e.g., Conway, 2005) by suggesting that the iterative retrieval process consisting of multiple memory-construction mappings continues even after a spatiotemporally AM is accessed.

Understanding the separable phases of memory retrieval can also provide important insights into AM across the life span and in clinical populations. First, turning to research in life-span development, fMRI was employed to examine the effects of age during the search and elaboration phases of AM retrieval (St. Jacques, Rubin, *et al.*, 2010). The main effect of healthy aging on AM retrieval is attenuation in episodic richness (Levine, Svoboda, Hay, *et al.*, 2002; Piolino, Desgranges, Benali, *et al.*, 2002; St. Jacques and Levine, 2007), but *when* during retrieval the age effect occurs is largely unknown. The results of this study suggest that the age-related attenuation in the episodic richness of AMs is associated with specific difficulty during elaboration, involving strategic retrieval processes underlying recovery of details. Age effects on AM activity were more pronounced during elaboration than search, with older adults showing less sustained recruitment of the hippocampus and lateral PFC (see Figure 7.2A). In linking the fMRI results to the age-related reductions in episodic richness observed behaviorally, it was found that functional activity in these regions was attenuated for AMs that were more episodically detailed. Further, there was an age-related decrease in the top-down modulation of the PFC on the hippocampus by episodic richness, possibly reflecting fewer controlled processes operating on the recovery of memory details in the hippocampus during elaboration. The present study shows that changes in the sustained response and coupling of the hippocampus and PFC underlie age-related reductions in episodic richness of the personal past. These results underscore the importance of decomposing the time course of retrieval processes when examining age-related effects by showing a differential pattern of functional activation across search versus elaboration processes in AM retrieval, and they provide greater understanding of the age-related reduction in episodic richness. For example, they suggest novel interventions to attenuate age-related

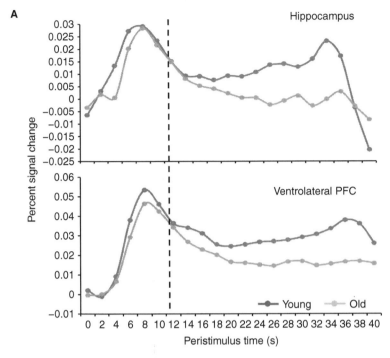

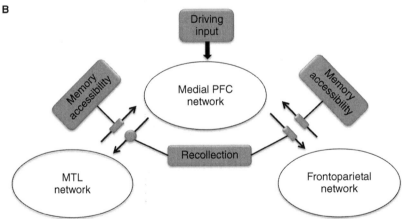

Figure 7.2. Complex retrieval of autobiographical memory (AM). A) Interrogating the search and elaboration phases of AM reveals age-invariant activity in the right hippocampus and left ventrolateral prefrontal cortex (PFC) during search, but age-related differences in these same regions during elaboration. Dotted line represents the peak of the average motor cortex response for the button press. B) Simplified

differences in episodic richness by providing retrieval support at separable time points during AM construction.

Second, turning to its use in clinical populations, we examined the neural mechanisms affected by post-traumatic stress disorder (PTSD) symptoms during the retrieval of emotionally intense AMs (St. Jacques, Botzung, *et al.*, 2011). PTSD affects a number of brain regions involved in AM (Etkin and Wager, 2007; Shin, Rauch, and Pitman, 2006), and the effects of emotional reactions extend beyond traumatic memories to non-trauma-related AMs (Rubin, Boals, and Berntsen, 2008). However, little is known regarding how PTSD would affect the neural basis of retrieval across a sample of emotionally intense AMs. We used the generic cue method and employed emotional words to elicit spontaneously generated memories during scanning, and then combined this with online ratings of emotional experience. This method allowed us to examine brain activity during search and elaboration that parametrically varied with the emotional intensity associated with retrieved memories on each trial. The fMRI results showed that there was greater recruitment of the MTL and other memory-related brain regions during the initial search versus elaboration of negatively intense AMs in PTSD when compared to controls. Thus, by segregating the time course of AM retrieval, using fMRI, we revealed that PTSD affects the initial reactivity of brain regions supporting emotion and memory. Understanding why PTSD leads to a boost in the initial recruitment of the memory network during retrieval of emotionally intense memories may provide novel insight into the alteration of AM in this disorder.

The findings reviewed thus far suggest that the complex retrieval of AM retrieval is supported by a distributed set of brain regions (Conway and Pleydell-Pearce, 2000; Norman and Bobrow, 1976); however, they do not consider the functional connections among these regions nor the potential influence of memory accessibility. AM retrieval encompasses multiple

---

Caption for Figure 7.2 (cont.)

version of a dynamic causal model showing the integration among networks contributing to AM retrieval and the influence of memory accessibility and recollection. The medial PFC network drives the construction and elaboration of AMs. Memory accessibility increases the bottom-up influence of the medial temporal lobe (MTL) and frontoparietal networks on the medial prefrontal cortex (PFC) network during the construction of AMs. In contrast, recollection influences the top-down influence of the medial PFC on the frontoparietal network (during construction; rectangle) and MTL network (during elaboration; circle).

neural systems that interact and are influenced by the properties of the retrieval process (Greenberg and Rubin, 2003; Rubin, 2005, 2006; also see Rubin, this volume). For example, the ease with which memories are accessed potentially influences whether generative or direct retrieval mechanisms are engaged (Conway and Pleydell-Pearce, 2000; Uzer, Lee, and Brown, in press; also see Moscovitch, 1992). To investigate these issues, we (St. Jacques, Kragel, et al., 2011) identified neural networks contributing to AM retrieval by independent-components analysis (ICA) (Calhoun, Adali, Pearlson, et al., 2001), and then examined whether memory accessibility (i.e., greater ease of retrieval) influenced the interaction among these networks in a dynamic causal model (DCM) (Friston, Harrison, and Penny, 2003; for a similar approach, see Stevens, Kiehl, Pearlson, et al., 2007). The fMRI results revealed several large-scale brain networks contributing to AM retrieval, including the following: (1) a left-lateralized frontoparietal network, including frontal and parietal cortices (primarily DPC extending into ventral parietal cortex [VPC]), which is linked to adaptive cognitive control processes (Dosenbach, Fair, Miezin, et al., 2007; Seeley, Menon, Schatzberg, et al., 2007; Vincent, Kahn, Snyder, et al., 2008); (2) the medial PFC network, involving anterior and posterior midline regions along with the bilateral VPC, which is a network associated with self-referential processes (Andrews-Hanna, Reidler, Sepulcre, et al., 2010; for a review, see Buckner, Andrews-Hanna, and Schacter, 2008); and (3) the MTL network, including the MTL and retrosplenial cortex, ventromedial PFC, and bilateral VPC, which is a network involved in declarative memory and the construction of mental scenes (Andrews-Hanna et al., 2010; Kahn, Andrews-Hanna, Vincent, et al., 2008; Vincent et al., 2006). These networks were differentially engaged across the separable phases of AM retrieval, such that the frontoparietal network was recruited only during the initial construction of AM, whereas the medial PFC and MTL networks were recruited across both phases. One interpretation of these results is that the initial construction of AM involves greater top-down control over memory, whereas recovery of memory details can occur throughout AM retrieval (also see Daselaar et al., 2008). These findings are potentially consistent with the attention to memory (AToM) model (for reviews, see Cabeza, 2008; Cabeza et al., 2008), which postulates that the DPC, observed here in the frontoparietal network, is associated with greater top-down attentional control during memory search, whereas the VPC, observed here in both the medial PFC and MTL networks, is linked to bottom-up attention processes as memory details are detected. Additionally, we also found that memory accessibility, defined as the fastest retrieval times within each participant, modulated the connectivity among the neural networks supporting AM. During construction, memory accessibility increased the influence of the MTL and frontoparietal networks (see Figure 7.2B) on the medial PFC network. There was no effect of memory accessibility during elaboration. Thus, the ease of retrieval influenced both the bottom-up networks associated with the recovery of the memory trace and the top-down control network, which impinged on a network linked to self-referential processes. These results suggest that memory accessibility increases the integration among the neural networks supporting AM retrieval, and potentially contributes to direct retrieval processes.

Self-reference

Self-reference is a critical and defining feature of AM (e.g., Brewer, 1986; Conway, 2005). Functional neuroimaging studies have shown that AM retrieval typically involves greater self-referential processes when compared to memory retrieval for stimuli encoded in the laboratory (for review, see Gilboa, 2004). For example, Cabeza *et al.* (2004) conducted an fMRI study in which participants were asked to recognize photographs of familiar locations taken by themselves compared to photographs encoded in the laboratory. Using the prospective method allowed control over most of the factors that could potentially differ between the conditions, such as the type of test (recognition in both), emotional content (minimal in both), memories' age (recent in both), retrieval success (measured and similar in both), semantic memory (similar in both), and internal structure (simple, disconnected events in both). With these six factors controlled, the AM and laboratory condition yielded very similar activations in several brain regions. Self-referential processing, however, was not controlled and likely accounted for the greater activity in the AM condition in the medial PFC based on previous functional neuroimaging evidence regarding the role of this region in self-reference (see Figure 7.3A; Kelley *et al.*, 2002; Raichle *et al.*, 2001). Others using different methods have also found greater involvement of the medial PFC in AM versus control tasks (Denkova *et al.*, 2006), as well as when self-referential processes were manipulated within the AM condition (Levine *et al.*, 2004; Maguire, Henson, Mummery, *et al.*, 2001; Muscatell, Addis, and Kensinger, 2010).

Self-referential processes in AM allow for the awareness of the self in time, or autonoetic awareness (Tulving, 1983; Wheeler, Stuss, and Tulving, 1997). The ability to self-project to the personal past is closely related to the ability to understand another person's perspective (Buckner and Carroll, 2007; Mitchell, 2009; Suddendorf and Corballis, 2007),

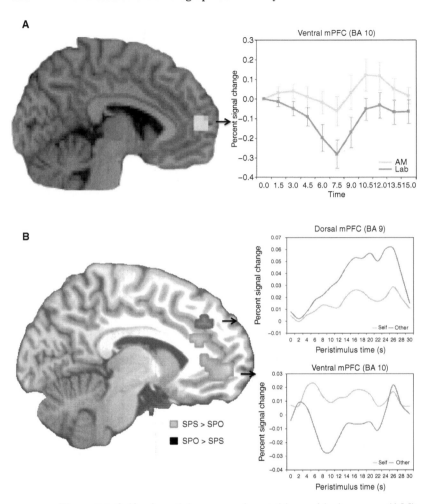

Figure 7.3. Self-referential processes in autobiographical memory (AM).
A) Autobiographical memory retrieval recruits greater medial prefrontal
cortex (mPFC) when compared to memory retrieval for simple laboratory
stimuli. B) There is a ventral versus dorsal distinction in the recruitment of
the mPFC during self versus other self-projection. SPS = self-projection of
oneself; SPO = self-projection of another's perspective.

such that there is overlap in the neural correlates supporting these processes (for meta-analysis, see Spreng, Mar, and Kim, 2009). Thus, in
order to fully understand the specificity of self-referential processes in
AM, it is important to determine the differential aspects involved in the
ability step into one's own personal past versus another individual's

perspective. In order to address this issue, we conducted an fMRI study that employed the first-person perspective cues generated by the SenseCam to examine neural differences in projection of self versus other (St. Jacques, Conway, *et al.*, 2011a). During functional scanning, participants were shown short event "movies" composed of photographs from their own life (self) or another individual's life (other) and were asked to re-experience or understand the self versus other perspectives, respectively. Our results showed that projection of self versus other differentially recruited distinct regions of the medial PFC. Projection to the personal past recruited the ventral medial PFC, whereas observing another person's perspective recruited the dorsal medial PFC (see Figure 7.3B). These results are consistent with studies linking ventral medial PFC to inferences about one's own self and dorsal medial PFC to mentalizing about another individual, such as during theory-of-mind tasks (Krueger, Barbey, and Grafman, 2009; Mitchell, 2009; Van Overwalle, 2009; also see Spreng and Grady, 2010). Further, parametric analyses linked the recruitment of each of these medial PFC subregions to online ratings tracking the ability to project. In order to gain further insight into the contribution of subregions of the medial PFC to projection of self versus other, we examined the functional connectivity of ventral versus dorsal medial PFC. These results revealed that the ventral medial PFC showed greater functional connectivity with the MTL network supporting memory (Kahn *et al.*, 2008; Vincent *et al.*, 2006), whereas dorsal medial PFC showed greater functional connectivity with the frontoparietal network supporting controlled processes (Vincent *et al.*, 2008). Our fMRI results suggest that the rich sense of re-experience of the personal past is functionally dissociable from similar shifts in perspective that contribute to inference of another person's mental state, and this is similar to findings observed by other research groups (Rabin, Gilboa, Stuss, Mar, *et al.*, 2010; Spreng and Grady, 2010; also see D'Argembeau, Ruby, Collette, *et al.*, 2007; Rosenbaum, Stuss, Levine, *et al.*, 2007).

The recruitment of the medial PFC is usually described for simplicity as *activations*; however, these differences typically occur because this region is *less deactivated* in the condition involving self-referential processing than in the control condition, as was also found in the aforementioned AM studies (see Figure 7.3; Cabeza *et al.*, 2004; St. Jacques, Conway, *et al.*, 2011a). That is, the AM condition does not elicit more activation in the medial PFC when compared to an implicit baseline condition where participants are asked to passively view a fixation. One explanation of this phenomenon is that self-referential processing, such as occurs during AM retrieval, is part of a *default state* of the brain (Gusnard and Raichle, 2001; Raichle *et al.*, 2001). Consistent with this suggestion, the pattern of activation observed during passive rest referred to as the *default network* overlaps with the regions supporting AM retrieval (for reviews, see Buckner *et al.*, 2008; Spreng *et al.*, 2009). Additionally, the content of thought during passive resting states appears to be largely composed of personally relevant events (e.g., Klinger and Cox, 1987). The fMRI findings reviewed here suggest that the number of personal memories that come to mind effortlessly may be much more prevalent than previously considered in the domain of AM, which has largely focused on voluntary and generative retrieval processes (but see Berntsen, 1996; also see Berntsen, 2007, this volume).

Not only are self-referential processes an important feature of AM, but they may also contribute to the construction of memory. The idea that the self modulates AM retrieval is consistent with theories of AM proposed by Conway (Conway, 2005; Conway and Pleydell-Pearce, 2000), but has been difficult to demonstrate behaviorally. Functional neuroimaging studies of AM provide direct evidence to support the widely accepted role of the self in memory construction. For example, in a previous fMRI study, Daselaar *et al.* (2008) found that the medial PFC was recruited to a greater extent during the initial search of AM than during the later maintenance or elaboration phase. This boost in the initial engagement of the medial PFC may help to initiate the construction of AM. Consistent with this idea, in another study, we found that the medial PFC network, rather than other candidate networks associated with memory (MTL network) or controlled processes (e.g., frontoparietal network), drove neuronal activation within the interacting neural networks supporting AM construction (see Figure 7.2B; St. Jacques, Kragel, *et al.*, 2011). Similarly, Muscatell *et al.* (2010), in an fMRI study that directly modulated the extent of self-involvement, found increased connectivity with the medial PFC within the network supporting AM retrieval. In sum, the results of these fMRI studies suggest that self-reference does not simply reflect the contents of AM, but actually helps to initiate and maintain AM construction, thereby providing support for current models of AM (Conway, 2005; Conway and Pleydell-Pearce, 2000) that emphasize the role of the self in modulating memory construction.

Recollection

Recollection, the ability to retrieve contextual details and to re-experience or relive a past event, is an integral feature of AM (e.g., Baddeley, 1992; Brewer, 1996). Functional neuroimaging studies have linked recollection processes in AM to regions such as the hippocampus, left PFC, and visual cortex (Cabeza and St. Jacques, 2007; St. Jacques and Cabeza, 2012; Svoboda *et al.*, 2006). For example, we found hippocampal activity associated with successful retrieval of both temporal and spatial context in AM (St. Jacques, Rubin, Lowder, *et al.*, 2009). However, the functional connectivity of the hippocampus differed according to source memory demands. There was greater co-activation between the hippocampus and visual cortex for spatial context, whereas the temporal context increased the connectivity between the hippocampus and left PFC. Because AMs are encoded in the rich multisensory environment of the real world, they often involve the recall of numerous contextual details, and thus recollection may tend to be more graded when it occurs (e.g., Mitchell and Johnson, 2009; Parks and Yonelinas, 2007) versus memory for simple laboratory stimuli (for review, see St. Jacques and Cabeza, 2012). For example, in the aforementioned photo study, Cabeza *et al.* (2004) found greater recruitment in the hippocampus for AM versus laboratory memory retrieval. This finding may be explained by the fact that the amount of visual detail was one of the additional factors not controlled in this study and contributed to the recruitment of additional contextual details, as is consistent with the observation that the AM condition also elicited greater activity in the visual cortex.

Visual imagery is an important component of the rich recovery of contextual information in AM (Rubin, Burt, and Fifield, 2003; Rubin, Schrauf, and Greenberg, 2003; for a review, see Greenberg and Rubin, 2003). Visual imagery impairment can disrupt the entire retrieval process, potentially because AM depends upon the interconnection and activation of many separate systems, of which the visual system plays an integral role (Greenberg and Rubin, 2003; Rubin and Greenberg, 1998; also see Rubin, 2006). In order to better understand the mechanisms by which visual imagery enhances recollection, we conducted an fMRI study in which we compared the functional connections among the regions supporting AM retrieval elicited via verbal descriptions or visual images (St. Jacques, Conway, Lowder, *et al.,* 2011b). We used the SenseCam to generate personal photographs to elicit AMs (visual) and compared this to memories retrieved via event descriptions (verbal) taken from logs of daily events that participants recorded. Following a week delay, participants were asked to recall the events depicted in short SenseCam clips or event descriptions, and then to rate the amount of reliving. We identified a common functional region of interest in the hippocampus based on parametric modulation analysis using the reliving ratings, which was then used in subsequent functional connectivity analysis. Given the central importance of visual imagery in AM, we predicted that visual images would foster integration among the brain regions supporting memory retrieval. Consistent with this prediction, the results indicated that AMs elicited using visual versus verbal cues involved greater co-activation among the

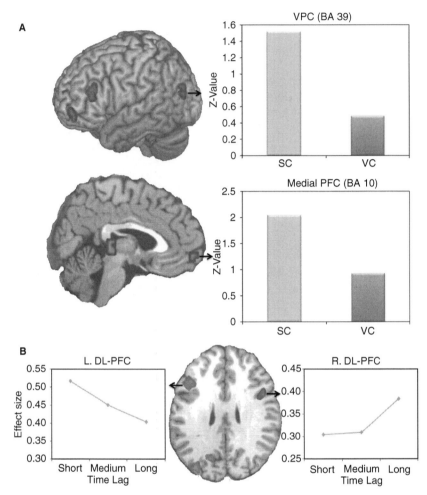

Figure 7.4. Recollection and familiarity processes in autobiographical memory (AM). A) Visual images augment AM recollection by increasing the functional connectivity of the hippocampus with the ventral parietal cortex (VPC) and medial prefrontal cortex (PFC). B) Left prefrontal cortex (PFC) was recruited to a greater extent when temporal-order judgments for AM events relied on recollection processes (shorter time lags), whereas right PFC showed a preferential recruitment when temporal-order judgments relied on familiarity (longer time lags).

hippocampus and critical regions of the retrieval network, including the lateral PFC involved in retrieval control, the medial PFC associated with self-referential processing, and the ventral parietal cortex linked to bottom-up attention processes (see Figure 7.4A). The fMRI results suggest that visual images augment the recollection of autobiographical experiences by strengthening the functional connections among the retrieval network.

Providing visual cues to elicit AMs could also potentially attenuate reported gender differences in recollection. Several studies document superior AMs in females compared to males. For example, compared to males, females recall longer and more detailed AMs (e.g., A. Friedman and Pines, 1991; Pillemer, Wink, DiDonato, *et al.*, 2003; Pohl, Bender, and Lachmann, 2005; Ross and Holmberg, 1992; Seidlitz and Diener, 1998), are more accurate at dating their AMs (e.g., Skowronski and Thompson, 1990), and are faster to recall AMs (e.g., Davis, 1999). However, previous studies examining gender differences in AM have relied upon verbal cues to elicit AMs and verbal processing strategies to determine the quality of retrieval, in which males might be at a disadvantage (for a review, see Andreano and Cahill, 2009). One means to examine gender differences in AM retrieval in a more unbiased way is to use functional neuroimaging to examine covert retrieval and also to manipulate the cue modality. We examined the interaction between gender and the type of cue (visual, verbal) on brain activity sensitive to reliving in a study using the SenseCam (St. Jacques, Conway, *et al.*, 2010). Based on reported gender differences in the reliance on spatial versus verbal processing (for a review, see Andreano and Cahill, 2009), we predicted that males would retrieve more richly experienced AMs when cued via the photographs versus the verbal descriptors, whereas females would show an equal benefit for both types of cues. The behavioral results indicated that there were no gender differences in subjective ratings of reliving, importance, vividness, emotion, and uniqueness, suggesting that gender differences in brain activity were not due to differences in these measures of phenomenological experience. Consistent with our predictions, the fMRI results revealed that, compared to females, males showed a greater difference in functional activity sensitive to reliving for AMs elicited by visual versus verbal cues in the hippocampus, retrosplenial cortex, and visual cortex. Other functional neuroimaging studies of AM have suggested that gender differences may be due to differences in retrieval strategy (Piefke, Weiss, Markowitsch, *et al.*, 2005), which may preferentially benefit some retrieval cues. The fMRI results emphasize the importance of using unbiased measures to elicit and evaluate AMs when examining gender differences, and they suggest that the female advantage in AM retrieval might be less robust once potential gender differences in cognitive strategies are controlled.

Emotion is an additional component of AM that contributes importantly to recollection during retrieval (e.g., Reisberg, Heuer, McLean, *et al.*, 1988; Talarico, LaBar, and Rubin, 2004). AMs infused with emotion are associated with greater recruitment of the amygdala and the hippocampus (Cabeza and St. Jacques, 2007; St. Jacques and Cabeza, 2012; Svoboda *et al.*, 2006). For example, Botzung, Rubin, Miles, Cabeza, *et al.* (2010) observed emotional modulation in the amygdala and hippocampus during retrieval of real-world memories for an emotionally charged college basketball game. Emotion may enhance AM recollection via the modulatory influence of the amygdala on the hippocampus (LaBar and Cabeza, 2006). For example, Greenberg *et al.* (2005) found greater amygdala–hippocampal interactions during AM compared to a neutral control task. In this study, activity in the amgydala was also correlated with activity in lateral PFC, suggesting a potential interaction between the emotional response and memory construction.

Given that both visual imagery and emotion contribute to AMs, an interesting question is whether their contributions occur simultaneously or at different points during AM construction. To investigate this issue, in the aforementioned study using the generic cue method, Daselaar *et al.* (2008) examined activity during search and elaboration phases of AM retrieval that was associated with online ratings of emotion and reliving. Whereas emotion ratings were correlated with early amygdala activity, reliving ratings were correlated with late visual cortex activity. This finding indicates that emotion contributes to AM even before event-specific memories are completely formed, whereas vividness develops late, as reflexive processes turn to recovered visual images. Similarly, in other studies using the generic cue method, we have observed that the effects of emotion tend to occur earlier (St. Jacques, Botzung, *et al.*, 2011), whereas the effects associated with vividness occur later (St. Jacques, Kragel, *et al.*, 2011; St. Jacques, Rubin, *et al.*, 2010). The fMRI results suggest that even though emotion and vividness ratings are positively correlated (e.g., Talarico *et al.*, 2004), the time course of the underlying processes is different.

In contrast with recollection, *familiarity*, the sense of knowing without being able to retrieve contextual information or to re-experience the past, is not typically considered to be an integral aspect of AM (e.g., Conway, 2001). This may be the result of the greater emphasis on recall versus recognition in AM research. In order to investigate the potential contribution of both recollection and familiarity processes in AM retrieval, we conducted an fMRI study that relied on a recognition memory paradigm involving temporal-order decisions (St. Jacques *et al.*, 2008). We used a prospective method employing a photo-paradigm in which participants took photos of many familiar campus locations in a particular order over a period of several hours. On the following day, they were scanned while making temporal-order judgments to pairs of photographs from different locations. We manipulated the extent to which temporal order of auto-biographical events relied on recollection versus familiarity processes by varying the time lag between pairs of photographs. For example, differ-ences in memory strength can be used to temporally parse photographs separated by longer distances (e.g., photo taken in morning vs. after-noon), but contextual information would need to be reconstructed in order to distinguish two photographs with similar memory strength (Friedman, 1993, 2004). Thus, we predicted that familiarity processes would be engaged to discriminate events farther away in time, whereas recollection processes would be required to discriminate events closer in time. Consistent with our hypotheses, parametric fMRI analyses linked shorter time lags to activations in regions previously associated with recollection (left PFC, parahippocampal, precuneus, and visual cortices) and longer time lags with regions previously associated with familiarity (right PFC; see Figure 7.4B). We also observed sub-threshold activity in the hippocampus proper for shorter time lags, consistent with the role of this region in memory in parsing temporal information (Kesner, Gilbert, and Barua, 2002). The current findings suggest that one factor explaining the predominantly left-lateralized recruitment of lateral PFC within AM is the bias toward retrieval tasks that emphasize recollection processes. Future studies of AM retrieval that incorporate retrieval tasks that rely on familiarity, such as recognition memory, may find greater involvement of the right lateral PFC and potentially lead to novel understanding of both recollection and familiarity processes in AM.

Conclusions

The evidence reviewed here suggests that functional neuroimaging studies of AM potentially provide novel insight by contributing to our understanding of the complex retrieval, self-referential, and recollective properties of the personal past. I focused on three critical components of AM retrieval, but this is certainly not an exhaustive list of the potential contributions of functional neuroimaging to our theoretical understand-ing of personal memory. Functional neuroimaging evidence contributes to issues of memory remoteness/consolidation (Moscovitch, this vol-ume), future simulation (D'Argembeau, this volume), child (Bauer, this volume) and life-span development (Fitzgerald and Broadbridge, this volume), and the contribution and interaction among separable systems underlying AM retrieval (Rubin, this volume). Further, although direct empirical studies are currently lacking, one could also foresee future areas where functional neuroimaging studies could provide important insight, such as understanding the retrieval mechanisms of involuntary AM (Berntsen, Hansen, Lee, *et al.*, this volume) or the organizational structure of AM (Brown, this volume). Understanding the neural correlates that orchestrate the recovery and conscious experience of our personal past is critical for a comprehensive theoretical understanding of autobiographical memory.

Acknowledgements

I thank Drs. Roberto Cabeza and David C. Rubin for helpful discussion in the development of my thinking on autobiographical memory, and to Dr. Morris Moscovitch for comments on an earlier draft. This work was supported by a post-doctoral NRSA AG038079 and a L'Oreal USA for Women in Science Fellowship.

References

Andreano, J. M. and Cahill, L. (2009). Sex influences on the neurobiology of learning and memory. *Learning & Memory*, **16**(4), 248–266.

Andrews-Hanna, J. R., Reidler, J. S., Sepulcre, J., Poulin, R., and Buckner, R. L. (2010). Functional-anatomic fractionation of the brain's default network. *Neuron*, **65**(4), 550–562.

Baddeley, A. D. (1992). What is autobiographical memory? In M. A. Conway, D. C. Rubin, H. Spinnler, and W. A. Wagenaar (eds.), *Theoretical perspectives on autobiographical memory* (pp. 13–29). Norwell, MA: Kluwer Academic.

Berntsen, D. (1996). Involuntary autobiographical memories. *Applied Cognitive Psychology*, **10**, 435–454.

   (2007). Involuntary autobiographical memories: speculations, findings and an attempt to integrate them. In J. Mace (ed.), *Involuntary memory* (pp. 20–49). Malden, MA: Blackwell.

Berry, E., Kapur, N., Williams, L., Hodges, S., Watson, P., Smyth, G., *et al.* (2007). The use of a wearable camera, SenseCam, as a pictorial diary to improve autobiographical memory in a patient with limbic encephalitis: a preliminary report. *Neuropsychological Rehabilitation*, **17**, 582–601.

Berryhill, M. E., Phuong, L., Picasso, L., Cabeza, R., and Olson, I. R. (2007). Parietal lobe and episodic memory: bilateral damage causes impaired free recall of autobiographical memory. *Journal of Neuroscience*, **27**(52), 14415–14423.

Botzung, A., Denkova, E., Ciuciu, P., Scheiber, C., and Manning, L. (2008). The neural bases of the constructive nature of autobiographical memories studied with a self-paced fMRI design. *Memory*, **16**(4), 351–363.

Botzung, A., Rubin, D. C., Miles, A., Cabeza, R., and Labar, K. S. (2010). Mental hoop diaries: emotional memories of a college basketball game in rival fans. *Journal of Neuroscience*, **30**(6), 2130–2137.

Brewer, W. F. (1986). What is autobiographical memory? In D. C. Rubin (ed.), *Autobiographical memory* (pp. 25–49). New York: Cambridge University Press.

(1996). What is recollective memory? In D. C. Rubin (ed.), *Remembering our past: studies in autobiographical memory* (pp. 19–66). New York: Cambridge University Press.

Buckner, R. L., Andrews-Hanna, J. R., and Schacter, D. L. (2008). The brain's default network: anatomy, function, and relevance to disease. *Annals of the New York Academy of Sciences*, **1124**, 1–38.

Buckner, R. L. and Carroll, D. C. (2007). Self-projection and the brain. *Trends in Cognitive Sciences*, **11**(2), 49–57.

Cabeza, R. (2008). Role of parietal regions in episodic memory retrieval: the dual attention process hypothesis. *Neuropsychologia*, **46**, 1813–1827. doi: 10.1016/j.neuropsychologia.2008.1003.1019

Cabeza, R., Ciaramelli, E., Olson, I. R., and Moscovitch, M. (2008). The parietal cortex and episodic memory: an attentional account. *Nature Reviews Neuroscience*, **9**(8), 613–625.

Cabeza, R., Prince, S. E., Daselaar, S. M., Greenberg, D. L., Budde, M., Dolcos, F., *et al.* (2004). Brain activity during episodic retrieval of autobiographical and laboratory events: an fMRI study using a novel photo paradigm. *Journal of Cognitive Neurosciences*, **16**(9), 1583–1594.

Cabeza, R. and St. Jacques (2007). Functional neuroimaging of autobiographical memory. *Trends in Cognitive Sciences*, **11**(5), 219–227.

Calhoun, V. D., Adali, T., Pearlson, G. D., and Pekar, J. J. (2001). Spatial and temporal independent component analysis of functional MRI data containing a pair of task-related waveforms. *Human Brain Mapping*, **13**(1), 43–53.

Conway, M. A. (2001). Sensory-perceptual episodic memory and its context: autobiographical memory. *Philosophical Transactions of the Royal Society of London. Series B, Biological Sciences*, **356**(1413), 1375–1384.

(2005). Memory and the self. *Journal of Memory and Language*, **53**, 594–628.

Conway, M. A. and Pleydell-Pearce, C. W. (2000). The construction of autobiographical memories in the self-memory system. *Psychological Review*, **107**(2), 261–288.

Conway, M. A., Pleydell-Pearce, C. W., Whitecross, S. E., and Sharpe, H. (2003). Neurophysiological correlates of memory for experienced and imagined events. *Neuropsychologia*, **41**(3), 334–340.

Conway, M. A., Turk, D. J., Miller, S. L., Logan, J., Nebes, R. D., Meltzer, C. C., *et al.* (1999). A positron emission tomography (PET) study of autobiographical memory retrieval. *Memory*, 7(5–6), 679–702.

Craik, F., Moroz, T., Moscovitch, M., Stuss, D., Winocur, G., Tulving, E., *et al.* (1999). In search of self: a positron emission tomography study. *Psychological Science*, **1**(1), 26–34.

Crovitz, H. F. and Schiffman, S. (1974). Frequency of episodic memories as a function of their age. *Bulletin of the Psychonomic Society*, **4**, 517–551.

D'Argembeau, A., Ruby, P., Collette, F., Degueldre, C., Balteau, E., Luxen, A., *et al.* (2007). Distinct regions of the medial prefrontal cortex are associated with self-referential processing and perspective taking. *Journal of Cognitive Neuroscience*, **19**(6), 935–944.

Daselaar, S. M., Fleck, M. S., Prince, S. E., and Cabeza, R. (2006). The medial temporal lobe distinguishes old from new independently of consciousness. *Journal of Neuroscience*, **26**(21), 5835–5839.

Daselaar, S. M., Rice, H. J., Greenberg, D. L., Cabeza, R., LaBar, K. S., and Rubin, D. C. (2008). The spatiotemporal dynamics of autobiographical memory: neural correlates of recall, emotional intensity, and reliving. *Cerebral Cortex*, **18**(1), 217–229.

Davis, P. J. (1999). Gender differences in autobiographical memory for childhood emotional experiences. *Journal of Personality and Social Psychology*, **76**, 498–510.

Denkova, E., Botzung, A., Scheiber, C., and Manning, L. (2006). Material-independent cerebral network of re-experiencing personal events: evidence from two parallel fMRI experiments. *Neuroscience Letters*, **407**(1), 32–36.

Diana, R. A., Yonelinas, A. P., and Ranganath, C. (2007). Imaging recollection and familiarity in the medial temporal lobe: a three-component model. *Trends in Cognitive Sciences*, **11**(9), 379–386.

Dosenbach, N. U., Fair, D. A., Miezin, F. M., Cohen, A. L., Wenger, K. K., Dosenbach, R. A., *et al.* (2007). Distinct brain networks for adaptive and stable task control in humans. *Proceedings of the National Academy of Sciences of the United States of America*, **104**(26), 11073–11078.

Etkin, A. and Wager, T. D. (2007). Functional neuroimaging of anxiety: a meta-analysis of emotional processing in PTSD, social anxiety disorder, and specific phobia. *American Journal of Psychiatry*, **164**(10), 1476–1488.

Friedman, A. and Pines, A. (1991). Sex differences in gender-related childhood memories. *Sex Roles*, **25**, 25–32.

Friedman, W. J. (1993). Memory for the time of past events. *Psychological Bulletin*, **113**(1), 44–66.

(2004). Time in autobiographical memory. *Social Cognition*, **22**(5), 591–605.

Friston, K. J., Harrison, L., and Penny, W. (2003). Dynamic causal modelling. *NeuroImage*, **19**(4), 1273–1302.

Gilboa, A. (2004). Autobiographical and episodic memory – one and the same? Evidence from prefrontal activation in neuroimaging studies. *Neuropsychologia*, **42**(10), 1336–1349.

Greenberg, D. L., Rice, H. J., Cooper, J. J., Cabeza, R., Rubin, D. C., and LaBar, K. S. (2005). Co-activation of the amygdala, hippocampus and inferior frontal gyrus during autobiographical memory retrieval. *Neuropsychologia*, **43**(5), 659–674.

Greenberg, D. L. and Rubin, D. C. (2003). The neuropsychology of autobiographical memory. *Cortex*, **39**(4–5), 687–728.

Gusnard, D. A. and Raichle, M. E. (2001). Searching for a baseline: functional imaging and the resting human brain. *Nature Reviews Neuroscience*, **2**(10), 685–694.

Hassabis, D. and Maguire, E. A. (2007). Deconstructing episodic memory with construction. *Trends in Cognitive Sciences*, **11**(7), 299–306.

Kahn, I., Andrews-Hanna, J. R., Vincent, J. L., Snyder, A. Z., and Buckner, R. L. (2008). Distinct cortical anatomy linked to subregions of the medial temporal lobe revealed by intrinsic functional connectivity. *Journal of Neurophysiology*, **100**(1), 129–139.

Kelley, W. M., Macrae, C. N., Wyland, C. L., Caglar, S., Inati, S., and Heatherton, T. F. (2002). Finding the self? An event-related fMRI study. *Journal of Cognitive Neuroscience*, **14**(5), 785–794.

Kesner, R. P., Gilbert, P. E., and Barua, L. A. (2002). The role of the hippocampus in memory for the temporal order of a sequence of odors. *Behavioral Neuroscience*, **116**(2), 286–290.

Klinger, E. and Cox, W. M. (1987). Dimensions of thought flow in everyday life. *Imagination, Cognition and Personality*, 7, 105–128.

Krueger, F., Barbey, A. K., and Grafman, J. (2009). The medial prefrontal cortex mediates social event knowledge. *Trends in Cognitive Sciences*, **13**(3), 103–109.

LaBar, K. S. and Cabeza, R. (2006). Cognitive neuroscience of emotional memory. *Nature Reviews Neuroscience*, **7**(1), 54–64.

Levine, B., Svoboda, E., Hay, J. F., Winocur, G., and Moscovitch, M. (2002). Aging and autobiographical memory: dissociating episodic from semantic retrieval. *Psychology and Aging*, **17**(4), 677–689.

Levine, B., Turner, G. R., Tisserand, D., Hevenor, S. J., Graham, S. J., and McIntosh, A. R. (2004). The functional neuroanatomy of episodic and semantic autobiographical remembering: a prospective functional MRI study. *Journal of Cognitive Neuroscience*, **16**(9), 1633–1646.

Macrae, C. N., Moran, J. M., Heatherton, T. F., Banfield, J. F., and Kelley, W. M. (2004). Medial prefrontal activity predicts memory for self. *Cerebral Cortex*, **14**(6), 647–654.

Maguire, E. A. (2001). Neuroimaging studies of autobiographical event memory. *Philosophical Transactions of the Royal Society of London. Series B, Biological Sciences*, **356**(1413), 1441–1451.

Maguire, E. A., Henson, R. N., Mummery, C. J., and Frith, C. D. (2001). Activity in prefrontal cortex, not hippocampus, varies parametrically with the increasing remoteness of memories. *Neuroreport*, **12**(3), 441–444.

McDermott, K. B., Szpunar, K. K., and Christ, S. E. (2009). Laboratory-based and autobiographical retrieval tasks differ substantially in their neural substrates. *Neuropsychologia*, **47**(11), 2290–2298.

Miller, E. K. and Cohen, J. D. (2001). An integrative theory of prefrontal cortex function. *Annual Review of Neuroscience*, **24**, 167–202.

Mitchell, J. P. (2009). Inferences about mental states. *Philosophical Transactions of the Royal Society of London. Series B, Biological Sciences*, **364**(1521), 1309–1316.

Mitchell, K. J. and Johnson, M. K. (2009). Source monitoring 15 years later: what have we learned from fMRI about the neural mechanisms of source memory? *Psychological Bulletin*, **135**(4), 638–677.

Moscovitch, M. (1992). Memory and working-with-memory. *Journal of Cognitive Neuroscience*, **4**(3), 257–267.

Muscatell, K. A., Addis, D. R., and Kensinger, E. A. (2010). Self-involvement modulates the effective connectivity of the autobiographical memory network. *Social, Cognitive, & Affective Neuroscience*, **5**(1), 68–76.

Norman, D. A. and Bobrow, D. G. (1976). On the role of active memory processes in perception and cognition. In C. N. Cofer (ed.), *The structure of human memory*. San Francisco, CA: Freeman.

Parks, C. M. and Yonelinas, A. P. (2007). Moving beyond pure signal-detection models: comment on Wixted (2007). *Psychological Review*, **114**(1), 188–202; discussion 203–189.

Pauly-Takacs, K., Moulin, C. J. A., and Estlin, E. J. (2010). SenseCam as a rehabilitation tool in a child with anterograde amnesia. *Memory*, **29**, 705–712. doi: 10.1080/09658211.09652010.09494046

Petrides, M. (2005). Lateral prefrontal cortex: architectonic and functional organization. *Philosophical Transactions of the Royal Society of London. Series B, Biological Sciences*, **360**(1456), 781–795.

Piefke, M., Weiss, P. H., Markowitsch, H. J., and Fink, G. R. (2005). Gender differences in the functional neuroanatomy of emotional episodic autobiographical memory. *Human Brain Mapping*, **24**(4), 313–324.

Pillemer, D. B., Wink, P., DiDonato, T. E., and Sanborn, R. L. (2003). Gender differences in autobiographical memory styles of older adults. *Memory*, **11**(6), 525–532.

Piolino, P., Desgranges, B., Benali, K., and Eustache, F. (2002). Episodic and semantic remote autobiographical memory in ageing. *Memory*, **10**(4), 239–257.

Pohl, R. F., Bender, M., and Lachmann, G. (2005). Autobiographical memory and social skills of men and women. *Applied Cognitive Psychology*, **19**, 745–759.

Rabin, J. S., Gilboa, A., Stuss, D. T., Mar, R. A., and Rosenbaum, R. S. (2010). Common and unique neural correlates of autobiographical memory and theory of mind. *Journal of Cognitive Neuroscience*, **22**, 1095–1111.

Raichle, M. E., MacLeod, A. M., Snyder, A. Z., Powers, W. J., Gusnard, D. A., and Shulman, G. L. (2001). A default mode of brain function. *Proceedings of the National Academy of Sciences of the United States of America*, **98**(2), 676–682.

Reisberg, D., Heuer, F., McLean, J., and O'Shaugnessy, M. (1988). The quantity, not the quality, of affect predicts memory vividness. *Bulletin of the Psychonomic Society*, **26**(2), 100–103.

Rosenbaum, R. S., Stuss, D. T., Levine, B., and Tulving, E. (2007). Theory of mind is independent of episodic memory. *Science*, **318**(5854), 1257.

Ross, M. and Holmberg, D. (1992). Are wives' memories for events in relationships more vivid than their husbands' memories? *Journal of Social and Personal Relationships*, **9**, 585–604.

Rubin, D. C. (2005). A basic-systems approach to autobiographical memory. *Current Directions in Psychological Science*, **14**(2), 79–83.

    (2006). The basic-systems model of episodic memory. *Perspectives in Psychological Science*, **1**(1), 277–311.

Rubin, D. C., Boals, A., and Berntsen, D. (2008). Memory in posttraumatic stress disorder: properties of voluntary and involuntary, traumatic and nontraumatic autobiographical memories in people with and without posttraumatic stress disorder symptoms. *Journal of Experimental Psychology: General*, **137**(4), 591–614.

Rubin, D. C., Burt, C. D., and Fifield, S. J. (2003). Experimental manipulations of the phenomenology of memory. *Memory & Cognition*, **31**(6), 877–886.

Rubin, D. C. and Greenberg, D. L. (1998). Visual memory-deficit amnesia: a distinct amnesic presentation and etiology. *Proceedings of the National Academy of Sciences of the United States of America*, **95**(9), 5413–5416.

Rubin, D. C., Schrauf, R. W., and Greenberg, D. L. (2003). Belief and recollection of autobiographical memories. *Memory & Cognition*, 31(6), 887–901.

Schacter, D. L., Addis, D. R., and Buckner, R. L. (2007). Remembering the past to imagine the future: the prospective brain. *Nature Reviews Neuroscience*, 8 (9), 657–661.

Seeley, W. W., Menon, V., Schatzberg, A. F., Keller, J., Glover, G. H., Kenna, H., *et al.* (2007). Dissociable intrinsic connectivity networks for salience processing and executive control. *Journal of Neuroscience*, 27(9), 2349–2356.

Seidlitz, L. and Diener, E. (1998). Sex differences in the recall of affective experiences. *Journal of Personality and Social Psychology*, 74(1), 262–271.

Shin, L. M., Rauch, S. L., and Pitman, R. K. (2006). Amygdala, medial prefrontal cortex, and hippocampal function in PTSD. *Annals of the New York Academy of Sciences*, 1071, 67–79.

Skowronski, J. J. and Thompson, C. P. (1990). Reconstructing the dates of events: gender differences in accuracy. *Applied Cognitive Psychology*, 4, 371–381.

Spreng, R. N. and Grady, C. L. (2010). Patterns of brain activity supporting autobiographical memory, Prospection, and theory-of-mind and their relationship to the default mode network. *Journal of Cognitive Neuroscience*, 22(6), 1112–1123.

Spreng, R. N., Mar, R. A., and Kim, A. S. (2009). The common neural basis of autobiographical memory, prospection, navigation, theory of mind, and the default mode: a quantitative meta-analysis. *Journal of Cognitive Neuroscience*, 21(3), 489–510.

St. Jacques, P. L., Botzung, A., Miles, A., and Rubin, D. C. (2011). Functional neuroimaging of emotionally intense autobiographical memories in post-traumatic stress disorder. *Journal of Psychiatric Research*, 45(630–637). doi:10.10 16/j.jpsychires.2010.1010.1011

St. Jacques, P. L. and Cabeza, R. (2012). Neural basis of autobiographical memory. In S. Ghetti and P. J. Bauer (eds.), *Origins and development of recollection: perspectives from psychology and neuroscience* (pp. 188–218). New York: Oxford University Press.

St. Jacques, P. L., Conway, M. A., and Cabeza, R. (2010). Gender differences in autobiographical memory for everyday events: retrieval elicited by SenseCam Images vs. verbal cues. *Memory*, 19(7), 723–732. doi: 10.1080/ 09658211.09652010.09516266

St. Jacques, P. L., Conway, M. A., Lowder, M. W., and Cabeza, R. (2011a). Watching my mind unfold versus yours: an fMRI study using a novel camera technology to examine neural differences in self-projection of self versus other perspectives. *Journal of Cognitive Neuroscience*, 23(6), 1275–1284.

(2011b). Two ways of accessing the personal past: an fMRI study examining the functional connectivity of the hippocampus during autobiographical memory retrieval. Under review.

St. Jacques, P. L., Kragel, P. A., and Rubin, D. C. (2011). Dynamic neural networks supporting memory retrieval. *NeuroImage*, 57(2), 608–616.

St. Jacques, P. L. and Levine, B. (2007). Ageing and autobiographical memory for emotional and neutral events. *Memory*, 15(2), 129–144.

St. Jacques, P. L., Rubin, D. C., and Cabeza, R. (2010). Age-related effects on the neural correlates of autobiographical memory retrieval. *Neurobiology of Aging.* doi: 10.1016/j.neurobiolaging.2010.1011.1007

St. Jacques, P. L., Rubin, D. C., Labar, K. S., and Cabeza, R. (2008). The short and long of it: neural correlates of temporal-order memory for autobiographical events. *Journal of Cognitive Neuroscience,* 20(7), 1327–1341.

St. Jacques, P. L., Rubin, D. C., Lowder, M. W., and Cabeza, R. (2009). Temporal vs. spatial source memory for autobiographical events: an fMRI study using a novel photo paradigm. Paper presented at the Society for Neuroscience, Chicago, October.

Steinvorth, S., Corkin, S., and Halgren, E. (2006). Ecphory of autobiographical memories: an fMRI study of recent and remote memory retrieval. *NeuroImage,* 30, 285–298.

Stevens, M. C., Kiehl, K. A., Pearlson, G. D., and Calhoun, V. D. (2007). Functional neural networks underlying response inhibition in adolescents and adults. *Behavioural Brain Research,* 181(1), 12–22.

Suddendorf, T. and Corballis, M. C. (2007). The evolution of foresight: what is mental time travel, and is it unique to humans? *Behavioral and Brain Sciences,* 30(3), 299–313; discussion 313–251.

Svoboda, E., McKinnon, M. C., and Levine, B. (2006). The functional neuro-anatomy of autobiographical memory: a meta-analysis. *Neuropsychologia,* 44(12), 2189–2208.

Talarico, J. M., LaBar, K. S., and Rubin, D. C. (2004). Emotional intensity predicts autobiographical memory experience. *Memory & Cognition,* 32(7), 1118–1132.

Tulving, E. (1983). *Elements of memory.* Oxford: Clarendon Press.

Uzer, T., Lee, P. J., and Brown, N. R. (in press). On the prevalence of directly retrieved autobiographical memories. *Journal of Experimental Psychology: Learning, Memory, and Cognition.*

Valenstein, E., Bowers, D., Verfaellie, M., Heilman, K. M., Day, A., and Watson, R. T. (1987). Retrosplenial amnesia. *Brain,* 110(Pt 6), 1631–1646.

Van Overwalle, F. (2009). Social cognition and the brain: a meta-analysis. *Human Brain Mapping,* 30(3), 829–858.

Vincent, J. L., Kahn, I., Snyder, A. Z., Raichle, M. E., and Buckner, R. L. (2008). Evidence for a frontoparietal control system revealed by intrinsic functional connectivity. *Journal of Neurophysiology,* 100(6), 3328–3342.

Vincent, J. L., Snyder, A. Z., Fox, M. D., Shannon, B. J., Andrews, J. R., Raichle, M. E., et al. (2006). Coherent spontaneous activity identifies a hippocampal-parietal memory network. *Journal of Neurophysiology,* 96(6), 3517–3531.

Wheeler, M. A., Stuss, D. T., and Tulving, E. (1997). Toward a theory of episodic memory: the frontal lobes and autonoetic consciousness. *Psychological Bulletin,* 121(3), 331–354.

Part III

Social and cultural aspects of autobiographical memory

The three chapters in this part all consider how each individual's memory is embedded in a larger social, cultural, and historical context, and how this affects the organization and content of autobiographical memories as well their retrieval and forgetting. Hirst and colleagues discuss the notion of collective remembering and reviews studies showing how the social context affects retrieval and forgetting of autobiographical memories. Their chapter describes the relevance of the experimental paradigm of retrieval-induced forgetting for our understanding of autobiographical remembering within a social context. The chapter by Brown and colleagues examines the effects of transitons on the organization of autobiographical memories. They argue that events that "change the fabric of everyday life" will have lasting effects on memory organization by defining new time periods in the individual life course. Such transitions can be both historical events affecting an entire community (e.g., end of World War II) and more private events (e.g., getting married), which may be culturally normative. Pillemer and Kuwabara discuss the directive functions of autobiographical remembering – that is, how autobiographical memories may help us to arrive at a better understanding of a given problem and also how our memories help to set the course for our behavior and goals in complex social situations. By discussing such functional aspects of remembering, Pillemer and Kuwabara address how autobiographical memories become adaptive in a larger social and cultural context.

8   Of sins and virtues: memory and collective identity

William Hirst, Alexandru Cuc, and Dana Wohl

Human memory seems ill equipped to handle the multitude of demands placed on it. Schacter (1999) has treated the widely recognized weaknesses of memory as sins, raising an ideal of a "perfect memory." For him, memory sins against people, and we assume that he would opine that people must simply learn to live with its corruption. They must accept that their memories are transient and perhaps undesirably persistent, and they must realize that memory is vulnerable to absent-mindedness, biases, source-monitoring errors, and the implantation of misinformation. These weaknesses are not what people might want out of their memory, but they are what evolution has provided.

In this volume on autobiographical memory, one might follow Schacter's lead and ask what the cost of these faulty memories is for identity formation. As Christopher Nolan's film *Memento* dramatically illustrates, the cost is no doubt severe. The central character in *Memento*, Leonard Shelby, struggles with a profound amnesia. This memory failure creates a tentative hold on the past that, as the movie progresses, leads to a slow disintegration of Lenny's identity. As his nemesis Teddy says: "You don't . . . know who you are, Lenny." And indeed, the audience watches as Lenny slips in and out of a slowly emerging realization that he might be a murderer. Although *Memento* captures the relation between autobiographical memory and identity *in extremis*, it underscores how the fallibility of memories might make the hold people have on their identity ever so tentative. From this perspective, the flaws of memory might be viewed as cardinal sins.

We want to explore here the possibility that the unreliability and malleability of memory might, in some contexts, be viewed as virtues rather than sins – and that when one steps back and views the many functions memory can serve, there are benefits, as well as costs, in memory's fallibility. The key to unlocking this claim is the realization that social

The support of National Science Foundation grant no. BCS-0819067 is gratefully acknowledged.

interactions around the past, and, in particular, the conversations about the past that flood everyday life, have the potential to shape and reshape memories, not because memory is reliable and nonmalleable, but because it is just the opposite – that it is unreliable and malleable. The claim is that as psychological mechanisms guide mnemonic reshaping, socially connected individuals will begin to converge on shared representations of the past. Couples will have in common an agreed upon rendering of their first meeting, and Americans, as a group, will possess similar recollections of Washington's destruction of a cherry tree. These shared memories are critically important for people because they can serve as *collective memories* – that is, shared memories that bear on collective identity.

We treat the formation of a collective memory as a virtue, not because their collective nature makes them more reliable than individual memories – it does not – but because of their relevance to collective identity. Just as autobiographical memories bear on individual identity, so do collective memories bear on collective identity. That a couple's first meeting was love at first sight has a bearing on how the couple view themselves as a unit. And that Americans remember that Washington cannot tell a lie about his destruction of a cherry tree underscores the moral high ground that Americans, as a collective, often feel they have as they act in the world. In promoting the formation of collective memory and, through that, collective identity, the unreliability and malleability of memory can be said to facilitate group cohesiveness and guide collective action as well. Moreover, the formation of a collective memory can serve as a means of grounding one of the most enduring characteristics of humans, their sociality. Indeed, sociality, in the sense used here, can be grounded in a community's collective identity, collective action, or more generally, the community member's shared reality (Festinger, 1950; Hardin and Higgins, 1996). Evolution may have supplied humans with a less-than-computer-perfect memory because the flaws it possesses promote the formation of collective memories, shape collective identity, guide collective actions, and ground human sociability. Each alone is worth striving for; together they present a compelling argument for maintaining a "defective" memory.

In what follows, we will articulate how many of the so-called sins of memory can promote the formation of collective memories. The memories we will be discussing here can be either episodic or semantic (Hirst and Manier, 2002; Manier and Hirst, 2008). A couple may share a memory of an event that they both directly experienced (their wedding); that only one directly experienced, but the other felt they lived through (the troubles one of them had at work); or that is relevant to both of them, but occurred before they met each other (that their grandmothers had known each other). The first may be thought of as a *shared episodic memory*; the second, a *shared lived-through memory*, which is, episodic for one, semantic for the other; the third, a *shared historical (semantic) memory*.

In exploring collective memories, many researchers focus on the actions of society in shaping collective memories (see Hirst and Manier, 2008, for a discussion of this point). Government authorities determine the content of textbooks; instigate, plan, and construct monuments and memorials; and devise commemorative celebrations, rituals, and more generally mnemonic practices – all with the intent to shape collective memory (Olick, 2002; Olick, Vinitzky-Seroussi, and Levy, 2010; Wertsch, 2002). By critiquing these actions, scholars hope to reveal the way the past is open to manipulation and underscore how something as fundamental to members of a community as their collective identity is a product of societal efforts, often those devised and executed by the powerful and the elite (e.g., Bodnar, 1993; but see Schwartz, 2000).

The present effort differs from this society-centered approach in two ways. First, rather than investigate mnemonic practices that can be traced to the efforts of a government or some other authority, such as the practice of building memorials and commemorations, we examine a more ephemeral practice, the conversations people frequently have with each other about the past (see also Fivush's chapter in this volume). Conversations appear particularly important in promoting the formation of vernacular or informal collective memories (Bodnar, 1993). For instance, Lithuanians of Lithuanian descent construct their collective memory around national historical events rather than events featured in the Russian textbooks they studied in school (Schuman, Rieger, and Gaidys, 1994). How did they learn about these events? Presumably through conversations with friends, relatives, and even acquaintances.

Second, and critically, with our focus on conversations, we explore not the social influences that shape what people remember conversationally, but the consequences of the conversation on subsequent memory. To a large extent, our concern about consequences raises psychological questions. What psychological mechanisms of memory would account for why some conversations, and not others, may be effective in altering group members' memory so that the group convergences onto a shared representation of the past? What would be the nature of this alteration and the content of the final emergent memory? We answer these questions mainly by considering cognitive aspects underlying memory performance. Motives could also play a role (see Echterhoff, Higgins, and Levine, 2008; see also the chapter by Habermas in this volume). Moreover, remembering and forgetting may be driven by normative considerations; for instance, people may forget a past event because they want to be a respected part of society. To remember it and speak about it to others could be considered offensive by many. Motivation and normative factors are worth considering, of course, but they are outside the scope of the present chapter.

The machinery of memory

What then are the psychological properties of memory that might lead to the formation of collective memories through conversational interaction? What machinery transforms individually held memories into shared memories? Surprisingly, these questions have not been addressed until recently. The "father" of collective memory research, Maurice Halbwachs (1925/1992), was skeptical about the role individual psychological mechanisms might play in investigating the topic. Although Halbwachs appears to accept that all remembering is in the final analysis individual, he found individual memory onion-like, in the sense that there is nothing left of it after peeling away one layer of social influence after another. Inasmuch as memory is social all the way down, he saw little recourse but to focus one's efforts, not on the psychology of individual memory, but on the social influences that shape collective memory. Most work on collective memory follows his lead.

As for psychologists interested in memory, they have generally ignored the topic. They do so in part because their agenda, until recently, was confined to uncovering universal mechanisms. The "father" of the experimental study of memory, Hermann Ebbinghaus, was perhaps the first to articulate this agenda as it applies to the study of memory (Ebbinghaus, 1913/1964). He recognized that social factors influence memory performance, but sought to minimize these influences through controlled experimentation. If social influences could be entirely eliminated, then the "raw material of memory" could be revealed. Something as socially determined as a collective memory could not be studied within this framework.

Another foundational figure in the study of memory, Frederic Bartlett, rejected both these approaches (Bartlett, 1932). He sought to understand what might be viewed as the interaction between universal psychological mechanisms and social factors. He disagreed adamantly with Halbwachs's (1925/1992) characterization of memory, in that, for him, there were universal psychological mechanisms. Moreover, he embraced rather than avoided studying social factors. If social factors shape memory, as even Ebbinghaus (1913/1964) conceded, then psychologists should study the underlying mechanisms. Bartlett's approach supplies the theoretical underpinnings for developing a psychology of collective memory.

Around the same time, Vygotsky (1978) argued that memory must be viewed from a socio-historical perspective. Of particular interest here is the role scaffolding plays in shaping acts of memorizing and remembering (see Fivush, this volume; and Bauer, this volume, for further exposition of this point). Conversations are, of course, one such scaffold. Bartlett and Vygotsky, and their many disciples, could be viewed as promoting a social constructionist view of memory. Whereas this perspective might be considered as contrary to the individualistic perspective of many cognitive approaches, there is no reason not to assume a role for the individual in such an approach (e.g., Sutton, Harris, Keil, *et al.*, 2010).

In what follows, we articulate several ways the cognitive machinery of memory may promote the formation of collective memories through conversational interaction.

The contribution of schema

According to Bartlett (1932), remembering is reconstructive. Rather than being stored away and later retrieved when needed, memories are built "on the run" out of the schemata people have formed through past experience, as well as their current attitudes and situations. Schemata are not simple traces of the past. Rather they are organized representations of the past into which new experiences are assimilated. Consequently, individual experiences are not necessarily represented in schemata, though what is represented is often sufficient to serve as a basis for reconstructing a memory. Just as each tennis stroke executed during a match is *not* stored away waiting to be retrieved, but constructed on the run out of past experience, present attitude, and present situation, so also are episodic and semantic memories similarly constructed out of schemata, attitude, and situation.

This notion of remembering not only underscores its unreliability, but also serves as a means of understanding how people in the same community come to remember similar things. As Bartlett (1932) noted,

Social organisation gives a persistent framework into which all detailed recall must fit, and it very powerfully influences both the manner and the matter of recall. Moreover, this persistent framework helps to provide those "schemata" which are the basis for the imaginative reconstruction called memory. (p. 296)

Recently, Wertsch (2008) has built on this observation in his work on *schematic narrative templates*. In contrast to specific narratives, these are "generalized structures used to generate multiple specific narratives with the same basic plots." According to Wertsch, members of a community tell their history through the lens of a schematic narrative template associated with that community. For instance, Wertsch suggested that a Russian schematic narrative template might contain the following elements:

(1) An initial situation in which Russia is peaceful and not interfering with others.
(2) The initiation of trouble in which a foreign enemy treacherously and viciously attacks Russia without provocation.
(3) Russia almost loses everything in total defeat as it suffers from the enemy's attempts to destroy it as a civilization.
(4) Through heroism, and against all odds, Russia and its people triumph and succeed in expelling the foreign enemy, thus justifying its claims of exceptionalism and its status as a great nation.

This template can be observed in the following description of World War II, offered by a Russian woman.

In 1939, Germany attacked Poland. In June of 1941, German forces, treacherously and without declaring war, invaded the territory of the USSR. The Great Patriotic War began. The Germans advanced almost all the way to Moscow, seizing a great deal of our country's territory: The turning point in the war was the Battle of Stalingrad. There the Germans received a well-deserved rebuff. After that, Soviet forces attacked and gradually drove the German forces from our territory. Then began the liberation of other countries: Czechoslovakia, Poland, Bulgaria, Hungary, Yugoslavia. The Soviet forces reached Berlin and routed Fascist Germany, bringing fascism in Europe to a halt. The allies of the USSR were England and the USA. They opened a second front. The main role in the victory over Fascist Germany was shouldered by the simple Soviet people, the simple Russian soldier. For the Russian people, the Great Patriotic War was emancipatory. (Wertsch, 2002, p. 154)

Any Russian can probably supply a number of historical examples that fit this template beyond this rendering of World War II, such as the Napoleonic invasion and defeat. As Wertsch (2002) cautioned, it is not that other nations cannot tell similar stories about historical events; it is just that, for Russians, this template is all pervasive, whereas for other nations, other schematic narrative templates prevail. The USA, for instance, has several templates, including the "reluctant hegemon" that seeks to better the world (Kagan, 1998). A schematic narrative template for Jews is often built around their victimhood, while the schematic narrative template for Israel is best captured by the image of the defiant *sabra* (Zerubavel, 1995).

What needs emphasizing here is that, whereas the schematic nature of remembering often leads to errors of omission and commission, the presence of socially shared schemata, such as schematic narrative templates, can also promote the formation of collective memory. As shared schema, they influence not just individuals but individuals within a group. (For a discussion of a concept related to the one Wertsch (2002) describes, but for autobiographical memories instead of collective memories, see the chapter by Berntsen and Rubin for reflections on cultural life scripts and their role for autobiographical memory.)

The contribution of social contagion

As Schacter (1999) pointed out, memory is open to suggestion. In a conversation, speakers will often intentionally or unintentionally introduce information their listeners are not privy to. Listeners will, in turn, often adopt this information as their own and come to remember it. In some instances, the information might be valid, thereby only enriching the listener's memory, but in other instances the introduced information may be new or misleading. The speaker's memory may be in error, or, alternatively, speakers may, perhaps with malice, introduce information they know to be wrong. This misleading information could serve as an alternative to the original memory of the listener. Whatever its origin, listeners can adopt the new or misleading information as their own. As a result, a memory that listeners previously did not share with the speaker is now shared, and the memories of speakers and listeners begin to converge. This spread of a memory is often referred to as *social contagion*.

The original work on the post-event misinformation effect viewed the malleability of memory as a deficiency. When Loftus first studied it, she couched the results in terms of the fallibility of eyewitness testimony (see Loftus, 2005, for a review). The introduction of misleading information during an interrogation of a witness, for instance, could create false memories. When these false recollections are of probative value – for example, a false memory of childhood sexual abuse – the malleability of memory clearly becomes problematic.

Yet, in addition to the obvious cost associated with memory's malleability, there are virtues as well, particularly the role social contagion may play in promoting the formation of collective memories. Information can spread quickly through a social network. It does not require broadcasting the information through a centralized media. As a result, a sequence of conversations can lead quickly to a shared memory. Harber and Cohen (2005), for instance, took their psychology class to see an autopsy and then tracked how news of the class outing spread. After three exchanges, 881 knew of the event, from the original class membership of 33, a multiplier of 26.7. Moreover, relatively short paths can be found between two members of even an extremely large network, creating what researchers often refer to as *small worlds* (Watts, 2004). Not only do people transmit information, but they can often find rather straightforward ways to get it transmitted from one person in the network to almost everyone else in the network. This was amply illustrated in the recent Egyptian revolution. Even with the shut-down of the internet, people learned about planned demonstrations in Tahrir Square and showed up in large numbers.

The point we want to emphasize here is that, in addition to circulating accurate information, each exchange in the transmission provides a means of both introducing and spreading misinformation. Presumably, as the spread of information circles repeatedly back to the original source and recycles through the group once again, the misinformation implanted by one person comes to be shared by the group as a whole. In other words, a collective memory could become formed around misinformation. This convergence might be viewed as a less-than-desirable outcome if the aim is accuracy. It seems much more reasonable if the aim is to create a shared representation of the past, regardless of its accuracy. The collective, albeit inaccurate, rendering could be a better vehicle for increasing group cohesion than an accurate one, as the existence of various national myths suggests (Hobsbawm and Ranger, 1983).

The contribution of retrieval effects

Retrieval effects are another mechanism by which memories can spread and converge onto a collective representation of the past. These can be broken down into two classes: those that reinforce existing memories and those that lead to induced forgetting.

Reinforcing existing memories   The ability of repetition to improve subsequent recollection can hardly be viewed as a weakness of memory (Karpicke and Roediger, 2008). Its usefulness can be easily appreciated in reinforcing both existing individual and collective memories. Consider a variation of Bartlett's (1932) serial reproduction task in which the last person in the chain then speaks to the first person. In this way, the chain of exchanges recycles through itself repeatedly. Although Bartlett emphasized how the memory changes as it is passed from one person to another, the repetition of a memory through the cycle should increase the likelihood that a particular memory will be recollected, not by one person, but by all individuals in the chain. One might imagine that, with repeated cycling, the memory would converge upon the repeated items. Blumen and Rajaram (2008) have shown the power of re-exposure in the context of a single conversational exchange on subsequent memory. Kashima (2008) has argued that, inasmuch as people are inclined to recollect stereotypic information, stereotypes can be formed and reinforced through the repetition of such information cascading through a chain of serial reproduction. Stereotypes can be viewed as a type of collective memory, albeit not necessarily a positive one.

Induced forgetting Conversational remembering is selective (Hirst and Echterhoff, 2012; Marsh, 2007; Pashupathi, 2001; Weldon, 2001). In conversations, people remember more than they might if remembering alone (*collaborative facilitation*), but they also remember less than the sum of each participant's capacity to remember (*collaborative inhibition*). This selective remembering will not only reinforce what is recollected but also induce forgetting for what goes unmentioned (Anderson and Levy, 2007; Hirst and Brown, 2011). Stone, Coman, Brown, *et al.* (2012) have argued that this unmentioned material can often be viewed as silences – that is, memories that participants in the conversation either fail or refuse to remember. They are instances in which the conversational participants fail to give voice to aspects of the past that in other circumstances they might be capable of articulating. There is a large literature concerned with such mnemonic silences (e.g., Ben-Ze'ev, Ginio, and Winter, 2010; Zerubavel, 2005). The following are two possible roots of mnemonic silence: in conversation, speakers can be silent because they might not want to talk about something that causes themselves or their audience stress; in national discourse, communities might be silent because they wish to avoid discussing troubling past actions that might even be viewed as criminal from the current vantage point. Whatever its cause, silence has consequences. Whereas mentioning something in a conversation may reinforce the recollected memories, failing to mention it can foster forgetting (Anderson and Levy, 2007). When these silences occur in a social setting, they can promote collective forgetting. Collective forgetting is as important to the study of collective memory as collective remembering inasmuch as a collective memory consists of not just what is remembered but also what is forgotten (Schudson, 1995).

Many scholars exploring the effect of silence on collective memory emphasize the role of decay or repression, but an important mechanism that receives less attention is *retrieval-induced forgetting* (RIF) (Hirst and Echterhoff, 2012). RIF refers to instances in which the act of retrieving will induce forgetting of related yet unretrieved memories. The phenomenon has mainly been studied outside the context of autobiographical memory (but see Barnier, Hung, and Conway, 2004, for an application to autobiographical memory). Indeed, many studies employ something as ecological invalid as word pairs. In such experiments (e.g., Anderson, Bjork, and Bjork, 1994), participants study and learn category-exemplar

Table 8.1. *Design of retrieval-induced forgetting (RIF) experiments*

Study phase	Practice phase	Testing phase	Condition
Fruit – apple	Fruit – ap____	List words paired with fruit	Practiced
Fruit – orange			Unpracticed, related
Vegetable – broccoli		List words paired with vegetable	Not practiced, unrelated
Vegetable – pea			Not practiced, unrelated

pairs and then receive selective practice. A final recall test on all the studied items then follows. As Table 8.1 indicates, this design creates three conditions: (1) a word pair is practiced, (2) a word pair is not practiced and is related to a practiced item, and (3) a word pair is not practiced and is unrelated to the practiced item. Obviously, the practiced items should be remembered better in the final recall test than the two types of unpracticed items. But is the rate at which the two unpracticed items are forgotten the same? Or are unpracticed, related items forgotten more rapidly than unpracticed, unrelated items? The unpracticed items might be viewed as analogs to mnemonic silences in a conversation. Do all mnemonic silences have the same impact on memory? Or do some induce forgetting more than others?

The RIF experiments repeatedly show that the relation between what is practiced and what goes unpracticed matters. Specifically, participants in the experiments fail to remember the unpracticed material more often in the final recall test if it is related to the practiced material than if it is unrelated (see Anderson and Levy, 2007, for a review). This difference is the telltale sign of RIF. It cannot be attributed to the decay that might occur to a memory if the memory is not practiced, in that a decay model would predict uniform forgetting. The most widely accepted account of RIF involves inhibition (Anderson and Levy, 2007; but see Dodd, Castel, and Roberts, 2006, for alternative accounts). The presentation of a retrieval cue activates related responses. Consequently, the rememberer must isolate the desired target from the array of activated responses and does so by inhibiting the non-target-activated material. This inhibition lingers, making it harder to remember in the final recall test the unpracticed related item than the unpracticed, unrelated responses, which were not among the activated responses. In some cases, the retrieval cue might actually facilitate remembering, but in many conditions, RIF strongly emerges in the final recall (Chan, McDermott, and Roediger, 2006).

The phenomenon of RIF is of interest to students of collective memory because RIF occurs not only when an individual overtly but selectively remembers the past but also when people listen to others overtly and selectively remember (*socially shared retrieval-induced forgetting* [SS-RIF]). Cuc, Koppel, and Hirst (2007) first demonstrated RIF in listeners by repeating the standard RIF experiment (using word pairs), but now introducing a second participant. Both participants studied the word pairs individually. In the practice phase, one of them recalled the selected material (hereafter referred to as the *speaker*), while the other monitored this recall (hereafter, the *listener*). The listener was asked to judge either the accuracy or the fluidity of the speaker's response. A final individual recall test followed.

Cuc *et al.* (2007) argued that listeners may concurrently, albeit covertly, retrieve along with the speaker in some circumstances. When this concurrent retrieval occurs, they will be in a state similar to that of the speaker and should, as a result, demonstrate RIF in a manner similar to that observed in the speaker. Cuc *et al.* examined this conjecture by contrasting two monitoring instructions. In the accuracy-monitoring condition, the listener was asked to specify on a 1–5 scale how accurate the speaker was as she recalled the studied material. For the fluidity-monitoring condition, the listener had to rate how fluidly the speaker recalled the material. RIF should be, and was, observed for both speaker and listener in the condition requiring monitoring for accuracy, but was only observed for the speaker in the condition requiring monitoring for fluidity (Cuc *et al.*, 2007).

Importantly, one can find RIF for speakers and listeners not just in contrived laboratory settings but also when people talk freely about previously studied material. In addition to carefully controlling the selective practice of two participants, Cuc *et al.* (2007) also asked their two participants to recall a previously studied story in a *free-flowing conversation*. The story was constructed to allow its episodes and events to be conceived of as category-exemplar pairs. For instance, the story might contain an episode *going to Coney Island*, with a set of embedded events: *ate a hot dog, rode a roller coaster, swam in the ocean*. Cuc *et al.* transcribed the conversation and, for each participant, used this transcription to code elements of the original story into practiced and unpracticed story elements – that is, story elements mentioned in the conversation and story elements that went unmentioned. The unmentioned items were further coded into those related to what was said in the conversation and those that were unrelated. Finally, for each element of the story, the coding for a participant was further classified as to the role the participant was playing in the conversation; that is, as a speaker or a listener. The coding produced a data matrix similar to the one produced in the studies using word pairs.

Moreover, the pattern of the data was similar to the word-pair study: unmentioned story elements related to the mentioned one were forgotten more often than unmentioned, unrelated story elements. That is, mnemonic silences in a conversation have a similar effect on memory for unmentioned items in a well-controlled, paired, associate learning experiment – some are more likely to produce forgetting than others. Follow-up conversational studies found similar RIF forgetting not just for story details but also for salient aspects of the story, for scientific material, and for autobiographical memories (Coman, Manier, and Hirst, 2009; Koppel, Wohl, Meksin, et al., 2010; Stone, Barnier, Sutton, and Hirst, 2010, submitted).

Inasmuch as the RIF pattern is found for both speakers and listeners, it can lead to collective forgetting (Cuc, Ozuru, Manier, et al., 2006; Stone et al., 2010a). More critically, this forgetting follows a specific pattern. Talking about a shared past event with others will not only reinforce the memories discussed in the conversation but also induce forgetting for unmentioned, related memories – not just for one participant in the conversation but possibly for all participants. One could use this principle to create a "desired" collective memory. If the current president, Barack Obama, wants people to forget the compromises he made in pushing the health bill through Congress, he might not avoid discussing the struggle to pass the bill. Rather he might just avoid discussing the parts that he wants forgotten. The latter strategy will lead to greater forgetting than the former and, as a result, an "American" collective memory that is silent about Obama's compromises. Of course, the effects of mnemonic silences in conversations may reshape the memory of participants without any intention on the part of speakers to do so. The selective remembering in the conversation may unfold in unintended ways. Whether intentional or not, the research suggests that induced forgetting across participants should occur.

Inducing forgetting of personal knowledge   In most of the work on socially shared RIF, speakers and listeners were exposed to the same material, yet, in the world outside the laboratory, a speaker often discusses something that the listener is learning about for the first time. Frequently, this new material is related to an event or material the listener already knows about.

Consider the following situation. A listener is learning about an accident for the first time. The speaker might recollect the speed with which the ambulance arrived, but remain silent about the reactions of passersby. Her overt recollection and silence might remind her listeners of their own traffic accidents, but, in doing so, might structure what listeners do and do not remember about their own accidents, even if their recollections are kept to themselves. As they attend to the speaker, listeners may, for instance, concurrently, but covertly, remember how quickly the ambulance arrived for their own accident, but fail to remember – even to themselves – the reactions of the passersby. In such an instance, the selective recollections of the speaker may lead to similar selective remembering on the part of listeners, inducing forgetting for the related, unmentioned material in both speaker and listeners. What the speaker and listeners mutually forget will not be the same – after all, they have different memories. Nevertheless, they will forget similar *classes* of information.

SS-RIF, then, might not be limited to events mutually experienced by speaker and listener. Coman *et al.* (2009) showed such "class-based" induced forgetting, using as stimulus material the memories people hold of how they spent their day on September 11, 2001. Although such memories are hardly a typical autobiographical memory, they are interesting when considering collective memories because they are one of the few instances in which the personal intersects with the historical (Neisser, 1982). The memories are no doubt autobiographical (they are about how *I* spent my day), but they concern a day that will have lasting historical importance.

The findings of Coman *et al.* (2009) offer a means of understanding how social taboos can allow speakers to influence listeners' memories of their personal past. If social taboos can shape what a person publicly recollects about their own autobiographical memories, then Coman *et al.*'s results indicate that the selective recollection of the speaker's own autobiographical memories will in turn shape how others recollect and forget their own, uniquely held, autobiographical memories. For instance, social taboos about the depiction of blood and gore often mean that war movies avoid portraying war at its worst. When a movie depicts war in this sanitized fashion, the claim of Coman *et al.* is that the movie may induce members of its audience to forget their own gruesome personal war experiences, in effect, sanitizing their personal memories. War memories may begin with personal details about the horrors of war, but, because of the way war is publicly depicted, will end with induced forgetting of the individual horrors. Through reasoning such as this, scholars can begin to understand how social taboos, and the silences they engender, can shape collective forgetting. The interaction between social taboos and the psychological mechanisms of memory grants both collective and individual memories a shared character that could, once again, serve to promote social cohesion.

Propagation of retrieval effects The research reviewed up to this point involved a single conversational interaction. The assumption has been that the effects observed in a single interaction can propagate through a sequence of social interactions, at least in many circumstances. Recently, Coman and Hirst (2012) have begun to study this claim. They examined a specific sequence of social interactions. A participant first learns about an event or a line of argument, for instance, by reading a newspaper or an essay. She then hears the details of the event or the argument repeated, but now by someone who has a clear bias – for instance, a political figure with an agenda. In part because of the bias, the presentation is selective, thereby providing conditions suitable for both practice effects and RIF to emerge. After the biased presentation, the participant then joins with others to discuss the event or line of argument. How much is the content of the original newspaper or essay altered by this sequence of exchanges? How much does the bias presentation shape what is said in the conversation? And does any effect that the biased presenter has on the memory of his listeners transfer through a conversation, so that it can be observed in probes of memory following the conversation? That is, are social memory effects, such as practice and socially shared RIF, transitive?

Coman and Hirst (2012) explored these issues in an experiment that proceeded as outlined in Figure 8.1, which captures the sequence of social interactions we just described. They chose, as the to-be-remembered material, arguments for or against the legalization of euthanasia. This topic allowed them to select participants who varied in their attitude toward legalization. There were two social interactions: (1) between participant and presenter (who is referred to as PERSON-PRO and who always presents arguments in favor of legalization), and (2) between a pair of participants in a conversation. There were three probes of memory: (1) an assessment of the influence of PERSON-PRO; (2) the conversation, here focusing both on what was recalled and what went unmentioned in the conversation; and (3) the final recall.

Ps = participants

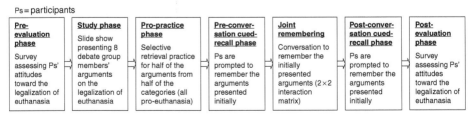

Figure 8.1. Phases of the experimental procedure.

The experiment produced a sequence of events that detailed how and when social interaction can produce mnemonic convergence. First, the selective presentation of PERSON-PRO led to a practice effect and to socially shared RIF. The size of the practice effect and RIF was not affected by the attitude of the participants. Second, both practice effects and RIF propagated into the conversation, but only when participants shared the same attitudes. When the conversing pair held different attitudes (one for legalization; the other, against it), the practice effects and RIF observed in the pre-conversational recall did not influence what was or was not recounted in the conversation.

Third, in instances in which practice effect and RIF propagated into the conversation, they also influenced what was remembered in the final recall test. Not only was the propagation transitive but it also accumulated across social interactions: For instance, RIF in the final recall was substantially stronger when it was also observed in both the pre-conversational recall and the conversation. Fourth, both practice effects and RIF led to a shift in attitude, with participants' attitudes changing in a manner concordant with what they remembered and forgot.

Finally, when the conversation was between like-minded people, the final memories clearly converged on the rendering offered by PERSON-PRO in his presentation. A political figure, then, could reshape memories to fit his bias if people spent most of their time after a presentation talking with those that share those attitudes. Critically, this holds whether participants in these homogeneous conversations agree or disagree with the biases of PERSON-PRO. The group simply becomes united with respect to the biases captured by PERSON-PRO.

Discussion

Seeming weaknesses of memory may mask an extremely useful benefit in that the weaknesses can promote the formation of collective memories and, in doing so, encourage sociality. We have focused here on three possible sources of mnemonic error: schema, social contagion, and retrieval effects. These errors are critical to the formation of collective memories because they can often occur in the midst of the social, particularly the conversational, exchanges that characterize every individual's daily life. What a speaker says will alter the memory of listeners in ways that lead to mnemonic convergence. A reinforcing circle emerges. As people interact, initially disparate memories become more similar. As the memories of members of a community become more similar, the group achieves a stronger collective identity. And as people form a stronger collective identity, members of the group will become more likely to interact with each other, making it ever more likely for the cycle to repeat itself (Visser and Mirabile, 2004). Moreover, this propensity to interact with like-minded people makes whatever effects social interactions have on memory even stronger, as the evidence presented here and elsewhere indicates (Coman and Hirst, 2012; Echterhoff, Higgins, and Levine, 2007). The results are ever-developing collective memories that, in turn, provide the foundation for well-defined and strong collective identities and a shared reality. Such identities and realities are beneficial, in that they can supply a sense of belonging, a place in the world, and a culture that can shape future behavior. We have articulated how some cognitive factors that are involved in this ever-developing collective memory, but, as we noted in the introduction, many others factors also come into play, including normative and motivational factors. Yet, even confining our concerns to cognitive factors, it is clear how the unreliability and malleability of memory unquestionably have benefits.

Of course, the formation of a collective memory can be something dangerous, in that it they can also lead to prejudice, dehumanization, and narrow-mindedness. While these detrimental consequences are grave, they should not be overemphasized. It is hard to understand how people would be people if they did not possess a well-developed and well-grounded collective memory, and, in turn, collective identity. As we have emphasized, human beings are social creatures. Any mechanism that promotes sociality should, *ceteris paribus*, be viewed as a benefit. What we want to stress here is that the human memory system seems well designed to offer this benefit, by promoting the formation of a collective memory and thereby fostering, among other things, a strong collective identity.

Interestingly, the role memory plays in promoting sociality may be a distinctly human virtue. The arguments we have been advancing suggest that human memory has evolved in such a way so as to take advantage of the social nature of humans and, in turn, to promote greater human sociality. Human memory can achieve this feature in large part because in humans, unlike in animals, remembering often takes place in a communicative setting. The resulting collaboration provides the foundation for at least two of the three sources of errors we have been discussing: social contagion and socially shared RIF. Inasmuch as it arises only in situations that encourage concurrent retrieval, RIF in the listener, in particular, is unlikely to occur outside communicative settings. If remembering merely occurred to allow a creature to locate food or avoid dangerous areas – that is, if it occurred outside a communicative setting – such induced forgetting would never arise. Evolutionary psychologists have argued that the "surplus" of intelligence humans possess grew in part out of a need to navigate and take advantage of complex social environments (Humphrey, 1976). These same social environments and social needs may have also produced an organism that relies on mnemonic unreliability and malleability to foster social cohesion. The sin becomes a virtue.

References

Anderson, M. C., Bjork, R. A., and Bjork, E. L. (1994). Remembering can cause forgetting: retrieval dynamics in long-term memory. *Journal of Experimental Psychology: Learning, Memory, and Cognition*, **20**, 1063–1087.

Anderson, M. C. and Levy, B. J. (2007). Theoretical issues in inhibition: insight from research on human memory. In D. S. Gorfein and C. M. MacLeod (eds.), *Inhibition in cognition* (pp. 81–102). Washington, DC: American Psychological Association.

Barnier, A. J., Hung, L., and Conway, M. A. (2004). Retrieval-induced forgetting of emotional and unemotional autobiographical memories. *Cognition and Emotion*, **18**, 457–477.

Bartlett, F. (1932). *Remembering: a study in experimental and social psychology*. New York: Cambridge University Press.

Ben-Ze'ev, E., Ginio, R., and Winter, J. (eds.) (2010). *Shadows of war: a social history of silence in the twentieth century*. New York: Cambridge University Press.

Blumen, H. M. and Rajaram, S. (2008). Influence of re-exposure and retrieval disruption during group collaboration on later individual recall. *Memory*, **16**, 231–244.

Bodnar, J. (1993). *Remaking America: public memory, commemoration, and patriotism in the twentieth century*. Princeton University Press.

Chan, J. C. K., McDermott, K. B., and Roediger, H. L. (2006). Retrieval-induced facilitation: initially nontested material can benefit from prior testing of related material. *Journal of Experimental Psychology: General*, **135**, 553–571.

Coman, A. and Hirst, W. (2012). Cognition through a social network: The propagation of induced forgetting and practice effects. *Journal of Experimental Psychology*, **141**, 321–336.

Coman, A., Manier, D., and Hirst, W. (2009). Forgetting the unforgettable through conversation: socially-shared retrieval-induced forgetting of 9/11 memories. *Psychological Science*, **20**, 627–633.

Cuc, A., Koppel, J., and Hirst, W. (2007). Silence is not golden: a case for socially-shared retrieval-induced forgetting. *Psychological Science*, **18**, 727–737.

Cuc, A., Ozuru, Y., Manier, D., and Hirst, W. (2006). The transformation of collective memories: studies of family recounting. *Memory & Cognition*, **34**, 752–762.

Dodd, M. D., Castel, A. D., and Roberts, K. E. (2006). A strategy disruption component to retrieval-induced forgetting. *Memory & Cognition*, **34**, 102–111.

Ebbinghaus, H. (1913/1964). *Memory: a contribution to experimental psychology*. New York: Dover.

Echterhoff, G., Higgins, E. T., and Levine, J. M. (2007). Shared reality: a product of the motivated sharing of inner states. *Perspectives in Psychological Science*, **4**, 496–521.

Festinger, L. (1950). Informal social communication. *Psychological Review*, **57**, 271–282.

Halbwachs, M. (1925/1992). *On collective memory*. L. A. Coser (trans.). University of Chicago Press.

Harber, K. D. and Cohen, D. J. (2005). The emotional broadcaster theory of social sharing. *Journal of Language and Social Behavior*, **24**, 382–400.

Hardin, C. D. and Higgins, E. T. (1996). Shared reality: how social verification makes the subjective objective. In R. M. Sorrentino and E. T. Higgins (eds.), *Handbook of motivation and cognition: the interpersonal context*, vol. III (pp. 28–84). New York: Guilford.

Hirst, W. and Brown, A. (2011). On the virtues of an unreliable memory: its role in grounding sociality. In G. Semin and G. Echterhoff (eds.), *Grounding sociality: neurons, minds, and culture* (pp. 95–114). New York: Psychological Press.

Hirst, W. and Echterhoff, G. (2008). Creating shared memories in conversation: toward a psychology of collective memory. *Social Research*, **75**, 183–216.

(2012). Remembering in conversation: the social sharing and reshaping of memory. *Annual Review of Psychology*, **63**, 55–79.

Hirst, W. and Manier, D. (2002). The diverse forms of collective memory. In G. Echterhoff and M. Saar (eds.), *Kontexte und Kulturen des Erinnerns: Maurice Halbwachs und das Paradigma des kollektiven Gedächtnisses* (pp. 37–58). Konstanz: UVK Verlagsgesellschaft mbH.

(2008). Towards a psychology of collective memory. *Memory*, **16**, 183–2000.

Hobsbawm, E. and Ranger, T. (eds.) (1983). *The invention of tradition*. New York: Cambridge University Press.

Humphrey, N. (1976). The social function of intellect. In P. P. P. G. Bateson and R. A. Hinde (eds.), *Growing points in ethology* (pp. 303–317). New York: Cambridge University Press.

Kagan, R. (1998). The benevolent empire. *Foreign Policy*, **111**, 24–35.

Karpicke, J. D. and Roediger, H. L. (2008). The critical importance of retrieval for learning. *Science*, **319**, 966–968.

Kashima, Y. (2008). A social psychology of cultural dynamics: examining how cultures are formed, maintained, and transformed. *Social and Personality Psychology Compass*, **2**, 107–120.

Koppel, J., Wohl, D., Meksin, R., and Hirst, W. (2010). The discrepant effects of expertise and mistrust on social contagion and socially-shared retrieval-induced forgetting: the pervasive influence of social factors. Manuscript in preparation.

Loftus, E. F. (2005). Planting misinformation in the human mind: a 30-year investigation of the malleability of memory. *Learning & Memory*, **12**, 361–366.

Manier, D. and Hirst, W. (2008). A cognitive taxonomy of collective memories. In A. Erll and A. Nünning (eds.), *Cultural memory studies: an international and interdisciplinary handbook* (pp. 253–262). New York: de Gruyter.

Marsh, E. (2007). Retelling is not the same as recalling: implications for memory. *Current Directions in Psychological Science*, **16**, 16–20.

Neisser, U. (1982). Snapshots or benchmarks? In U. Neisser (ed.), *Memory observed: remembering in natural contexts* (pp. 34–48). San Francisco, CA: W. H. Freeman.

Olick, J. K. (2002). Collective memory: the two cultures. *Sociological Theory*, 17, 333–348.

Olick, J. K., Vinitzky-Seroussi, V., and Levy, D. (2010). *The collective memory reader*. New York: Oxford University Press.

Pashupathi, M. (2001). The social construction of the personal past and its implications for adult development. *Psychological Bulletin*, 127, 651–672.

Schacter, D. L. (1999). The seven sins of memory: insights from psychology and cognitive neuroscience. *American Psychologist*, 54, 182–203.

Schudson, M. (1995). Dynamics of distortion in collective memory. In D. L. Schacter (ed.), *Memory distortions: how minds, brains, and societies reconstruct the past* (pp. 246–365). Cambridge, MA: Harvard University Press.

Schwartz, B. (2000). *Abraham Lincoln and the forge of national memory*. University of Chicago Press.

Stone, C. B., Barnier, A. J., Sutton, J., and Hirst, W. (2010). Building consensus about the past: schema consistency and convergence in socially shared retrieval-induced forgetting. *Memory*, 18, 170–184.

(submitted). *Forgetting our personal past: socially shared retrieval-induced forgetting of autobiographical memories*.

Stone, C., Coman, A., Brown, A., and Koppel, J. (2012). Towards a science of silence: consequences of leaving a memory unsaid. *Perspectives in Psychological Science*, 7, 39–53.

Sutton, J., Harris, C. B., Keil, P. G., and Barnier, A. J. (2010). The psychology of memory, extended cognition, and socially distributed remembering. *Phenomenology and Cognitive Science*, 9, 521–560.

Visser, P. S. and Mirabile, R. R. (2004). Attitudes in the social context: the impact of social network composition on individual-level attitude strength. *Journal of Personality and Social Psychology*, 87, 779–795.

Vygotsky, L. S. (1978). *Mind in society: the development of higher psychological processes*. Cambridge, MA: Harvard University Press.

Watts, D. J. (2004). *Six degrees: the science of connected age*. New York: Norton.

Weldon, M. S. (2001). Remembering as a social process. In G. H. Bower (ed.), *The psychology of learning and motivation*, vol. X (pp. 67–120). New York: Academic Press.

Wertsch, J. V. (2002). *Voices of collective remembering*. New York: Cambridge University Press.

(2008). Collective memory and narrative templates. *Social Research*, 75, 133–156.

Zerubavel, E. (2005). *The elephant in the room: silence and denial in everyday life*. New York: Oxford University Press.

Zerubavel, Y. (1995). *Recovered roots: collective memory and the making of Israeli national tradition*. University of Chicago Press.

9   Historically defined autobiographical periods: their origins and implications

*Norman R. Brown, Tia G. B. Hansen, Peter J. Lee,
Sarah A. Vanderveen, and Fredrick G. Conrad*

Historically significant public events sometimes organize autobiographical memory, acting as temporal landmarks and providing the thematic content which defines the lifetime periods they spawn (Brown and Lee, 2010; Brown, Lee, Krslak, *et al.*, 2009). We begin this chapter by briefly reviewing a research program that has demonstrated the existence of these *historically defined autobiographical periods* and that has allowed us to identify the conditions that bring them about. In this section, we also present data from four samples of World War II-generation adults, data which prove that historically defined autobiographical periods endure over time. Next, we consider the theoretical implications of these findings. In particular, we introduce a new approach to autobiographical memory called the *transition theory*. This approach assumes that autobiographical memory is organized by transitional events and that these transitions can be self-initiated or externally imposed. On this view, historically defined autobiographical periods are formed by externally imposed transitions. We develop this point in the third and final section of this chapter.

The living-in-history project

War, terrorism, and natural disasters can have far-reaching effects on the lives of those involved (Blaikie, Cannon, Davis, *et al.*, 1994; Levy and Sidel, 1997; McNally, 2003). Collective memory for extraordinary social events can also play a critical role in the construction and maintenance of group identities and in the persistence of intergroup hostility (Bar-Tal, 2007; Cairns and Roe, 2003; Halbwachs, 1992; Hirst, Cuc, and Wohl, this volume). Our project examined the mnemonic impact of public events at the individual level in order to understand when autobiographical memory and historical events can become intertwined. More

This research was supported in part by an NSERC grant awarded to the first author. We thank Connie Svob and Tugba Uzer-Yildiz for their input to this project and their comments on this chapter.

160

specifically, the program of research was undertaken to determine whether public events affect the organization of autobiographical memory and to specify the conditions that result in the creation of historically defined autobiographical periods. We were interested in this issue because we suspected that people who had "lived in history" might understand the recent past in a different way than those who had not, and that this understanding might ground current and future beliefs about that past. For this reason, we wanted to identify public events that caused people to "live in history" and to distinguish these *epoch-defining* events from other significant public events.

We developed a two-stage procedure to address this issue. In phase 1, we present participants with about 20 neutral cue words[1] (e.g., *automobile, bag, ball, book, box, bread, chair, coat, dog, pencil, piano, pill, radio, river, snow, spoon, stone, street, tree, window*). Participants see these cues one at a time in a unique random order, and are asked to respond to each cue by recalling a specific autobiographical memory related to the cue word, and to write a brief description of this event onto separate cue cards. The word-cue task is believed to elicit a representative sample of autobiographical memories from across the life span (Rubin and Schulkind, 1997).

In phase 2, we present the participants with the written descriptions of their Phase-1 memories and ask them to provide think-aloud protocols as they attempt to date each of their phase-1 events. In autobiographical memory, personal periods are blocks of time dominated by a particular set of event features, with landmark events signaling the transition from one period to the next (Belli, 1998; Conway and Rubin, 1993; Loftus and Marburger, 1983; Shum, 1998). When dating autobiographical events, individuals often justify their responses by mentioning personal periods (e.g., "When I was in elementary school, 5th grade, so it maybe during the winter of 1998") or period-bounding personal landmarks (e.g., "That was right after we moved to our second apartment – let's say May, 1982") and use this information to support one or more temporal inferences (Brown, 1990; Friedman, 1993; Thompson, Skowronski, Larsen, *et al.*, 1996).

At the outset of this project, we hypothesized that people might also refer to public periods and news events when dating autobiographical memories (e.g., "during the war"; "soon after the earthquake"), but only when historically significant events had brought about fundamental

---

[1] The exact number of stimulus words has ranged from 18 to 22 across samples, and the cue set has been modified slightly across samples to reflect obvious cultural differences. For example, when we collected data in Lebanon, we replaced the cue word *piano* with the cue word *derbake* (a kind of Arabic drum) because pianos are rare in Lebanon and derbakes are common.

changes in the fabric of a person's daily life. These changes might come about, for example, through the destruction of people's dwellings, workplaces, shops, or places of worship; the death of family members or close friends; the rise of famine; or the end of statutory medical care, schooling, and many other public services – in summary, a catastrophic and long-lasting change in people's normal activities, and how they are able to lead their lives.

We also assumed that the percentage of references to historical periods and public events would be related to the degree to which a given population was impacted by forces beyond their control. This is to say that the duration of a conflict or disaster, and the intensity of its effects, should predict the percentage of historical references observed in the phase-2 dating protocols. These intuitions were confirmed during our initial studies, which demonstrated the presence of a *living-in-history* effect[2] in some samples but not others (Brown et al., 2009; Brown and Lee, 2010). For example, people from Sarajevo, Bosnia-Herzegovina, often mentioned the civil war that occurred in the aftermath of the break-up of Yugoslavia (1992–5) – these references were present in about 24% of the justified date estimates. In contrast, Montenegrins who were not at the center of the Bosnian conflict were much less likely to mention it. Likewise, Serbs in Belgrade rarely mentioned the conflicts of the 1990s. This research also indicated that natural disasters can spawn historically defined autobiographical periods, but only in populations that were directly affected by them. Two Turkish samples supported these claims; one sample was made up of people who were living in Izmit during the earthquake of 1999 and the other was made up of people who were living in Ankara, some 250 km away. References to the earthquake appeared in 14% of protocols collected in Izmit and in hardly any of the protocols collected in Ankara. Finally it is worth noting that the living-in-history effect has been observed in two Lebanese samples (Zebian and Brown, 2012) and that it was absent (or very modest) in samples collected from young adults living in Canada, Demark, the USA (including post-9/11 New York City), Israel, and Russia (Brown and Lee, 2010).

In previous studies we have focused on the presence or absence of the living-in-history effect in samples comprised of young adults (Brown et al., 2009; Brown and Lee, 2010). These data make it clear that conflict and natural disaster can produce historically defined autobiographical periods in younger people. What is not clear from these data is whether

---

[2] The living-in-history effect is observed when people from a given population frequently refer to public events (e.g., "that was after Dayton") or historical periods (e.g., "that was during the civil war") when dating mundane personal memories.

these structures last a lifetime or whether they fade over time. To address this issue, we used the two-phase cueing procedure on four samples of World War II-generation noncombatants (M age $= 82$ years, $SD = 4.6$ years) – Canadians, Americans, Danes, and Dutch immigrants who arrived in Canada shortly after the war. The data were collected between 2006 and 2008.

These samples were interesting in part because our participants transitioned into, and out of, an epoch-defining period in twentieth century history, and in part because World War II impacted countries differentially. Of the samples, the Dutch were arguably the most affected by the war. The Dutch experience began with the disruption caused during the Battle of the Netherlands and the destruction of Rotterdam in May 1940, and included the *Hongerwinter* or Dutch Famine that killed 16,000 civilians in 1944. The Dutch Central Bureau of Statistics puts the total number of direct casualties during World War II at 210,000 people (~2.4% of the population). By comparison, the Danish experience of occupation was much mitigated (Futselaar, 2008; Giltner, 2001). The initial invasion was over within two hours, and the total number of wartime casualties was 3,249 people (~0.09% of the population). This is not to suggest that transitions wrought by the Nazi occupation did not have profound personal consequences for many Danes – 1,502 Danes were executed, died in concentration camps, or were killed in resistance actions, coupled with many day-to-day changes in the lives of Danish citizens. These included a ban on public assembly, rationing, price shocks, and a shift to designing and producing goods destined for Germany.

We compared these occupied countries with Canadian and American noncombatants, whose lives were impacted by the transition from peace to war, but to a far lesser extent than were the lives of the Danes or the Dutch. Canadians and Americans experienced changes in the availability of goods, and the type of work opportunities open to them (e.g., increased employment, and a massive increase in the role of women within industry). In addition, the existence of universal conscription in the USA and massive enlistment in Canada had a marked effect on family life and other social institutions. Given these between-nation differences, and assuming that the prevalence of historically defined autobiographical periods for a given population is related to the degree of psychological and material transition, we predicted that historical references would be most frequent for the Dutch sample, followed by Danes, and considerably less frequent in the protocols of Canadians or Americans.

We analyze each phase-2 dating protocol by assigning them to one of three response types: unjustified due to the absence of any verbal report, justified with reference to personal/generic information only, and justified with reference to historical information. For this study, we created a fourth category for references to immigration on the grounds that immigration also involves a major lifetime transition at the individual rather than group level (we return to the issue of transitions and the structure of autobiographical memory later on).

This taxonomy allows us to categorize the justified reports as those that reference only personal information, those that include historical references, and those that refer to immigration. Examples of these three response types are presented in Table 9.1. Our analysis of these older participants shows that our Dutch respondents who lived in the Netherlands during the Nazi occupation referred to World War II in 12.6% of their justified protocols, while Danes mentioned the war 10.7% of the time. These figures are more than twice as high as those for Canadians (4.8%) and Americans (4.9%) who did not experience the war directly. Furthermore, these results concur with the principle that frequency of the historical references in the protocols is related to the degree of externally imposed change people experience when transitioning from one period to another. Here, the effect is predicted by the proximity, intensity, and duration of conflict experienced by these different populations.

Overall the percentage of references to historically defined autobiographical periods in these samples was not especially high (and should not be for elderly populations whose long lives have been characterized by decades of stability rather than conflict). However, these references do cluster around 1939 to 1945. Figure 9.1 shows the percentage of memories by their estimated year of occurrence for each of our four samples, with the proportion of memories dated by referencing historically defined autobiographical periods color coded in black. This figure indicates that many events that happened during this period were dated with reference to the war, and that very few of the events that happened outside this period were dated with reference to the war or other public events. These data also indicated that the Dutch and the Danes were much more likely to refer to Word War II when dating events from the war period (1939–45) than were the Americans and the Canadians. The Dutch referred to the war when dating war-period memories 61% of the time, and the Danes 41% of the time, whereas the Canadians and Americans mentioned the war 22% and 19% of the time, respectively.

In brief, we have observed that historically defined autobiographical periods are formed only when and where external events alter the fabric of daily life in dramatic ways. War and natural disaster are agents of change, and it is the transition wrought by these agents, the direct and pervasive impact they have on the lives of people who experience them, that heralds the creation of new autobiographical periods. Of course, war and natural

Table 9.1. *Examples of historically defined autobiographical references, immigration references, and personal references from the Dutch immigrant sample*

Cue	Reported memory	Verbalized date estimates	Response type
House	We ate all the food in our house	Oh … that would be 19 … May 1940 … because it was in the spring in Holland and I remember the, the ah … Germans in ah, um … (how do you say that) … came over on Holland in 1940 and it was in May and ah … then we begun to realize what they were doing … how they were taking out, emptying out all warehouses and everything because we might as well eat everything in the house because we don't want them … our enemies to have it.	Historical
Coat	I got a hand-me-down coat, but it was too long	Hand-me-down coat … that was also before the war … Coat. I got a hand-me-down coat but it was too long. I was probably already around twelve. I wasn't a little kid that I didn't care to know how you would look. I would say I was 12 years old or something, you know. During the war more or less. It could have been before. In 1940 the war broke out in Holland, you know. So it could have been around that time. It could have also been '39 … but it was around that time that it happened.	Historical
Car	I bought a 1937 Dodge which cost $300	Well my first … the '37 Dodge I bought in the summer of 1950, because that's the year I came to Canada … but it wasn't the summer it was more the fall … I don't know the month exactly.	Immigration
window	Jumped through a window while sleep walking	When we came here [to Canada]. That was 1954. That was the first little house. That was … let me think … yeah, we came in May … June … say, July …	Immigration
stone	Inherited a pair of earrings from mother	From my mother, that was in 1949 she died. Ah, December the 7th.	Personal
ball	Football through window	When I was a boy in the 6th grade in Holland we were playing football with wooden shoes on [laughs] and we give it a good kick and it went through that hallway window in our schoolhouse … next morning we had to bring 5 cents … every boy who played football to replace the window … how is that?	Personal

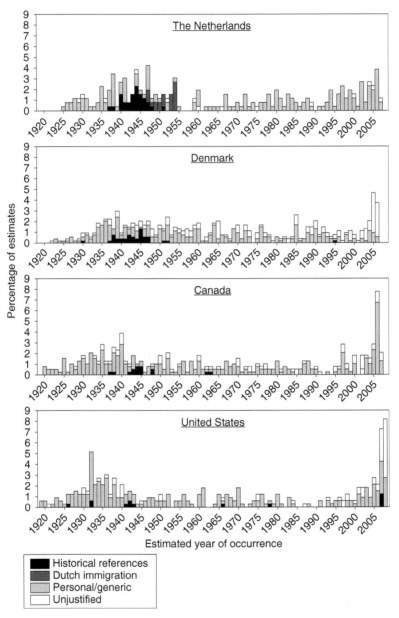

Figure 9.1. Percentage of response type as function of estimated year for WWII-generation samples from the Netherlands, Denmark, Canada, and the United States.

disaster are not the only agents of change; people can and do "change their lives." And when they do, these transitions should also spawn identifiable autobiographical periods.

Data from our sample of Dutch immigrants speak to this point. Emigrating from one country to another involves a major transition; from a life characterized by one set of features to one characterized by a new set of features. For example, immigrants often experience changes in career (or begin training for new careers) and engage in new activities (e.g., exposure to different sports, new leisure interests, and cultural events), as well as coming to terms with different social customs. In addition, there are outwardly superficial changes that permanently alter the day-to-day lives of people who have moved from one country to another. For example, it is inevitable that immigrants are exposed to new foods and consumer products and to differences in the natural world (e.g., weather conditions, plants, and animals).

Given the impact of immigration on the fabric of daily life and assuming that that these changes mark the transitions from one significant lifetime period to the next, it follows that we should observe an immigration effect in the Dutch sample that parallels the living-in-history effect. Evidence regarding this prediction is presented in the top panel of Figure 9.1. It is clear from this figure that people in the Dutch sample frequently referred to immigration and that these references were most common during the late 1940s and early to mid 1950s. Overall, immigration references appeared in 9% of the justified responses produced by the Dutch. However, when we focus only on the time period between 1947 and 1960, immigration is mentioned in almost half (49%) of the justified date estimates.

In summary, this research has shed light on how major lifetime periods are created, how these periods are characterized by the historical and personal content of the memories that populate them, and the durability of this content across the life span. Broadly speaking, new autobiographical periods are permanent mnemonic structures created when people experience profound changes in their material circumstances – whether they are experienced as part of a collective transition that binds historical content to personal information, or as private transitions evoked by personal choice.

Transition theory

In the preceding section, we argued that public events spawn historically defined autobiographical periods only when they produce a marked and enduring change in the fabric of daily life. We also noted that wars and natural disasters are not the only processes that alter the fabric of daily life and correctly predicted the existence of an emigration effect in our Dutch sample, an effect that closely parallels the living-in-history effect. In addition, we have argued elsewhere that historically significant events, even very important ones (e.g., the 9/11 attacks), will not organize auto-biographical memory if they fail to change the way people live (Brown *et al.*, 2009; Brown and Lee, 2010; Nourkova and Bernstein, 2010; Zebian and Brown, 2012; also see below). Taken as a whole, these findings have led us to speculate about the nature of lifetime periods. Specifically, we proposed that a lifetime period covers a span of time during which there is relatively little change in the fabric of daily life and that these periods are bounded by transitional events that bring about a marked change in a person's material circumstances. In this section we develop this position more fully and in the process introduce an approach to understanding the organization of autobiographical memory that we call transition theory. We begin our description of this approach with a discussion of the "fabric of daily life," lifetime periods, and major transitions, and then move on to consider a wider range of transitions and periods. Finally, we briefly discuss links between these concepts and those that have been put forward by other researchers in the area.

Major lifetime periods and temporally delineated event components

One way to understand what we mean by the fabric of daily life is to consider the experience of a person who has moved from one region (e.g., Pittsburgh, Pennsylvania) to another, very distant, region (e.g., Edmonton, Alberta). Intuitively, a move of this sort is a major transition, and it is easy to imagine this person using phrases like "when I lived in Pittsburgh" or "after I moved to Alberta" when dating personal events. In other words, this move can be seen as having put an end to one major lifetime period, "the Pittsburgh years," and providing the starting point for another, "life on the Canadian prairies."

A relocation like this one need not change everything – possessions are movable, as are partners, children, pets, careers, and interests – but, it does, necessarily, change a great deal. Consider what gets left behind: *the people* – friends, neighbors, coworkers, acquaintances, clerks, tradespeople; *the things* – local products and produce, local flora and fauna, the climate and topography of the region; *the places* – a house or apartment, the work-place, local shops, malls, restaurants, bars, cafés, schools, athletic facilities, parks, neighborhoods and cycle routes; and *the activities* – the recurring events that characterize work, home life, and leisure time, which can also involve these people, places, and things. All of this is left behind when someone relocates. Prior to the relocation, these people, places, activities, and things constitute what we call the fabric of daily life; they provide both content and context for most personal experiences, and as a result these *event components* define the autobiographical memories that are formed during the periods they populate.

There are two important things to note about these event components. First, typically, we know a great deal about each component, and we gain this knowledge through repeated, often massively repeated, exposure. Some of this knowledge is tied to events and hence linked to specific autobiographical memories, but certainly not all. For example, knowledge of a close friend would include information about his or her background, profession, personality, tastes, and personal life, along with memories of shared experiences (Hastie and Kumar, 1979). Similarly, knowledge of a recurring activity, such as a daily swim at the university pool, might consist of information about the layout of the sports complex, the identities of some regulars and staff, and an understanding of the conventions that determine lane selection. In addition, there would be script-like knowledge of the actions that constitute a typical swim and, perhaps, specific memories of a few distinctive or noteworthy trips to the pool (Barsalou, 1988).

We assume that each event component is linked to a rich mix of specific memories, generic memories, and event-independent facts and that this is true regardless of whether the component refers to people, places, activities, or objects. We also assume that temporal knowledge is integral to the mix. This is the second important aspect of our conceptualization of event components and the reason that we refer to them as *T-DEC*s (*temporally delineated event components*). Specifically, it seems people know, at least roughly, when individual event components entered their lives and when they ceased to be part of them. This knowledge can be coarse or fine-grained; it can be couched in terms of conventional periods, idiosyncratic ones, or calendar dates; and it can indicate that experiences involving a given component spanned the whole of a lifetime period or some portion of a period, or that they cut across periods. It is access to this temporal knowledge that supports the various temporal inferences that enable people to estimate dates of personal and public events with a fair degree of accuracy (Brown, 1990; Friedman, 1993; Thompson *et al.*, 1996).

Once established as part of the autobiographical knowledge-base, a T-DEC can last a lifetime. However, the real-world entities represented by this knowledge are transient. Simply put, things change, and we are aware of these changes. This is true even when we stay put. People come and go; businesses open and close; possessions wear out and are replaced; styles and technologies evolve at a rapid pace, etc. In general, these changes and our experiences with them are temporally uncoordinated, and thus T-DEC onsets and offsets tend to be staggered. In other words, even when our lives are relatively stable, they are lightly punctuated by the beginnings and endings of T-DECs. But this is not always the case.

Returning to the relocation example, consider how a move from one region to another affects things. Such a move causes an abrupt and (near)[3] total shift in the fabric of daily life for the individual involved. It concludes (almost) all of his or her interactions with the local social and material environment; it signals an end to (almost) all activities involving elements specific to those environments; and, from a memory perspective, it "terminates" a large number of T-DECs, and thus aligns their offsets. Although a major transition aligns the offsets of pre-transitional T-DECs, it does not necessarily align onsets of the T-DECs that come online following the move. This is because it takes time to establish a social network, to settle into a daily routine, to explore a new environment, and to decide on a preferred set of activities and venues.

In brief, a major transitional event, like a relocation, causes and marks the simultaneous offsets for a very large number of T-DECs and enables the (often staggered) onset for another set. On this view, a major lifetime period is the span of time that falls between such transitions; each period consists of a fairly stable set of T-DECs, and, for the most part, T-DECs that comprise one period differ from those that comprise other periods and are identified with the period to which they belong.

Transition types

There is, of course, a wide range of transitional events (Hobson and Delunas, 2001; Holmes and Rahe, 1967), and most do not conclude an existing way of life and initiate a new one. Rather, they alter some circumscribed aspect(s) of a person's experience, leaving many others untouched. Consider what happens when a person purchases a new house and moves from one side of town to the other. In this case, some things change, but many do not. Obviously, domestic events henceforth will be played out against a new and different backdrop. And all homes come complete with a new batch of neighbors, a novel commute, another corner store, and their own set of galling and expensive maintenance issues. In the language of transition theory, the cross-town move has caused and marked the simultaneous termination of one set of T-DECs – T-DECs that were directly associated with life at the prior residence. At the same time, the move has

---

[3] We qualify these claims because we recognize that interpersonal relationship can be maintained at a distance and that people sometimes return to their old haunts. However, it seems likely that these post-transition experiences are marked as being exceptional.

created a number of new T-DECs and has established the conditions for the introduction of many more.

In describing a local-move scenario, we have focused on change that involves the large-scale, if partial, introduction and termination of T-DECs. However, in contrast to the transcontinental move described above, these changes are carried out against a stable backdrop of unaffected T-DECs. The commute still leads to the same workplace, job, and colleagues; the social network remains intact; and the move is unlikely to affect the availability of previously favored consumer goods, cultural activities, or recreations.

There are two important points here. The first is that transitions are graded. Some transitions radically alter the fabric of daily life, abruptly redefining much of what a person experiences on a daily basis (e.g., relocation to a distant city). Others bring about many changes (e.g., becoming a parent), but leave many aspects of a person's life intact. Still others are very focused, affecting only one aspect of a person's life or at most a few (e.g., joining a swim team).

The second point is that transitions differ in the way that they affect the current stock of active T-DECs. Some diminish this stock. For example, when a good friend moves away, it will disrupt what had previously been regular social interactions and might spell the end of shared recreations. Other transitions augment our supply of active T-DECs. Consider a person who has acquired a dog for the first time. This individual is plunged into a new world, one with its own consumer culture (pet stores, dog toys), social circle (the neighborhood dog people, the local veterinarian), and required activities (dog walks, feedings, grooming). These kinds of transitions are single-sided as they either add or subtract T-DECs to or from the existing stock.

As pointed out above, there are also transitions that simultaneously terminate one set of T-DECs and enable the creation of another set. These double-sided transitions come in two forms. One type terminates a set of T-DECs associated with a particular theme while establishing the conditions for the acquisition of a new set of T-DECs of the same theme – a new set of TDECs is substituted for the old set. The local-move scenario provides one example of this sort of transition since T-DECs associated with living at the old house will most likely be replaced by a similar set of T-DECs after moving into the new one.

There are also double-sided transitions that mark an end to one period and initiate the beginning of a new period of a different sort. The transitions that involve major role changes are often of this type. Some of these are normative (e.g., marriage, parenthood, retirement), others are not (e.g., a major illness, incarceration), but they all bring about important changes in the fabric of daily life. Married people do many things that they did not do when they were single and do not do many things they used to do; likewise, for parents, retirees, patients, and convicts. People sometimes undergo less important transitions that have the same structure. For example, a time-pressed and cash-strapped student who quits the chess club to take on a part-time job would undergo such a transition. Regardless of their impact, transitions of this sort have two things in common: they terminate one set of T-DECs and enable the establishment of a qualitatively different set of T-DECs.

In summary, we conceptualize transitions as being graded depending on how extensively they impact the current stock of active T-DECs; we recognize that transitions can be single-sided or double-sided, depending on how T-DECs are added to or subtracted from that stock; and we distinguish between double-sided transitions that involve thematically related or thematically unrelated changes in T-DEC content. This framework is useful because it allows us to describe and categorize different transitions. For example, our Dutch participants experienced a major double-sided transition in 1940. In this case, the transition involved the extinction of many old T-DECs and the creation and imposition of many T-DECs of a sort not previously experienced.

Themed periods

Transition theory distinguishes between major lifetime periods and what might be called *themed periods*. Again, a lifetime period represents a span of time during which there is a high degree of stability in the fabric of daily life. These periods are marked by major transitions that simultaneously affect many aspects of a person's life, and provide the backdrop against which minor transitions are carried out. In contrast, themed periods are created by transitions that affect a single aspect of a person's life, or sometimes a few highly integrated aspects.

These periods are themed in two senses. First, when a person undergoes a themed transition, the T-DECs it creates are obviously related to one another – they share a common theme (e.g., people, places, and activities related to a particular job). Second, across their lifetimes, people often experience a number of periods from the same thematic class – they hold more than one job; they live in more than one house; they involve themselves in more than one serious relationship. We assume that people know the relative ordering of periods sharing a common theme and can identify the major lifetime period(s) during which each occurred. In addition, it seems that people can often place the transitional events that define the onset and offset of a given themed period relative to those that define the onset and offset of the contemporaneous lifetime period (e.g., "I was involved with D. [relationship theme] during my last few years in Chicago [major lifetime period]," "I bought my first house [residence theme] a few years after moving to Edmonton [major lifetime period]").

Transition theory and existing accounts of autobiographical memory

In brief, transition theory holds that transitional events structure autobiographical memory, and it defines transitions in a functional manner. On the current view, transitions are events that alter the fabric of daily life and their importance is gauged by the impact they have the current stock of active T-DECs – important transitions cause the addition or termination of a large number T-DECs; unimportant ones affect only a few. This approach recognizes that a wide variety of events can play a transitional role and that these events can differ in terms of normative status, predictability, goal-relatedness, and the number of people affected. Transition theory also implies that nominally similar events can sometimes differ greatly in their transitional impact.[4]

To the best of our knowledge, the functional approach to transitions that is at the core of transition theory is a novel one. Nonetheless, there are obvious links between this account and the existing literature. We conclude this section by mentioning several of them. First, we use the term "major lifetime period" in much the same way that Barsalou (1988) uses the term "extended-event time line" and Reiser uses the term "era" (Reiser, Black, and Kalamarides, 1986). Second, we use the term "themed period" in much the same way that Conway uses the term "lifetime period" (Conway, 2005, this volume; Conway and Pleydell-Pearce, 2000), Thomsen uses the term "life chapter" (Thomsen and Berntsen, 2008), and Linton uses the term "extenditure" (Linton, 1986). Third, on the current view, most "life-script events" (e.g., getting married, having children, first job; Berntsen and Bohn, 2009; Berntsen and Rubin, 2004; Rubin and Berntsen, 2003) would be considered "transitional events," though there are also important transitions that are not part of the life script. Fourth, several researchers have noted that people represent their knowledge of repeated events sequences in autobiographical memory. Barsalou (1988) refers to these structures as "summarized events"; Neisser (1981) refers to them as "repisodes"; and Conway identifies them as one type of "general event" (Conway and Pleydell-Pearce,

---

[4] Consider, for example, the marriage of two people who have cohabited for several years. It is likely that this event would have less transitional impact than the marriage of two people who have never lived together.

2000). In transition theory, these representations have their counterpart in activity-based T-DECs. Fifth, T-DECs that pick out individuated aspects of our material experience (i.e., specific people, places, and things) have also been identified in the literature; Linton (1986) calls them "elements," and Barsalou (1988) calls them "exemplars."

A final point of possible overlap moves us from theories that concern the organization of autobiographical memory to those that concern the process of event dating. These latter theories assume that people typically date personal events by relating them to *temporal landmarks* (Brown, 1990; Friedman, 1993; Shum, 1998; Thompson *et al.*, 1996). We suspect that most temporal landmarks are transitional events and that major transitions play a more important role in event dating than minor ones.

Historically defined autobiographical periods as major lifetime periods

Earlier, we claimed that historically defined autobiographical periods are lifetime periods that arise when (and where) public events have caused a profound and enduring change in the fabric of daily life. We can now restate this claim in terms of transition theory. On this view, historically defined autobiographical periods are formed the same way personally defined autobiographical periods are formed. Simply put, such periods are spawned by public events that put an end to one way of life and give rise to another; they terminate a large number of pre-existing T-DECs and establish conditions that lead to the creation of a large number of new T-DECs.

Consider how the invasion of the Netherlands impacted the individuals and families concerned. Dutch citizens would go on to see the price of vegetables treble even as the quality of foodstuffs (and their health) deteriorated, their ration of soap slashed by half just as tuberculosis, diphtheria, dysentery, and influenza became epidemic, and the availability of fuel drop by 90% when average winter temperatures were barely above 1°C. By 1945 the Dutch way of life had become so impoverished that the Danes donated to them over 43,000 pairs of used shoes, 2,000 kettles, and 200,000 pieces of cutlery (Futselaar, 2008). Many farmers, who had been comparatively fortunate, ultimately saw livelihoods disappear when their fields were flooded by the Germans as a defensive measure. At the same time these effects were overlaid by the imposition of a new system of regulations and restrictions aimed at totalitarian control over Dutch society (*Gleichschaltung*), and men were forced to leave home to work in German factories (*Arbeitseinsatz*). Added to this human catastrophe were civilians unfortunate enough to live in the path of the Atlantic Wall defenses, who were forcibly evacuated – such as residents of The Hague, where 65,000 people were removed and over 25,000 houses destroyed or commandeered. By any measure, the Dutch transition from freedom to occupation signaled the end of one way of life, and the beginning of something very different.

In contrast to epoch-defining events like World War II or the siege of Sarajevo, public events, even very important ones like the 9/11 attacks on the World Trade Center, will not spawn historically defined autobiographical periods if they do not terminate one set of T-DECs and establish another in its place. We do not deny that such events can have lasting effects. We know that people remember important public events (Booth, 1971; Findahl and Hoijer, 1985; Schuman and Scott, 1989), that such events sometimes give rise to flashbulb memories (Berntsen and Thomsen, 2005; R. Brown and Kulik, 1977; Conway, Anderson, Larsen, et al., 1994; Hirst et al., 2009; Lee and Brown, 2003), and that they can alter public opinion and have a negative impact on mental health (Galea, Viahov, Resnick, et al., 2003; Li and Brewer, 2004; Schuster, Stein, Jaycox, et al., 2001). In addition, we suspect that some of these events create their own collective *interludes*. For example, there is evidence that the 9/11 attacks were followed by a brief period during which people shifted their attention from the personal sphere to the public sphere and engaged in memorable activities unique to that period (Cohn, Mehl, and Pennebaker, 2004; Mehl and Pennebaker, 2003). However, because such interludes are followed by a return to "business as usual," they do not spawn historically defined autobiographical periods.

We believe that historically defined autobiographical periods are formed by the same processes as other major lifetime periods. However, we also acknowledge that they differ from conventional epochs in several potentially important ways. First, the living-in-history project demonstrates that historically defined autobiographical periods formation is driven by external events, events over which the individual has little or no control. In contrast, the transitions that give rise to conventional lifetime periods are often goal-related, reflecting an individual's actions, motives, and decisions (Conway, 2005). Second, to date, we have only observed the formation of historically defined autobiographical periods in response to negative events – wars and natural disasters – whereas conventional lifetime periods are defined by both positive (e.g., graduation) and negative events (e.g., death of a spouse). Third, events that spawn historically defined autobiographical periods affect a large segment of society, simultaneously altering the lives of many people regardless of their age, sex, or class. This is not the case with transitions that generate conventional lifetime periods; such events generally operate at the level of the individual, though there are some that affect families (e.g., divorce), tight-knit social networks (e.g., lay-offs at work), or age cohorts (e.g., graduation).

At present we do not know whether any or all of these features are necessary for creating and maintaining historically defined autobiograph-ical periods or whether one or all are related to the magnitude of the living-in-history effect. Thus, a more detailed investigation of these issues is required. However, in the absence of evidence to the contrary and given the parallel role transitions appear to play in defining historically defined autobiographical periods and personally defined autobiographical peri-ods, it makes sense to treat them as being fundamentally the same type of structure.

Conclusion

We initiated the current line of research because we wanted to understand the relationship between history and autobiographical memory. Above we reviewed research indicating that historically significant public events can have an enduring effect on the organization of autobiographical memory, sometimes leading to the creation of historically defined autobiographical periods. This research also indicated that the formation of these periods is the exception rather than the rule. We have found that historically defined autobiographical periods occur only when public events produce a marked change in how people live and only in places where these changes are most directly felt.

The discovery of historically defined autobiographical periods raised two sets of issues. One concerned the role these periods play in defining collective memories and altering and/or reinforcing group identity; we have speculated briefly about these topics elsewhere (Brown *et al.*, 2009; Brown and Lee, 2010; Svob and Brown, in press; Zebian and Brown, 2012). The second set concerned the origins and nature of historically defined autobiographical periods and the implications their existence has for an understanding of the organization of autobiographical memory.

It was the consideration of this second set of issues that led us to transition theory. This account is committed to three central claims. The first is that T-DECs are the fundamental building blocks of autobio-graphical memory; the second is that autobiographical memory is organ-ized by transitional events, events that change the fabric of daily life by terminating one set of T-DECs and/or enabling another; and the third is that transitions are graded, some affecting only one aspect of a person's life and others affecting many.

Admittedly, there are a number of important issues that are not covered by this position. For example, at present, transition theory is not concerned with the retrieval of autobiographical memories (Berntsen, this volume; Uzer, Lee, and Brown, in press) or with the processes that associate event memories with one another to create event clusters (Brown, 2005; Brown and Schopflocher, 1998a, 1998b) and other narrative-like structures (Bruner, 1991; Burt, Kemp, and Conway, 2003; Robinson, 1992; Schank and Abelson, 1995). Also, there are important issues concerning the ways people generalize over experiences to create abstract period knowledge that have not yet been addressed (Barsalou, 1988; Reiser *et al.*, 1986). Despite these gaps, we feel that the current approach advances theory in this area by assigning transitional events a central role in the organization of autobiographical memory. Put another way, this research has led us to realize that the organization of autobiographical memory necessarily tracks the organization of our lives, and that our lives are necessarily organized by the transitions we experience.

References

Barsalou, L.W. (1988). The content and organization of autobiographical memories. In U. Neisser and E. Winograd (eds.), *Remembering reconsidered: ecological and traditional approaches to the study of memory* (pp. 193–243). Cambridge University Press.

Bar-Tal, D. (2007). Sociopsychological foundations of intractable conflicts. *American Behavioral Scientist*, **50**, 1430–1453.

Belli, R. F. (1998). The structure of autobiographical memory and the event history calendar: potential improvements in the quality of retrospective reports in surveys. *Memory*, **6**, 383–406.

Berntsen, D., and Bohn. A. (2009). Cultural life scripts and individual life stories. In P. Boyer and J. V. Wertsch (eds.), *Memory in mind and culture* (pp. 62–82). Cambridge University Press.

Berntsen, D. and Rubin, D. (2004). Cultural life scripts structure recall from autobiographical memory. *Memory & Cognition*, **32**, 427–442.

Berntsen, D. and Thomsen, D. K. (2005). Personal memories for remote historical events: accuracy and clarity of flashbulb memories related to World War II. *Journal of Experimental Psychology: General*, **134**, 242–257.

Blaikie, P., Cannon, T., Davis, I., and Wisner, B. (1994). *At risk: natural hazards, people's vulnerability and disasters*. London: Routledge.

Booth, A. (1971). The recall of news items. *Public Opinion Quarterly*, **34**, 604–610.

Brown, N. R. (1990). Organization of public events in long-term memory. *Journal of Experimental Psychology: General*, **119**, 297–314.

(2005). On the prevalence of event clusters in autobiographical memory. *Social Cognition*, **23**, 35–69.

Brown, N. R. and Lee, P. J. (2010). Public events and the organization of autobiographical memory: an overview of the living-in-history project. *Behavioral Sciences of Terrorism and Political Aggression*, **2**, 133–149.

Brown, N. R., Lee, P. J., Krslak, M., Conrad, F. G., Hansen, T., Havelka, J., and Reddon, J. (2009). Living in history: how war, terrorism, and natural disaster affect the organization of autobiographical memory. *Psychological Science*, 20, 399–405.

Brown, N. R. and Schopflocher, D. (1998a). Event clusters: an organization of personal events in long-term memory. *Psychological Science*, 9, 470–475.

(1998b). Event cueing, event clusters, and the temporal distribution of autobiographical memories. *Applied Cognitive Psychology*, 12, 305–319.

Brown, R. and Kulik, J. (1977). Flashbulb memories. *Cognition*, 5, 73–99.

Bruner, J. (1991). The narrative construction of reality. *Critical Inquiry*, 18, 1–21.

Burt, C. D. B., Kemp, S., and Conway, M. A. (2003). Themes, events, and episodes in autobiographical memory. *Memory & Cognition*, 31, 317–325.

Cairns, E., and Roe, M. D. (ed.) (2003). *The role of memory in ethnic conflict*. New York: Palgrave Macmillan.

Cohn, M. A., Mehl, M. R., and Pennebaker, J. W. (2004). Linguistic markers of psychological change surrounding September 11, 2001. *Psychological Science*, 15, 687–693.

Conway, M. A. (2005). Memory and the self. *Journal of Memory and Language*, 53, 594–628.

Conway, M. A., Anderson, S. J., Larsen, S. F., Donnelly, C. M., McDaniel, M. A., McClelland, A., *et al.* (1994). The formation of flashbulb memories. *Memory & Cognition*, 22, 326–343.

Conway, M. A. and Pleydell-Pearce, C. W. (2000). The construction of autobiographical memories in the self-memory system. *Psychological Review*, 107, 261–288.

Conway, M. A. and Rubin, D. C. (1993). The structure of autobiographical memory. In A. E. Collins, S. E. Gathercole, M. A. Conway, and P. E. M. Morris (eds.), *Theories of memory* (pp. 103–137). Mahwah, NJ: Lawrence Erlbaum Associates.

Findahl, O. and Hoijer, B. (1985). Some characteristics of news memory and comprehension. *Journal of Broadcasting and Electronic Media*, 29, 379–396.

Friedman, W. J. (1993). Memory for the time of past events. *Psychological Bulletin*, 35, 1–36.

Futselaar, R. (2008). *Lard, lice, and longevity: the standard of living in occupied Denmark and the Netherlands, 1940–1945*. Amsterdam: Askant.

Galea, S., Vlahov, D., Resnick, H., Ahern, J., Susser, E., Gold, J., *et al.* (2003). Trends of probable post-traumatic stress disorder in New York City after the September 11 terrorist attacks. *American Journal of Epidemiology*, 158, 514–524.

Giltner, P. (2001). The success of collaboration: Denmark's self-assessment of its economic position after five years of Nazi occupation. *Journal of Contemporary History*, 36, 485–506.

Halbwachs, M. (1992). *On collective memory*. L. Coser (trans.). University of Chicago Press.

Hastie, R. and Kumar, P. A. (1979). Person memory: personality traits as organizing principles in memory for behaviors. *Journal of Personality and Social Psychology*, 37, 25–38.

Hirst, W., Phelps, E. A., Buckner, R. L., Budson, A. E., Cuc, A., Gabrieli, J. D. E., *et al.* (2009). Long-term memory for the terrorist attack of September 11: flashbulb memories, event memories, and the factors that influence their retention. *Journal of Experimental Psychology: General*, **138**, 161–176.

Hobson, C. J. and Delunas, L. (2001). National norms and life-event frequencies for the revised Social Readjustment Rating Scale. *International Journal of Stress Management*, **8**, 299–314.

Holmes, T. H. and Rahe, R. H. (1967). The Social Readjustment Rating Scale. *Journal of Psychosomatic Research*, **11**, 213–218.

Lee, P. J. and Brown, N. R. (2003). Delay related changes in personal memories for September 11th 2001. *Applied Cognitive Psychology*, **17**, 1007–1015.

Levy, B. S. and Sidel, V. W. (eds.) (1997). *War and public health*. New York: Oxford University Press.

Li, Q. and Brewer, M. B. (2004). What does it mean to be an American? Patriotism, nationalism, and American identity after 9/11. *Political Psychology*, **25**, 727–739.

Linton, M. (1986). Ways of searching and the contents of memory. In D. C. Rubin (ed.), *Autobiographical memory* (pp. 50–67). Cambridge University Press.

Loftus, E. F. and Marburger, W. (1983). Since the eruption of Mt. St. Helens, has anyone beaten you up? Improving the accuracy of retrospective reports with landmark events. *Memory & Cognition*, **11**, 114–120.

McNally, R. J. (2003). *Remembering trauma*. Cambridge, MA: Belknap Press/ Harvard University Press.

Mehl, M. R. and Pennebaker, J. W. (2003). The social dynamics of a cultural upheaval: social interactions surrounding September 11, 2001. *Psychological Science*, **14**, 579–558.

Neisser, U. (1981). John Dean's memory: a case study. *Cognition*, **9**, 1–22.

Nourkova, V. V. and Bernstein, D. M. (2010). Why historical becomes personal? Spontaneous historical content of individual autobiographical memory. In Y. P. Zinchenko and V. F. Petrenko (eds.), *Psychology in Russia: state of the art – 2010* (pp. 1–21). Moscow: Lomonosov Moscow State University.

Reiser, B., Black, J., and Kalamarides, R. (1986). Strategic memory search processes. In D. C. Rubin (ed.), *Autobiographical memory* (pp. 100–121). New York: Cambridge University Press.

Robinson, J. A. (1992). First experience memories: context and functions in personal histories. In M. A. Conway, D. C. Rubin, H. Spinnler, and W. A. Wagenaar (eds.), *Theoretical perspective on autobiographical memory* (pp. 223–239). Dordrecht: Kluwer.

Rubin, D. C. and Berntsen, D. (2003). Life scripts help to maintain autobiographical memories of highly positive, but not highly negative, events. *Memory & Cognition*, **31**, 1–14.

Rubin, D. C. and Schulkind, M. D. (1997). The distribution of autobiographical memories across the lifespan. *Memory & Cognition*, **25**, 859–866.

Schank, R. C. and Abelson, R. P. (1995). Knowledge and memory: the real story. In R. S. Wyer (ed.), *Advances in social cognition*, vol. VII (pp. 1–85). Hillsdale, NJ: Erlbaum.

Schuman, H. and Scott, J. (1989). Generations and collective memories. *American Sociological Review*, **54**, 359–381.

Schuster, M. A., Stein, B. D., Jaycox, L., Collins, R. L., Marshall, G. N., Elliott, M. N., *et al.* (2001). A national survey of stress reactions after the September 11, 2001, terrorist attacks. *New England Journal of Medicine*, **345** (20), 1507–1512.

Shum, M. (1998). The role of temporal landmarks in autobiographical memory processes. *Psychological Bulletin*, **124**, 423–442.

Svob, C. and Brown, N. R. (in press). Intergenerational transmission of the reminiscence bump and biographical conflict knowledge. *Psychological Science*.

Thompson, C. P., Skowronski, J. J., Larsen, S. F., and Betz, A. (1996). *Autobiographical memory: remembering what and remembering when*. Mahwah, NJ: Lawrence Erlbaum Associates.

Thomsen, D. K. and Berntsen, D. (2008). The cultural life scripts and life story chapters contributed to the reminiscence bump. *Memory*, **16**, 420–435.

Uzer, T., Lee, P. J., and Brown, N. R. (in press). On the prevalence of directly retrieved autobiographical memories. *Journal of Experimental Psychology: Learning, Memory, and Cognition*, **38**.

Zebian, S. and Brown, N. R. (2012). *Living in history in Lebanon: the influence of chronic social upheaval on the organization of autobiographical memories*. Under review.

10 Directive functions of autobiographical memory: theory and method

David B. Pillemer and Kie J. Kuwabara

In 1929, at the age of 4 years, prominent African-American activist Malcolm X experienced a horrifying event that became his "earliest vivid memory":

I remember being suddenly snatched awake into a frightening confusion of pistol shots and shouting and smoke and flames. My father had shouted and shot at the two white men who had set the fire and were running away. Our home was burning down around us. We were lunging and bumping and tumbling all over each other trying to escape. My mother, with the baby in her arms, just made it into the yard before the house crashed in, showering sparks. I remember we were outside in the night in our underwear, crying and yelling our heads off. The white police and firemen came and stood around watching as the house burned down to the ground. (Malcolm X, 1965, pp. 5–6)

Why was this early childhood experience so memorable? One answer to this question focuses on well-known and carefully studied mental and affective processes known to enhance memory vividness (e.g., Rubin and Kozin, 1984). The episode was highly emotional; it was distinctive and unique; it carried immense personal and familial importance; and as a result it was repeatedly thought about, talked about, and written about in the years that followed. The memory represents these qualities so strongly that it would be far more difficult to explain its absence than its prominent place in Malcolm's life history.

A second answer to the question of why the episode was vividly remembered focuses on *adaptive functions* rather than *mental processes*. Autobiographical memory is much more than a passive record of things that happened years ago – it also actively influences current thoughts, attitudes, and behaviors. Malcolm X's memory seemed to anchor a continuing set of attitudes and deeply felt feelings that helped to set the course of his career as an activist and leader (Pillemer, 1998, pp. 75–76). He referred back to episodes of childhood trauma and harassment when speaking publicly about racial hatred and injustice (Malcolm X, 1965, p. 6).

Mainstream research on the psychology of memory has focused primarily on cognitive and affective mechanisms – *how* memories are kept alive by mental activities and emotional reactions. This chapter focuses instead on recent work on functional or adaptive significance – *why* remembering distinctive personal episodes is valuable for survival and life enrichment. Certain properties of life events – emotional salience, distinctiveness, and personal importance – enhance memory vividness. Vivid memories in turn support important life functions, one of which is to inform, guide, or direct present and future behaviors (Pillemer, 1998, 2003, 2009). Malcolm's memories of childhood trauma served as a painful warning of the real dangers posed by a culture that was unsympathetic and vengeful toward African-Americans, and encouraged protective and even aggressive countermeasures on his part in the years that followed.

In this chapter we examine the functional approach to autobiographical memory. We begin by exploring the origins of current scientific work on memory functions. We then describe prominent functions identified by memory theorists and researchers. Next, we focus our analysis on directive functions. We identify strengths and weaknesses of several empirical strategies for examining memory directives: case studies, self-report surveys, correlational studies, and experiments. We propose a new methodological framework for designing and evaluating experimental studies of directive functions. Finally, we suggest ways to increase the ecological validity of research on memory functions.

Origins of the functional approach to autobiographical memory

Current scientific interest in autobiographical memory functions was piqued by several landmark publications (see Pillemer, 1998, ch. 1; Pillemer, 2009, for more complete histories). Brown and Kulik's (1977) classic paper on *flashbulb memories* explored people's recollections of their own personal circumstances when they learned of unexpected events, such as the assassination of a US president or the untimely death of a close relative. Subsequent research on flashbulb memories has focused primarily on mechanisms supporting memory vividness and persistence, including the roles played by emotion, surprise, importance, and rehearsal. Yet Brown and Kulik were especially interested in functional questions. They asked, "When – ever – would such memories have had survival value?" (p. 97). Their explanation emphasized the adaptive advantages of remembering vivid details of emotional and important events. For example, information contained in a memory of a life-threatening episode may provide a blueprint for avoiding similar dangers in the future.

Brown and Kulik's paper was followed closely by the publication of Neisser's influential book, *Memory Observed* (1982a). Neisser presented a collection of studies examining memories of everyday events rather than memories of laboratory stimuli. Neisser (1982b) also pointedly questioned Brown and Kulik's preferred functional explanation for flashbulb memories. Rather than focusing on survival value, Neisser emphasized the personal and interpersonal benefits of remembering and sharing stories of momentous past events. This public debate between prominent leaders in psychology helped to expand the almost exclusive focus on memory mechanisms to include questions about functional significance.

Interest in memory functions was sharpened further by Baddeley's (1988) paper provocatively titled, "But what the hell is it for?" Like Neisser, Baddeley is well known for his seminal contributions to experimental cognitive psychology, and his admonition to examine the underlying value of autobiographical remembering helped to validate the functional approach. Baddeley's own analysis highlighted identity-building features of retaining personal memories: "If you lose contact with your past, then presumably you lose contact with much of yourself" (1988, p. 13).

The study of autobiographical memory functions also was advanced by an increased emphasis on the narrative study of lives and stories (e.g., Bruner, 1986, 1987; McAdams, 1993; Schank, 1990; Spence, 1982) and on memory models that feature representations of the self (e.g., Conway and Pleydell-Pearce, 2000; Singer and Salovey, 1993). Experimental research on memory had focused primarily on recall of impersonal information presented by an experimenter in a laboratory setting. Broadening the scope of research topics to include memories of authentic life experiences led naturally to questions about function, including how remembering supports or undermines a stable and healthy sense of self.

A shared interest in memory functions could provide an important bridge between contemporary researchers embracing laboratory and narrative approaches. For example, Nairne, Pandeirada, and Thompson (2008) introduced the term "adaptive memory" to describe enhanced recall of experimentally presented words that were processed with respect to their relevance to survival needs. Schacter and Addis (2007) cited neuroimaging studies in support of a possible connection between episodic memory and the ability to imagine future events (also see D'Argembeau, this volume). Their observation that "the past is useful only to the extent that it allows us to anticipate what may happen in the future" (p. 27) fits well with work on directive functions of autobiographical memory to be described in this chapter. Functional theories may be enriched by closer intellectual connections between memory researchers representing different methodological perspectives.

What is an autobiographical memory function?

There are at least two meanings of the term *autobiographical memory function* (Bruce, 1985, 1989; Pillemer, 1998, 2009). First, function can refer to practical applications, such as the role played by memory in legal testimony or treatment of psychiatric disorders. Examples demonstrating the real-world usefulness of research on autobiographical memories are plentiful (Pillemer, 2009). This chapter also addresses a second meaning of memory function: its adaptive or evolutionary significance, survival value, or contribution to fitness and life enrichment. Theoretical analyses have identified several prominent categories of memory functions, and researchers have begun to examine these functions empirically. This new work is promising, although shortcomings are also apparent and additional conceptual development is needed.

Defining autobiographical memory functions

Building on the work of Brown and Kulik (1977) and Neisser (1982b), Pillemer (1992) identified three broad categories of memory functions. *Communicative* functions involve sharing personal memories with others in order to convey special meaning and achieve interpersonal goals. *Psychodynamic* functions target the emotional and psychological impact of remembering past episodes. *Directive* functions are operative when specific autobiographical memories guide or direct present or future attitudes and behaviors.

Current theoretical models of autobiographical memory functions have retained these three general categories, but with significant modifications. Bluck and colleagues (Bluck, 2003; Bluck and Alea, 2002; Bluck, Alea, Habermas, *et al.*, 2005) identified social, self, and directive functions:
- *Social functions* facilitate interpersonal interactions through memory sharing.
- *Self functions* promote personal identity and support a sense of coherence or continuity over time.
- *Directive functions* involve using memories to make decisions in the present and to guide future behaviors.

The three functional categories are defined broadly and rather imprecisely. For example, social functions include such diverse communicative goals as enhancing feelings of intimacy (Alea and Bluck, 2007) and persuading the listener (Pillemer, 1992). In addition, some unique functions may not be fully captured by the three categories (Bluck, 2003; Pillemer, 2009), including emotional regulation (e.g., Pasupathi, 2003) or boredom reduction (Webster, 2003). A promising alternative research strategy, discussed later in this chapter, involves shifting the focus from broad functional categories to more precisely defined and measurable effects of memory on feelings, attitudes, and behaviors.

Examining directive functions of autobiographical memory

In this section we describe and evaluate four empirical strategies for examining directive functions of autobiographical memory: case studies, surveys, correlational studies, and experiments. Although the primary focus is on directive functions, we extend our analysis to social and self functions when appropriate parallels exist.

Case studies

Directive functions are well illustrated by memories published in celebrity interviews and autobiographies and recounted by participants in research studies. For example, consider the career of renowned basketball player Michael Jordan. Jordan's accomplishments are legendary. He led his Chicago Bulls professional team to six league championships, he was a five-time league most valuable player, and he won two gold medals playing for the US Olympic team. How was Jordan able to achieve at such a high level? He had great physical size, strength, and agility; close and supportive relationships with his parents; a healthy sibling rivalry with his talented older brother Larry; and superb coaches at the college and professional levels.

Jordan was not the only aspiring athlete who is physically gifted, and had strong family support and excellent mentors. What made him different? Some observers identified his unusual ability to motivate himself – where did this come from? Jordan described how he used a memory of a momentous failure to provide continuing motivation (Pillemer, 1998). As a teenager, he experienced the shock of not making his high-school basketball team:

It was embarrassing, not making that team. They posted the roster and it was there for a long, long time without my name on it. I remember being really mad, too, because there was a guy who made it that really wasn't as good as me . . . Whenever I was working out and got tired and figured I ought to stop, I'd close my eyes and see that list in the locker room without my name on it, and that usually got me going again. (May, 1991, p. 105)

Part of Jordan's own explanation for his famous work ethic is his purposeful and strategic recall of this humiliating formative event. It suggests one answer to Alan Baddeley's (1988) famous question: "But what the hell is it [memory] for?" For Jordan, the memory served a directive function: it informed and motivated future behaviors.

Michael Jordan was a one-of-a-kind athlete, yet his purposeful use of autobiographical memory is by no means unique. Jonathan Papelbon, a star pitcher for the Boston Red Sox professional baseball team, also used a memory of a humiliating defeat as a continuing source of inspiration. Papelbon's role on the Red Sox is to pitch effectively at the end of games, and in a key contest in 2009 he failed miserably, ending the Red Sox season. In an interview after the game, Papelbon was already thinking about the next season, and how to use his failure memory as motivation:

When I leave the clubhouse, I won't take anything home, or to the off-season with me. But when you do go home for an off-season after [a season] ends the way it did today, I will definitely, definitely remember this situation when I'm in the weight room [exercising]. Who knows? I may be playing this on TV when I'm in the weight room for motivation ... I'm going to use this as fuel. (Ryan, 2009, p. C12)

Using memories to direct, motivate, or improve performance is not limited to accomplished athletes. One college student's memory focused on a relatively mundane but uncomfortable ethical breach in an art history course:

I wrote about a sculpture from a picture I had, rather than going to the museum to view it as we had been instructed. When I received the paper back it had no grade, but instead a note which said 'see me.' Upon meeting with the instructor I was informed that the piece about which I wrote was currently being restored. Since I had not followed instructions and written about a piece I had seen, I was required to write another paper. In addition to being extremely embarrassed, I learned a valuable lesson about not taking short-cuts. (Pillemer, Picariello, Law, et al., 1996, p. 331)

All three examples portray a lesson generated by a disappointment or mishap of some kind – illustrating what Roger Schank (1999) has called "failure-driven memory." The case illustrations are consistent with the more general finding that memories serving a directive function frequently are associated with negative emotions (Rasmussen and Berntsen, 2009). But directive memories are not limited to negative events. A final example recounted by a college graduate illustrates how a positive moment can provide continuing inspiration:

[A professor] said to us that the most talented people he'd ever known in his life he had seen come through his classrooms at Wellesley, and the obvious high esteem in which he held Wellesley students was an added boost to me. My self-esteem and self-awareness of my own abilities has not ever been low, but in moments since my Wellesley years when my own doubts, or the doubts of others as to my ability to do something have bothered me, I hear this man's words and know I can give it as good a try as *anyone* else could. (Pillemer *et al.*, 1996, p. 331)

The potential directive effects of specific memories are apparent in case examples taken from a diverse array of individuals and life contexts (Pillemer, 1998, 2001, 2003; Pillemer *et al.*, 1996). Yet case-based evidence is lacking in several respects. First, directive functions are identified somewhat informally, without a precise operational definition or formal coding scheme to guide the analysis. Second, isolated cases illustrate how particular memories can offer continuing guidance and inspiration, but they do not provide an estimate of how frequently directive functions occur during everyday remembering. Third, the person providing the memory frequently identifies a causal connection between the recounted event and later attitudes and behaviors, but case examples do not have the power to establish causality. In the example given earlier in this chapter, Michael Jordan believed that the memory of failing to make his high-school basketball team inspired him to work harder, but we will never know the intensity of Jordan's work ethic if he had made that team instead.

Surveys

In an effort to obtain systematic information about autobiographical memory functions, researchers have constructed questionnaires that assess respondents' self-reported memory activities. The Reminiscence Functions Scale (RFS) developed by Webster (Robitaille, Cappeliez, Coulombe, *et al.*, 2010; Webster, 1993, 1995, 2003) contains 43 items representing different purposes of reminiscence, defined for respondents as "the process of recalling memories from our personal past" (Robitaille *et al.*, 2010, p. 186); for each item, respondents rate on a 6-point scale how frequently they reminiscence for that particular purpose. Webster and colleagues identified eight distinct reminiscence functions: boredom reduction, death preparation, identity, problem-solving, conversation, intimacy maintenance, bitterness revival, and teach/inform (Robitaille *et al.*, 2010). For example, a problem-solving item assesses how frequently reminiscence is used to "help resolve some current difficulty." Because some RFS items reflect memory functions that may be prevalent among older adults, its applicability to younger age groups may be somewhat limited. In particular, items targeting death preparation (e.g., reminiscing "because it gives me a sense of personal completion or wholeness as I approach the end of life") and teach/inform (e.g., reminiscing "to teach younger family members what life was like when I was young and living in a different time") appear to be less relevant to the everyday concerns of young adults. Accordingly, Webster and McCall (1999) found that ratings of both the death preparation and teach/inform functions increased with age.

The Thinking About Life Experiences (TALE) questionnaire (Bluck et al., 2005) was designed to examine the three theoretically motivated autobiographical memory functions – social, self, and directive – described earlier in this chapter. For each of 28 test items, respondents are instructed to rate on 6-point scales how often they "think back over or talk about my life or certain periods of my life" for a particular purpose. Notably, this request identifies activities associated with general life review, which can include but are not limited to remembering specific episodes. Example items include "when I want to develop a closer relationship with someone" (social function), "when I want to understand who I am now" (self function), and "when I want to make plans for the future" (directive function). Statistical analyses of college student responses identified four factors: directive, self-continuity, nurturing relationships, and developing relationships. The authors concluded that the directive function is broader than originally defined; the self function focused narrowly on self-continuity; and the social function is composed of two components (nurturing and developing relationships). Mean scores (averaged across items) for how often students thought about or talked about the past to fulfill different functions were 3.62 (developing relationships), 3.86 (directive function), 4.01 (self-continuity), and 4.70 (nurturing relationships), where 3 = seldom, 4 = occasionally, and 5 = often.

Although surveys indicate that people intentionally use reminiscence or life review to fulfill theoretically derived functions, questionnaire studies share several basic limitations (Bluck et al., 2005; Pillemer, 2003, 2009). First, the test items only tap purposeful or deliberate memory activities, thereby excluding functions that operate relatively automatically. Memories that direct or influence attitudes and behaviors may come to mind spontaneously, without a conscious attempt to retrieve them for a particular purpose (also see Berntsen, this volume). Second, survey ratings depend on people's metacognitive ability to accurately estimate how often they use memory for different purposes. How do respondents decide how often they think or talk about the past for example, "to understand who I am now" or "to make plans for the future"? When memory activities are difficult to count or quantify, the validity of frequency estimates is questionable. Third, functional analyses based on questionnaires depend directly on which items happen to be included in the survey. For example, self items tapping self-continuity may produce different results than self items focusing on self-enhancement (Pillemer,

2009). Broadly defined functions (such as using memories when making decisions) may produce different frequency estimates than functions defined more precisely (such as using memories when deciding on a location for your next vacation). Limitations of questionnaire studies qualify conclusions about both absolute and relative frequencies of autobiographical memory functions.

Correlational approaches

Directive functions are evident when past episodes are recalled during the process of solving current problems (e.g., Bluck *et al.*, 2005; Pillemer, 2003). Some researchers have elicited self-reports of memory use and then looked for an association between memory and successful task performance. In particular, the role played by episodic memory in problem solving has been examined in two domains: classroom tests and social problem-solving tasks.

Although educational research has focused primarily on the acquisition of general or factual knowledge, several studies document the significant role played by episodic learning and memory in academic contexts (Conway, Gardiner, Perfect, *et al.*, 1997; Herbert and Burt, 2004; MacKenzie and White, 1982; Nuthall and Alton-Lee, 1995). For example, when elementary and middle-school students talk aloud as they solve test items, they frequently refer to an original classroom learning episode, including how the lesson was presented and what the teacher and other students said (Nuthall and Alton-Lee, 1995). Importantly, remembering relevant classroom activities was positively related to test performance. Similarly, when Conway *et al.* (1997) asked college students to indicate how they had solved problems on classroom exams, they frequently responded that they answered the test items by remembering a specific learning episode. Doukas, Bemis, Leichtman, *et al.* (2010) also found a high frequency of episodic memory-based solutions to questions on middle-school science exams, including the following answer to a question on rock and water cycles:

Mrs. X had us draw or paste pictures for each cycle. And we even did this thing for the rock cycle where we got in a huge circle and we laid [it] out because she made arrows and she laminated them... And she had us place everything where it goes. And say something about it that we knew... Like there is green that represented weathering and erosion, which turned all three of the rocks into sediments. And magma cooling which would be the blue arrow turns into igneous. And it had like those kind of things. And cooling and compaction were only one arrow and everything else had a lot of arrows.

Goddard and colleagues (Goddard, Dritschel, and Burton, 1996, 1998, 2001; Goddard, Howlin, Dritschel, *et al.*, 2007) examined the association between recall of autobiographical memories during social problem solving and the quality of generated solutions. Hypothetical social problems included arguments with a romantic partner, developing relationships in a new neighborhood, and difficulties with a work supervisor. Following Williams' (1996) theoretical model, the researchers hypothesized that recall of specific memories enhances problem solving because the memories contain detailed cues to possible solutions. Although findings are mixed, some evidence provides support for a connection between problem-solving effectiveness and retrieval of specific memories, whereas recall of repeated or "categoric" events was a negative indicator of performance (Goddard *et al.*, 1996). In other studies, failure to retrieve any type of memory during problem solving was associated with poorer quality solutions for normally functioning participants (Goddard *et al.*, 2007).

Although research has identified an association between academic and social problem-solving skills and the concurrent activation of autobiographical memories, results of correlational studies are subject to important qualifications. The studies rely on participants' meta-awareness of ongoing memory processes and on their ability to report their memory activities accurately as they engage in problem solving. Importantly, causal links between memory activation and the quality of problem solving are unclear. Self-reported memory use could be a by-product of some unspecified factor that is related to successful problem solving, such as self-awareness or intelligence. Causal inferences about memory's effects on performance are strengthened by adopting an experimental approach, as described in the next section.

Experimental approaches

In experimental studies of memory functions, participants are prompted to recall certain types of memories, and subsequent effects on feelings, attitudes, or behaviors are observed. Unlike surveys, which examine people's awareness of how they use memory for broadly defined purposes, experimental outcomes are narrowly defined and measurable within the specific research context. Unlike correlational studies, memories are actively recruited in response to researchers' specific probes.

Two recent experiments were designed specifically to examine the directive impact of autobiographical remembering (Beike, Adams, and Naufel, 2010; Kuwabara and Pillemer, 2010). Beike *et al.* (2010) prompted college students to remember a specific past failure to donate to a charity and assessed subsequent donation behaviors. Some participants were asked to think of reasons why their past failure to donate was still "unfinished business" (decreased closure), some participants provided reasons why their past donation failure was a "closed book" (increased closure), and some participants were not asked to provide a memory. Donation behavior following the experimental manipulations was assessed by students' persistence on a button-clicking task which resulted in actual monetary donations to the American Red Cross, and by students' voluntary efforts to explore websites of prominent charities. Students in the decreased closure memory condition produced a higher number of donation button-clicks than did students in both the increased closure and no memory conditions. The memory manipulation had no effect on students' willingness to explore charity websites; as might be expected in a study where participation fulfilled a course requirement, students rarely chose to explore the websites on their own. Finally, the memory manipulation did not have a significant effect on students' ratings of their general motivation to donate to charity; the effects were specific to observable button-clicking behaviors. Directive effects of autobiographical remembering were apparent only when students were encouraged to think of their past failure to donate as unfinished business, suggesting that "a person lacking closure may be inspired to engage in behaviours that he or she expects to remedy the remembered experience" (p. 46).

Kuwabara and Pillemer (2010) also examined the directive impact of autobiographical remembering on donation behaviors. Students attending the University of New Hampshire (UNH) filled out a questionnaire about college. To measure general attitudes toward the university, students rated the quality of their experiences at UNH. Then, students were assigned to one of three memory conditions. Students in a positive memory condition described a past experience when they felt pleased and satisfied with UNH; students in a negative memory condition described a past experience when they felt disappointed and dissatisfied with UNH; and students in a no memory condition did not provide a memory. Students also rated the intensity of positive or negative emotions associated with their reported memory. Students' future plans concerning UNH were assessed by ratings of intentions to recommend the university to prospective students, to attend a class reunion, to maintain contact with faculty members, and to donate to UNH. Finally, students donated $2 (supplied by the researchers) to either the UNH Annual Fund (which supports university programs) or to the United Way (which is not affiliated with UNH).

Results demonstrated a clear effect of the memory manipulation on students' future intentions and actual donation behaviors. After statistically controlling for general attitudes toward the university, students who recalled a positive memory were most likely to plan to recommend UNH to prospective students, to attend a future class reunion, and to donate money to UNH. In addition, they were significantly more likely than students in the no memory condition to designate their $2 donation to UNH rather than to the United Way. Future intentions and donation behaviors were also predicted by intensity of positive emotion ratings. Students who chose to donate their $2 to UNH and who planned to donate to UNH in the future had more intensely positive memories of UNH than did students who chose to donate to the United Way and whose future intentions to donate to UNH were weaker. Students who recalled a negative memory also were more likely than control participants to direct their $2 donation to UNH, although this effect did not reach statistical significance at the $p = 0.05$ level and the intensity of negative emotions did not significantly predict either future intentions or actual donation choices.

Recent experimental research has also targeted social and self functions of autobiographical memory. Alea and Bluck (2007) assigned adults who were currently in long-term relationships (marriage or cohabitation) to one of two conditions. People in the autobiographical memory condition were asked to think about a positive vacation and a romantic evening that they had experienced with their partner. People in the fictional vignette condition listened to stories about another couple's vacation and romantic evening. Participants who reminisced about personal episodes felt warmer toward their partners than participants who listened to impersonal stories; females in the autobiographical memory condition also felt closer to their partners.

Research on nostalgia (Wildschut, Sedikides, Arndt, et al., 2006; Zhou, Sedikides, Wildschut, et al., 2008) also supports the idea that autobiographical memory serves social and self functions. Wildschut et al. (2006) asked college students to think of a nostalgic personal event, with nostalgia defined as a "sentimental longing for the past," or to think of "an ordinary event in your life that took place in the last week" (p. 987). Students who remembered a nostalgic rather than an ordinary event reported lower attachment anxiety and greater self-esteem, and they also rated themselves more highly in the domains of initiating interactions and relationships, self-disclosure, and providing emotional support.

Experimental studies of autobiographical memory functions share several strengths and weaknesses. Assigning participants to different memory conditions strengthens causal inferences. By precisely defining attitudinal and behavioral outcomes within the context of a particular study, ambiguities associated with overly broad and vaguely defined functional categories are minimized. Ecological validity is limited, however, because the memories are necessarily elicited in somewhat artificial circumstances, usually in response to a request from a researcher. In addition, questions remain about the exact mechanisms that lead from memory to behavior. In the following section, we introduce an organizational scheme for designing and analyzing experiments on memory functions that could help answer theoretical questions about mechanisms of influence. We also suggest how experimental studies may achieve a higher level of ecological validity.

An analytical framework for experimental studies of memory functions

In this section we identify three key dimensions of research on memory functions: memory structure (specific or general), conscious awareness of memory processes (implicit or explicit), and quality of measured outcomes (self-reported attitudes or observable behaviors). Examining these dimensions can inform both the design of new research and theoretical analyses of autobiographical memory.

Memory specificity

Michael Jordan's foundational early memory of failing to make his high-school basketball team, described earlier in this chapter, focused on a particular painful event: the varsity roster was posted without his name on it. Yet some influential memories refer instead to more general or repeated occurrences. Ray Allen, star player for the Boston Celtics professional basketball team, reported using a general memory of a recurring event to motivate his performance: "One thing I always say about when I am playing is that I think about my mom and she always told me, 'You're the best out there on the floor no matter where you are'. . . I just always tell myself that. When I am practicing, it's like do what you do and focus on the things you need to focus on" (Washburn, 2010, p. C10).

Do specific and general memories have similar effects on intentions and behaviors? Under what circumstances is each memory type especially influential? Research studies can examine memory structure by coding reported memories into specific and general categories (e.g., Brunot and Sanitioso, 2004; Pillemer, Goldsmith, Panter, *et al.*, 1988). For example, Kuwabara and Pillemer (2010) conducted separate data analyses for memories coded as specific or general. The probability of students' donating to their university after recalling a positive college memory was enhanced for students who provided either specific or general memories; there was no clear advantage for either memory type.

The distinction between specific and general memories has potential theoretical and practical importance. Cognitive and clinical theories of autobiographical memory define several levels of representation, organized hierarchically: extended lifetime periods, general events, and event-specific knowledge (e.g., Brewin, Dalgleish, and Joseph, 1996; Conway and Pleydell-Pearce, 2000; Thomsen and Berntsen, 2008; also see Conway, this volume). Pillemer (1992, 1998, 2003) emphasized the potential power of specific episodes to influence thoughts and behaviors, but functional distinctions between memory levels have rarely been examined empirically. Experiments could selectively prompt recall of specific episodes, general memories, or extended life chapters and then compare their directive impact. Similarly, studies could examine the influence of general versus specific remembering on feelings about the self or social relationships. One theoretical perspective holds that general memories are especially important for self-definition, in part because they provide a broader perspective on the self than do memories of particular instances (Brunot and Sanitioso, 2004).

Aware versus unaware uses of memory

When recall of an autobiographical memory influences subsequent attitudes or behaviors, the individual may be aware or unaware of this connection. In the example presented earlier in this chapter, Michael Jordan clearly articulated his purposeful activation of a failure memory in order to motivate his current performance. Yet a robust literature on the distinction between explicit and implicit memory convincingly demonstrates that memory processes often operate outside conscious awareness (e.g., Roediger, Marsh, and Lee, 2002; Schacter, 1987), and theories of autobiographical memory identify implicit as well as explicit processes (Brewin, 1989; Brewin et al., 1996; Pillemer, 1998, 2003). For example, Brewin (1989) analyzed memory processes relevant to psychotherapy and concluded that "powerful emotional and behavioral effects can be observed without the necessity for representing relevant past experiences at a conscious level" (p. 382). Similarly, Schacter's (1987) historical account of psychiatric theories identified the prominent role of implicit memory: "experiences that are not available to conscious or voluntary recall nevertheless influence cognition and behavior in everyday life" (p. 504). Contemporary work in the psychology laboratory also has documented very long-lasting implicit memory effects (e.g., Mitchell, 2006).

Kuwabara and Pillemer's (2010) study, described earlier, examined students' awareness of memory effects on their donation choices by asking them to explain how they had made their decision. Although students in the positive college memory condition were far more likely than control group students to designate their donation to their university, they never mentioned the content of their reported memory as a reason for giving, and even indirect connections between memory themes and donation rationales were generally lacking. The authors concluded that the impact of memory activation on donation decisions was implicit, although it is possible that more extensive and targeted questioning of participants could have uncovered conscious links between memory and behavior. Assessments of directive functions that rely solely on respondents' descriptions of purposeful mental activities (e.g., Bluck *et al.*, 2005) will miss these unaware uses of memory.

Kuwabara and Pillemer (2010) proposed a tentative theoretical model to explain how positive memories of college may have influenced donation decisions implicitly. According to the model displayed in Figure 10.1, a recently activated memory of a positive experience at UNH enhanced positive feelings toward the university, which in turn influenced donation behaviors even in the absence of conscious awareness of this connection. The model is supported by the strong association between students' ratings of the intensity of positive emotions connected to the remembered event and their subsequent donation behaviors. It is consistent with more general theories of emotional effects on behavior (e.g., Izard, 2007), which hold that emotion schemas can be activated by memories; that emotions influence "thought, decision making, and actions" (p. 260); and that "different levels of the intensity of an emotion have different levels of effects and perhaps that even quite subtle emotion feelings have measurable as well as personally and socially significant consequences" (p. 274).

In Kuwabara and Pillemer's (2010) study, the implicit effect of memory on behavior appeared to be transmitted via the activation of positive emotions. Under other circumstances, memory effects will be more direct and explicit, and the role played by emotion may change accordingly. To explore more fully the complex moderating effects of affect, it is necessary to assess the emotional valence and intensity of recalled memories and to include this information in analytical models. To better understand how the level of conscious awareness influences the directive impact of

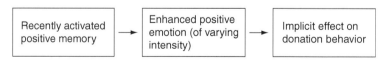

Figure 10.1. A theoretical model of donation decisions.

autobiographical memories, research participants should be interviewed about reasons underlying their behavioral choices and perhaps even encouraged to "think aloud" as they make their decisions.

Self-reported outcomes versus observable behaviors

How should directive effects of memory be measured? One research strategy relies on self-reported outcomes. In the case examples given earlier in the chapter, people simply described how memory influenced their attitudes and behaviors. Survey studies rely entirely on people's subjective ratings of how frequently and for what purposes they use memory. But fundamental questions exist about the validity of self-reports. Baumeister, Vohs, and Funder (2007) identified a broad under-representation of published psychological studies that include behavioral outcomes. They observed that people's intentions and predictions often are at odds with their actual behaviors, and they recommended "a renewed commitment to including direct observation of behavior whenever possible" (p. 396).

Recent experimental studies of directive functions have included both attitudinal and behavioral measures. In Beike *et al.*'s (2010) study, prompting students to recall a failed opportunity to give to charity did not affect their general motivation to donate, but there was an effect on participants' button-clicking to increase the amount of an actual donation (provided by the researchers). The memory manipulation had no effect on the most naturalistic behavioral outcome: participants' willingness to explore charitable organizations on their own. In Kuwabara and Pillemer's (2010) study, prompting UNH students to remember a positive college experience increased both self-reported intentions to donate to UNH in the future and the probability of directing a real monetary donation (provided by the researchers) to UNH rather than to a competing charity.

With some ingenuity and effort, studies could examine directive effects of autobiographical memory in more ecologically valid contexts. For example, authentic donations to a particular charity could be solicited under different conditions of memory activation. With the cooperation of fundraisers, a call for donations could be accompanied by a request for personal memories of topics related to the charity, and giving could be compared to donations when solicitations do not include a memory prompt. Experimental paradigms could potentially be used to examine a variety of topics including food preferences (e.g., Bernstein and Loftus, 2009), consumer decision making (e.g., Braun-LaTour and LaTour, 2007; LaTour, LaTour, and Zinkhan, 2010), political choices (e.g., Han, 2009), and academic performance (e.g., Ivcevic, Pillemer, and Brackett, 2010). For each of these topics, an intervention prompting selective memory of relevant past experiences would precede measurement of the targeted behaviors.

Conclusions

Research on autobiographical memory has exploited and will continue to exploit a natural connection between personal remembering and fundamental scientific and practical questions about adaptive functions and real-world usefulness. The memories represent salient and emotional events that happened in real time, under everyday circumstances, and as such they are intimately connected to decisions and actions that affect our daily lives.

Case studies and surveys represent a good first step toward identifying and cataloging the diversity of functions served by autobiographical remembering. Self-reported memory operations during targeted activities, including academic or social problem solving, can identify potential connections between memory and successful performance. Experimental studies in which participants are prompted to recall particular types of past experiences provide the clearest evidence about the causal impact of remembering on attitudes and behaviors. The next important scientific and practical leap forward may be achieved by conducting experimental studies of autobiographical memory functions within the ecologically valid contexts of everyday life decisions and activities.

References

Alea, N. and Bluck, S. (2007). I'll keep you in mind: the intimacy function of autobiographical memory. *Applied Cognitive Psychology*, **21**, 1091–1111.

Baddeley, A. (1988). But what the hell is it for? In M. M. Gruneberg, P. E. Morris, and R. N. Sykes (eds.), *Practical aspects of memory: current research and issues* (pp. 3–18). Chichester: Wiley.

Baumeister, R. F., Vohs, K. D., and Funder, D. C. (2007). Psychology as the science of self-reports and finger movements. *Perspectives on Psychological Science*, **2**, 396–403.

Beike, D. R., Adams, L. P., and Naufel, K. Z. (2010). Closure of autobiographical memories moderates their directive effect on behaviour. *Memory*, **18**, 40–48.

Bernstein, D. M. and Loftus, E. F. (2009). The consequences of false memories for food preferences and choices. *Perspectives on Psychological Science*, **4**, 135–139.

Bluck, S. (2003). Autobiographical memory: exploring its functions in everyday life. *Memory*, **11**, 113–123.

Bluck, S. and Alea, N. (2002). Exploring the functions of autobiographical memory: why do I remember the autumn? In J. D. Webster and B. K. Haight (eds.), *Critical advances in reminiscence work: from theory to application* (pp. 61–75). New York: Springer.

Bluck, S., Alea, N., Habermas, T., and Rubin, D. C. (2005). A tale of three functions: the self-reported uses of autobiographical memory. *Social Cognition*, **23**, 91–117.

Braun-LaTour, K. A. and LaTour, M. S. (2007). Using childhood memory elicitation to gain insights into a brand at a crossroads: the In-N-Out Burger situation. *Cornell Hotel and Restaurant Administration Quarterly*, **48**, 246–273.

Brewin, C. R. (1989). Cognitive change process in psychotherapy. *Psychological Review*, **96**, 379–394.

Brewin, C. R., Dagleish, T., and Joseph, S. (1996). A dual representation theory of posttraumatic stress disorder. *Psychological Review*, **103**, 670–686.

Brown, R. and Kulik, J. (1977). Flashbulb memories. *Cognition*, **5**, 73–79.

Bruce, D. (1985). The how and why of ecological memory. *Journal of Experimental Psychology: General*, **114**, 78–90.

(1989). Functional explanations of memory. In L. W. Poon, D. C. Rubin, and B. A. Wilson (eds.), *Everyday cognition in adulthood and late life* (pp. 44–58). New York: Cambridge University Press.

Bruner, J. S. (1986). *Actual minds, possible worlds*. Cambridge, MA: Harvard University Press.

(1987). Life as narrative. *Social Research*, **54**, 11–32.

Brunot, S. and Sanitioso, R. B. (2004). Motivational influences on the quality of memories: recall of general autobiographical memories related to desired attributes. *European Journal of Social Psychology*, **34**, 627–635.

Conway, M. A., Gardiner, J. M., Perfect, T. J., Anderson, S. J., and Cohen, G. M. (1997). Changes in awareness during learning: the acquisition of knowledge by psychology undergraduates. *Journal of Experimental Psychology: General*, **126**, 393–413.

Conway, M. A. and Pleydell-Pearce, C. W. (2000). The construction of autobiographical memories in the self-system. *Psychological Review*, **107**, 261–288.

Doukas, A. M., Bemis, R. H., Leichtman, M. D., Pillemer, D. B., and Malahy, S. (2010). Episodic memory in a middle school science classroom: a think-aloud study. Conference on Human Development, New York City.

Goddard, L., Dritschel, B., and Burton, A. (1996). Role of autobiographical memory in social problem solving and depression. *Journal of Abnormal Psychology*, **105**, 609–616.

(1998). Gender differences in the dual-task effects on autobiographical memory retrieval during social problem solving. *British Journal of Psychology*, **89**, 611–627.

(2001). The effects of specific retrieval instruction on social problem-solving in depression. *British Journal of Clinical Psychology*, **40**, 297–308.

Goddard, L., Howlin, P., Dritschel, B., and Patel, T. (2007). Autobiographical memory and social problem-solving in Asperger syndrome. *Journal of Autism and Developmental Disorders*, **37**, 291–300.

Han, H. C. (2009). Does the content of political appeals matter in motivating participation? A field experiment on self-disclosure in political appeals. *Political Behavior*, **31**, 103–116.

Herbert, D. M. B. and Burt, J. S. (2004). What do students remember? Episodic memory and the development of schematization. *Applied Cognitive Psychology*, **18**, 77–88.

Ivcevic, Z., Pillemer, D. B., and Brackett, M. A. (2010). Self-esteem memories and school success in early adolescence. *Applied Cognitive Psychology*, **24**, 1265–1278.

Izard, C. E. (2007). Basic emotions, natural kinds, emotion schemas, and a new paradigm. *Perspectives on Psychological Science*, **2**, 260–280.

LaTour, K., LaTour, M. S., and Zinkhan, G. M. (2010). Coke is It: how stories in childhood memories illuminate an icon. *Journal of Business Research*, **63**, 328–336.

Kuwabara, K. J. and Pillemer, D. B. (2010). Memories of past episodes shape current intentions and decisions. *Memory*, **18**, 365–374.

MacKenzie, A. A. and White, R. T. (1982). Fieldwork in geography and long-term memory structures. *American Educational Research Journal*, **19**, 623–632.

Malcolm X. (1965). *The autobiography of Malcolm X: as told to Alex Haley*. New York: Grove Press.

May, P. (1991). The man who beat out Jordan. *Boston Globe*, June 11, pp. 105, 110.

McAdams, D. P. (1993). *The stories we live by: personal myths and the making of the self*. New York: Morrow.

Mitchell, D. B. (2006). Nonconscious priming after 17 years: invulnerable implicit memory? *Psychological Science*, **17**, 925–929.

Nairne, J. S., Pandeirada, J. N. S., and Thompson, S. R. (2008). Adaptive memory: the comparative value of survival processing. *Psychological Science*, **19**, 176–180.

Neisser, U. (ed.) (1982a). *Memory observed: remembering in natural contexts*. San Francisco, CA: W. H. Freeman.

  (1982b). Snapshots or benchmarks? In U. Neisser (ed.), *Memory observed: remembering in natural contexts* (pp. 43–48). San Francisco, CA: W. H. Freeman.

Nuthall, G. and Alton-Lee, A. (1995). Assessing classroom learning: how students use their knowledge and experience to answer classroom achievement test questions in science and social studies. *American Educational Research Journal*, **32**, 185–223.

Pasupathi, M. (2003). Emotion regulation during social remembering: differences between emotions elicited during an event and emotions elicited when talking about it. *Memory*, **11**, 151–163.

Pillemer, D. B. (1992). Remembering personal circumstances: a functional analysis. In E. Winograd and U. Neisser (eds.), *Affect and accuracy in recall: studies of "flashbulb" memories* (pp. 236–264). New York: Cambridge University Press.

  (1998). *Momentous events, vivid memories: how unforgettable moments help us to understand the meaning of our lives*. Cambridge, MA: Harvard University Press.

  (2001). Momentous events and the life story. *Review of General Psychology*, **5**, 123–134.

(2003). Directive functions of autobiographical memory: the guiding power of the specific episode. *Memory*, **11**, 193–202.

(2009). Twenty years after Baddeley (1988): is the study of autobiographical memory fully functional? *Applied Cognitive Psychology*, **23**, 1193–1208.

Pillemer, D. B., Goldsmith, L. R., Panter, A. T., and White, S. H. (1988). Very long-term memories of the first year in college. *Journal of Experimental Psychology: Learning, Memory, and Cognition*, **14**, 709–715.

Pillemer, D. B., Picariello, M. L., Law, A. B., and Reichman, J. S. (1996). Memories of college: the importance of specific educational episodes. In D. C. Rubin (ed.), *Remembering our past: studies in autobiographical memory* (pp. 318–337). New York: Cambridge University Press.

Rasmussen, A. S. and Berntsen, D. (2009). Emotional valence and the functions of autobiographical memory: positive and negative memories serve different functions. *Memory & Cognition*, **37**, 477–492.

Robitaille, A., Cappeliez, P., Coulombe, D., and Webster, J. D. (2010). Factorial structure and psychometric properties of the reminiscence functions scale. *Aging and Mental Health*, **14**, 184–192.

Roediger, H. L., III, Marsh, E. J., and Lee, S. C. (2002). Kinds of memory. In H. Pashler and D. Medin (eds.), *Stevens' handbook of experimental psychology*, 3rd edn. (vol. II, pp. 1–41). Hoboken, NJ: Wiley.

Rubin, D. C. and Kozin, M. (1984). Vivid memories. *Cognition*, **16**, 81–95.

Ryan, B. (2009). Usually reliable fireballer has a hellish outing. *Boston Globe*, October 12, pp. C1, C12.

Schacter, D. L. (1987). Implicit memory: history and current status. *Journal of Experimental Psychology*, **13**, 501–518.

Schacter, D. L. and Addis, D. R. (2007). The ghosts of past and future. *Nature*, **445**, 27.

Schank, R. C. (1990). *Tell me a story: a new look at real and artificial memory*. New York: Charles Scribner.

(1999). *Dynamic memory revisited*. New York: Cambridge University Press.

Singer, J. A. and Salovey, P. (1993). *The remembered self: emotion and memory in personality*. New York: The Free Press.

Spence, D. P. (1982). *Narrative truth and historical truth*. New York: Norton.

Thomsen, D. K. and Berntsen, D. (2008). The cultural life script and life story chapters contribute to the reminiscence bump. *Memory*, **16**, 420–435.

Washburn, G. (2010). Swayed by cavalier attitude. *Boston Globe*, May 8, p. C10.

Webster, J. D. (1993). Construction and validation of the reminiscence functions scale. *Journal of Gerontology*, **48**, 256–262.

(1995). Adult age differences in reminiscence functions. In B. K. Haight and J. D. Webster (eds.), *The art and science of reminiscing: theory, research, methods, and applications* (pp. 89–102). Washington, DC: Taylor & Francis.

(2003). The reminiscence circumplex and autobiographical memory functions. *Memory*, **11**, 203–215.

Webster, J. D. and McCall, M. E. (1999). Reminscence functions across adulthood: a replication and extension. *Journal of Adult Development*, **6**, 73–85.

Wildschut, T., Sedikides, C., Arndt, J., and Routledge, C. (2006). Nostalgia: content, triggers, functions. *Journal of Personality and Social Psychology*, **91**, 975–993.

Williams, J. M. G. (1996). Depression and specificity of autobiographical memory. In D. C. Rubin (ed.), *Remembering our past: studies in autobiographical memory* (pp. 244–267). New York: Cambridge University Press.

Zhou, X., Sedikides, C., Wildschut, T., and Gao, D. (2008). Counteracting loneliness: on the restorative function of nostalgia. *Psychological Science*, **19**, 1023–1029.

Part IV

Development of autobiographical memory from infancy to old age

The three chapters in this part together address the development of autobiographical memory from infancy to old age. The chapters offer different perspectives on this topic and focus on different parts of the life span. The chapter by Bauer reviews and discusses research on memory in infancy and early childhood. Bauer identifies different rates of forgetting for very early childhood memories as compared to memories later in life. She discusses the implications of these findings for our understanding of infantile amnesia. The chapter by Fivush reviews and discusses how sociocultural factors affect autobiographical memory development. She proposes that although episodic representations are available from a very early age, the ability to construct and integrate such episodes into temporally and thematically coherent autobiographical stories of the personal past emerges gradually during the preschool years and continues to develop through adolescence under the influence of sociocultural factors. The chapter by Fitzgerald and Broadbridge examines the development of autobiographical memory from a life-span perspective and also discusses the implications of this perspective for research on autobiographical memory more broadly. Among other things, Fitzgerald and Broadbridge discuss possible explanations of the reminiscence bump (i.e., the increase of memories from young adulthood relative to the surrounding periods) from a life-span developmental perspective.

11 The life I once remembered: the waxing and waning of early memories

Patricia J. Bauer

One of the most intriguing phenomena in the memory literature is infantile or childhood amnesia. The amnesia has two components: a relative paucity among adults of memories of specific past events from the first 3 to 4 years of life, and from the ages of 3 or 4 to age 7 or 8, a smaller number of memories than would be expected on the basis of forgetting alone (Pillemer and White, 1989). The amnesia made its debut in the psychological literature in 1893, with a report by C. Miles on adults' responses to a questionnaire designed to gain information about the phenomenal experience of childhood. One of the questions included in the survey was, "What is the earliest thing you are sure you can remember? How old were you?" The average earliest memory of Miles' 89 respondents was age 3.04 years. The amnesia was named in 1905 by Sigmund Freud, who remarked on "the peculiar amnesia which veils from most people (not from all) the first years of their childhood, usually the first six or eight years" (1905/1953, p. 581). For much of the twentieth century, efforts were made to describe the amnesia by characterizing adults' earliest memories along dimensions of detail and completeness (highly detailed or fragmentary), perspective (first or third person), emotionality (predominantly positive, negative, or devoid of emotion), and so forth (see, e.g., Bauer, 2007; White and Pillemer, 1979, for reviews). Explanatory accounts ranged from theories of repression and "screening" of psychically unacceptable recollections (Freud, 1905/1953) to cognitive theories characterizing the ability to remember specific past events as a developmentally late achievement due to changes in representational processes (Piaget, 1962), or non-mnemonic developments, such as the dawning of

The author's work reported in this chapter was supported by the National Institutes of Health (NICHD HD28425, HD42483), and by the College of Arts and Sciences, Emory University. The author also thanks members of the Memory at Emory laboratory group for their contributions to the research program, and the children and families who took part in the research.

Correspondence may be addressed to Patricia J. Bauer, Department of Psychology, 36 Eagle Row, Emory University, Atlanta, Georgia 30322, USA; patricia.bauer@emory.edu.

autonoetic awareness (e.g., Perner and Ruffman, 1995), for example. Largely missing from the literature, however, were data on the memories of children within the age period eventually veiled by the amnesia. As a result, there was little to constrain accounts of the origins or development of the amnesia.

The end of the twentieth century was marked by emergence of interest in autobiographical memory in development, with special attention to the early childhood years. A consistent finding was that even young children were able to encode, store, and later retrieve memories of past events. In infancy, the evidence came from nonverbal tests of recall of sequences of actions produced with props (see Bauer, 2006, for a review). In the preschool years, the evidence came from conversations between parents and their children about everyday events and routines, such as going to McDonald's (Nelson, 1986), and unique experiences and episodes, such as a trip to Disney World (Hamond and Fivush, 1991). The research made clear that the paucity among adults for memories of events from the first years of life could not be due to an absence of such memories in childhood. It thus paved the way for research on the development of autobiographical or personal memory in early childhood and beyond, and on the "fates" of early memories over the course of the first decade of life. The major purpose of this chapter is to discuss the literatures on young children's early memories and on the fates of those memory traces, thereby capturing both the waxing and the waning of early autobiographical memories.

The waxing of autobiographical memories

When adults describe the events of their lives, they do so in rich narrative terms. Adults' narratives typically feature all of the elements of a good story, including *who* participated in the event, *what* happened, *where* and *when* the event took place, and *why* the sequence of actions unfolded as it did. Their narratives also typically feature information about *how* the participants in the event reacted to it at the time and the perspective that they now take on it, including how it has become integrated into the life story or personal past (e.g., Bauer, Stennes, and Haight, 2003; Weigle and Bauer, 2000; West and Bauer, 1999). Furthermore, the elements are presented in a coherent manner, allowing the listener (or reader) to understand the theme of the event, the context in which it took place, and the chronology of actions (Reese, Haden, Baker-Ward, *et al.*, 2011).

Children's earliest narratives are neither complete nor coherent. In their earliest reports, young children typically merely confirm or deny information provided by another. For example, an adult offers the observation that the child had fun at a party, and the child responds with an enthusiastic "Yes!" At around the age of 3 years, when children begin contributing memory content, they typically include only the most crucial elements such as who and what ("I fell"). They omit many of the elements that make for a good story, such as where and when the event occurred, and why it happened as it did (see Fivush, this volume; Nelson and Fivush, 2004, for reviews). These elements are uncommon in young children's accounts of past events and when they are included, they are not necessarily provided in a coherent manner. In the preschool years, children score no more than one point on a 4-point scale for coherence on the dimensions of context, chronology, and theme (Reese *et al.*, 2011). Although memories and the narratives that describe them are not one and the same, the relatively impoverished nature of children's early autobiographical accounts is diagnostic of the status of the memories themselves. Children's incomplete reports imply that important elements of what happened to whom and when may be left unspecified in the memory trace. Even if these elements are encoded at the time of the event, unless they are rehearsed – through narrative retelling – they are unlikely to be remembered. Thus, the fact that early narratives are incomplete and incoherent implies that their memories are, or eventually will be, as well.

A paucity of research on later childhood

The fact that preschoolers tell incomplete narratives that are low in coherence, and that adults tell complete narratives that are highly coherent, implies substantial development in narrative form and structure between early childhood and adulthood. It is a "quirk" of the autobiographical memory literature that relatively little is known about changes in autobiographical narratives during this period, however. There are at least two reasons for the lack of attention to the middle childhood years. First, much of the developmental work on autobiographical memory has been with children aged 6 and younger because of a preoccupation with the period eventually obscured by childhood amnesia. The concentration of effort was logical given explanations of the amnesia that emphasized the late development of autobiographical memory ability. Information about the emergence of autobiographical competence was critical to evaluation of these explanations.

The second reason for the lack of attention to developments in autobiographical narrative beyond the preschool years is the suggestion that the age of 8 years marks the beginning of an adult-like distribution of autobiographical memories. This assumption is apparent in Wetzler and Sweeney's (1986) oft-cited empirical demonstration of childhood amnesia. Wetzler and Sweeney used data from Rubin (1982, Experiment 1) in which young adults located in time personal memories associated with a large number of different cue words (e.g., *ice cream*; see below for further description). To the data, Wetzler and Sweeney fitted a power function that in many investigations (e.g., Crovitz and Schiffman, 1974; Rubin and Wenzel, 1996; Rubin, Wetzler, and Nebes, 1986) has been shown to capture the distribution of memories across the life span. As discussed by Rubin and Wenzel (1996), the power function (e.g., Wickelgren, 1974, 1975) implies that equal ratios of time ($t_1/t_2 = t_3/t_4$) will result in equal ratios of recall ($recall_1/recall_2 = recall_3/recall_4$). Thus, for example, if Time 2 recall was 90% of Time 1 recall, then Time 4 recall would be 90% of Time 3 recall (assuming equal ratios of time, that is). If total recall at Time 1 was of 100 memories, then Time 2 recall would be 90% of Time 1 or 90 memories; Time 3 recall would be 90% of Time 2 or 81 memories; Time 4 would be 90% of Time 3 or 73 memories; and so forth. As a result of the constant ratio, over time, forgetting actually slows (i.e., smaller absolute numbers of memories are lost over each unit of time), presumably as a result of consolidation of memory traces (see Moscovitch, this volume, for discussion of the contribution of autobiographical memory research to our understanding of consolidation). In Wetzler and Sweeney's analysis, the power function was a poor fit to data from birth to age 6 years, implying accelerated forgetting of memories from ages 6 and below. Memories from age 7 years were excluded from the analysis because age 7 years is considered the "inflection point" for childhood amnesia: after age 7 years, the rate of forgetting is assumed to be adult-like. Consistent with this suggestion, Wetzler and Sweeney found that the power function was a good fit to data from age 8 to adulthood (see Bauer, 2007, for additional discussion). As outlined below, data from adults are no substitute for data from children, however.

Elaborating the intervening years

Although the literature on autobiographical narratives from children beyond the preschool years is limited, it is highly consistent in pointing to substantial developmental change throughout childhood and adolescence. Developmental changes are apparent in the breadth of narratives that children tell, in the coherence of their narratives, and in terms of the integration of individual episodes into a life story. For example, between the ages of 7 and 11 years, there are changes in the length and complexity of children's autobiographical narratives (Habermas, Negele, and Mayer, 2010; Van Abbema and Bauer, 2005). The amount of information that children report nearly doubles over this period (Van Abbema and Bauer,

2005), as does the temporal organization of the narratives that children produce (Morris, Baker-Ward, and Bauer, 2009). Ten- to 12-year-old children also produce narratives that more effectively orient the listener to the time and place of the event, and they maintain and elaborate on topics more effectively than 7- to 9-year-old children (e.g., O'Kearney, Speyer, and Kenardy, 2007; Reese *et al.*, 2011). Yet even at age 11 to 12 years, children's narratives still are lacking in the causal connections that characterize older adolescents' and adults' narratives (e.g., Bauer, Stark, Lukowski, *et al.*, 2005; Habermas *et al.*, 2010). It is only in adolescence that individuals construct an extended life narrative (e.g., Bohn and Berntsen, 2008; Habermas and Bluck, 2000).

The most compelling form of demonstration of the protracted course of development of autobiographical narratives is afforded by direct comparison of narratives from children and adults. Unfortunately, such comparisons are rare because, for the most part, the adult and developmental literatures on autobiographical memory are separate (see Fitzgerald and Broadbridge, this volume, for discussion of a life-span developmental perspective on autobiographical memory). To accomplish direct comparisons, the same method must be used with children and adults. The cue-word technique that was the source of data for Wetzler and Sweeney's (1986) empirical demonstration of childhood amnesia is well suited to the task. The cue-word technique has been used heavily in the adult autobiographical memory literature (e.g., Rubin, 1982, 2000; Rubin and Schulkind, 1997). Participants are given a word (e.g., *chair, dog, plant*) and asked to "think of a specific memory" associated with the word and to estimate their age at the time of the event. Bauer, Burch, Scholin, *et al.* (2007) adapted the technique for use with children aged 7 to 11 years (see also Fitzgerald, 1991, for an earlier application). We have since used the technique with both children and adults, to examine age-related changes in narrative ability from ages 7 to 11, relative to young adults (college students) and middle-aged adults.

In Bauer and Larkina (2011), we provided children 7 to 11 years of age, college-age adults, and middle-aged adults with 20 cue words and asked them to provide brief narratives describing memories associated with each word. We then coded the narratives for the eight narrative categories described in Bauer *et al.* (2007): who, what-object, what-action, where, when, why, how-description, and how-explanation. The resulting narrative breadth scores – the average number of narrative categories included in the reports – are depicted in Figure 11.1. The figure reveals gradual increase in narrative breadth throughout childhood. Surprisingly, the narrative breadth scores of the young adults ($M = 19$ years) did not differ from those of children aged 9 to 11 years; the breadth of the young adults'

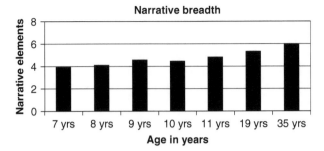

Figure 11.1. Average narrative breadth scores, reflecting the number of elements included in narratives, at each of ages 7, 8, 9, 10, 11, 19, and 35 years (maximum = 8). Data from Bauer and Larkina (2011).

narratives was significantly different from that of the 7- and 8-year-olds only. One could view this either as the glass half full or the glass half empty. The "full" perspective on the glass is that adult-like narrative breadth is achieved by age 9 years. However, the "empty" perspective on the glass is that the narrative breadth scores of the middle-aged adults (M = 35 years) were significantly greater than those of all child groups. Thus, although narrative breadth scores at age 9 years did not differ from those of young adults, neither had they reached their full adult potential. These data indicate a protracted course of development in narrative breadth.

Summary

The developmental literature on autobiographical memory makes clear that the ability to remember personal past events begins to develop early in childhood (see also Fivush, this volume). It also makes clear that the course of development of the skills to report on and otherwise share autobiographical memories is protracted indeed. Although a report and a memory are not the same thing, they are intimately related. An accurate report can never feature more than is "in" the memory; the elements of a memory trace that are rehearsed and shared with others are those most likely to remain accessible over time. As such, the fact that age-related changes in autobiographical narratives continue throughout the first decade of life (and even beyond) has implications for the robustness of memories from this period in life. Direct tests of the fates of memories from this period are the subject of the next section.

The waning of autobiographical memories

The fact that children narrate past events – even if incompletely – is ample evidence that they form and retain memories of their experiences. On the other hand, the phenomenon of childhood amnesia is a compelling demonstration that early childhood memories are not written in indelible ink: at least by adulthood, memories from early childhood are largely inaccessible. When does the amnesia begin to set in? This question is not only a matter of curiosity but also of substantial theoretical importance, in that the "onset" of childhood amnesia marks the achievement of an adult-like distribution of autobiographical memories. As such, the loss of memories from early childhood is an important developmental achievement.

There are essentially two means by which to chart the development of childhood amnesia: prospective tests and retrospective tests. Within the broad category of retrospective tests are examinations of the age of earliest memory among children and the distribution of memories across the life span. I examine each broad category below.

Prospective examinations of the "fates" of childhood memories

Prospective examinations involve collection of data on children's memories of specific past events and then testing memory for the same events at a later time (or times), to determine whether an event is still remembered. Because prospective studies of memory for early childhood memories take a long time (months to years) and are thus expensive to conduct, there are relatively few of them. The small literature is largely consistent, however, and suggests that forgetting of childhood memories sets in relatively early in childhood.

Cleveland and Reese (2008) obtained conversations between mothers and their children about past events at each of ages 19, 25, 32, 40, and 65 months. The fact that the children talked about the events provided evidence that they had formed memory traces of them. When the same children were 66 months of age, the authors asked the children about events from each of the prior data collection points. Thus, at 66 months, Cleveland and Reese tested children's memories for events that were 1, 26, 34, 41, and 47 months in the past. As reflected in Figure 11.2, the amount that the 66-month-old children remembered decreased steadily as the retention interval increased. Fivush and Schwarzmueller (1998) reported a similar trend, though higher rates of retention, from 8-year-old children interviewed about events from ages 3.5 and 4 (77% of events remembered) versus 5 and 6 (92% of events remembered) years of age. The data from both studies are consistent with the suggestion that as time

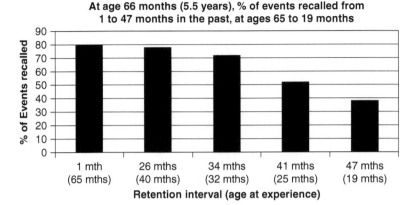

Figure 11.2. The percentage of events recalled by children 66 months of age, from 1 to 47 months in the past, when the children were 65 to 19 months of age. Data from Cleveland and Reese (2008).

goes by, forgetting becomes more pronounced. However, the data must be interpreted with caution because, in both studies, the age at the time of encoding and the length of the delay were confounded. That is, the events with the longest delays between the initial and later tests also were events with the earliest age of encoding (i.e., 19 months in the case of Cleveland and Reese, 2008). This feature of the designs makes it difficult to determine whether age at the time of experience or the length of the delay was the critical variable in the forgetting equation.

My laboratory has conducted a pair of experiments that permit unconfounding of age at experience and delay. The studies demonstrate the importance of both variables as determinants of the fates of autobiographical memories from early in life. In Van Abbema and Bauer (2005), we collected data from a large group of 3-year-old children and their mothers; each dyad discussed a number of events from the recent past. We tested different subgroups of the children 3.5, 4.5, or 5.5 years later, to see how many of the events discussed at age 3 years they still remembered. At the time of test, the children were 6.5, 7.5, or 8.5 years of age. As reflected in the right-most three bars of Figure 11.3, forgetting set in as time went by. Whereas the children 6.5 years of age remembered 64% of the events from age 3 years, the 7.5- and 8.5-year-olds remembered only 36% and 34% of the past events, respectively. Subsequent to publication of the work by Van Abbema and Bauer (2005), we tested groups of children 1.5 and 2.5 years after their age 3 interviews (at ages 4.5 and 5.5 years). Over the shorter retention intervals, the children remembered 79% and 88% of the

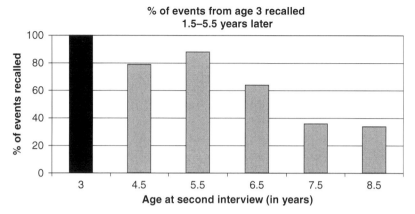

Figure 11.3. The percentage of events experienced at age 3 years (i.e., age at first interview) and recalled by children 1.5 to 5.5 years later, when children were 4.5 to 8.5 years of age. Data from time points 6.5 to 8.5 from Van Abbema and Bauer (2005). Data from time points 4.5 and 5.5 are unpublished.

events from age 3 years (see Figure 11.3). These data are consistent with Fivush and Schwarzmueller (1998) and Cleveland and Reese (2008) in suggesting that, as time goes by, children begin to forget experiences from early in life.

Data from a study that held retention interval constant and varied age at the time of experience of events provide evidence that forgetting of early childhood events also is influenced by the child's age at the time of experience of the event. In Morris *et al.* (2010), we enrolled children at ages 4, 6, and 8 years. Each child discussed a number of events from the recent past. All of the children were interviewed about the events again 1 year later. Children who had been older at the time of the events remembered more of them over the 1-year delay. Specifically, children 4, 6, and 8 years of age at the time of the events remembered 67%, 78%, and 91% of the events 1 year later, when they were 5, 7, and 9 years of age. These results are consistent with suggestions in Cleveland and Reese (2008) and Fivush and Schwarzmueller (1998). Together with the results of Van Abbema and Bauer (2005), they make it clear that forgetting of events from early childhood is apparent by 5.5 to 7.5 years of age; that with time, early childhood memories become less accessible; and that the younger the child at the time of the experience, the greater is the loss from memory.

Retrospective examinations of the "fates" of childhood memories

Prospective tests of remembering and forgetting of early childhood memories are valuable yet rare. They also are limited in the comparisons they afford: none permit direct comparison of the rate of forgetting of events in children and adults. Direct comparisons require that children and adults participate in the same paradigm. Two such approaches are available in the literature. In the first, adults and children are asked to report on the age of their earliest childhood memory. In the second, adults and children generate memories in response to cue words, thus permitting charting of the shape of the distribution of memories over the lifespan.

Age of earliest memory   As noted earlier, among adults, the age of earliest memory typically is 3 to 3.5 years (36 to 42 months), though individual differences in the age of earliest memory among adults are pronounced (see Bauer, 2007, for a review). This age estimate is robust to the method used to obtain the earliest memories, whether with a questionnaire, free recall, or a targeted event, such as birth of a sibling. The age estimate also is robust to cohort: the estimate has remained the same for over 100 years (e.g., compare Miles, 1893, to West and Bauer, 1999).

Investigations of the age of earliest memory reported by children have a much shorter history. As reflected in Table 11.1, the estimates largely are consistent with those obtained from adults. Across four separate studies (Jack, MacDonald, Reese, *et al.*, 2009; Larkina, Merrill, Fivush, *et al.*, 2009; Peterson, Grant, and Boland, 2005; Reese, Jack, and White, 2010), queries about the age of earliest memory among children as young as 6 years of age and as old as 19 years have produced estimates of the average age of earliest memory at 38 months, with a range of 28 months to 45 months. The estimates fit comfortably around the 36–42-month range obtained from adults (the 28-month estimate from Jack *et al.* [2009] is an exception that may be due to unique methodological features of the study, including the fact that the children and mothers discussed early memories repeatedly during childhood and that the adolescent interviews began with a life review; see Reese *et al.*, 2010, for discussion). The results of these studies suggest that developmental events establish a floor for the age at which enduring memories are formed (around 30–36 months of age); the floor is not altered by the passage of time.

Distribution of memories   The age of earliest memory is only one of the components of childhood amnesia. The second is the distribution of memories, such that, among adults, the number of memories from the first 7 years of life is smaller than would be expected by normal forgetting

Table 11.1. *Ages of earliest memories of adults, and adolescents and children, estimated from retrospective tests*

Subjects	Source	Age at test (years)	Age of earliest memory (months)
Adults	Various/numerous	Adults	36 to 42
Adolescents and children	Peterson et al. (2005)	17 to 19	42
	Peterson et al. (2005)	14 to 16	45
	Larkina et al. (2009)	14	42
	Jack et al. (2009)	12 to 13	28
	Reese et al. (2010)	12 to 13	32
	Peterson et al. (2005)	10 to 13	44
	Peterson et al. (2005)	6 to 9	36
	Overall adolescents/ children	Adolescents/ children	38

Note: The data for adults are the means derived from numerous studies in the literature as opposed to any single study. Jack et al. (2009); Larkina et al. (2009); Peterson et al. (2005); Reese et al. (2010).

alone, implying an accelerated rate of forgetting of memories from early childhood. The retrospective approach of retrieving memories in response to cue words can inform the shape of the distribution of memories in children as well as adults.

In Bauer et al. (2007), we used the cue-word technique to examine autobiographical memories in children 7 to 10 years of age (see also Fitzgerald, 1991). The children successfully generated memories in response to the cue words and accurately dated them, according to parental report. A provocative finding was that the distribution of memories produced by the children was better fit by an exponential than by a power function. That is, in contrast to adults, for whom forgetting seemingly slows over time, for children, over each unit of time (e.g., a year) the number of memories in the corpus decreases by one-half. This pattern implies that memories remain vulnerable to disruption and interference even as they age, suggesting that they do not consolidate. Bauer et al. (2007) thus provided evidence to suggest that the distributions of autobiographical memories in children and adults are not the same.

The study by Bauer et al. (2007) was an important demonstration of the efficacy of the cue-word technique for use with children, as well as a source of intriguing evidence of developmental differences in the shapes of the distributions of autobiographical memories from childhood to adulthood. Yet the study was limited by the fact that the sample was of

20 children aged 7 to 10 years. Tests of the best-fitting function to the distribution of memories were conducted across the entire age range; the sample was too small to permit a test of the possibility of change in the best-fit function over this wide developmental span. Because the study included children only, Bauer *et al.* also could not inform comparisons of the shapes of the distribution of memories in children and adults. Accordingly, in Bauer and Larkina (2011), introduced earlier, we tested 20 children at each of the ages of 7, 8, 9, 10, and 11 years (100 children total). We also included two groups of adult participants. One group of adults were college undergraduate students. College students commonly participate in research on autobiographical memory and have been the source of data for many studies using cue words (including Rubin, 1982, Experiment 1, which was the source of data for Wetzler and Sweeney's [1986] empirical demonstration of childhood amnesia). The second group of adult participants comprised the middle-aged parents of some of the child participants. Including the older group of adults allowed us to cover more of the life span, thus allowing for a more comprehensive test of similarities and differences in the shapes of the distribution of memories. All participants provided memory responses to 20 cue words, for a total of 2,800 data points.

Analysis of the data from the children provided a replication of the results of Bauer *et al.* (2007). As reflected in Table 11.2, for the entire sample of children and for each group of children (7-, 8-, 9-, 10-, and 11-year-olds) separately, the best-fitting function to the distribution was the exponential. In contrast, for both adult samples, the best-fitting function was the power. These data clearly suggest that, as old as 11 years, the distribution of children's autobiographical memories is not adult-like. The data are consistent with the suggestion that, at least until the age of 11 years, children experience an accelerated rate of forgetting of memories from their childhoods.

What is the significance of the apparent difference in the form of forgetting for children than adults? As discussed earlier, the power function implies that equal ratios of time ($t_1/t_2 = t_3/t_4$) result in equal ratios of recall ($recall_1/recall_2 = recall_3/recall_4$; Wickelgren, 1974, 1975; Rubin and Wenzel, 1996; Wixted, 2004). As a result, over time, forgetting slows, presumably as a result of consolidation of memory traces. In contrast, the exponential function implies a constant half-life. That is, over each unit of time (e.g., a year) the number of memories in the corpus decreases by one-half. To use the earlier example, if Time 1 recall was of 100 memories, then recall at Times 2, 3, and 4 would be of 50, 25, and 12.5 memories, respectively (contrast this rate of loss with the distribution conforming to the power function: Time 1 to Time 4 change of 100 memories at T1 to 73 memories at T4). This pattern implies that memories remain vulnerable

Table 11.2. *Fit statistics for the power and exponential functions applied to data from Bauer and Larkina (2011)*

	Fit by function	
Age group	Power function	Exponential function
7 years	.86	.96
8 years	.87	.94
9 years	.91	.95
10 years	.90	.92
11 years	.78	.92
Overall children	.85	.95
19 years	.84	.61
35 years	.93	.70

Note: For all child groups (ages 7 to 11 years and overall), the exponential is the best-fitting function. For the adult groups (ages 19 and 35 years), the power is the best-fitting function.

to disruption and interference even as they age, suggesting that they do not consolidate. As discussed in Bauer *et al.* (2007) and Bauer and Larkina (2011), although interference is not typically thought to play a large role in forgetting of autobiographical memories, in young children, in whom consolidation processes may be less efficient and effective, interference (and attendant trace degradation) may exert a more pronounced effect, resulting in continued vulnerability and forgetting (see Bauer, 2006, 2007, for discussions). The consequence would be a smaller pool of early memories from which to draw. The findings of Bauer *et al.* (2007) and Bauer and Larkina (2011) indicate that the pool continues to shrink at least throughout the first decade of life. Over time, the smaller pool would contribute to the appearance of a "childhood amnesia component" – a smaller number of memories than expected by normal forgetting (i.e., with "normal" forgetting equated with an adult rate; see Rubin, 2000).

Summary

Taken together, the results of prospective and retrospective tests of auto-biographical memories from early in life indicate that the amnesia that adults suffer for the events of their early childhoods begins in childhood. Although the estimates vary across the small number of studies that inform the question most directly, it appears that by 5.5 to 7.5 years of age, children experience substantial loss of memories of events from earlier in their lives. The younger the child at the time of the event, the greater is the loss from memory. The result is that when children are asked about their earliest memories, they nominate events from the third to fourth years of their lives, with an average age of 38 months (3.17 years). Moreover, throughout the first 10 years of life, the distribution of memories that children produce in response to cue words is better fit by the exponential than by the power function. This implies less efficient and effective consolidation of memories from this period of life.

Crossover of two functions

The data summarized in this chapter present a major paradox: over the course of the development, autobiographical memories include more and more of the features of a "good narrative," yet, as adults, we have few personal memories from early in life. Resolution of the paradox requires that we consider changes in both the richness of the autobiographical memories that children form (the "waxing" of autobiographical memories), and the rate at which they are forgotten (the "waning" of autobiographical memories). Although the preschool years are marked by developmental improvements in the quality of autobiographical memories that are formed, they also are marked by an accelerated rate of forgetting, relative to the rate of forgetting in later childhood and adulthood. The result is that, of early childhood, adults have a smaller number of memories than would be expected on the basis of adult rates of forgetting.

Increase in the richness of autobiographical memories

As early as they are able to use past tense markers, children refer to past events of relevance to themselves. Yet even 11-year-old children's narratives are not as complete or as coherent as those of adults. Although the fact that a child does not report when an event occurred, or where, or why, does not imply that the information is missing from the memory trace, it raises the possibility of omission. Similarly, although the fact that a child does not provide a coherent narrative account of a past event does not imply that the memory trace is itself poorly organized, it raises that possibility. Moreover, verbal rehearsal is one of the major means by which memories – and the elements and organization thereof – are kept alive. Thus, omission from the narrative and poor organization of the narrative will, over time, contribute to forgetting. Conversely, developmental increases in the breadth of narratives and in narrative coherence reflect improvements in the quality of the memory trace. With development, children's narratives about past events also take on more and more elements of drama, and they contain an increasing amount of evidence of the significance of the event for the child. Children's narratives also increasingly include elements that provide a sense of the intensity of experience, elements of suspense, and information about the internal states of the participants, for example (e.g., Ackil, Van Abbema, and Bauer, 2003; Fivush and Haden, 1997). Narratives also become organized into a life story that is informed by cultural life scripts (Bohn and Berntsen, 2008). In sum, over the course of the preschool years, children's stories about the times of their lives bear more and more of the marks of a typical autobiography.

Decrease in the rate at which autobiographical memories are forgotten

The results of the retrospective cue-word studies (Bauer *et al.*, 2007; Bauer and Larkina, 2011) imply that, throughout the first decade of life, children experience an accelerated rate of forgetting of autobiographical memories. Why would this be the case? There are two related reasons why we should predict exactly this effect. First, there are neurodevelopmental changes that make memories formed in early childhood more vulnerable to consolidation and storage failures, relative to memories formed later in life. Autobiographical memory relies on a multi-component neural network for the encoding, consolidation, storage, and subsequent retrieval, of memories (see also St. Jacques, this volume; Moscovitch, this volume; Rubin, this volume). As discussed in Bauer (2006, 2007, 2008), some of the components of the network develop early, whereas others continue to develop well into the second decade of life. As a result, we should expect age-related neurodevelopmental changes to affect autobiographical memory processes throughout early childhood.

The second reason why we should expect an accelerated rate of forgetting in early childhood, relative to later childhood and adulthood, is that the memory representations that younger children have available for consolidation and storage contain fewer of the features that ensure long-term retention, relative to memory representations from later in life. As discussed earlier (and in more detail in Bauer, 2007), the memories that the young child is asking her or his immature brain to consolidate and store contain fewer of the features that typify autobiographical memories. In terms of narrative elements, for example, younger children likely encode fewer of the elements that make for a good narrative, relative to older children, thereby denying themselves an effective retrieval tool (and perhaps contributing to a "fragmented" quality of early memories: Bruce, Wilcox-O'Hearn, Robinson, *et al.*, 2005). Given that in early childhood we have less than optimal processes operating on less than optimal raw materials, we should expect – rather than be surprised by – output the quality of which simply is not as high as that in later childhood and adulthood, when we have more optimal processes operating on more optimal materials.

The point(s) of intersection

The net effect of this analysis is a model that suggests that we see an increase in autobiographical memories dating from the age period of 4 to 6 years because this is the point at which the functions that characterize the increasing richness of memories formed and the rate at which they are forgotten "crossover" (Bauer, 2007). Prior to the age of 4 years, the rate at which memories are lost is faster than the rise in the quality of the memories that are formed; after the age of 6 years, the richness of the memories that are formed increases faster than the rate at which memories are lost. Considering the phenomenon of childhood amnesia to be a result of the crossover of two functions – the rise in formation of elaborated autobiographical memories and the rate of forgetting – has at least two distinct advantages. One advantage is that it does not require that we invoke pronounced developmental changes or special mechanisms to account either for the increase in autobiographical memories at age 4 to 6 years, or for the relative paucity of autobiographical memories from the first years of life. That is, we need not invoke a later developmental change, such as the dawning of a subjective perspective (e.g., Fivush, this volume), or autonoetic awareness (e.g., Perner and Ruffman, 1995), that comes online at 4 to 6 years of age and "jump-starts" the autobiographical memory system. The system has been "up and running" for some time. We begin to see substantial evidence of it at the end of the preschool years because, by that time, the rate of memory formation has outstripped the rate of forgetting. Nor do we need to invoke a mechanism such as "repression" (e.g., Freud, 1905/1953) to explain why early memories that we know were formed (from studies with preschoolers) later are inaccessible – they are lost to normal (for the age period) forgetting.

Another advantage of the conceptualization in terms of a crossover of two functions is that it provides a ready account of individual and group differences in the apparent offset of childhood amnesia. Although the mean age of adults' earliest memories is 3 to 3.5 years, samples routinely yield a range of earliest memories from as early as the second year of life to as late as age 8 or 9 years (see Bauer, 2007, for discussion). There also are group differences in the age of adults' earliest memory. For example, adults in Western societies routinely report earlier earliest memories, relative to adults in Eastern societies (e.g., Mullen, 1994; Wang, 2003). Conceptualizing early autobiographical memory development in terms of a crossover of two functions provides a ready means of explanation for these patterns. For example, two individuals who as children had the same rate of forgetting may nevertheless have vastly different "offsets" of childhood amnesia as a function of differences in the slopes of change in the function that characterizes the richness or quality of autobiographical memories formed. Children in a family and cultural environment that places a premium on narrative, that encourages reflection on the meanings of events and their significance for the child – as in the Maori culture in New Zealand (MacDonald, Uesiliana, and Hayne, 2000) – may have autobiographical memories from early in the preschool years. In contrast, children in a family and cultural environment that uses a less elaborative style and which does not encourage reflection on the self – as in some Asian cultures (Wang, Leichtman, and Davies, 2000) – may have autobiographical memories from later in the preschool years.

Individual differences also could result from differences in the slopes of the forgetting function. That is, individuals whose rates of improvement in the quality of autobiographical memories formed are the same could nevertheless experience a different course of development of autobiographical memory because of differences in the rate at which memories are forgotten. Variability in the forgetting function no doubt is associated with a variety of factors, including different rates of developmental change in the neural structures that subserve autobiographical memory and associated differences in the basic mnemonic processes of encoding, consolidation, storage, and retrieval. As such, the conceptualization provides a ready account of individual and cultural differences: they result from differences in the "quality" of the autobiographical memories that are formed during the period and from the likelihood of survival of the memories over time.

Conclusions

As is apparent from the literature reviewed in this chapter, autobiographical memory is with us virtually for our lifetime. The earliest narrative reports of autobiographical memories occur in the second year of life; they are our companions from that time forward. Early in development we represent the times of our lives without much specificity or detail, and without much longevity. We represent them nonetheless. With development, autobiographical memory changes from a wispy sapling to a sturdy tree. It brings along with it a perspective on the events of our lives that is personal and unique. Also with age develops the capacity to share the experiences of our lives with others, through narratives that tell not only what happened to whom, but why things happened, and how they impacted the individuals involved in and thus touched by the events.

The analysis provided in this chapter makes clear that the development of autobiographical memory and the story of the phenomenon of childhood amnesia are not one and the same. For much of the history of the field of psychology – between the time the phenomenon of childhood amnesia was "discovered" and the end of the twentieth century – the onset of autobiographical memory was defined, almost by default, as the offset of childhood amnesia. Yet autobiographical memory develops early in childhood, whereas childhood amnesia makes its debut in middle childhood. We must be especially cautious about making the equation between the development of autobiographical memory and the offset of childhood amnesia, because it leads to the erroneous assumption that at the end of the preschool years autobiographical memory changes qualitatively. This contributes to models that explain the acceleration of memories beginning at 4 to 6 years of age in terms of something that is, in effect, "turned on" to permit their rapid formation. Alternatively, it contributes to models that acknowledge that autobiographical memories are formed prior to 4 to 6 years of age, but that at roughly that time something happens to make them inaccessible, thereby accounting for the accelerated forgetting of early memories observed among adults.

In this chapter, I have argued that a more productive approach is to view the change in distribution of memories near the end of the preschool years in terms of a "crossing over" of the two complementary functions of remembering and forgetting. Early in the preschool years, forgetting outstrips remembering; by later in the preschool years, remembering begins to outstrip forgetting. Because the rate of forgetting of events from early childhood is more rapid than that from later childhood and adulthood, if one looks back, it appears that something has happened to accelerate forgetting. However, if one looks forward from the perspective afforded by developmental lenses, one sees that what has happened is that the rate of forgetting has begun to approach the rate in adulthood. What this perspective lacks in glamour and mystery, it makes up for by permitting us to see the continuity of autobiographical memory that may otherwise be obscured.

References

Ackil, J. K., Van Abbema, D. L., and Bauer, P. J. (2003). After the storm: enduring differences in mother–child recollections of traumatic and nontraumatic events. *Journal of Experimental Child Psychology*, **84**, 286–309.

Bauer, P. J. (2006). Event memory. In W. Damon and R. M. Lerner (eds.), *Handbook of child psychology* (6th edn.). Vol. II: D. Kuhn and R. Siegler (vol. eds.), *Cognition, perception, and language* (pp. 373–425). Hoboken, NJ: Wiley.

(2007). *Remembering the times of our lives: memory in infancy and beyond.* Mahwah, NJ: Lawrence Erlbaum Associates.

(2008). Infantile amnesia. In M. M. Haith and J. B. Benson (eds.), *Encyclopedia of infant and early childhood development* (pp. 51–61). San Diego, CA: Academic Press.

Bauer, P. J., Burch, M. M., Scholin, S. E., and Güler, O. (2007). Using cue words to investigate the distribution of autobiographical memories in childhood. *Psychological Science*, **18**, 910–916.

Bauer, P. J. and Larkina, M. (2011). *Childhood amnesia in the making: different distributions of autobiographical memories in children and adults.* Manuscript in review.

Bauer, P. J., Stark, E. N., Lukowski, A. F., Rademacher, J., Van Abbema, D. L., and Ackil, J. K. (2005). Working together to make sense of the past: mothers' and children's use of internal states language in conversations about traumatic and non-traumatic events. *Journal of Cognition and Development*, **6**, 463–488.

Bauer, P. J., Stennes, L., and Haight, J. C. (2003). Representation of the inner self in autobiography: women's and men's use of internal states language in personal narratives. *Memory*, **11**, 27–42.

Bohn, A. and Berntsen, D. (2008). Life story development in childhood: the development of life story abilities and the acquisition of cultural life scripts from late middle childhood and adolescence. *Developmental Psychology*, **44**, 1135–1147.

Bruce, D., Wilcox-O'Hearn, A., Robinson, J. A., Phillips-Grant, K., Francis, L., and Smith, M. C. (2005). Fragment memories mark the end of childhood amnesia. *Memory & Cognition*, **33**, 567–576.

Cleveland, E. S. and Reese, E. (2008). Children remember early childhood: long-term recall across the offset of childhood amnesia. *Applied Cognitive Psychology*, **22**, 127–142.

Crovitz, H. F. and Schiffman, H. (1974). Frequency of episodic memories as a function of their age. *Bulletin of the Psychonomic Society*, **4**, 517–518.

Fitzgerald, J. M. (1991). A developmental account of early childhood amnesia. *Journal of Genetic Psychology*, **152**, 159–171.

Fivush, R. and Haden, C. A. (1997). Narrating and representing experience: preschoolers' developing autobiographical accounts. In P. van den Broek, P. J. Bauer, and T. Bourg (eds.), *Developmental spans in event representation and comprehension: bridging fictional and actual events* (pp. 169–198). Mahwah, NJ: Erlbaum.

Fivush, R. and Schwarzmueller, A. (1998). Children remember childhood: implications for childhood amnesia. *Applied Cognitive Psychology*, **12**, 455–473.

Freud, S. (1905/1953). Childhood and concealing memories. In *The basic writings of Sigmund Freud*. A. A. Brill (trans. and ed.). New York: Modern Library.

Habermas, T. and Bluck, S. (2000). Getting a life: the emergence of the life story in adolescence. *Psychological Bulletin*, **126**, 748–769.

Habermas, T., Negele, A., and Mayer. F. B. (2010). "Honey, you're jumping about": mothers' scaffolding of their children's and adolescents' life narration. *Cognitive Development*, **25**, 339–351.

Hamond, N. R. and Fivush, R. (1991). Memories of Mickey Mouse: young children recount their trip to Disney World. *Cognitive Development*, **6**, 433–448.

Jack, F., MacDonald, S., Reese, E., and Hayne, H. (2009). Maternal reminiscing style during early childhood predicts the age of adolescents' earliest memories. *Child Development*, **80**, 496–505.

Larkina, M., Merrill, N., Fivush, R., and Bauer, P. J. (2009). Linking children's earliest memories and maternal reminiscing style. Poster presented to the Cognitive Development Society, San Antonio, Texas, October.

MacDonald, S., Uesiliana, K., and Hayne, H. (2000). Cross-cultural and gender differences in childhood amnesia. *Memory*, **8**(6), 365–376.

Miles, C. (1893). A study of individual psychology. *American Journal of Psychology*, **6**, 534–558.

Morris, G., Baker-Ward, L., and Bauer, P. J. (2009). What remains of that day: the survival of children's autobiographical memories across time. *Applied Cognitive Psychology*, **24**, 527–544.

Mullen, M. K. (1994). Earliest recollections of childhood: a demographic analysis. *Cognition*, **52**, 55–79.

Nelson, K. (1986). *Event knowledge: structure and function in development*. Hillsdale, NJ: Erlbaum.

Nelson, K. and Fivush, R. (2004). The emergence of autobiographical memory: a social cultural developmental theory. *Psychological Review*, **111**, 486–511.

O'Kearney, R., Speyer, J., and Kenardy, J. (2007). Children's narrative memory for accidents and their post-traumatic distress. *Applied Cognitive Psychology*, **21**(7), 821–838.

Perner, J. and Ruffman, T. (1995). Episodic memory and autonoetic consciousness: developmental evidence and a theory of childhood amnesia. *Journal of Experimental Child Psychology*, **59**, 516–548.

Peterson, C., Grant, V. V., and Boland, L. D. (2005). Childhood amnesia in children and adolescents: their earliest memories. *Memory*, **13**, 622–637.

Piaget, J. (1962). *Play, dreams and imitation in childhood*. New York: W. W. Norton & Co.

Pillemer, D. B. and White, S. H. (1989). Childhood events recalled by children and adults. In H. W. Reese (ed.), *Advances in child development and behavior*, vol. XXI (pp. 297–340). Orlando, FL: Academic Press.

Reese, E., Haden, C., Baker-Ward, L., Bauer, P. J., Fivush, R., and Ornstein, P. A. (2011). Coherence of personal narratives across the lifespan: a multidimensional model and coding method. *Journal of Cognition and Development*, **12**, 424–462.

Reese, E., Jack, F., and White, N. (2010). Origins of adolescents' autobiographical memories. *Cognitive Development*, **25**, 352–367.

Rubin, D. C. (1982). On the retention function for autobiographical memory. *Journal of Verbal Learning and Verbal Behavior*, **21**, 21–38.

(2000). The distribution of early childhood memories. *Memory*, **8**, 265–269.

Rubin, D. C. and Schulkind, M. D. (1997). The distribution of important and word-cued autobiographical memories in 20-, 35-, and 70-year-old adults. *Psychology and Aging*, **12**, 524–535.

Rubin, D. C. and Wenzel, A. E. (1996). One hundred years of forgetting: a quantitative description of retention. *Psychological Review*, **103**, 734–760.

Rubin, D. C., Wetzler, S. E., and Nebes, R. D. (1986). Autobiographical memory across the adult lifespan. In D. C. Rubin (ed.), *Autobiographical memory* (pp. 202–221). New York: Cambridge University Press.

Van Abbema, D. L. and Bauer, P. J. (2005). Autobiographical memory in middle childhood: recollections of the recent and distant past. *Memory*, **13**, 829–845.

Wang, Q. (2003). Infantile amnesia reconsidered: a cross-cultural analysis. *Memory*, **11**, 65–80.

Wang, Q., Leichtman, M. D., and Davies, K. I. (2000). Sharing memories and telling stories: American and Chinese mothers and their 3-year-olds. *Memory*, **8**, 159–177.

Weigle, T. W. and Bauer, P. J. (2000). Deaf and hearing adults' recollections of childhood and beyond. *Memory*, **8**, 293–309.

West, T. A. and Bauer, P. J. (1999). Assumptions of infantile amnesia: are there differences between early and later memories? *Memory*, **7**, 257–278.

Wetzler, S. E. and Sweeney, J. A. (1986). Childhood amnesia: an empirical demonstration. In D. C. Rubin (ed.), *Autobiographical memory* (pp. 191–201). New York: Cambridge University Press.

White, S. H. and Pillemer, D. B. (1979). Childhood amnesia and the development of a socially accessible memory system. In J. F. Kihlstrom and F. J. Evans (eds.), *Functional disorders of memory* (pp. 29–73). Hillsdale, NJ: Erlbaum.

Wickelgren, W. A. (1974). Single-trace fragility theory of memory dynamics. *Memory & Cognition*, **2**, 775–780.

(1975). Alcoholic intoxication and memory storage dynamics. *Memory & Cognition*, **3**, 385–389.

Wixted, J. T. (2004). On common ground: Jost's (1897) law of forgetting and Ribot's (1881) law of retrograde amnesia. *Psychological Review*, **111**, 864–879.

12 Subjective perspective and personal timeline in the development of autobiographical memory

Robyn Fivush

> I try desperately to conquer the transitory nature of my existence, to trap moments before they evanesce, to untangle the confusion of my past . . . to elucidate the ancient secrets of my childhood, to define my identity, to create my own legend. In the end, the only thing we have in abundance is the memory we have woven. (Allende, 2001, pp. 303–304)

Autobiographical memory is best defined as the construction of a coherent narrative woven from the fleeting memories of our past experiences. Through telling and sharing our stories with ourselves and others, we reconstruct and reinterpret what happened in ways that provide an evolving sense of meaning and narrative identity: who we are over time. More provocatively, although autobiographical memory is defined as memories of one's own experiences, individual life narratives incorporate and integrate cultural interpretative frameworks. In a very real sense, autobiographical memory is memory beyond the individual to include how an individual life is understood, modulated, and transformed through socially and culturally constructed narratives.

In this chapter, I present an overview of the development of autobiographical memory from a sociocultural developmental perspective. I make two related arguments. First, I argue that the emergence of autobiographical memory during the preschool years depends on the development of a subjective perspective (what Tulving, 2002, has called autonoetic consciousness). A subjective perspective is the ability to link mental states across time to create a continuous sense of inner subjectivity (James' [1890] stream of consciousness). Second, I argue that autobiographical memory continues to develop through middle childhood and adolescence, as individuals begin to compose a personal timeline. Personal timelines are constructed from life scripts (Berntsen and Rubin, 2004) and master narratives (McAdams, 2004) that define what a life looks like, how it should be lived, and how it should be evaluated. These life scripts and master narratives provide both structural and moral frameworks for constructing an individual life narrative in ways that produce autobiography in the true sense of the word, a biography of one's own life interwoven with sociocultural events and the lives of others (Fivush, 2008, 2010a, 2010b). Before delving into these arguments in more detail, I first set the stage by defining autobiographical memory and providing an overview of the sociocultural theory of autobiographical memory development.

Defining autobiographical memory

In 1972, Tulving made a distinction between two forms of declarative memory, semantic and episodic. Whereas semantic memory is gleaned from experience, it is not tied to a specific time and place, but represents general knowledge about the world (e.g., the Empire State Building is the tallest building in New York City). In contrast, episodic memory is memory of a specific episode occurring at a specific time and place (e.g., I remember the day I went to the top of the Empire State Building and the exhilarating view over the city). In Tulving's conceptualization, there are two components of episodic memory, spatial-temporal tagging and auto-noetic knowing – that is, the subjective sense that one experienced this event at a particular place and time in the past, or what has now come to be called mental time travel (Tulving, 2002). Much of the research on epi-sodic memory assumes that demonstrating spatial-temporal tagging simul-taneously demonstrates autonoetic knowing, but, in fact, these are two theoretically and empirically separable components. Whereas the former demonstrates an episodic memory representation, only the latter demon-strates an *autobiographical* memory, a memory of a self engaging in that past event that is linked in a continuous stream to the present (see Fivush, 2010a; Nelson, 2003; Nelson and Fivush, 2004, for related arguments).

The ability to take a *subjective perspective* on the past requires at least three additional layers beyond an episodic spatial-temporal tag: (1) a representation of a self that experienced the event – not simply that an event happened, but that it happened *to me*; (2) that this self has mental states that provide a perspective, or point of view, on the past, and that these mental states are continuous in time – that when I was there I had specific thoughts and feelings that I can now recall; and that (3) earlier mental states are causally related to later mental states, that the way I thought and felt then may be the same as or different than I think and feel now, and these internal states are linked through time in meaningful ways. Each of these, in turn, relies on the development of multiple social and cognitive skills that emerge across the preschool years and allow for the emergence of autobiographical memory (see Fivush and Nelson, 2006; Nelson and Fivush, 2004, for related arguments).

The concept of autonoetic knowing, or mental time travel, additionally implies more than the ability to link a single past event to the present through subjective perspective: it implies the ability to create a coherent personal timeline that stretches back into a continuous past (and perhaps into the future as well; see D'Argembeau, this volume). For true auto-biography, the individual must be able to link multiple events together into an overarching life narrative, the "story of me" (Barnes, 1998; Conway, Singer, and Tagini, 2004; Fivush, 2001; Fivush and Haden, 2005; McAdams, 2001; Pillemer, 1998). This ability relies on at least two additional components beyond simple subjective perspective: (1) a devel-oping understanding of both conventional time (e.g., calendars) and cultural time (e.g., life scripts that define life periods); and (2) the incor-poration of culturally defined master narratives, or life motifs, that define evaluative and moral frameworks of how a life should be lived and what it means (Bruner, 1990; Fivush, 2010b; McAdams, 1992; Thorne, McLean, and Lawrence, 2004). Both the development of subjective perspective and the construction of a personal timeline depend on the individual interacting with others in socially rich contexts that allow the individual to appropriate culturally provided models of selves and lives. Thus, although animals may be capable of episodic representations, only humans are capable of autobio-graphical memory (see Fivush, 2010a; Nelson and Fivush, 2004, for related arguments).

The sociocultural developmental model

Vygotsky (1978) argued that human lives develop within cultures that define what it means to be a competent member of that culture, and that activities are structured in such a way that children are exposed to and invited to participate in graded activities in which they will learn necessary adult skills. To put some flesh on these ideas, think about virtually any home with an infant in a modern industrialized culture. Even in the first few months of life, the infant will be surrounded by picture books, alpha-bet books, and toys with letters and numbers. Well before these strange markings hold any meaning for the infant, the infant will already be drawn into contact and activities with these cultural artifacts, exactly because these are artifacts of literacy, which has become the most important cultural skill a child will need to master. Parents will sing the alphabet and play counting games with infants even in the first months of life, structuring the environment in such a way that the infant is drawn into critical cultural activities.

Similarly, having and telling the stories of our lives, of who we are, is an essential cultural skill, again especially in modern industrialized societies (see McAdams, 1992; Nelson, 2003, for related arguments), in which individuals are frequently called upon to explain themselves through their experiences, and these social interactions serve multiple functions, including self-defining, social bonding, and directive functions (see Pillemer and Kuwabara, this volume). Even preschoolers are expected to provide coherent accounts of their daily activities to Daddy and Grandma; school-age children are expected to provide coherent accounts of what they learned from their summer vacation. Students and job applicants are expected to provide coherent statements that integrate personal, academic, and occupational experiences and draw lessons and conclusions from these experiences in compelling ways. In medical settings, patients are expected to provide coherent narratives of their experiences of relations between symptoms and behaviors. And obviously, in social interaction, whether we are meeting new people, catching up with old friends, or simply reuniting with family at the end of the day, we are expected to have coherent and meaningful stories of our experiences to share with others (hence the frustration of receiving the response "nothing" when asking someone what happened that day!).

From the moment of birth, as they are holding and soothing their infants, parents and grandparents are already telling infants stories about the family, exploits of adventurous and successful family members, stories about how silly the parents were when they were children, and projected stories about what the world holds for this new life (Fiese, Hooker, Kotary, *et al.*, 1995). Obviously, in the first months of life, the infant does not understand these stories, but the importance of these stories is underscored by their prevalence in everyday social activity.

Intriguingly, children begin participating in conversations about their own past experiences virtually as soon as they begin talking. At about 16 months of age, children will make references to recently past events (this morning's breakfast, yesterday at the park) although these references are brief and are heavily structured or scaffolded by the parent (Eisenberg, 1985; Hudson, 1990). For example, the child may say "swings" and the mother says, "Yes, we played on the swings in the park this morning. You went up so high! Wasn't that fun?" In this way, mothers draw a fleeting reference into a story with a beginning, middle, and end, and, perhaps most importantly, provide an evaluative framework for what the event means and how it should be understood. It is through participating in parentally scaffolded narratives about past experiences that children are learning the forms and functions of autobiographical memory. Moreover, from a Vygotskian perspective, the way in which parents scaffold autobiographical narratives is critical. Parents who co-construct more elaborated, detailed, and coherent narratives of the past have children who internalize these culturally canonical forms, and come to tell more elaborated and coherent stories on their own (Fivush, 1991; Fivush, Haden, and Reese, 2006).

Language, narrative, and autobiographical memory

These arguments obviously rest on the assumption that language, and especially narrative, is critical in the development of autobiographical memory. Although memory itself is clearly not linguistically based (e.g., Conway and Pleydell-Pearce, 2000; Rubin, 2006, this volume), and is apparent well before language (e.g., Carver and Bauer, 1999, 2001; see Bauer, this volume, for a review), narratives are a primary cultural tool for organizing and expressing memories. First, language allows us to share our memories with others in ways that would simply not be possible outside a language system. Although references to past objects and events may not require language, the only way that individuals can express an experience that occurs over time and that includes their thoughts and emotions about that experience in a coherent way is through language. Language allows us to unite what Bruner (1990) has called the landscape of action with the landscape of consciousness into an integrated account of what occurred. Second, by sharing our memories with others, we are confronted with the possibility that others may recall events differently than we do (e.g., I saw giraffes at the zoo but Mommy does not remember that). Without language, memory is conceptualized by the individual as a copy of reality; what is remembered is what occurred. With language, and especially through sharing stories that are contested, negotiated, negated, or validated, individuals come to understand that memory is a subjective system; what is remembered may be partly what happened but is also partly reconstructed from the perspective of a personal present (Fivush and Haden, 2005; Fivush and Nelson, 2006). Importantly, it is not only facts about what happened that may be contested but also interpretations and evaluations (I liked the roller coaster but my brother was scared). It is only through sharing our stories with others that we come to own our experiences as uniquely ours and different from others. Memories may not be true to the world but they are true to the self; through language we share our memories with others and through sharing our memories with others we come to understand that our memories are our own subjective perspective on our personal past.

Moreover, because narratives provide culturally canonical forms for sharing our past with others, they ultimately provide organizational schemes for ourselves. Narratives move beyond simple chronologies, to provide events with a beginning, middle, and end; what happened and why; who were the actors; what were their intentions and emotions; and how did this all play out? A story is not a story if we do not understand why people acted as they did and how these intentions and motivations were or were not shared with others in ways that lead to comedy or tragedy (Bruner, 1990).

Thus, language and narratives are critical in organizing the events of our lives into meaningful sequences and allowing us to share these experiences with others. This, in turn, allows for renegotiation and reconstruction that provides a sense of subjective perspective: this is not *a* story – this is *my* story (Barnes, 1998). Developmentally, the question is, how do children develop from simple representations of past events (i.e., episodic representations) to a coherent life narrative that provides perspective and meaning for the self across time (i.e., autobiographical memory)? Autobiographical memories build on episodic representations, but they are not the same as episodic representations; autobiographical memories include subjective perspective and personal timeline. Following from sociocultural theory, it is the culture that provides the tools for autobiographical memory, and these tools are displayed and internalized through everyday local social interactions.

Parental reminiscing style

There is now abundant evidence both that there are individual differences in children's developing autobiographical narrative skills, and that these differences are linked to earlier, parentally scaffolded, co-constructed narratives (see Bauer, 2007; Fivush, 2007; Fivush, Haden, and Reese, 2006; Reese, 2002, for reviews). Moreover, many of these developmental relations are quite specific. Parents who use more temporal and causal language in their co-constructed narratives with their 2- to 3-year-old children have 4- to 5-year-old children who use more temporal and causal language when narrating an autobiographical event to an unfamiliar adult (Fivush, 1991; Peterson and McCabe, 1992, 1996). Parents who co-construct more elaborated detailed narratives with their young preschool children have children who come to tell more detailed autobiographical narratives later in the preschool years (e.g., Bauer and Burch, 2004; Farrant and Reese, 2000; Fivush and Vasudeva, 2002; Flannagan, Baker-Ward, and Graham, 1995; Harley and Reese, 1999; Hudson, 1990; McCabe and Peterson, 1991; Welch-Ross, 1997, 2001). And parents who co-construct narratives that focus more on internal states have children who use more of this kind of language in their own autobiographical narratives later in development (Fivush, 1991; Fivush and Haden, 2005; Kuebli, Butler, and Fivush, 1995; Rudek and Haden, 2005). In addition to longitudinal correlational studies, there is converging experimental evidence that mothers who are trained to be more elaborative subsequently have children who narrate more coherent and elaborated autobiographical memories (Peterson, Jesso, and McCabe, 1999; Peterson and McCabe, 1994).

Intriguingly, differences in parental reminiscing style are linked to child and parent gender, and to culture, but it is beyond the scope of this chapter to review that research (see Fivush and Buckner, 2003, for a review of gender, and Wang and Ross, 2007, for a review of culture as it relates to parental scaffolding and children's developing autobiographical narratives). Equally important, parental reminiscing style is not a general conversational style; parents who are more elaborate and coherent when co-constructing the past are not necessarily more elaborate in other conversational contexts, such as book-reading, free play, or care-giving routines (see Fivush et al., 2006, for a full discussion). Rather, the evidence indicates that reminiscing is a critical and unique context of social interaction in which children are encouraged to participate, and that individual differences in how parents scaffold co-constructed narratives during reminiscing is directly related to the specific narrative skills children are learning to construct their own autobiography. Moreover, through sharing memories with others, children become aware that their memories are subjective representations; memories evolve from representations of external events to memories of a personal past. To flesh out these arguments, I now turn to a more detailed discussion of what is involved in the development of subjective perspective.

The development of subjective perspective

Subjective perspective relies on three interrelated developments: (1) the representation of a self; (2) the understanding that the self has internal states (thoughts, emotions, beliefs, desires) that are coherently linked to behavior; and (3) the understanding that others also have internal states and that others' internal states may be the same or different than one's own. Understanding internal states is critical in creating a perspective on an event; not simply that something happened but that one has thoughts and feelings about it that provide an evaluative framework. Moreover, unless one realizes that others can have a different evaluative perspective on an event, the perspective cannot be truly subjective. Much of the research focused on these developments has been conducted within the framework of a "theory of mind," and there is general consensus that these abilities have early precursors even in infancy, with the development of intersubjectivity (see Tomasello, 1999, for full theoretical review and discussion). By late in the first year of life, infants will follow eye gaze and finger points, with the seeming understanding that the other is looking at and referring to something interesting, and infants will begin to engage in "show and share" behavior, holding up an object that they are delighted in just to show it to another and see their responses. The back and forth looking at the person and the object indicates that the infant is interested in "sharing the moment." By age 2, children indicate an understanding of a physical self through mirror self-recognition (Lewis and Brooks-Gunn, 1979), as well as an understanding of a mental self, that the child and others have desires on which they both act (for example, other children grab a toy because they "want" it – they have an intention) (see Wellman, 2002, for an overview of the development of theory of mind).

Much of this early ability to understand subjective perspective is in the here-and-now, in the moment of the interaction. However, the ability to extend subjective perspective across time develops much later. More specifically, several component abilities develop, including the ability to understand (1) that one has internal states that persist over time, and thus that earlier mental states may cause later behavior; (2) that mental states, while persistent, can also change such that, for example, something that made you happy earlier now makes you sad; (3) that others have mental states that persist over time as well, and that others' mental states can also change over time; and (4) that self and other may have the same or different states over time. These are complex sets of skills, and, not surprisingly, they are reasonably late in developing (Fivush and Nelson, 2006). There are two lines of evidence suggesting how protracted this developmental process is – the use of internal state language within narratives of the personal past, and the ability to link internal states across time, such that one understands that earlier internal states are connected in some way to current internal states. The development of each of these abilities is discussed in turn.

Internal state language within personal narratives

Although preschoolers talk a good bit about ongoing internal states (Bretherton, Fritz, Zahn-Waxler, *et al.*, 1986; Dunn, Bretherton, and Munn, 1987; Dunn, Brown, and Beardsall, 1991), it is not until the end of the preschool years that children begin to integrate much internal state language into personal narratives, and the inclusion of mental state language in personal narratives continues to increase across childhood and into early adulthood. For example, in parentally scaffolded narratives about everyday emotional events (a time you were sad, happy, scared, or angry), 4-year-old children used a mean of 1.18 emotion words in any given narrative, whereas their parents used a mean of 4.61 emotion words (Fivush, Brotman, Buckner, *et al.*, 2000). Even when narrating highly emotional events, 3- to 4-year-olds recalling a natural disaster used a mean of 1.54 emotion words, and a mean of 0.59 cognitive processing words, words such as *think* and *believe*, indicative of mental states. These same children, interviewed 6 years later, increased their inclusion of emotion words to a mean of 2.30 and cognitive processing words to a mean of 3.79 (Sales, Fivush, Parker, *et al.*, 2003). This may partly reflect an increasing vocabulary, but there is reasonably good evidence that preschoolers have a fairly wide vocabulary of emotion words and use them when describing ongoing experience (e.g., Bretherton *et al.*, 1986; Dunn *et al.*, 1991). Moreover, even school-age children do not incorporate internal state language to the same extent as adolescents and adults in their personal narratives. When asked to narrate scary and frustrating events, 8- to 12-year-olds use a mean of 2.32 negative emotion words and 1.48 cognitive processing words, whereas adults used a mean of 4.85 negative emotion words and 4.02 cognitive processing words (Fivush, Sales, and Bohanek, 2008). Bauer and colleagues (Bauer, Burch, Van Abbema, *et al.*, 2007; Bauer, Stark, Lukowski, *et al.*, 2005) obtained similar results in examining internal state language used by mothers and their children when narrating about a devastating tornado; children as old as 11 years used only half the number of emotion and cognition terms in their narratives as their mothers, indicating that the integration of internal state language into personal narratives continues well into early adulthood.

Moreover, consistent with sociocultural theory, there is evidence that children are learning how to integrate mental state language into their personal narratives through participating in parentally scaffolded co-constructed narratives. Those parents who use more mental state language in co-constructing narratives with their preschool children, have children who 1 to 2 years later are using more mental state language when narrating their past to an unfamiliar adult (Fivush, 1991; Kuebli *et al.*, 1995; Rudek and Haden, 2005). These relations continue through middle childhood. Seven- to 11-year-old children whose mothers use more mental state language when co-constructing narratives of both highly stressful and everyday events, subsequently use more mental state language in their own personal narratives (Bauer *et al.*, 2007).

Importantly, maternally structured reminiscing that includes more internal state language is related to children developing theory of mind, the idea that self and others have thoughts, emotions, and desires, and that these internal states may be the same or different across self and other (Reese, 2002; Reese and Cleveland, 2006; Welch-Ross, 1997). From a sociocultural perspective, the argument is that children develop this understanding through participating in reminiscing with others who structure these conversations in such a way to highlight subjective perspective. There are critical conversational junctures where parents and children will disagree about what happened, and parents who explicate these moments by using more internal state language have children who come to understand that each individual remembers events from their own subjective perspective. For example, here is a mother and her 4-year-old daughter discussing when the latter's friend slept over for the weekend:

MOTHER: I remember when you were sad. You were sad when Melinda had to leave on Saturday, weren't you?
CHILD: Uh-huh.
MOTHER: You were very sad. And what happened? Why did you feel sad?
CHILD: Because Melinda, Melinda say, was having [unintelligible word].
MOTHER: Yes.
CHILD: And then she stood up on my bed and it was my bedroom. She's not allowed to sleep there.
MOTHER: Is that why you were sad?
CHILD: Yeah. Now it makes me happy. I also, it makes me sad. But Melinda just left.
MOTHER: Uh-huh.
CHILD: And then I cried.
MOTHER: And you cried because . . .
CHILD: Melinda left.
MOTHER: Because Melinda left? And did that make you sad?
CHILD: And then I cried [makes "aaahhhh" sounds] like that. I cried and cried and cried and cried.
MOTHER: I know. I know. I thought you were sad because Melinda left. I didn't know you were also sad because Melinda slept in your bed.

There is actually quite a lot of complexity in this simple exchange. The mother indicates that she did not understand how the child felt, suggesting that internal states are subjective and not always shared. The mother further helps the child understand that the child herself could have multiple emotions at different points during the event, being both sad and happy. Finally the mother scaffolds a coherent narrative that integrates what happened with how the child felt in a way that creates a meaningful story. It is through this kind of reminiscing that children are learning to create a personal past infused with complex mental states that are the glue of the story.

Linking mental states across time

An additional component of subjective perspective is the understanding that mental states persist over time such that earlier mental states are related to and predict current mental states and behavior. Research by Lagattuta and Wellman (2001, 2002) indicates that it is not until the end of the preschool years that children are able to link mental states across time in this way. In this series of studies, children are presented with vignettes about children being approached by a friendly dog in the park or seeing a friend at the playground. Virtually all children agree that the children in the story will be happy due to these events. However, some children are given a back-story about an individual child who a week before had a scary experience with a dog, or had a fight with their friend. Preschoolers do not use this information to predict current behavior. In fact, even among 5-year-olds, only 39% of the children spontaneously referred to previous mental states as persisting over time (the child will be scared of the friendly dog or will be angry with the friend), and even when prompted, only 60% claim that previous mental states will predict current behavior. As a comparison, among adults, 89% spontaneously refer to thoughts persisting over time (Lagattata and Wellman, 2001). These findings suggest that preschoolers do not yet quite understand that individuals have mental states that persist over time in ways that link past experiences to current behavior.

Thus, evidence both from more naturalistic studies examining maternally scaffolded reminiscing and children's developing personal narratives, and more experimental work on theory of mind and the understanding that mental states persist over time converges on the conclusion that a subjective perspective does not emerge until the end of the preschool years. Although infants and young children certainly have episodic representations – that is, that an event happened at a particular time and place in the past – the understanding that memories of the past are constructed from a personal perspective that may be the same as or different from those of others develops gradually across the preschool years. This is the first step in transforming episodic memories into autobiographical memories. However, the full transformation of episodic into autobiographical memory involves what Tulving (2002) has called mental time travel, and relies on the further development of a personal timeline. Not only did this event happen in the past to me in ways that link my past self to my current self; this event occurred in relation to other past events as well, and all of these events are related to each other on a timeline that creates a continuous sense of self through time. Note that the development of both subjective perspective and a personal timeline depends on the ability to recall past episodes, but they are not in and of themselves mnemonic developments. Rather they are skills that allow episodic memories to become autobiographical (see Nelson and Fivush, 2004, for full arguments).

The development of a personal timeline

A personal timeline depends on two related developments. First, the developing understanding of conventional time (e.g., the division of time into weeks and months) that allows for the temporal sequencing of multiple episodes onto an overarching timeline, and, second, the developing understanding of cultural time in terms of both life scripts (e.g., the division of time into life periods such as childhood and adolescence) that provide an organization for a life narrative, and master narratives that provide culturally canonical ways of evaluating a life narrative.

There has been surprisingly little research examining children's developing understanding of time, and the understanding of time seems to be a surprisingly late development (Friedman, 1993, 2003, 2004). Infants demonstrate some understanding of the temporal order of a sequence of actions within an event; for example, by the end of the first year, infants will reasonably accurately re-enact sequences of actions leading to a goal, such as putting a ball into two interlocking cups to make a rattle (Bauer, Wenner, Dropik, et al., 2000). But the ability to put a series of events in order, such as making a rattle on Monday and a drum on Tuesday, seems to be much more difficult. Although preschool children will use temporal terms such as "yesterday" and "tomorrow," they seem to use these words indiscriminately to mean any time in the past or the future (Harner, 1982). By the end of the preschool years, children can judge which of two events happened more recently or in the more distant past (e.g., the rattle was made before the drum), but only if these events occurred in the previous few months. Even 8-year-olds perform at chance in judging the relative recency of events that occurred over multiple months (Friedman, 1992, 2003; Friedman and Kemp, 1998). Understanding of calendar time, and the ability to date events by conventions (e.g., July 3, 2003), appears to be even later developing, and, indeed, although adults can use conventional time, they have great difficulty in dating personal events in this way (Belli, Smith, Andreski, et al., 2007). Instead, even as adults, we rely mostly on culturally defined life periods, such as "when I was in high school" or "before I was married" (Conway and Pleydell-Pearce, 2000), that form a life script. Life scripts provide templates for prototypical life events and when they occur that help organize individual timelines (Berntsen and Rubin, 2004), and may also help integrate personal timelines with historical events in ways that organize autobiographical memory (Brown, Hansen, Lee, et al., this volume).

These kinds of cultural life scripts, or culturally canonical biographies (Habermas and Bluck, 2000), rely on an amalgam of conventional and cultural time. Cultures define the shape of a life, in the sense of defining life periods and appropriate experiences. Although some life periods could be argued to be biologically based (e.g., infancy), others are clearly culturally defined. For example, the age of consent for marriage is culturally and historically variable due to shifting understanding of when childhood ends and adulthood begins. Puberty is no longer the criterion for adulthood; indeed, in modern Western culture, we are extending childhood and have added life periods such as "tweeners" and "emerging adulthood" to extend adolescence to begin earlier and end later (see Meyer, 1988, for related arguments).

What is particularly interesting is that recent research indicates that children begin to understand life scripts at about the same time they begin to understand conventional time, between the ages of 8 and 12 years. Children of this age are able to provide information about expected life events (e.g., high-school graduation, marriage, children, retirement) and the ages at which they may be expected to occur (Berntsen and Bohn, 2010; Bohn and Berntsen, 2008). It is more interesting that children who provide more "adult-like" life scripts also provide more coherent narratives about their own personal experiences, suggesting that knowledge of the life script helps children to create a more organized personal timeline as well. At age 8, children begin to be able to provide "chapters" for their lives (when I was in kindergarten, when I was in summer camp), and, with increasing age, children provide more sophisticated and complex life chapters (Reese, Yan, Jack, et al., 2010). By late adolescence, individuals provide reasonably coherent life narratives, defined as an overarching narrative that incorporates and unifies separate experiences in ways that create a coherent account across a lifetime (Habermas and de Silveira, 2008; Habermas and Paha, 2001; McAdams, 2001).

But life scripts do not yet form autobiographical memory; as argued here, autobiographical memory depends on subjective perspective. The life script provides a culturally canonical framework for organizing a personal timeline; master narratives provide culturally available evaluative frameworks (McAdams, 2001; Thorne and McLean, 2002). For example, a highly prevalent master narrative in American culture is the Horatio Alger "rags to riches" story: one starts with nothing, works hard, and ends up materially successful. This master narrative infuses cultural media, stories, books, movies, in ways that allow individuals to appropriate this evaluative framework to make sense of their own lives (Harbus, 2011). McAdams (2004) has identified a similar, highly prevalent American master narrative, "the redemptive self," in which the individual overcomes great hardship and as a result becomes a better person. This master narrative has infused the current self-help culture, as can be seen in the widespread acceptance of 12-step programs that focus on initial acceptance of oneself as tragically flawed and create a redemptive narrative of overcoming the odds and ultimately helping others. When master narratives are integrated with life scripts, they provide evaluative frameworks that both describe and prescribe how a life should be lived.

Whereas some master narratives are culture-wide, others are more sub-culturally specific. For example, Thorne and McLean (2002) identified gender-specific master narratives, such that male adolescents told "John Wayne" personal stories and female adolescents told "Florence Nightingale" personal stories. It is also the case that some evaluative frameworks are considered culturally inappropriate, and are silenced. These may change over historical time; for example, prevalent American master narratives changed with the advent of the US civil rights movements and the second wave of the women's movement (see Fivush, 2010b, for full discussion of voice and silencing). These culturally available and appropriated life scripts and master narratives merge to provide evaluative frameworks for individuals living in specific socio-cultural contexts and provide both descriptive and prescriptive models for constructing a meaningful personal life narrative.

Moreover, in line with the sociocultural perspective outlined here, there is emerging evidence that adolescents learn how to create this kind of a personal timeline through participating in maternally structured life narratives (Habermas, Negele, and Brenneisen-Mayer, 2010). With 8-year-olds, mothers focus on creating a coherent temporal timeline, helping their children to learn conventional and cultural timelines. As children get older mothers begin to focus more on evaluative aspects of the life story, providing interpretative and moral frameworks, perhaps scaffolding the integration of perspective into the personal timeline. However, although there is theoretical agreement that adolescence is a critical period for the formation of a life narrative, research on how this occurs is just beginning (e.g., McLean and Pasupathi, 2010).

Summary and conclusions

Autobiographical memory, defined as a subjective life narrative, is a uniquely human and surprisingly late developing skill. Although episodic representations are clearly available from very early in development, the ability to construct a personal past that provides a temporally organized sequence of events that are related to each other and to the present through an evaluative subjective perspective emerges gradually during the preschool years and continues to develop through adolescence. It is important to emphasize that the developments of a subjective perspective and of a personal timeline are not necessarily explicit mnemonic developments, but rely on more overarching social and cognitive skills. What transforms episodic memory into autobiographical memory is the gradually developing ability to integrate these emerging skills into episodic representations such that they become representations of the experiences of a continuous self over time (see Donald, this volume, for theoretically related arguments about the evolution of autobiographical memory). Indeed, this is likely a life-span process; the evaluative frameworks brought to bear on creating meaning from life experiences most likely continue to develop across adulthood (McAdams, 2004). Rather than a set of memories collected over time, autobiographical memory is best conceptualized as an evolving perspective on oneself through the past. To return to the quotation that opened this chapter, perhaps autobiography is more legend than memory.

References

Allende, I. (2001). *Portrait in sepia*. New York: HarperCollins.

Barnes, H. E. (1998). *The story I tell myself: a venture in existentialist autobiography*. University of Chicago Press.

Bauer, P. J. (2007). *Remembering the times of our lives: memory in infancy and beyond*. Mahwah, NJ: Lawrence Erlbaum Associates.

Bauer, P. J. and Burch, M. M. (2004). Developments in early memory: multiple mediators of foundational processes. In J. M. Lucariello, J. A. Hudson, R. Fivush, and P. J. Bauer (eds.), *The development of the mediated mind* (pp. 101–125). Mahwah, NJ: Lawrence Erlbaum Associates.

Bauer, P. J., Burch, M. M., Van Abbema, D. L., and Ackil, J. K. (2007). Talking about twisters: relations between mothers' and children's contributions to conversations about a devastating tornado. *Journal of Cognition and Development*, **8**, 371–399.

Bauer, P. J., Stark, E., Lukowski, A., Rademacher, J., Van Abbema, D., and Ackil, J. (2005). Working together to make sense of the past: mothers' and children's use of internal states language in conversations about traumatic and nontraumatic events. *Journal of Cognition and Development*, **6**, 463–488.

Bauer, P. J., Wenner, J. A., Dropik, P. L., and Wewerka, S. S. (2000). Parameters of remembering and forgetting in the transition from infancy to early childhood. *Monographs of the Society for Research in Child Development*, **65** (4, Serial No. 263).

Belli, R. F., Smith, L. M., Andreski, P. M., and Agrawal, S. (2007). Methodological comparisons between CATI event history calendar and standardized conventional quiostionnaire instruments. *Public Opinion Quarterly*, **71**, 603–622.

Berntsen, D. and Bohn, A. (2010). Cultural life scripts and individual like stories. In P. Boyer and J. Wertsch (eds.), *Memory in mind and culture* (pp. 130–147). New York: Cambridge University Press.

Berntsen, D. and Rubin, D. C. (2004). Cultural life scripts structure recall from autobiographical memory. *Memory & Cognition*, **32**, 427–442.

Bird, A. and Reese, E. (2006). Emotional reminiscing and the development of an autobiographical self. *Developmental Psychology*, **42**, 613–626.

Bohn, A. and Berntsen, D. (2008). Life story development in childhood: the development of life story coherence abilities and the acquisition of cultural life scripts from late middle childhood to adolescence. *Developmental Psychology*, **44**, 1135–1147.

Bretherton, I., Fritz, J., Zahn-Waxler, C., and Ridgeway, D. (1986). Learning to talk about emotions: a functionalist perspective. *Child Development*, **57**, 529–548.

Bruner, J. (1990). *Acts of meaning*. Cambridge, MA: Harvard University Press.

Carver, L. J. and Bauer, P. J. (1999). When the event is more than the sum of its parts: Nine-month-olds' long-term ordered recall. *Memory*, **7**, 147–174.

(2001). The dawning of a past: the emergence of long-term explicit memory in infancy. *Journal of Experimental Psychology: General*, **130**, 726–745.

Conway, M. A. and Pleydell-Pearce, C. W. (2000). The construction of autobiographical memories in the self-memory system. *Psychological Review*, **107**, 261–288.

Conway, M. A., Singer, J. A., and Tagini, A. (2004). The self in autobiographical memory: correspondence and coherence. *Social Cognition*, **22**, 491–529.

Dunn, J., Bretherton, I., and Munn, P. (1987). Conversations about feeling states between mothers and their young children. *Developmental Psychology*, **23**, 132–139.

Dunn, J., Brown, J., and Beardsall, L. (1991). Family talk about feeling states and children's later understanding of others' emotions. *Developmental Psychology*, **27**, 448–455.

Eisenberg, A. (1985). Learning to describe past experience in conversation. *Discourse Processes*, **8**, 177–204.

Farrant, K. and Reese, E. (2000). Maternal style and children's participation in reminiscing: stepping stones in children's autobiographical memory development. *Journal of Cognition and Development*, **1**, 193–225.

Fiese, B. H., Hooker, K. A., Kotary, L., Scwagler, J., and Rimmer, M. (1995). Family stories in the early stages of parenthood. *Journal of Marriage and the Family*, **57**, 763–770.

Fivush, R. (1991). The social construction of personal narratives. *Merrill-Palmer Quarterly*, **37**, 59–82.

(2001). Owning experience: the development of subjective perspective in autobiographical memory. In C. Moore and K. Lemmon (eds.), *The self in time: developmental perspectives* (pp. 35–52). Mahwah, NJ: Lawrence Erlbaum Associates.

(2007). Maternal reminiscing style and children's developing understanding of self and emotion. *Clinical Social Work*, **35**, 37–46.

(2008). Remembering and reminiscing: how individual lives are constructed in family narratives. *Memory Studies*, **1**, 45–54.

(2010a). The development of autobiographical memory. *Annual Review of Psychology*, **62**, 1–24.

(2010b). Speaking silence: the social construction of voice and silence in cultural and autobiographical narratives. *Memory*, **18**, 88–98.

Fivush, R., Brotman, M., Buckner, J. P., and Goodman, S. (2000). Gender differences in parent–child emotion narratives. *Sex Roles*, **42**, 233–254.

Fivush, R. and Buckner, J. P. (2003). Creating gender and identity through autobiographical narratives. In R. Fivush and C. Haden (eds.), *Autobiographical memory and the construction of a narrative self: developmental and cultural perspectives* (pp. 149–168). Hillsdale, NJ: Lawrence Erlbaum Associates.

Fivush, R. and Fromhoff, F. (1988). Style and structure in mother–child conversations about the past. *Discourse Processes*, **11**, 337–355.

Fivush, R. and Haden, C. A. (eds.) (2003). *Autobiographical memory and the construction of a narrative self: developmental and cultural perspectives*. Mahwah, NJ: Lawrence Erlbaum Associates.

(2005). Parent–child reminiscing and the construction of a subjective self. In B. D. Homer and C. S. Tamis-LeMonda (eds.), *The development of social cognition and communication* (pp. 315–335). Mahwah, NJ: Lawrence Erlbaum Associates.

Fivush, R., Haden, C. A., and Reese, E. (2006). Elaborating on elaborations: maternal reminiscing style and children's socioemotional outcome. *Child Development*, **77**, 1568–1588.

Fivush, R. and Nelson, K. (2006). Parent–child reminiscing locates the self in the past. *British Journal of Developmental Psychology*, **24**, 235–251.

Fivush, R., Sales, J. M., and Bohanek, J. G. (2008). Meaning making in mothers' and children's narratives of emotional events. *Memory*, **16**, 579–594.

Fivush, R. and Vesudeva, A. (2002). Remembering to relate: maternal reminiscing style and attachment. *Journal of Cognition and Development*, **3**, 73–90.

Flannagan, D., Baker-Ward, L., and Graham, L. (1995). Talk about preschool: patterns of topic discussion and elaboration related to gender and ethnicity. *Sex Roles*, **32**, 1–15.

Friedman, W. J. (1992). Children's time memory: the development of a differentiated past. *Cognitive Development*, 7, 171–188.

(1993). Memory for the time of past events. *Psychological Bulletin*, 11, 44–66.

(2003). The development of a differentiated sense of the past and the future. *Advances in Child Development and Behavior*, **31**, 229–269.

(2004). Time in autobiographical memory. *Social Cognition*, **22**, 591–605.

Friedman, W. J. and Kemp, S. (1998). The effects of elapsed time and retrieval on young children's judgments of the temporal distances of past events. *Cognitive Development*, **13**, 335–367.

Habermas, T. and Bluck, S. (2000). Getting a life: the emergence of the life story in adolescence. *Psychological Bulletin*, **126**, 748–769.

Habermas, T. and de Silveira, C. (2008). The development of global coherence in life narratives across adolescence: temporal, causal, and thematic aspects. *Developmental Psychology*, **44**, 707–721.

Habermas, T., Negele, A., and Brenneisen-Mayer, F. (2010). "Honey, you're jumping about": mothers' scaffolding of their children's and adolescents' life narratives. *Cognitive Development*, **25**, 339–351.

Habermas, T. and Paha, C. (2001). The development of coherence in adolescents' life narratives. *Narrative Inquiry*, **11**, 35–54.

Harbus, A. (2011). Exposure to life-writing as an impact on autobiographical memory. *Memory Studies*, **4**, 206–220.

Harley, K. and Reese, E. (1999). Origins of autobiographical memory. *Developmental Psychology*, **35**, 1338–1348.

Harner, L. (1982). Talking about the past and future. In W. J. Friedman (ed.), *The developmental psychology of time*. New York: Academic Press.

Hudson, J. A. (1990). The emergence of autobiographic memory in mother–child conversation. In R. Fivush and J. A. Hudson (eds.), *Knowing and remembering in young children* (pp. 166–196). New York: Cambridge University Press.

James, W. (1890). *The principles of psychology*. New York: Henry Holt [Dover reprint].

Kuebli, J., Butler, S., and Fivush, R. (1995). Mother–child talk about past events: relations of maternal language and child gender over time. *Cognition and Emotion*, **9**, 265–293.

Lagattuta, K. H. and Wellman, H. M. (2001). Thinking about the past: early knowledge about links between prior experience, thinking and emotion. *Child Development*, **72**, 82–102.

   (2002). Differences in early parent–child conversations about negative versus positive emotions: implications for the development of psychological understanding. *Developmental Psychology*, **38**, 564–580.

Lewis, M. and Brooks-Gunn, J. (1979). *Social cognition and the acquisition of the self*. New York: Plenum.

McAdams, D. P. (1992). Unity and purpose in human lives: the emergence of identity as a life story. In R. A. Zucker, A. I. Rabin, J. Aronoff, and S. J. Frank (eds.), *Personality structure in the life course* (pp. 323–375). New York: Springer.

   (1993). *The stories we live by: personal myths and the making of the self*. New York: William Morrow.

   (2001). The psychology of life stories. *Review of General Psychology*, **5**, 100–122.

   (2004). The redemptive self: narrative identity in America today. In D. R. Beike, J. M. Lampinen, and D. A. Behrend (eds.), *The self and memory* (pp. 95–116). New York: Psychology Press.

McCabe, A. and Peterson, C. (1991). Getting the story: a longitudinal study of parental styles in eliciting narratives and developing narrative skill. In A. McCabe and C. Peterson (eds.), *Developing narrative structure* (pp. 217–253). Hillsdale, NJ: Lawrence Erlbaum Associates.

McLean, K. and Pasupathi, M. (2010). *Narrative development in adolescence: creating the storied self*. New York: Springer.

Meyer, J. W. (1988). *The social construction of the psychology of childhood: some contemporary processes*. In R. M. Lerner and E. M. Hetherington (eds.), *Child development in life span perspective* (pp. 47–66). Hillsdale, NJ: Lawrence Erlbaum Associates.

Nelson, K. (2001). From the experiencing I to the continuing me. In C. Moore and K. Lemmon (eds.), *The self in time: developmental perspectives* (pp. 15–33). Mahwah, NJ: Lawrence Erlbaum Associates.

   (2003). Narrative and self, myth and memory. In R. Fivush and C. Haden (eds.), *Connecting culture and memory: the social construction of an autobiographical self*. Hillsdale, NJ: Lawrence Erlbaum Associates.

Nelson, K. and Fivush, R. (2004). The emergence of autobiographical memory: a social cultural developmental theory. *Psychological Review*, **111**, 486–511.

Peterson, C., Jesso, B., and McCabe, A. (1999). Encouraging narratives in pre-schoolers: an intervention study. *Journal of Child Language*, **26**, 49–67.

Peterson, C. and McCabe, A. (1992). Parental styles of narrative elicitation: effect on children's narrative structure and content. *First Language*, **12**, 299–321.

(1994). A social interactionist account of developing decontextualized narrative skill. *Developmental Psychology*, **30**, 937–948.

(1996). Parental scaffolding of context in children's narratives. In C. E. Johnson and J. H. V. Gilbert (eds.), *Children's language*, vol. IX (pp. 183–196). Hillsdale, NJ: Lawrence Erlbaum Associates.

Pillemer, D. (1998). *Momentous events, vivid memories*. Cambridge, MA: Harvard University Press.

Reese, E. (2002). A model of the origins of autobiographical memory. In J. W. Fagen and H. Hayne (eds.), *Progress in infancy research*, vol. II (pp. 215–260). Mahwah, NJ: Lawrence Erlbaum Associates.

Reese, E. and Cleveland, E. (2006). Mother–child reminiscing and children's understanding of mind. *Merrill-Palmer Quarterly*, **52**, 17–43.

Reese, E. and Fivush, R. (1993). Parental styles for talking about the past. *Developmental Psychology*, **29**, 596–606.

Reese, E., Haden, C. A., and Fivush, R. (1993). Mother–child conversations about the past: relationships of style and memory over time. *Cognitive Development*, **8**, 403–430.

Reese, E., Yan, C., Jack, F., and Hayne, H. (2010). Emerging identities: narrative and self from early childhood to early adolescence. In K. C. McLean and M. Pasupathi (eds.), *Narrative development in adolescence: creating the storied self* (pp. 23–44). New York: Springer-Verlag.

Rubin, D. C. (2006). The basic-systems model of episodic memory. *Perspectives on Psychological Science*, **1**, 277–311.

Rudek, D. and Haden, C. A. (2005). Mothers' and preschoolers' mental state language during reminiscing over time. *Merrill-Palmer Quarterly*, **51**, 557–583.

Sales, J. M., Fivush, R., Parker, J., and Bahrick, L. (2003). Stressing memory: Long-term relations among children's stress, recall, and psychological outcome following Hurricane Andrew. R. Fivush (Chair), Focusing in the internal in memories of trauma. Symposium presented at the biennial meetings of the Society for Applied Research in Memory and Cognition, Aberdeen, Scotland, July.

Thorne, A. and McLean, K. C. (2002). Gendered reminiscence practices and self-definition in late adolescence. *Sex Roles*, **46**(9–10), 267–277.

Thorne, A., McLean, K. C., and Lawrence, A. M. (2004). When remembering is not enough: reflecting on self-defining memories in late adolescence. *Journal of Personality*, **72**, 513–520.

Tomasello, M. (1999). *The cultural origins of human cognitions*. Cambridge, MA: Harvard University Press.

Tulving, E. (1972). Episodic and semantic memory. In E. Tulving and W. Donaldson (eds.), *Organization of memory* (pp. 382–403). New York: Academic Press.

(2002). Episodic memory: from mind to brain. *Annual Review of Psychology*, **53**, 1–25.

Vygotsky, L. S. (1978). *Mind in society: the development of higher psychological processes.* Cambridge, MA: Harvard University Press.

Wang, Q. and Ross, M. (2007). Culture and memory. In Shinobu Kitayama and Dov Cohen (eds.), *Handbook of cultural psychology* (pp. 645–667). New York: Guilford Press.

Welch-Ross, M. K. (1997). Mother–child participation in conversation about the past: relationship to preschoolers' theory of mind. *Developmental Psychology*, **33**, 618–629.

(2001). Personalizing the temporally extended self: Evaluative self-awareness and the development of autobiographical memory. In C. Moore and K. Skene (eds.), *The self in time: developmental issues* (pp. 97–120). Hillsdale, NJ: Lawrence Erlbaum Associates.

Wellman, H. M. (2002). Understanding the psychological world: developing a theory of mind. In U. Goswami (ed.), *Blackwell handbook of childhood cognitive development* (pp. 167–187). Malden, MA: Blackwell.

13 Theory and research in autobiographical memory: a life-span developmental perspective

Joseph M. Fitzgerald and Carissa L. Broadbridge

The title of this chapter reflects two important organizing features. The first is that it is about autobiographical memory, and the second is that it takes a life-span developmental perspective on that topic. Following chapters by Bauer and Fivush, this is the third of three explicitly developmental chapters in this volume. Developmentalists generally agree that when individuals report a memory, that report may be influenced by memory functions related to encoding, storage, retrieval, and forgetting; the development of the individual since the moment of the event across cognitive, social cognitive, and personality domains; and environmental and cultural factors. Thus, the developmental approach provides a great many challenges.

This chapter is structured to provide the reader with an image of the life-span development of autobiographical memory, but not an exhaustive review of the literature. That would not be possible within the available space. Research on the various topics discussed here is growing rapidly. According to the Web of Science, from 2005 to 2009, over 1,000 articles were published in the area of autobiographical memory, and almost 20 percent of those articles were developmental in nature. The pace of data collection, however, is running ahead of theoretical integration.

We have taken on the following tasks: (1) outline the life-span perspective, (2) describe a perspective on memory development, and (3) discuss enough exemplars from the literature to provide the reader with a sense of the fit of that perspective to enduring issues, methods, theories, and hypotheses relevant to autobiographical memory development.

The life-span perspective

The present chapter shares many common reference points with the chapters on development by Bauer and Fivush in this volume. We differ in that we take a life-span developmental perspective. The life-span perspective emerged during the 1970s in reaction to the division of developmental psychology into a series of age by topic segments, such as infant memory or the aging of intelligence, marked by little interaction among investigators. The life-span movement enlisted developmental scientists into an integrated contextualist discipline. A thorough introduction to the life-span perspective is provided by Baltes, Lindenberger, and Staudinger (2006). We focus on the core themes and questions.

Contextualism

The contextualist world view (Pepper, 1942) hypothesizes that individual change is embedded in an ever-changing context. It is at the core of the life-span approach. The contextualist metaphor for science is the study of historical events. For example, an event such as the American Civil War must be viewed from multiple perspectives in order to be understood. The work of Fivush and her colleagues (Fivush, this volume) is good example of the application of a contextualist approach.

In the life-span perspective, contextual influences are generally categorized as normative, age-graded events, normative, history-graded events, and non-normative events. Starting school at age 5 or getting married in early adulthood are normative age-related events. These are the type of events discussed in life-script theory (Berntsen and Rubin, 2004; Rubin, Berntsen, and Hutson, 2009). The use of the atomic bomb in World War II is a normative, history-related event experienced directly or indirectly by everyone alive at the time. An explicit attempt to understand the role of history in autobiographical memory is provided by Brown, Hansen, Lee, *et al.* (this volume). Finally, experiencing a life-threatening illness at age 8 months or alcohol abuse in adulthood are non-normative events. The life-span model directs us to study both intraindividual and interindividual differences, implying that we must study not only changes in the mean levels of the various properties of autobiographical memory but also variability within individual performance from moment to moment and decade to decade. This effort requires a comprehensive approach to the conceptualization and measurement of change, which we turn to next.

Modeling and measuring change

Schaie (1965) drew attention to the fact that every observation in a developmental design reflects the age of individuals, their birth cohort, and the time of measurement. The value of any two of these sets the third. The standard approach employed in most developmental research is the cross-sectional design, which is useful for the study of age differences. Although the longitudinal design is regarded as the reference standard for the study of age changes, Schaie (1965) and Baltes (1997) developed sequential designs that had the purpose of disentangling age differences, age changes, and cohort differences. Unfortunately, these designs require time and resources beyond the limits of most researchers. The life-span approach is associated with multivariate methodologies capable of addressing the multidimensional nature of development, frequently in large interdisciplinary research such as the Berlin Aging Study (Gertsorf, Smith, and Baltes, 2006).

Developmental models need not assume unidirectional explanations, but rather are open to bidirectional or transactional models. In the memory domain, the development of the self is one of the most important milestones in the development of autobiographical memory (Howe and Courage, 1997). Once memory and the self emerge, the two are mutually interactive, with each one fostering the growth of the other (Conway and Jobson, this volume). For instance, once children develop autonoetic awareness, they use this ability to think about the past and plan for the future through temporal extension of the self, and such temporal organization helps them to form a more coherent self (Friedman, 2005). In this way, individuals actively shape their own development.

Intraindividual variability

The importance of intraindividual variability for developmental theory and research is now widely recognized. Theorists recognize that complete models of behavior must incorporate both enduring traits and transient states (Nesselroade, 1991). In the current context, the question is how accurately one property of memory, such as vividness (y), is predicted by other properties ($x_1, x_2, x_3 \ldots x_k$) such as rehearsal, coherence, or sensory information, $y = f(x_1, x_2, x_3 \ldots x_k)$. For example, if an individual recalls multiple episodes, each memory recalled is a state with multiple properties. Those properties may be correlated across memories. Groupings of individuals can be created to allow us to study whether the relationship between y and x_1 is the same within groupings such as males and females or demented or nondemented individuals (Hamaker, Molenaar, and Nesselroade, 2007).

In autobiographical memory, on average, individuals report high levels of detail, but individual memory reports vary in levels of detail. Each individual memory report can be "scored" for memory details and ratings of properties such as coherence. Analysis of such data can clarify the relationship among the variables for each individual. Such data can be collected in a narrow time frame in a single context, such as an individual sitting at a computer responding to word prompts: one context, one time of measurement, and no audience. Greater richness of context, however, can be achieved in diary studies or experience-sampling studies, in which participants are signaled to record and rate their most recent memory. In an experience-sampling study of personality, Fleeson and Jolley (2006) report that within-subject variance actually exceeded between-subject variance.

Several factors might produce variability in individual distributions, including the interpretation of the testing situation, goals, motives, desired identities, temporal trends (depression), stabilizing forces (genetics), and resource availability (brain functioning, stimulating social environments, or loss of sensory acuity). Rubin, Schrauf, and Greenberg (2003, 2004) provide examples of within-subject data collected in both the single context/occasion and across a 2-week interval. Diary studies and experience-sampling methods also provide opportunities to study variability in the specificity, accuracy, and frequency of memory types.

Autobiographical memory and development

Autobiographical memory has been defined in a number of different ways over the past several decades. A common view fractionalizes declarative memory into varying numbers of declarative memory systems, most often semantic and episodic (Tulving, 1983). In a contrasting view, autobiographical memory operates in the context of a single declarative memory system with features typically termed semantic knowledge and memory for episodes (Roediger, 1984; Rubin, 2006; Westmacott, Freedman, Black, *et al.*, 2004). Nelson (2006, p. 183) captured the issue succinctly when she wrote, "experiential memory and knowledge representation are inextricably interrelated in the human cognitive system and are kept separate only arbitrarily."

The Tulving model gave rise to research in which participants are asked to select whether they remember or know whether a stimulus was presented. The alternatives are presented as a dichotomy. "Remember" is meant to imply that the individual has an episodic memory and "know" that they have knowledge that an event took place but have no actual memory. This implies that remember and know are *negatively* correlated. Autobiographical memory research supports an alternative model with two empirically correlated and conceptually interdependent constructs: recollection and belief (Rubin *et al.*, 2003). We have confirmed a model of memory experience consistent with the hypothesis that recollection and belief are distinct but *positively* correlated constructs for several types of autobiographical memories (Fitzgerald and Broadbridge, 2012).

Development and memory

We must begin by acknowledging the important influence of Katherine Nelson (1986, 2006) on the psychology of memory development. Among her many contributions to the field was the recognition that the development of memory must be understood in the context of maturing children constantly interacting with others in their environment. For example, once children develop the capacity to mentally represent events, they may not only represent events from their own experience but also appropriate the experiences of others as their own. Children must develop metacognitive skills that allow them to navigate increasingly complex contextual demands.

Figure 13.1 builds on a figure from Fitzgerald (1986, p. 128), which in turn was developed from Kvale (1974) by Riegel (1978). We attempt to make explicit the relevant contextual dimensions of autobiographical memory development. A fundamental premise is that perceptual and memory experiences exist only momentarily. At Time 2, event A is constructed as A′ influenced by B, and at Time 3, A is experienced as A″. At Time 3, our perception of event C as it occurs is influenced by events A and B that have come before it. This account emphasizes the similarity of the acts of perception and retention (Rubin, 2006); both are momentary states allowing humans to adapt to change either within or external to the individual. Suppose event A is a man's wedding day, event B is the birth of his child, and C is that child's wedding. His wedding and the birth of his

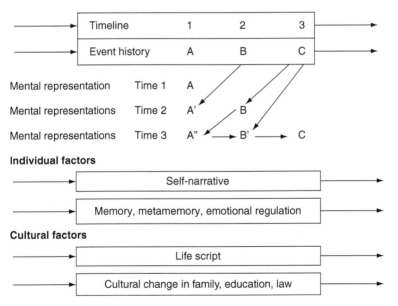

Figure 13.1. Timeline model of the multiple influences on memory construction.

child color the perception of the child's wedding. At the same time, his memory for his own wedding is colored by his son's wedding.

In constructing the current version of Figure 13.1, we considered two domains, the individual and sociocultural. Each is both a product of and a contributor to memory development. We further differentiated the individual and sociocultural dimensions. The first individual domain is the self-narrative. The self-narrative represents the self in storied form. We could not have a self-narrative without autobiographical memories. The self-narrative motivates and influences further development. The second individual dimension is labeled memory, metamemory, and emotional regulation. This refers to the development of relevant functional capacity of the self with age.

At the cultural level, the first track refers to the normative life scripts acquired by individuals during socialization. The other sociocultural track refers to characteristic structures and functions including education, family, legal systems, and media. Depending on the history of the culture, these factors may promote change or stability during development. We employ this framework to discuss research on the accuracy and specificity of autobiographical memories, and the distribution of memories over time and age.

Aging and characteristics of autobiographical memory

Accuracy of autobiographical memories

Most autobiographical memory researchers working in adulthood and aging have set aside the issue of accuracy because (1) there is often no record of the original event, and (2) many functions of autobiographical memory do not rely upon the accuracy of memory. Accuracy has been studied in the context of diary or experience sampling studies. Most have been short-term studies of college students (Thompson, 1982) or cognitive psychologists who have studied their own memory performance (Conway, Collins, Gathercole, et al., 1996; Linton, 1978; Wagenaar, 1986). A significant concern in these studies is that participants record relatively few low-distinctive events, perhaps because the participants believe that such events will be difficult to recall.

Lhost-Catal and Fitzgerald (2004) reported a diary study of recall of events recorded by a 78-year-old woman and her 79-year-old husband. Each day she recorded events that she wanted to have available as an objective record of family activity, but in many cases she was the only participant and the events were highly repetitive (low distinctiveness). She recorded the *who*, *where*, *what*, and *when* of daily events, quite like the methods that cognitive psychologists had employed in their studies (Wagenaar, 1986). Elements from these records were used as cues for recall.

What-cues were the most effective cues when presented as the only cue, and *when*-cues were the least effective single cue. The combination of *what-when* was the best two-cue combination. The data for both cued-recall performance and memory ratings were consistent with the power function model (Rubin and Wenzel, 1996). Recent performance was very high but declined steeply over a relatively short period, and then leveled off. Distinctiveness was assessed by an independent rater and, along with rehearsal, was a predictor of memory performance.

Specificity of recall

Age differences in the number of episodic details reported have been interpreted by some as a decline in memory specificity or more broadly as a decline in voluntary episodic autobiographical memory (Levine, Svoboda, Hay, *et al.*, 2002). Alternatively, older adults may report fewer details because they revise their communicative goals or they may view errors of omission as more desirable than errors of commission. (Errors of commission the researcher actually could not detect.) Below we illustrate the issues that need to be disentangled in classifying memories.

Consider these three memories

Memory 1: *Letters from banks are usually sad. I don't like getting them. They never bring good news, do they?*

Memory 2: *I received a letter from the bank last Monday. I hated seeing it. I never like getting those things. It seems they are always charging for something. It seems they had made an error sometime in the past and sent me a credit. It's good to know someone is honest these days when we always read about the banks as crooks. I get angry thinking that we bailed them out.*

Memory 3: *I went for a long walk last week. While I was out I ran into my talkative neighbor, who told me about a coyote attack on a dog in the neighborhood. I was so distracted by the news that I took a wrong turn on the way home. I ended up walking a lot longer than I had expected.*

Memory 1 would be termed a generic memory, stringing together pieces of semantic information about letters along with an evaluation of a type of experience. This would be considered a memory failure if the experimenter only accepted specific memories located in space and time.

Memory 2 refers to a specific event located in time and place, but contains more semantic information than internal details of the episode. In contrast, Memory 3 consists almost entirely of episodic information with a small amount of semantic detail concerning the neighbor. The issue of specificity is in part an issue of whether the report in Memory 2 should be regarded as a failure because it bears some resemblance to Memory 1. Does this represent a decline in episodic autobiographical memory functioning?

Levine *et al.* (2002) reasoned that detailed levels of cognitive representation are more prone to disruption because of changes to the prefrontal cortex in normal aging. They tested their hypothesis by comparing internal (episodic) and external (semantic) details of autobiographical recall in highly educated, healthy, younger and older (66–89 years) adults. Before any probing, they found a significant age difference in the mean number of internal details (approximately 23 and 17), but not for external details. Following specific probes, the younger adults added, on average, 35 internal details and the older adults added 25, reflecting significant plasticity in both age groups.

Levine *et al.* (2002) noted that few of the semantic (external) details were repetitions or refer to external specific events that might confuse listeners. Memory 2, for example, reflects adequate constructive processes and metacognitive awareness of storytelling principles such as maintaining listener interest. Trunk and Abrams (2009) asked young adults to rate procedural or episodic recall by young and older adults. The young listeners rated the episodic stories of both age groups as equally well focused, but rated the procedural recall of the younger adults as more focused. The results support the following conclusion: older adults know how to tell a story and for the most part are viewed positively for this ability.

Do older adults omit episodic details because they opt to do so or because the details are unavailable to them due to declining neural function? Can interventions alter the observed pattern? In one intervention, researchers manipulate the method of collecting the information. The cognitive interview (CI) (Fisher, 1995), for example, is an interview methodology based on forensic cognitive research. Witnesses to and victims of crimes are instructed to apply imagery and cognitive mechanisms in recalling the event. The CI increases recall without increasing errors. In a prototypic CI study, Mello and Fisher (1996) presented a videotape of a crime to younger and older adults. After a brief delay, they interviewed participants using either a standard interview (SI), similar to specific probing, or the CI. The CI was most effective for the older adult, more than doubling the amount of detail, while maintaining a true information/total information ratio of 88 percent. Fisher, Falkner, Trevision, *et al.* (2000) interviewed older adults about events from 35 years in the past and found similar evidence favoring the CI.

Using another approach, Rudoy, Weintraub, and Paller (2009) hypothesized that retrieval orientation is a habit subject to modification over time (age). If individuals experience retrieval failures for details, they may shift to an orientation less reliant on details, such as reporting gist or increasing the number of external details. For example, consider an older adult who is recounting a story about taking her children out on a particular Halloween to a new acquaintance. She may refer to going out "with the neighbors" rather than stating the names of particular neighbors that were with her on that specific Halloween, names unfamiliar to her audience anyway. Rudoy *et al.* (2009) tested participants who were aged 67–78 with no known cognitive impairment. Participants recalled events following two different manipulations, *episodic* or *gist-oriented*, administered in counterbalanced order. Following each manipulation, the older adults recalled autobiographical events that took place between the ages of 18 and 30. After the *episodic* manipulation, the number of episodic details *increased* 40% relative to baseline, whereas after exposure to the *gist orientation* the number of episodic details *decreased* (38%). The effectiveness of very brief manipulations highlights the plasticity of recall specificity.

The distribution of memories across retention intervals

Investigators have studied the distribution of memories across retention intervals by a number of techniques. Some of these are designed to simulate as best as possible the conditions of retention of daily human experience. Other methods target memories for more atypical experiences such as highly important, highly vivid, or particularly emotional events. We review two categories of study: (1) those that place very little restriction on the participants in terms of what to recall, and (2) those that require participants to report a memory that satisfies a specific criterion related to the self. The distributions of event ages for these two tasks are often quite different.

Studies of minimally restricted autobiographical recall

In autobiographical memory research, memory strength, the number of memories per day or hour, is plotted against time to produce a retention function. Three components provide a reasonably complete description of autobiographical memory retention when subjects can essentially report whatever autobiographical memory they choose. First, normal forgetting is described by the power function, which is graphed as a log function, memory strength = f log (time). The power function accounts for the bulk of retention data with the strong recency effect, a period of steep decline, and then a period of gradually slowing decline. The logarithmic transformations produce a linear function. The second component is childhood amnesia. For children over 6, adolescents, and adults of all ages, the power function does not fit the data for memories of the first 6 years of life. Very low levels of recall, a phenomenon termed "childhood amnesia," mark this period. The third element is that memories are reported at a stronger rate (more memories per day) than expected for a period in adolescence or early adulthood. This last phenomenon was termed "the bump" (Rubin, Wetzler, and Nebes, 1986).

This bump has been discussed thoroughly in several recent reviews including Conway (2005), Fitzgerald (1996), and Rubin (2002). It has proved to be a robust phenomenon; it does not matter if the cues are words, phrases, pictures, or smells or if no cues are used (see Rubin, 2002, for review). Rubin notes that one can eliminate the bump by asking people to report memories from three, four, or five segments of their lives for 10 minutes. Participants do not exhaust their available memories for any portion of the life span, so the retention function is flat (Howes and Katz, 1992).

Research indicates substantial variability in properties of the bump. Rubin (1989) reported an intensive study of two older adults who each reported a total of 125 memories. One individual reported roughly 50% of his or her memories from the interval between birth and age 30; while the other individual showed a more modest bump effect but a very strong recency effect. A highly exaggerated appearance of the bump was found in a study comparing recently detoxified alcoholics to normal controls with mean ages of 47 and 49 (Fitzgerald and Grove, 1999). The bump was more pronounced in the alcoholic group even without the exclusion of recent retention intervals because they report very few recent memories.

The timing of the bump also shows effects of culture. Schrauf and Rubin (1998) reported a delayed bump in a sample of individuals who moved after spending at least 20 years in a Spanish-speaking culture and then at least 30 years in an English-speaking culture. A secondary bump was found among a sample of older Bangladeshi who endured great upheaval between the ages of 35 and 55, leading to a bump for that period (Conway and Haque, 1999).

Rubin and Shulkind (1997) tested multiple univariate hypotheses regarding mean differences between bump and non-bump memories for such constructs as novelty, vividness, rehearsal, and effort. They did not find support for these hypotheses and concluded that an enhanced ability to encode events during the bump period (Rubin, Rahhal, and Poon, 1998) was responsible for this effect rather than factors related to the self.

Although the bump for cue-word memories is sometimes portrayed as very strong, such memories actually have very low memory strength (memories per day) compared to recent time periods. Therefore, it is important to characterize features of the retention function by using designs with adequate power. A recent paper by Janssen, Rubin, and St. Jacques (2011) addressed the power issue by collecting data over the internet. They collected 10 memories for each of 2,341 participants. They found consistent support for the bump. By one estimate, the bump covers the range 6 to 10, and by another, 11 to 20. The widest definition of the bump (ages 6 to 20) accounts for 28% of the memories *that took place more than 15 years ago*. Extrapolating from their data, if a group of 10 older adults produced a pool of 1,000 memories, approximately 560 (56%) would be recent memories, and 125 (12.5%) of all memories would be from the bump period. They also provide evidence of the nonuniversal nature of the cue-word bump, as 13.62% of their sample did not report a memory from the bump period (ages 6 to 20 years). Memories from the bump period were not rated significantly higher for vividness or sense of reliving. This suggests that *extraordinary* vividness does not explain the presence of the bump. The overall correlations of these rating variables to the age of the event and the age at the event are both low. For older adults, the correlation is 0.09 between age at event and reliving, which indicates a very flat function. Participants may employ a rating rubric such as "If I remember something from my past, it must be at least somewhat vivid." Such a rubric would bias the results toward stability, and lessen the utility of ratings for testing the hypothesis presented by Janssen *et al.* (2011). Alternative measures of vividness such as the CI also show only small effects of age.

Janssen *et al.* (2011) attribute their findings to the existence of a pool of highly available memories. Such a pool could be explained either by the nature of encoding during the bump period, the nature of the events during the bump period, or the "role of the events in the life story or identity formation, which would lead to better encoding and to greater rehearsal" (p. 6). To date, however, no data have affirmatively supported any of these alternatives directly.

Is superior encoding during the bump period the best explanation for the bump in cue-word memories (Rubin *et al.*, 1998)? Clearly, the adolescent/early adult memory works very well for academically oriented and laboratory tasks, but young adults are relative novices at the application of narrative reasoning. Some of the factors that explain the bump may actually occur after the bump period. Shifts in the timing of the bump for different cultures, for different subgroups such as immigrants within a culture suggest the need for a multidimensional contextual explanation.

Highly restricted autobiographical memory searches

Cue-word studies, which place minimally restrictive criteria on memory search, yield consistent evidence of a subtle but notable departure from standard retention models. In contrast, researchers employing more restricted searches report results with very weak recency effects and very strong evidence for a very strong bump effect related to the early adult-hood era (ages 21–30).

Fitzgerald (1988) found an "accentuated" bump by asking older adult participants to report three highly vivid memories; the proportion of memories in the bump for older adults was remarkably higher than found in a cue-word study by Fitzgerald and Lawrence (1984). In a further analysis, Fitzgerald (1992) reported a similar result for older and middle-aged adults. The results were interpreted in terms of a self-narrative hypothesis reflecting the influence of Erikson (1956), Bruner (1986), and Riegel (1978), who each emphasize an ongoing dialectic between individual and cultural forces during development and multiple forms of self-knowledge. Pillemer (2001) further developed our understanding of the role of momentous life events in the development of the life story.

An exaggerated bump is also found when individuals discussed the important events of their lives in free-form narratives or a book about their lives (Fitzgerald, 1992). When individuals placed events on a time line of their lives (Elnick, Margrett, Fitzgerald, *et al.*, 1999), a significant bump appeared for the age range of 20–29 for all age groups over 40. Unlike cue-word studies, family and relationship events dominated the bump. The most common items were marriage, birth of a child, and divorce (self or parents). In addition, they report that men and women who scored higher on self-complexity reported *fewer* family-personal events, which is consistent with the independent, non-normative tendencies of high self-complexity individuals. Those low in self-complexity organize self-related thoughts in terms of social norms. Similarly, Holmes and Conway (1999) documented a bump for private events (ages 20–29). Among the private events, the most common memory category was relationships, followed by memories of death and birth.

Berntsen and Rubin (2002) asked individuals to report their happiest, saddest, most traumatic, most important, and most recent involuntary memory. They reported a strong bump in early adulthood for happiest and most important memories, but a flatter distribution of saddest memories over the adult years. Given that many of the reported happiest and important events are commonly considered life-script events, their data are also consistent with the hypothesized correspondence between cultural life scripts and life stories proposed in life-script theory (Berntsen and Rubin, 2004; see under "Life-script hypothesis" below).

In addition to the highly vivid, benchmark, life-script, and positive memories that belong in our life stories, several other forms of memory have been found to display exaggerated bumps along with a diminished recency component. These include studies in which participants report their most pleasant and important memory, or their favorite movie, record, or book (Schulkind, Hennis, and Rubin, 1999; Sehulster, 1996).

A construct unifying these observations must capture the memory properties identified in the literature. These include involvement of the self and close others; high levels of accessibility, importance, and pleasantness; and perceived centrality to identity. Singer (1995) proposed the construct of self-defining memories. A number of different memories have been collected in studies of self-defining memories including turning point, most important, and earliest memories (McAdams, 2001). The term "self-defining memory," however, implies a degree of permanence of both the self and memories inconsistent with contemporary theory and research. In addition, not all the memories that show the accentuated bump distribution can be regarded as self-defining. The *Godfather* movies may be the favorite films of many aging baby boomers, but few of them define themselves as sociopathic gangsters.

As an alternative, we suggest the term "currently central memories." In the existing studies, the participants are asked to report a memory for an event that *currently* satisfies some criterion relevant or *central* to the self. A limitation of existing studies is the lack of information regarding the reliability of the methods in terms of either memory content, memory themes, or the age of individuals at the event. Use of the term "central" links this idea to the work on PTSD and centralization of trauma events to current identity (Berntsen and Rubin, 2006). As Berntsen and Rubin note, however, it is more normative for individuals to place positive events central to their life stories.

As noted, the clearest published "failure" to find that currently central memories cluster in the third decade of life was the case of saddest memories; such events tend to distribute more evenly across the life span (Berntsen and Rubin, 2002). A wide variety of self-related events remain to be studied, including the most important work-related event, the most startling accident, or the best sporting event witnessed. Any of these categories could plausibly be associated with another portion of the life span. The internet provides a good vehicle for the needed normative, cross-cultural research on this topic. In addition, longitudinal studies are needed to document the degree of long- and short-term stability of currently central memories. Next we outline three explanations that have been put forward to account for the available data.

The self-narrative hypothesis

The self-narrative hypothesis proposed that during the period of late adolescence and early adulthood the individual develops a sense of identity that is expressed in story form (Fitzgerald, 1988, 1992). These stories are formed in the context of signals from the cultural setting about what important successes and failures belong in their overall self-narrative. Not all vivid memories may fit our current self-narrative, and not all of the topics and events contained in our self-narratives are associated with vivid memories (Robinson and Taylor, 1998).

In Figure 13.1, we characterize the self-narrative as an influence on perception, encoding, retention, and retrieval of an event. The narrative form of representation provides a cognitive economy by which individuals can represent complex, identity-related information in story form. Rummens (2003) discusses a model for the complexity of representing a comprehensive model of identity. She identifies twelve identity domains; within each domain, an individual can have one or more specific identities. The identity domains include gender, language, ability, ethnicity, religion, and socioeconomic status. Rummens proposes that each identity is context dependent; that is, in some contexts, a specific identity may be completely irrelevant. In narrative terms, there may be aspects of an individual's self-narrative that are unknown to some associates because she would not share them with those others.

When prompted to identify one's most important memory, the answer is likely to reflect the aspect(s) of the self-narrative most strongly associated with the retrieval context. For example, if discussing the question with some fellow parents, a father may recall a critical event in that role, while the same question might prompt a career-oriented memory in discussing memories with fellow professionals.

The available data also need to be considered in the context of the nature of emotional functioning in older adults. Research on the socio-emotional selectivity theory supports the presence of positivity bias in older adults. The theory predicts that, with age, adults focus more on positive experiences, both seeking out and recalling more such experiences. The positivity bias has been replicated many times in different contexts. Older adults show a retrospective positivity effect. For example, in the study by Kennedy, Mather, and Carstensen (2004), older adults gave more positive ratings to their emotional states from 14 years prior. This may lead them to look for the positive features of events that were earlier regarded as neutral or even negative.

Life-script hypothesis

Berntsen and Rubin (2002, p. 640) argue for a shift in the conversation from self-oriented narratives to life scripts, from the individual to the cultural level: "Life script deals with a fixed temporal order of events, whereas life memories deal with a lived temporal order. Life script is a form of semantic knowledge, whereas life narrative represents autobiographical memory characterized by a belief in the truthfulness of the memories and reliving their perceptual content."

As noted earlier, Berntsen and Rubin reported that the happiest and most important memories showed a strong bump, while negative memories showed either no bump or a modest one. Although they make no such claim, their study has been incorrectly used to characterize cue-word studies as demonstrating that the bump is only found for positive memories. In fact,the life-script model is presented as a model of the recall of affectively intense and important memories.

Rubin and Berntsen (2003) provided evidence that cultures appear to allocate many important, positive life events to young adulthood. Berntsen and Rubin (2004) largely replicated the finding of earlier studies of a pattern of allocating emotionally charged positive memories to the bump. The data for negative script events were less regular. Berntsen and Rubin (2004) report that memories for highly positive transitional events were most often from the bump; in contrast, recall of negative events shows a variety of different patterns. Some are consistent with normal forgetting and others appear unrelated to time.

Berntsen and Rubin (2004) argue that cultural context has an impact on memory and memory development. Many developmentalists have grappled with related questions. How are the contents of culture conveyed to the individual so that they can develop a representation of the life script? Is it a unidirectional process in which each new generation passively receives the script from the parent generation? If so, what mechanisms account for individual and subgroup differences in the socialization process? Some individuals, classes, or even generations develop idiosyncratic interpretations of norms. In a bidirectional model, the recipient generation can adopt or selectively adapt life scripts to life circumstances. Bohn and Berntsen (2008) demonstrated that life scripts are reported by middle-school children before they can use that knowledge to construct a life story. Researchers distinguish between acquiring knowledge and incorporating it into life stories.

We have incorporated both the life script hypothesis and cultural change as influences on memory into Figure 13.1. As with the self-narrative, we believe that encoding, retention, and retrieval may be influenced by these variables. Life scripts help individuals to understand, evaluate, and remember large segments, such as marriage, of their lives and those of others, just as scripts for smaller, shorter events, such as weddings, serve similar functions. Change in cultural institutions, such as marriage, family, and the workplace, influences the representation of these insitutions by individuals, albeit to differing degrees for different individuals or groups.

Self-memory system

Another emergent theory of autobiograpical memory is the self-memory system (SMS) proposed by Conway and Pleydell-Pearce (2000) and recently updated in Conway, Singer, and Tagini (2004); Conway (2005); and Conway and Jobson (this volume). Conway *et al.* (2004) argue that self-defining memories differ from other personally important memories in two ways: (1) strong linkages to other memories with similar themes, and (2) high relevance to enduring personal concerns and unresolved conflict. Robinson and Hawpe (1986) discussed similar themes in narrative thinking.

Rathbone, Moulin, and Conway (2008) proposed that the addition of significant elements to the self-concept generates cognitive activity within the individual. Events that occur in close proximity to these alterations add a set of memories that in essence provide a justification for that alteration. Some of these additions are abstract (*I am open-minded*) and others are more concrete (*I am a truck driver*). Their research supported the hypotheses that bumps form around the addition of salient self-descriptors and that such changes are more frequent early in life. Evidence for the continuation of this process in later adulthood is reported by Lhost-Catal and Fitzgerald (2004), who found bumps in memory accuracy over a 20-year period (ages 55–75); the bumps appear to be associated with significant life events, scripted or unique, such as the death of a parent or movment to a new state. As with self-narratives and life-script theories, moving from insights and hypotheses to empirical research will be challenging.

In closing

The life-span developmental approach provides a helpful framework for the theoretical and emprical integration of the topics discussed throughout this volume with the study of adult development and aging. In only three decades, much has been accomplished in the domains of the development and aging of autobiographical memory. The bulk of the research has focused on the distribution of memories over the life span. We believe that the literature on that topic is best understood by distinguishing between word-cued relatively unselected versus highly selected memories, which we term "currently central memories." The tendency to merge them together has not been productive. The evidence to date has not provided affirmative evidence for any theoretical account for the retention function of cue-word memories.

We have presented three hypotheses that seem to be well suited to account for the presence of currently central memories. Each hypothesis has strong potential for advancing the field, because there may be multiple reasons why an event is currently central at one time and not very central a short time later. We have attempted to explicitly present ideas from each of the three in the simplest of terms. Simplicity can cut off corners and smooth edges in ways that proponents of the theories find uncomfortable, but it may be useful in the early stages of theory and research to regard each theory as a source of hypotheses.

We have learned a great deal with very straightforward investigative methods; the challenges in moving forward will be met only by continued methodological innovation. Considerable work remains to be done on life-span issues concerning basic characteristics of autobiographical memory such as accuracy and specificity. But unless our ability to measure performance and behavior improves, progress may be slow.

References

Baltes, P. B. (1997). On the incomplete architecture of human ontogeny: selection optimization, and compensation as foundation of developmental theory. *American Psychologist*, **52**, 366–380.

Baltes, P. B., Lindenberger, U., and Staudinger, U. M. (2006). Life-span theory in developmental psychology. In R. M. Lerner (ed.), *Handbook of child psychology*. Vol. I: *Theoretical models of human development* (6th edn., pp. 569–664). New York: Wiley.

Berntsen, D. and Rubin, D. C. (2002). Emotionally charged autobiographical memories across the lifespan: the recall of happy, sad, traumatic, and involuntary memories. *Psychology and Aging*, **17**, 636–652.

(2004). Cultural life scripts structure recall from autobiographical memory. *Memory & Cognition*, **32**, 427–442.

(2006). The centrality of event scale: a measure of integrating a trauma into one's identity and its relation to post-traumatic stress disorder symptoms. *Behavior and Research Therapy*, **44**, 219–231.

Bohn, A. and Berntsen, D. (2008). Pleasantness bias in flashbulb memories: positive and negative flashbulb memories of the fall of the Berlin Wall among East and West Germans. *Memory & Cognition*, **35**(3), 565–577.

Bruner, J. (1986). *Actual minds, possible worlds*. Cambridge, MA: Harvard University Press.

Conway, M. A. (2005). Memory and the self. *Journal of Memory and Language*, **53**, 594–628.

Conway, M. A., Collins, A. F., Gathercole, S. E., and Anderson, S. J. (1996). Recollections of true and false autobiographical memories. *Journal of Experimental Psychology: General*, **125**, 69–95.

Conway, M. A. and Haque, S. (1999). Overshadowing the reminiscence bump: Memories of a struggle for independence. *Journal of Adult Development*, **6**, 35–44.

Conway, M. A. and Pleydell-Pearce, C. W. (2000). The construction of autobiographical memories in the self-memory system. *Psychological Review*, **107**(2), 261–288.

Conway, M. A., Singer, J. A., and Tagini, A. (2004). The self and autobiographical memory: correspondence and coherence. *Social Cognition*, **22**, 491–529.

Elnick, A., Margrett, J., Fitzgerald, J. M., and Labouvie-Vief, G. (1999). Benchmark memories in adulthood: Central domains and predictors of their frequency. *Journal of Adult Development*, **6**, 45–59.

Erikson, E. (1956). *Childhood and society*. New York: Norton.

Fisher, R. P. (1995). Interviewing victims and witnesses of crime. *Psychology, Public Policy, and Law*, **1**, 732–764.

Fisher, R. P., Falkner, K. L., Trevisan, M., and McCauley, M. R. (2000). Adapting the cognitive interview to enhance long-term (35 years) recall of physical activities. *Journal of Applied Psychology*, **85**, 180–189.

Fitzgerald, J. M. (1986). Autobiographical memory: a developmental perspective. In D. C. Rubin (ed.), *Autobiographical memory* (pp. 122–133). New York: Cambridge University Press.

(1988). Vivid memories and the reminiscence phenomenon: the role of a self-narrative. *Human Development*, **31**, 261–273.

(1992). *Autobiographical memory and conceptualizations of the self*. In M. A. Conway, D. C. Rubin, H. Spindler, and W. Wagenaar (eds.), *Theoretical perspectives on autobiographical memory* (pp. 99–114). Dordrecht: Kluwer.

(1996). Intersecting meanings of reminiscence in adult development and aging. In D. C. Rubin (ed.), *Remembering our past: studies in autobiographical memory* (pp. 360–383). New York: Cambridge University Press.

Fitzgerald, J. M. and Broadbridge, C. L. (2012). Latent constructs of autobiographical memory ratings: a recollection-belief model of memory experience. Unpublished manuscript.

Fitzgerald, J. M. and Grove, S. (1999). Memory and affect: autobiographical memory in recently detoxified alcoholics. *Journal of Adult Development*, **6**, 11–19.

Fitzgerald, J. M. and Lawrence, R. (1984). Autobiographical memory retrieval across the lifespan. *Journal of Gerontology*, **39**, 692–699.

Fleeson, W. and Jolley, S. (2006). A proposed theory of the adult development of intraindividual variability in trait-manifesting behavior. In D. Mroczek and T. D. Little (eds.), *Handbook of personality development* (pp. 41–59). Mahwah, NJ: Lawrence Erlbaum Associates.

Friedman, W. J. (2005). Developmental and cognitive perspectives on humans' sense of the times of past and future events. *Learning and Motivation*, **36**, 145–158.

Gertsorf, D., Smith, J., and Baltes, P. B. (2006). A systematic-wholistic approach to differential aging: longitudinal findings from the Berlin Aging Study. *Psychology and Aging*, **21**, 645–653.

Hamaker, E. L., Molenaar, P., and Nesselroade, J. R. (2007). The integrated trait state model. *Journal of Research in Personality*, **41**, 295–315.

Holmes, A. and Conway, M. A. (1999). Generation identity and the reminiscence bump: memory for public and private events. *Journal of Adult Development*, **6**, 21–34.

Howe, M. L. and Courage, M. L. (1997). Independent paths in the development of infant learning and forgetting. *Journal of Experimental Child Psychology*, **67**, 131–163.

Howes, J. L. and Katz, A. N. (1992). Remote memory: recalling autobiographical and public events across the lifespan. *Canadian Journal of Psychology*, **46**, 92–116.

Janssen, S. M., Rubin, D. C., and St. Jacques, P. L. (2011). The temporal distribution of autobiographical memory: changes in reliving and vividness over the lifespan do not explain the reminiscence bump. *Memory & Cognition*, **39**, 1–11.

Kennedy, Q., Mather, M., and Carstensen, L. L. (2004). The role of motivation in the age-related positivity effect in autobiographical memory. *Psychological Science*, **15**, 208–214.

Kvale, S. (1974). The temporality of memory. *Journal of Phenomenological Psychology*, **5**, 7–31.

Levine, B., Svoboda, E., Hay, J., Winocur, G., and Moscovitch, M. (2002). Aging and autobiographical memory: dissociating episodic from semantic retrieval. *Psychology and Aging*, **17**, 677–689.

Lhost-Catal, L. and Fitzgerald, J. M. (2004). Autobiographical memory in two older adults over a twenty-year retention interval. *Memory & Cognition*, **32**, 311–323.

Linton, M. (1978). Real-world memory after six years: an in vivo study of very long-term memory. In M. M. Gruneberg, P. E. Morris, and R. N. Sykes (eds.), *Practical aspects of memory* (pp. 69–76). New York: Academic Press.

McAdams, D. (2001). The psychology of life stories. *Review of General Psychology*, **5**, 100–122.

Mello, E. W. and Fisher, R. (1996). Enhancing older adult eyewitness memory with the cognitive interview. *Applied Cognitive Psychology*, **10**, 403–417.

Nelson, K. (1986). *Event knowledge: structure and function in development*. Hillsdale, NJ: Lawrence Erlbaum Associates.

  (2006). Development of representation in childhood. In E. Blaystock and F. I. M. Craik (eds.), *Lifespan cognition* (pp. 178–192). New York: Oxford University Press.

Nesselroade, J. R. (1991). Interindividual differences in intraindividual change. In L. M. Collins and J. L. Horn (eds.), *Best methods for the analysis of change: recent advances, unanswered questions, future directions* (pp. 92–105). Washington, DC: American Psychological Association.

Pepper, S. C. (1942). *World hypotheses.* Berkeley, CA: University of California Press.

Pillimer, D. B. (2001). Momentous events and the life story. *Review of General Psychology,* 5, 123–134.

Rathbone, C. J., Moulin, C., and Conway, M. A. (2008). Self-centered memories: the reminiscence bump and the self. *Memory & Cognition,* 36, 1403–1414.

Riegel, K. F. (1978). *Psychology mon amour: a countertext.* New York: Houghton-Mifflin.

Robinson, J. A. and Hawpe, L. (1986). Heuristic uses of narrative thinking. In T. R. Sarbin (ed.), *Narrative thinking: the storied nature of human conduct.* New York: Praeger.

Robinson, J. A. and Taylor, L. R. (1998). Autobiographical memory and self-narratives: a tale of two stories. In C. P. Thompson, D. Bruce, D. Read, D. G. Payne, and M. P. Toglia (eds.), *Autobiographical memory: theoretical and applied perspectives* (pp. 125–143). Mahwah, NJ: Lawrence Erlbaum Associates.

Roediger, H. L. (1984). Does current evidence from dissociation experiments favor the episodic semantic distinction? *Behavioral and Brain Sciences,* 7, 252–254.

Rubin, D. C. (1989). Issues of regularity and control: confessions of a regularity freak. In L. W. Poon, D. C. Rubin, and B. A. Wilson (eds.), *Everyday cognition in adult and later life* (pp. 84–103). Cambridge University Press.

  (2002). Autobiographical memory across the lifespan. In P. Graf and N. Ohta (eds.), *Lifespan development of human memory* (pp. 159–184). Cambridge, MA: MIT Press.

  (2006). The basic systems model of episodic memory. *Perspectives on Psychological Science,* 1, 277–311.

Rubin, D. C. and Berntsen, D. (2003). Life scripts help to maintain autobiographical memories of highly positive, but not highly negative, events. *Memory & Cognition,* 31, 1–14.

Rubin, D. C., Berntsen, D., and Hutson, M. (2009). The normative and the personal life: individual differences in life scripts and life stories among U.S.A. and Danish undergraduates. *Memory,* 17, 54–68.

Rubin, D. C., Rahhal, T. A., and Poon, L. W. (1998). Things learned in early adulthood are remembered best. *Memory & Cognition,* 26, 3–19.

Rubin, D. C., Schrauf, R. W., and Greenberg, D. L. (2003). Belief and recollection of autobiographical memories. *Memory & Cognition,* 31(6), 887–901.

Rubin, D. C., Schrauf, R. W., and Greenberg, D. L. (2004). Stability in autobiographical memories. *Memory,* 12, 715–721.

Rubin, D. C. and Schulkind, M. D. (1997). Distribution of important and word-cued autobiographical memories in 20-, 35-, and 70-year old adults. *Psychology and Aging,* 17, 524–535.

Rubin, D. C. and Wenzel, A. E. (1996). One hundred years of forgetting: a quantitative description of retention. *Psychological Review,* 103, 61–72.

Rubin, D. C., Wetzler, S. E., and Nebes, R. D. (1986). Autobiographical memory across the lifespan. In D. C. Rubin (ed.), *Autobiographical memory* (pp. 202–221). Cambridge University Press.

Rudoy, J. D., Weintraub, S., and Paller, K. A. (2009). Recall of remote episodic memories can appear deficient because of a gist-based retrieval orientation. *Neuropsychologia*, **47**, 938–941.

Rummens, J. A. (2003). Conceptualising identity and diversity: overlaps, intersections, and processes. *Canadian Ethics Studies*, **25**(3), 10–25.

Schaie, K. W. (1965). A general model for the study of developmental problems. *Psychological Bulletin*, **64**, 92–107.

Schrauf, R. W. and Rubin, D. C. (1998). Bilingual autobiographical memory in older adult immigrants: a test of cognitive explanation of the reminiscence bump and the linguistic encoding of memories. *Journal of Memory and Language*, **39**, 437–457.

Schulkind, M. D., Hennis, L. K., and Rubin, D. C. (1999). Music, emotion, and autobiographical memory. *Memory & Cognition*, **27**, 948–955.

Sehulster, J. R. (1996). In my era: evidence for the perception of a special period of the past. *Memory*, **4**, 145–158.

Singer, J. (1995). Seeing one's self: locating narrative memory in a framework of personality. *Journal of Personality*, **63**, 429–457.

Trunk, D. and Abrams, L. (2009). Do younger and older adults' communicative goals influence topic speech in autobiographical narratives? *Psychology and Aging*, **24**, 324–337.

Thompson, C. P. (1982). Memory for unique personal events: the roommate study. *Memory & Cognition*, **10**, 324–332.

Tulving, E. (1983). *The elements of episodic memory*. New York: Oxford University Press.

Wagenaar, W. A. (1986). My memory: a study of autobiographical memory over six years. *Cognitive Psychology*, **18**, 225–252.

Westmacott, R., Freedman, M., Black, S. E., Stokes, K. A., and Moscovitch, M. (2004). Temporally graded semantic memory loss in Alzheimer's disease: cross-sectional and longitudinal studies. *Cognitive Neuropsychology*, **21**, 353–378.

Evolution and basic processes of autobiographical memory

The three chapters in Part V attempt to make theoretical and empirical connections between autobiographical memory (as most frequently studied) and other basic mental processes. All three chapters address relatively new topics of autobiographical memory research. Donald's chapter discusses the development of autobiographical memory in an evolutionary perspective. Donald proposes that many nonhuman species are capable of episodic remembering when triggered by concrete cues in the environment, but are unable to initiate the recall process in a decontextualized and controlled fashion. It is primarily this ability for autocuing (strategic recall) which renders human autobiographical memory unique, according to Donald. Berntsen addresses the phenomenon of involuntary (spontaneously arising) autobiographical memories and proposes that such memories form a basic mode of remembering that may be evolutionarily earlier than the much more cognitively demanding (and much more studied) voluntary mode of accesing the past. The chapter by D'Argembeau reviews an accumulating amount of findings showing that the ability to remember the personal past and imagine the personal future is supported by many of the same cognitive and neural processes. D'Argembeau discusses the possible component processes underlying future thinking.

14 Evolutionary origins of autobiographical memory: a retrieval hypothesis

Merlin Donald

The evolutionary origins of autobiographical memory (AM) are a challenge for evolutionary cognitive science. The search for a theory is complicated by theoretical biases regarding the special nature of human memory, which seems so different from its primate predecessors. Why is it so different? How did human memory evolve, and where does AM fit into an evolutionary theory of human memory?

This chapter focuses on the evolution of one key feature of human memory: voluntary retrieval, or recall. Human memory is special in many of its superficial manifestations, but, from an evolutionary standpoint, its major distinguishing feature is the ease with which its contents are made accessible to consciousness. The evolution of voluntary conscious access to memory may account for many, if not most, of the distinguishing characteristics of human memory. The unique human capacity for accessing our memory banks provided a platform on which the spiraling co-evolution of human cognition and culture could be constructed.

The distinctiveness of human memory

Human memory researchers use a distinctive vocabulary to describe the memory systems of the human brain. It does not correspond to that used to describe animal memory. For example, in the extensive review edited by Kendrick, Rilling, and Denny (1986), no animal equivalents of semantic or episodic memory were mentioned, and the focus was on a monolithic concept of "long-term memory," as if no further distinctions were needed. Does this difference in terminology imply that the distant ancestors of modern humans must have evolved one or more radically new long-term memory systems?

In human memory research, it is common to speak of explicit/declarative versus implicit/nondeclarative memory, a distinction not normally made in animal memory research. This is sometimes taken as evidence that explicit or declarative memory is absent in animals. For example,

Tulving (1985, 2002) has claimed that episodic memory is uniquely human. Others disagree; Morris (2001) claims that there is a convergence of evidence from neuroscience, learning research, and ethology supporting the existence of episodic memories in various species of birds and mammals. Further evidence for this is provided by Griffiths, Dickenson, and Clayton (1999). I also concluded that many animals seem able to record (or encode) both episodic and semantic memories (Donald, 1991, 1993, 2001). However, this does not apply to their ability to recall. They are poor at recall tasks, and can only retrieve their memories passively – that is, by means of involuntary cues. It follows that voluntary retrieval might be the missing element in animals, and the key to uniquely human memory capabilities.

Procedural memory also seems to have different properties in animals and human beings. Animals can be trained to perform complex procedural routines, which resemble simple human skills, but cannot rehearse and refine skills on their own. As a result, they cannot acquire most of the complex skill hierarchies that define human society – for example, piano playing, driving a car, or using complex tools – which cannot be learned without extensive self-paced rehearsal. Humans are unique in being able to learn in this manner, and this might imply that humans have evolved a radically different procedural memory system.

If it were true that the human brain evolved as many as three new memory systems (episodic memory, explicit semantic memory, and a distinctive class of procedural memory), it would be a remarkable evolutionary phenomenon. Such a complex of adaptations would represent a huge cognitive distance traveled in only three major speciation events within the same line (the successive speciations, from an ancestral Miocene ape, of australopithecines, *Homo erectus*, and *Homo sapiens*, respectively). Moreover, each of these human memory systems falls into a distinct cognitive domain, making such a scenario even less likely.

The emergence of AM in modern humans complicates the situation even more. In theory, AM is a "higher" form of memory than semantic, episodic, or procedural memory, in that it cuts across these basic categories, integrating semantic and episodic memory material with selected procedural memory content. AM supposedly integrates all this disparate material into a time-based framework built around a virtual self (Conway, 2005, this volume) – a truly monumental achievement of cognitive integration. Does it follow that AM should be classified as yet another evolutionarily novel human memory system, perhaps a superordinate memory system able to coordinate and integrate material imported from "lower-level" systems?

Such a hypothesis assumes a great deal about the speed with which major evolutionary changes occur in the nervous system. The brain is a very conservative organ, not inclined to evolve radically new "modules" easily or fast. In order to accept that humans have evolved several novel memory systems, a very strong case must be made. It must be shown how primate memory systems could have been modified by natural selection to produce the constellation of memory systems we routinely study in humans. No answer to those questions is found in the biological or comparative literature. A simpler approach would be useful at this point.

Resolving a neuropsychological dilemma: a co-evolutionary approach

Since AM has no equivalent in other primate species, this may imply that the ancestors of human beings evolved a radically different kind of brain, and that AM is the product of a uniquely human brain design. However, in view of the similarities between the functional neuroanatomy of humans and the great apes (Passingham, 1982), this hypothesis seems less attractive than its alternative, that AM evolved without fundamentally redesigning the primate brain.

This hypothesis may seem unlikely, but that depends on how we define the expression "radically different brain." There are certainly some important differences between the human brain and those of other primates. The human brain has greater connectivity and plasticity, especially of the cerebral cortex and cerebellum, and is much larger, in relative terms, than other primate brains, with at least twice the number of neurons as those of our closest relatives, gorillas and chimpanzees. There are other distinctive features, such as a disproportionate volumetric expansion of certain regions of the cerebral cortex and lateral cerebellum, but these entail a quantitative, not qualitative, difference from the known properties of the brains of great apes. The same applies to such features as spindle (Von Economo) neurons, once thought to be special to Anthropoidea (Allman, Hakeem, Erwin, et al., 2001; Allman, Hakeem, and Watson, 2002) but also found in whales and elephants (Butti, Sherwood, Hakeem, et al., 2009).

These differences, while significant, are not truly radical. A radical innovation should involve a qualitative change – for example, a novel anatomical structure, such as a new cortical region with a novel connectivity pattern; a new neurotransmitter system; or a distinct, language-related anatomical system, similar in principle to the song neuroanatomy of songbirds (cf. Nottebohm, 1994). We might then try to attribute our unique capacity for AM to such an innovation, but no such thing has been discovered.

There is a credible alternative theoretical approach that does not postulate a qualitative change to the primate nervous system, and is nevertheless quite feasible in neuropsychological terms: brain–culture co-evolution. This postulates an evolutionary feedback loop between culture and brain that amplifies the formative role of culture in human cognitive development. In effect, it is the spiraling brain–culture interface, combined with increased plasticity, that provides the truly radical feature in such a theory. Culture (as a modifiable cognitive ecology) changes the mind, and vice versa. Both sides of this interaction affect selection pressure and influence the direction of evolution.

Because culture is unpredictable, and accumulates new knowledge rapidly at the group level, this co-evolutionary scenario would select for greater plasticity and improved learning capacity, favoring adaptable individuals who can assimilate the accumulating and unpredictable cultural knowledge base. Plasticity, combined with the continuing late maturation of certain anatomical structures, and a capacity for lifelong learning, would make the evolving hominin brain more flexible in its functional architecture, and better able to reorganize itself in response to a culturally imposed and variable cognitive load. I proposed (Donald, 1991, 1993, 1998b, 2001) that this is what happened in human evolution: a co-evolutionary process tethered neural epigenesis to culture, and made the human brain subject to radical functional reorganization by cultural forces, especially at the highest and most abstract level of the cognitive system.

This set the stage for a major cultural role in shaping human higher cognition, by developmentally rewiring the functional architectures supporting various cognitive skills. This approach is gaining ground in cognitive evolutionary theory (see Donald, 1991; Deacon, 1997; Dehaene, 2007; Tomasello, 1999). It postulates a cognitive symbiosis between the archaic human brain and its emerging cultural environment, whereby culture played an increasingly important role in formatting the adult mind and brain. This created new selection pressures whereby individuals with greater neural plasticity and openness to cultural reformatting were favored over their less flexible conspecifics. The human brain thus evolved a greater learning capacity, and more sophisticated social cognitive skills, to optimize the ability of individuals to access and assimilate the knowledge stored in cultural networks.

Of course, shifting the onus for change from brain to culture leaves the question of how and where this change in the role of culture might have come from. The answer proposed here is that it came from a quantitative change to the nervous system, which affected the way the brain accesses is own memory banks.

Nelson's hypothesis about the evolution of AM

Katherine Nelson (1993) has proposed that AM might have emerged in three evolutionary steps:
(1) generic event-memory, found in all mammals and birds
(2) episodic recognition memory, found in social animals
(3) autobiographical memory, found only in humans.
This proposal is essentially an evolutionary epistemology based on an evolving hierarchy of event-representations. Generic event-memory is the ability to remember and recognize different classes of events – generic categories – to know how to behave appropriately within the context of each category. Since the meaning of a given stimulus can change as a function of the event category into which it falls, this ability is vital for survival.

The evolution of episodic recognition memory took this event-recognition process one step further, by enabling animals to record the specific contextual details that mark an event –such as the identities of participants, attributions of agency and causality, and specific spatial and temporal features, such as colors, sounds, and microdetails. Sherry and Schacter (1987) made a somewhat similar distinction in their theory, proposing two kinds of memory in animals: system I (memory for generalities) and system II (memory for specific details).

Why would vertebrates have evolved several different long-term memory systems, rather than one all-inclusive system? One possible answer is that different kinds of memories impose incompatible storage requirements. In songbirds, learning a new song involves procedural learning of general rules for producing a sound sequence. In learning where food is located, the bird must remember specific details of where food was hidden. These tasks impose two incompatible kinds of memory loads, general rules versus event-specific details. Remembering the specific details of each previous song performance would presumably interfere with abstracting out the essential features of the song, which, to be successful, must maintain a consistent perceptual identity across many different conditions.

Language carried this evolutionary process one step further; it enabled people to construct large-scale life narratives into which much longer sequences of specific event-memories could be inserted selectively. Language served as the highest integrative device in this operation, gathering material from generic event-memory and episodic memory, and placing it in a wider context. Nelson theorized that the impact of language on memory was so important that many of the signature features of adult higher cognition could be attributed to the radical effect of language on the cognitive system. AM differentiates from episodic memory around 4 years of age, when children construct their first narrative accounts of experience. The functional significance of AM is that it enables human beings to share memories; construct and refine them together; and, most importantly, reinstate them. This is what she meant in coining the expression "mediated mind" (Nelson, 1996). In her theory, language is an essential tool in mediating later-developing cognitive skills such as analytical thought, a sense of time, a sense of personal identity, and, especially, AM.

Nelson's approach has great attraction, and is consistent with a great deal of available behavioral data. It is also simple and testable. Moreover, it seems true to the basic observation that human memory encodes wider and more abstract events than animal memory, this being perhaps its most distinctive feature. Her model also provides us with a clear epistemological hierarchy of knowledge that fits in well with developmental evidence and constructivist theory.

However, her model remains silent on neural mechanisms, and neutral on the question of why human memory structure is so distinctive. The challenge is that there is no evidence (yet) in brain physiology to support the existence of radically new neural memory systems in the human brain. Both episodic memory, as conceived by Tulving (2002), and AM are often regarded as specialized and novel human memory systems, but their origin remains a mystery.

A simplifying assumption: recall evolved independently

I am proposing a parsimonious, nonmodular theory to explain how our distinctively human memory configuration evolved. It places less emphasis on what is remembered, and more on the underlying process of gaining access to memories; that is, on recall. It is a retrieval theory of human memory evolution. It cuts across the classification systems commonly used in memory research, and focuses instead on the most basic distinction in the field, that between encoding and retrieval.

This theory proposes that *the distinctive structure of human memory emerged mostly as a byproduct of evolving neural machinery for voluntary recall.* Moreover, it proposes that this neural machinery simply took the form of *increased connectivity between certain crucial structures.*

The apparent restructuring of explicit memory in humans might simply be the result of evolving a general neural foundation for recall. In addition, the evolution of a recall mechanism triggered a revolutionary change in the nature of culture, especially in its cognitive role. The emergence of a capacity for recall triggered a chain of evolutionary events that led to the sharing of cognitive resources in culture, with a subsequent reorganization of the human memory system by cultural forces.

A corollary is that the machinery supporting two distinct aspects of human memory, encoding and retrieval, evolved at different times, with encoding mechanisms emerging much earlier than retrieval mechanisms, each following its own distinctive evolutionary trajectory. The neural mechanisms of voluntary retrieval were subject to different selection pressures, in a different evolutionary environment, at a different time, and in a different species.

Voluntary recall is the signature behavioral manifestation of retrieval from memory in humans. Animal memory lacks any capacity for *self-initiated* recall. Our capacity for voluntarily retrieving memories might be the major reason why human memory looks so different on the behavioral surface, and affords such different experimental paradigms in the laboratory. Passive episodic memories – that is, detailed, involuntary memories of specific events in their past lives – are found in many animal species, and documented in human memory, and even AM (Berntsen, 2009, this volume). However, humans have an option to initiate a search-and-retrieval process, whereas nonhuman animals do not.

Semantic memory, a memory for facts and general properties of the world drawn from experience, can be demonstrated in animals; however, such memories are retrievable only when elicited by passive association. The same applies to animal procedural memory. Nonhuman animals can learn skills with appropriate conditioning, but their performances can be retrieved only by external cues that elicit conditioned responses. Voluntary recall, as in self-triggered conscious retrieval, the kind of recall needed to practice a skill, is absent.

The missing element in all three examples of animal memory is a capacity for voluntary search and retrieval. I argue here that humans initially evolved the neural means for recalling memories through evolving the ability to recall procedural memories. This enabled the species to evolve a consensual morpho-phonological basis for language, and eventually transformed the surface architecture of semantic and episodic memory in our species. Changes in human memory structure are due mostly to the fact that we possess the neural means of voluntarily initiating a search process, and of consciously controlling that process, to gain access to specific memories, retrieve them, and validate the relative success or failure of the search-and-retrieval process.

This idea presents a theoretically useful alternative to a multiple memory system theory, in which each system has its own distinctive brain organization for encoding, storing, and retrieving specific kinds of memories. It also simplifies the challenges of making memory theory compatible with evolutionary cognitive neuroscience. Research could then focus on retrieval mechanisms as a distinct, and possibly superordinate, brain adaptation, and abandon the search for three or more distinctly human memory systems. This also implies a much simpler evolutionary scenario than the traditional mainstream theory, in which humans supposedly evolved several qualitatively new kinds of memory systems in parallel, within the relatively short span of hominin evolution.

The evolutionary rationale for this model is described in the next section, with special reference to procedural memory, where this evolutionary transformation started. This model is then expanded to explain not only the unique human ability to recall but also the emergence of special forms of encoding in human explicit/declarative memory and AM.

The origins of autocuing in procedural memory: mimesis

I have suggested elsewhere (Donald, 1991, 1999, 2005a, 2012) that the remote origins of human symbolic thought lie in an early cognitive revolution, which resulted in our remarkable capacity for refining and rehearsing skill. This is where the evolution of a memory retrieval mechanism begins. Skilled rehearsal is a voluntary performance. There can be no systematic rehearsal of skill without accurate voluntary recall of previous performances.

The act of recalling a procedural memory is itself a performance that usually entails implicit or covert motor acts. Recall is thus an essential component of human procedural learning. The refinement of skill assumes a capacity to self-trigger a specific procedural memory. The ability to initiate and guide the selective internal cuing process that triggers such a memory is called "autocuing." Thus, in terms of its evolution, autocuing may be viewed as an integral part of a radically modified primate procedural learning mechanism, linked to the brain's action systems. Self-triggering a memory – any memory – entails an action on the part of the subject, even if it is, more often than not, nothing more than a covert or indefinitely delayed action.

The most basic case in which autocuing is necessary is the practice and rehearsal of skilled performances, toward their improvement. To practice and refine an action, the subject must self-trigger an accurate memory of previous performances: this entails autocuing. A capacity for autocuing is also evident in another common human practice, exploring personal memories in fantasy (say, family memories from childhood) and relying largely on an imaginative process of internal recollection and reflection. This also requires individuals to exercise control over an internal memory search, which presumably relies on the same basic neural mechanism for recall as procedural autocuing, because evolutionary breakthroughs of this magnitude are extremely unlikely to evolve twice, in parallel brain systems, in the same line.

Procedural autocuing is inherently creative. As Bartlett (1932) observed almost a century ago, each act of recall is distinct from every other, because it entails actively reconstructing the memory in question, and not literal retrieval (in the manner of, say, a computer). The constructive factor implies that there is a creative dimension to recall, even in the case of retrieving an action-memory or body-memory, such as an act of throwing, a way of walking, or a dance step.

One reason why autocuing is a challenge for neuroscience is that it involves searching one's memory banks in a systematic manner. A nervous system is a cluster of impression-forming neural nets; it has no means of tagging memories for later retrieval. A brain lacks the equivalent of the file-allocation table (FAT), which computers use to locate a stored memory item. FATs require a fixed address system that can locate specific memories by means of something stable, searchable, and predictable, such as an assigned location. No neural net system can have such markers built in, because, in neural nets, memories are randomly assigned according to the history of the organism and the exact state of the nervous system at the time of learning, which is, in principle, completely unpredictable.

Even if the human brain had a FAT equivalent built into its basic anatomy, the timing of an experience would greatly affect where and how certain memory locations were allocated in the brain, defeating its usefulness as a retrieval device. Other potential vehicles for labeling a specific memory, such as time-tagging, would also fail as accurate retrieval devices. There appears to be very little precise time-tagging of long-term memories in the mammalian brain, other than through association, and some variation in vividness, with old memories fading in comparison to new ones (although this is reversed somewhat in old age, usually without affecting the ability of the subject to locate memories accurately in time and space). Moreover, even if time-tagging were a reliably available cue, as it is not, due to the unpredictability of environmental priming, it would convey extremely limited information for any retrieval system to use, likely proving useful for only a short period, soon after a simple event was experienced. Thus, evolving a built-in, precise neural address system for retrieval appears to be impossible in principle.

Without tagging, how are memories found? There is an alternative that might work: humans might have evolved a direct linkage between event-memory and voluntary movement – *evolving retrieval as a performance skill*, as it were. This hypothesis amounts to a motor theory of retrieval, where conscious recall taps into the decision mechanisms and action-generating systems driving voluntary movement.

The hypothesis boils down to this: humans are able to recall by performing a covert motor act that sends a fairly precise activation signal from voluntary motor regions to the appropriate event-perceptual circuitry, and vice versa, converging on a final target version of an imagined action. Why cannot nonhuman animals do this? Presumably, they cannot because they lack the neural connection and feedback pathways needed to activate event-memories from the cortical regions initiating and planning voluntary actions, even covert ones.

By this logic, autocuing must have originated in an expanded and more precise reciprocal mapping between the anterior "motor brain" (including various prefrontal and premotor regions) and the posterior, event-perceptual regions of the brain. It is not yet known whether mirror neurons play a role in these reciprocal circuits; their presence in monkeys, who lack imitative and mimetic skills, suggests that mirror neurons are not in themselves sufficient to enable such performances (Donald, 2005b, 2012). However, they might have been important evolutionary forerunners of mimetic skills and autocuing.

Core hypotheses

This retrieval hypothesis may be summarized as follows:
(1) Autocuing emerged first in the domain of procedural memory, in australopithecines.
(2) This adaptation incorporated the actions of the self into an event-perceptual framework, enabling a form of conscious self-observation that subjected those actions to critical review. This was the basis for the "review-rehearsal loop" which permitted the refinement of skill.
(3) Its emergence in the hominin line is evident in a documented breakthrough in the domain of skill, evident in refined tool manufacture at least 2.5–3.5 million years ago, probably appearing first in afarensis australopithecines (McPherron, Alemseged, Marean, *et al.*, 2010), but certainly present by the time habilines emerged (Donald, 1991).
(4) The neurocognitive foundation for rehearsing skill lies in a process called mimesis, or mimetic action, made possible by the evolution of the review-rehearsal loop. Mimetic capacity enabled humans to initiate a specific pattern of learned action, review it, and then repeat it, or modify it, to improve the performance.
(5) The anatomical foundation of the review-rehearsal loop emerged from an expansion of the connections of prefrontal cortex to posterior cortical regions, and an enlarged path to the lateral cerebellum. Both of these changes to the primate brain have been demonstrated in modern humans (Deacon, 1997), but the exact time when they

appeared is not yet known. Recent data on stone toolmaking suggest they had already started to evolve in afarensis australopithecines over 3 million years ago (McPherron *et al.*, 2010).

(6) The review-rehearsal loop was not restricted to the literal reproduction of highly specified action patterns, as in practice or mimicry of highly constrained patterns of action; it also applied to covert actions, and those not specified in detail. Thus, it formed the neural foundation for a cluster of expressive behaviors that were potentially creative, such as generic imitation, pantomime, and fantasy play.

(7) A capacity for mimetic action enabled our ancestors to focus attention on their own actions in context, not only to refine them, but also to produce more effective public performances. This opened up the possibility of nonlinguistic gestures that could be conventionalized in the actions of social groups, and established some of the preconditions for the later evolution of language (Donald, 1999).

Mimetic action evolved primarily because of the selection advantages associated with toolmaking and refined skill in general, but carried other (exaptive) benefits, especially gains in expressive behavior, which were a product of the same neural adaptation that created the neural foundation for fantasy play and pantomime. This occurred without further radical changes to the nervous system, because fantasy play and pantomime were also a direct result of having a retrieval mechanism that could subject performances to scrutiny and change them. In turn, these capacities had enormous social and cultural ramifications, creating the neural potential for the emergence of conventional nonlinguistic gesturing, and ritualized sequences of gestures that could express group emotions, such as grief and victory, in a conventional manner. In short, the emergence of mimetic capacity inevitably generated a "mimetic vernacular," and this created further selection advantages favoring a rapid spread of this capability in the ancient hominin line.

Mimetic expression was, and still is, driven by an analog logic – the logic of impression-formation, resemblance, and metaphor. This same logic energizes animal generic event-perceptions, but not their motor behavior. The difference in hominins was their ability to translate perceptual analog logic into public acts and performances, generating a public expressive space. This allowed them to capture analog logic in the public arena, distribute it widely in a shared set of public skills and expressions, and create the possibility of a culture in which there was some sharing of mind.

Mimetic expression works through selective re-enactment. Such expressions can be remembered in both individual and collective memory; hence, skills and mimetic representations can outlive individuals (cf. Hirst, Cue, and Wohl, this volume). In essence, mimesis started the process of culture as a shared storehouse of collective memory, which could evolve in its own right. In this sense, mimesis was the beginning of a uniquely human adventure: the power to represent past experience in collective memory, a population-level adaptation whose origin, paradoxically, stemmed from an adaptation for learning to refine skills.

Two additional points are central to the idea of mimesis. The first is that the perception of context is important for accurate mimetic recall. The rehearsal of any skill demands the voluntary recall of past performances *in an appropriate context*. Nonhuman animals are very sensitive to context, and it is fair to assume that early hominins were as well. The emergence of recall would have created selection pressures to evolve that sensitivity ever further. Adjustment of response to context necessitates very accurate recall of detail, along with noticing different contexts, to allow finer adjustments according to current context. Only with this kind of precise information can the brain achieve the systematic improvement of past performances.

Archaeologists and anthropologists have provided solid evidence that this capacity had already evolved by the time we find the earliest stone tools. These tools were finished to the point where even modern anthropologists need several weeks of practice to perfect their manufacture (Toth, Schick, and Semaw, 2003). Even the most primitive Oldowan tools could not have been manufactured without a significant amount of practice and rehearsal, and sensitivity to context – in this case, specific materials used for the hammer stone and different ones for the tool itself, as well as specific contextual adjustments in the manufacturer's strategy for striking.

It is significant that the enculturated bonobo Kanzi, who was trained (Toth, Schick, Savage–Rumbaugh, *et al.*, 1993) almost two decades ago to make a stone cutting tool by banging two rocks together to produce a flake sharp enough to cut a rope and release food, has never improved on his previous performances, even after 18 years. Kanzi does not practice his skill, or try to refine it; he simply breaks rocks until a piece is sharp enough to cut. To produce a true Oldowan tool, Kanzi would have to possess some mimetic ability, which, among other things, would give him accurate recall of previous performances, and better ability to adjust to context.

The second point is that a cognitive system that could support skilled rehearsal of toolmaking could also support mimetic skills in general, across virtually all modalities of voluntary movement. Toolmaking is a complex skill system embedded in a social network of practice, which maintains a shared system for identifying and locating appropriate materials, dividing the labor of tool use and manufacture, and the social management of the network (a very complex political matter). Mimesis is inherently an amodal system, and functions at a supramodal level – literally, above modality – and there are good reasons to postulate that it was amodal from the start (see Donald, 1991, 1998a, 1999).

This is central to one of the main principles underlying this theory: *once you evolve an amodal capacity to rehearse a skill, you get pantomime and fantasy play free*. Pantomime is formally identical to skilled rehearsal, in terms of the role played by the underlying rehearsal-review loop mechanism. The cognitive operations involved in practicing refined skills, and mimetic performance, in the wider sense of public fantasy play and ritual, are similar, and can generate a public "theater" of embodied expression and event re-enactment. In every case, the actions of both individuals and groups are guided and evaluated in mimetic imagination.

Human imaginative acts can project ahead in time (see also D'Argembeau, this volume); this is a crucial feature of mimetic imagination in its role of performance control. The same cognitive system that enables mimetic reduplication of behavior also provides the neural foundation for expanding the range of planned (imagined) action. Primates, including apes, cannot "design" or examine their future actions the way humans can. Humans do this very well, even at an early age. Apes cannot rehearse or practice an imagined action-pattern, to improve or modify it. Nor can they pantomime. Both practice and pantomime require mimetic imagination, which enables the performance of an imagined action, followed by its review in imagination.

Episodic and semantic retrieval: a common link to language

This argument can be extended to the challenge presented by the emergence of modern explicit memory systems. Mimesis was a major advance in gaining voluntary access to procedural memory, and establishing the cognitive foundation for creating a simple nonverbal expressive culture. However, it falls short of accounting for the abstractions and complexities of semantic memory and AM. The next evolutionary step, or steps, for ancient hominins, bridged the enormous gap between procedural retrieval, and explicit memory and AM, as they exist today in anatomically modern humans.

The bridging of that gap was tied to the evolution of language, which was scaffolded on mimesis; even a simple protolanguage could not have evolved without mimesis being in place (Donald, 1999). The review-rehearsal loop is also indispensable for lexical invention (cf. Donald, 1993). Languages are a product of group interaction, and it is impossible for a population of human beings to invent a voluntary consensual system of expressions, or even a shared morpho-phonology, without having mimetic expressive skill in the first place. Thus, mimesis was a necessary preadaptation for the evolution of both protolanguage and fully evolved language. Mimesis and language were both impossible without voluntary recall from procedural memory.

The dependency of language on mimesis stems from another of the inherent properties of mimesis: group performance. The capacity to create original expressive performances in a group lies at the heart of every language act. Mimesis is an integrative performance skill, and it can support activities that range from toolmaking (an ancient, but deceptively complex, multimodal skill) to speaking (a more abstract, and recently evolved, multimodal skill). The learning and refinement of language skills is similar to the practice and performance of other skills; however, their acquisition is much more socially intricate.

Mastering a language entails more than acquiring a vocabulary and learning some basic rules of grammar; the latter is a relatively low level of skill, and is often reached early in development, around 2 years of age. The mature use of language entails original storytelling, and children typically take 4 years or more to reach the point where they can construct a simple story of their own, based on their own experience (Nelson, 1996, 2007). They must serve a longer apprenticeship in society before they meet the demanding performance standards for entering a human linguistic community, even as very junior members.

This process undoubtedly entailed additional major modifications to the human nervous system, and these will not be discussed here. The point is that language is mimetic in its essence, and so is the process of constructing an elaborate system of AM. Living in a linguistic community is largely a question of mastering and performing conceptually complex representational skills in a social context. Because of the overwhelming presence of language, human social life has become dominated by a public theater of language acts, and *narrative accounts of experience are constructed essentially as real or latent public performances*.

The link between knowledge and performance is the key to accurate retrieval, and explicit recall combines some of the properties associated with posterior cortical systems (event-perception) with some of the properties commonly identified with anterior cortical and cortico-cerebellar systems (voluntary action and the conscious supervision of performance). The performance of language acts in a social context requires humans to use detailed social knowledge (which is largely dependent on posterior brain mechanisms that support event-perception) to guide and plan expressive action (which is dependent upon anterior cortical systems for its voluntary execution).

This emphasizes the most fundamental difference between the way humans learn and the way other animals learn. The difference has nothing to do with language as such. It concerns autocuable control of procedural memory. *Human beings can voluntarily self-direct and supervise the perform-ance of learned skills, but other primates cannot.* This capacity remains the foundation of our powers of recall and recollection, even in the more abstract realms of semantic memory.

Rubin (1995) documented how various cultures have capitalized on linkages between meaning and procedural memory to sustain an enduring oral tradition – for example, the use of rhyme schemes to make epic poetry more memorable. He singled out "serial cuing" as the foundation on which oral traditions have been maintained for centuries. I would remark that, in most of the examples he cited, the order of cuing proceeded from the procedural to the semantic and conceptual. This does not rule out the possibility of reversing the cuing order. However, it illustrates a natural preference for procedural autocuing, and supports the notion that it remains the primary voluntary access point into the human memory system. For serial cuing to be brought under voluntary control, a link to the action brain – even in the form of covert phonological acts – is necessary. Procedural autocuing is the primary entry point in the chain at which this kind of conscious intervention can take place.

The critical role of language

The evolution of language appears to have been an indispensable part of the emergence of AM, but how can this be proven? Developmental studies of the growth of AM in children have shown a positive correlation between language mastery and AM development (Fivush, this volume; Nelson, 1996). This confirms the canonical developmental pattern, but does not address the question of the indispensability of language, because language and AM develop in parallel and cannot easily be disentangled.

One way to address this question is to examine the development of AM in adults with normal brains, who nonetheless lack language. This presents us with a significant challenge, since, given our extremely social nature, very few neurologically normal humans ever reach adulthood without language. Studies of "feral" children raised outside society are a flawed sample, given that such children usually suffer from impairments other than an absence of language.

However, confirming evidence for the indispensability of language in developing AM can be found in cases of deaf people who learned sign language as adolescents or adults. Schaller (1991) documented several case histories of deaf people who acquired sign language very late in their development, as late as age 30, long after the normal period of language learning, and found no evidence supporting the existence of AM in this population before learning sign language. However, some considerable time after they acquire sign language, usually several years, their AM improves greatly. Significantly, once they are sufficiently expert in sign language to construct a self-narrative, AM develops rapidly.

Yet they cannot apply this new skill retroactively to earlier memories. Even after acquiring sign language, they continued to have a very poor memory record of their earlier (prelinguistic) lives. Despite having been able, in their earlier lives, to acquire skills and hold simple occupations without sign language, their memories of that period could not be recalled clearly. In these subjects, acquiring sign late did not help them recover memories of the distant past, even though it enabled them to construct an AM record of their lives after learning language.

This demonstrates that language must be in place when specific events are being recorded in AM. Otherwise, these events will remain lost to long-term recollection, unless they are accidentally cued by an external signal. This idea is not new: a century ago, the most famous of late language learners, Helen Keller, described her prelanguage self as "Phantom" (1902). Her own autobiographical writings suggested strongly that her AM system existed only in a very primitive and vague form prior to her learning language. The subjective impressions of Schaller's subjects, as well as her clinical observations, served to confirm Keller's self-reports. Language, even when learned well into adulthood, radically changes the mental life of the subject, sharpening not only recollection, but also the sense of self and the experience of temporal continuity.

Why should late language learning have such a revolutionary effect on the ability to construct and access personal memories? There is no *a priori* neurological reason to predict a failure of basic episodic memory, and this is supported by behavioral data: Schaller's reports indicate that episodic memory of a given event was reasonably good, if measured soon after its occurrence. This is also true of prelinguistic children: Bauer (2006, this volume) reviewed an extensive literature on young children's ability to recall, and found that they retain episodic knowledge of when an event takes place; but those memories apparently fade if they cannot weave them into a personal narrative. The same applies to Schaller's subjects. In the absence of sign language, fragmented episodic memories retained for a short time following an event were not sufficient to sustain a significant, long-term AM record. Language proved to be essential.

On the surface, the reason why language mattered so much is that it can help provide an effective mnemonic system capable of capturing and reconstructing an elaborate event-representation – say, of a family tragedy – for later recall. Language is an effective organizational tool for memory, and, importantly, its products remain accessible long after the memory is recorded, presumably through a chain of associative cues that are available to a mechanism of voluntary internal autocuing. Narrative structures enable speakers to string together the fragmented pieces of an experience systematically, giving them later access to the episodes that comprise the event, in a coherent order.

Without this organizational tool, the prelinguistic mind is left only with the fragmented and disorganized episodic subcomponents of events, easily lost in a maze of other memories. The episodic details of prelinguistic experience remain vague and largely outside voluntary reach. Learning sign language late in life did not help Schaller's subjects recall their early experiences because those experiences were not entered into an accessible memory system in the first place.

An important corollary follows: mimetic expression alone, which these subjects had mastered long before acquiring sign language, was not sufficient to help them build an effective AM system. Mimetic expressions enabled them to acquire skills and participate in human social life, but did not support the construction of a personal system for remembering personal life experiences in detail. The development of an explicit AM system appears to depend on language mastery.

This is consistent with the evolutionary model proposed here: procedural access came first, followed by the invention of languages by societies that had reached a point of communicative complexity where the disambiguation of mimetic expressions acquired adaptive significance. Only after that second stage could AM start to evolve, but that second stage could not be reached, or even begin, until the neural basis for procedural autocuing had been secured.

Distributed networks and evolution of modern memory structure

The ancestors of humans evolved, first and foremost, into unusually adept learners of complex skills, but the rudimentary communicative skills that accompanied mimesis also started them on the road to becoming supremely social beings capable of developing knowledge networks in culture. The cultures of the Lower Paleolithic had already evolved a potential for becoming distributed knowledge networks – perhaps limited in terms of their cognitive or representational range, but nevertheless able to influence the direction of an evolving cognitive-cultural system. Those simple archaic networks may have held only a few shared algorithms that guided practices related to the maintenance of skill systems, such as toolmaking and fire-tending, but their importance should not be underestimated; and they were prototypes of what was yet to evolve. The knowledge involved in, for instance, successful toolmaking was stored in networks of practice (cf. Hutchins, 1995) that evidently endured for many generations. As brain–culture co-evolution gained momentum, culture assumed a radically novel, and leading, role in human brain evolution and development.

As cultures accumulated more knowledge, and individuals were increasingly dependent upon culture for survival, the human brain came under selection pressure to assimilate the knowledge stored in culture-based cognitive systems more effectively. The balance of influence in the brain–culture interaction gradually shifted toward more abstract habits and expressions, especially those determining the forms of social rituals and conventions, and the public regulation of emotional expression in groups. This process further engaged social cognition, and stimulated the refinement of social systems that regulate shared emotional behavior (Tomasello, 2008). In the longer run, human culture evolved into a storehouse of custom and knowledge that vastly exceeded the memory capacity of the individual brain. The specific intellectual capabilities of anatomically modern humans were shaped by a cognitive ecology that was largely man-made, and started with the establishment of an ancient mimetic culture based on the evolution of the neural underpinnings of the review-rehearsal loop and procedural autocuing.

This aspect of the theory bears some resemblance to the biological theory of niche construction; however, there is a fundamental difference. The "niche" constructed in the case of human cognition is open-ended, or open-loop. Whereas niche construction is normally closed-loop and conservative in its dynamics, the human cognitive ecology is an *open-loop* system, subject to the unpredictable vicissitudes of cultural innovation. Human cultures, and especially their material byproducts such as technology, can generate changes so quickly that they can finesse the protections inherent in a closed, and slower-moving, system. They can also *design* change, to advance some shared objective. This is an evolutionarily novel process, restricted to the human species. Its implications have not been fully explored.

Summary and conclusion

This theory does not attempt to explain every aspect of the evolution of AM, but claims only to address its deepest evolutionary roots. A complete theory would have to address the question of language evolution, which was not examined here in detail. Moreover, enculturation was not discussed here, even though it is highly relevant to AM theory, because particular cultures and subcultures can influence the manner and degree to which AM is cultivated (see Fivush and Nelson, 2004; Marcowitsch and Welzer, 2005; Nelson, 1996, 2007; Rubin, 1995). However, these influences on AM could not have emerged without the more basic evolutionary trigger: gaining conscious access to the procedural memory system.

Another topic that was not addressed was involuntary AM recall. Autobiographical memories, especially those with strong emotional content, are often recalled involuntarily (Berntsen, 2009, this volume). This does not contradict the notion that AM evolved because of an archaic brain adaptation that permitted humans to gain voluntary access to memory. That adaptation enabled human ancestors to create cultures that evolved into distributed memory systems, starting the process of brain–culture co-evolution. Once AM had become a reality, much later in evolution, these kinds of memories, like all memories, were susceptible to cuing by every force of association inherent in the environment, as well as in the associative stream of the individual mind.

Finally, the importance of distributed cognition in evolving AM should be re-emphasized. AM is shaped as much by the distributed network as by individual experience. The specific content of AM reflects knowledge contained in the larger social system, not merely the experiences of an individual. Autobiographical memories are thus personal instantiations of a collective cultural-cognitive process, which shapes and reshapes the internal networks of memory, incorporating technology into the collective memory system, and reconfiguring cognition in the process.

In sum, the deep roots of AM lie in the interplay of two factors: (1) the early evolution of procedural recall in the hominin line, and (2) the emergence and differentiation of distributed cultural-cognitive networks made possible by the first development. The convergence of these two forces – voluntary access to memory, and cultural-cognitive networks that can change what is stored in memory – created a co-evolutionary spiral, and a representational revolution, leading eventually to language, which raised memory representation to a new level of abstraction, giving culture a central role in shaping the evolving AM capacity of the human species.

References

Allman, J. M., Hakeem, A., Erwin, J. M., Nimchinsky, E., and Hof, P. (2001). Anterior cingulate cortex: the evolution of an interface between emotion and cognition. *Annals of the New York Academy of Sciences*, **935**, 107–117.

Allman, J. M., Hakeem, A., and Watson, K. (2002). Two phylogenetic specializations in the human brain. *Neuroscientist*, **8**(4), 335–346. doi: 10.1177/107385840200800409. PMID 1219450

Bartlett, F. (1932). *Remembering*. Cambridge University Press.

Bauer, P. (2006). *Remembering the times of our lives: memory in infancy and beyond.* Mahwah, NJ: Lawrence Erlbaum Associates.

Berntsen, D. (2009). *Involuntary autobiographical memories: an introduction to the unbidden past.* New York: Cambridge University Press.

Butti, C., Sherwood, C. C., Hakeem, A. Y., Allman, J. M., and Hof, P. R. (2009). Total number and volume of Von Economo neurons in the cerebral cortex of cetaceans. *Journal of Comparative Neurology*, **515**(2), 243–259.

Conway, M. (2005). Memory and the self. *Journal of Memory and Language*, **53**, 624–628.

Deacon, T. (1997). *The symbolic species: the co-evolution of language and the brain.* New York: Norton.

Dehaene, S. (2007). Cultural recycling of cortical maps. *Neuron*, **56**, 384–398.

Donald, M. (1991). *Origins of the modern mind: three stages in the evolution of culture and cognition.* Cambridge, MA: Harvard University Press.

(1993). Précis of *Origins of the modern mind* with multiple review and author's response. *Behavioral and Brain Sciences*, **16**, 737–791.

(1998a). Mimesis and the executive suite: missing links in language evolution. In J. R. Hurford, M. Studdert-Kennedy, and C. Knight (eds.), *Approaches to the evolution of language: social and cognitive bases* (pp. 44–67). Cambridge University Press.

(1998b). Hominin enculturation and cognitive evolution. In C. Renfrew and C. Scarre (eds.), *Cognition and material culture: the archaeology of symbolic storage* (pp. 7–17). McDonald Institute Monographs. University of Cambridge.

(1999). Preconditions for the evolution of protolanguages. In M. C. Corballis and I. Lea (eds.), *The descent of mind* (pp. 355–365). Oxford University Press.

(2001). *A mind so rare: the evolution of human consciousness.* New York: W. W. Norton.

(2005a). Imitation and mimesis. In S. Hurley and N. Chater (eds.), *Perspectives on imitation: from neuroscience to social science.* Vol. II: *Imitation, human development, and culture* (pp. 282–300). Cambridge, MA: MIT Press.

(2005b). The application of ideomotor theory to imitation. In S. Hurley and N. Chater (eds.), *Perspectives on imitation: from neuroscience to social science.* Vol. I: *Mechanisms of imitation and imitation in animals* (pp. 217–218). Cambridge, MA: MIT Press.

(2012). Mimesis theory re-examined, 20 years after the fact. In G. Hatfield and H. Pittman (eds.), *The evolution of mind, brain and culture*. Philadelphia: University of Pennsylvania Press.

Fivush, R. and Nelson, K. (2004). Culture and language in the emergence of autobiographical memory. *Psychological Science*, **15**, 573–577.

Griffiths, D., Dickinson, A., and Clayton, N. (1999). Episodic memory: what can animals remember about their past? *Trends in Cognitive Sciences*, **3**, 74–80.

Hutchins, E. (1995). *Cognition in the wild.* Cambridge, MA: MIT Press.

Keller, H. (1902). *The story of my life*. New York: Grosset & Dunlap.

Kendrick, D. F., Rilling, M. E., and Denny, M. R. (eds.) (1986). *Theories of animal memory*. New York: Lawrence Erlbaum Associates.

Marcowitsch, H. J. and Welzer, H. (2005). *The development of autobiographical memory*. D. Emmans (trans). Hove: Psychology Press.

McPherron, S. P., Alemseged, Z., Marean, C. W., Wynn, J. G., Reed, D., Geraads, D., Bobe, R., and Béarat, H. A. (2010). Evidence for stone-tool-assisted consumption of animal tissues before 3.39 million years ago at Dikika, Ethiopia. *Nature*, **466**, 857–860. doi: 10.1038 /nature09248

Morris, R. G. L. (2001). Episodic-like memory in animals. *Philosophical Transactions of the Royal Society of London. Series B, Biological Sciences*, **356**, 1453–1465.

Nelson, K. (1993). The psychological and social origins of autobiographical memory. *Psychological Science*, **4**, 7–14.

(1996). *Language in cognitive development: the emergence of the mediated mind*. New York: Cambridge University Press.

(2007). *Young minds in social worlds: experience, meaning, and memory*. Cambridge, MA: Harvard University Press.

Nottebohm, F. (1994). *The song circuits of the avian brain as a model system in which to study vocal learning, communication and manipulation. Discussions in Neurosciences*, **10**, 72–81.

Passingham, R. (1982). *The human primate*. New York: Freeman.

Rubin, D. C. (1995). *Memory in oral traditions: the cognitive psychology of epic, ballads, and counting-out rhymes*. New York: Oxford University Press.

Schaller, S. (1991). *A man without words*. New York: Summit Books.

Sherry, D. F. and Schacter, D. L. (1987). The evolution of multiple memory systems. *Psychological Review*, **94**, 439–454.

Tomasello, M. (1999). *The cultural origins of human cognition*. Cambridge, MA: Harvard University Press.

(2008). *Origins of human communication*. Cambridge, MA: MIT Press.

Toth, N., Schick, K., Savage-Rumbaugh, E. S., Sevcik, R., and Rumbaugh, D. (1993). Pan the tool-maker. *Journal of Archaeological Science*, **20**, 81–91.

Toth, N., Schick, K., and Semaw, S. (2003). A comparative study of the toolmaking skills of *Pan*, *Australopithecus*, and *Homo sapiens*. In N. Toth and K. Schick (eds.), *The Oldowan: case studies of the earliest Stone Age*. Bloomington, IN: Craft Press.

Tulving, E. (1985). How many memory systems are there? *American Psychologist*, **40**, 385–398.

(2002). Episodic memory: from mind to brain. *Annual Review of Psychology*, **53**, 1–25.

15 Spontaneous recollections: involuntary autobiographical memories are a basic mode of remembering

Dorthe Berntsen

> I was running in the Botanical Gardens, while planning my day. It was a frosty, quiet, and beautiful day. I was running lost in my thoughts – and suddenly I ran over some *slippery*, frozen puddles. I suddenly remembered another run, also on a frosty day. I had passed another runner, with long, ruffled hair, and a big smile, who yelled: "Take care on the ice!"

Autobiographical memories often arise involuntarily, that is, with no preceding retrieval effort, as illustrated by the example. However, most research on autobiographical/episodic memory still works under the assumption that conscious recollections of past events normally require a goal-directed and controlled (voluntary) retrieval process. For example, in his seminal book, Tulving (1983) argued that "access to, or actualization from, the episodic memory system tends to be deliberate and usually requires conscious effort" (p. 46). Mandler (1985) observed that episodic retrieval in general is "deliberate and consciously accessed" (p. 94), while acknowledging that "much of everyday memory experiences are in fact non-deliberate" (pp. 102–103). More recently, Davachi and Dobbins (2008) stated, "Occasionally, a memory will just pop into one's head wholly uninvited. Although we have all had such involuntary recollections, they are arguably not the norm..." (p. 115). Here I am going to challenge this view by arguing that involuntary recollections are a basic mode of remembering.

A basic mode of remembering

On the first pages of his groundbreaking book on memory, Ebbinghaus (1885) identified three basic modes of remembering, a voluntary conscious mode, an involuntary conscious mode, and a non-conscious mode. However, since Ebbinghaus, modern cognitive psychologists have generally ignored the category of involuntary conscious memories (see Berntsen, 2009; Hintzman, 2011, for reviews). In contrast, involuntary conscious memories have received substantial attention in the field of clinical psychology, but almost always in relation to emotionally stressful experiences or psychological disorders (e.g., Brewin, Dalgleish, and Joseph, 1996; Ehlers, Hackmann, and Michael, 2004).

Only recently have involuntary autobiographical memories been the focus of systematic research in cognitive psychology. Among other things, this research has shown that involuntary autobiographical memories are common in everyday life and that they are generally emotionally positive – in contrast to the focus on negative involuntary memories in clinical psychology (e.g., Ball and Little, 2006; Berntsen, 1996, 2009; Berntsen and Hall, 2004; Berntsen and Rubin, 2002; Kvavilashvili and Mandler, 2004; Mace, 2004, 2005, 2007; Rubin, Boals, and Berntsen, 2008; Schlagman, Kvavilashvili, and Schulz, 2007). In the following, I shall pick up the threads from the early pioneers on research on memory and consciousness (Ebbinghaus, 1885/1964; James, 1890) and outline a theory that considers involuntary autobiographical memories as a basic mode of remembering.

At a more detailed level, this claim has the following implications. First, involuntary autobiographical memories are universal, and this means that everyone with intact autobiographical memory has them. Second, involuntary autobiographical memories are frequent in daily life – at least as frequent as voluntary autobiographical memories. Third, involuntary autobiographical memories operate on the same episodic memory system as voluntary memories. This means that they are subject to the same basic encoding mechanism. However, they differ with regard to mechanisms of retrieval. Involuntary remembering evolves from association through distinctive situational cues, whereas voluntary recall involves a self-initiated, top-down search with elaborated search descriptions. Fourth, the involuntary mode predates voluntary autobiographical memories evolutionarily and is therefore likely to be present (in species-specific forms) in many nonhuman animals. Fifth, involuntary autobiographical memories are as functional and adaptive as are voluntary memories. One important function is to provide an obligatory rehearsal of novel or emotional events in ongoing situations with a distinctive feature overlap with the memory. This allows potentially relevant episodic information to be transferred from the past to the present situation, and this may lead to a change in ongoing behavior or the extraction of regularities. This also contributes to the construction of a mental model of the particular social and physical environment of the individual (e.g., whom to trust, where to find food). These functional aspects of involuntary memories may have maladaptive consequences after highly negative/traumatic events – for example, in terms of spontaneous recollections or flashbacks of the traumatic event in neutral situations, as observed in relation to post-traumatic stress disorder (PTSD) (American Psychiatric Association, 2000). In the following sections, I shall elaborate on these claims.

Universality and frequency

Involuntary autobiographical memories take place in all people with intact autobiographical memory. Like all claims of universality, this claim may eventually be refuted. However, it is consistent with diary studies showing that large, nonselective samples of subjects, with very few exceptions, are capable of reporting involuntary memories as they occur in their daily life (e.g., Ball and Little, 2006). Survey studies with large stratified samples (e.g., Berntsen and Rubin, 2002; Rubin and Berntsen, 2009) also show that involuntary autobiographical memories are generally a well-known phenomenon.

Frequency estimates of involuntary autobiographical memories vary. When interviewed subsequent to their participation in a diary study (e.g., Berntsen, 1996), most participants retrospectively assessed that they had had about 5–6 involuntary memories per day, but also that their frequency varied greatly as a function of duties and activity level. Because frequency was not the focus of these diary studies and the estimates were done retrospectively, these numbers should be considered with caution. In a more controlled study, Rubin and Berntsen (2009) asked large stratified samples of Danes to assess how often they had involuntarily, as well as voluntarily, thought about a self-chosen important event from the last week as well as an important childhood event selected by the experimenter. Consistent with the idea that involuntary remembering forms a basic mode of remembering, the participants reported the involuntary remembering of the events to have taken place about as frequently as the voluntary counterpart. Only one study (Rasmussen and Berntsen, 2011) has involved online recording of the frequency of involuntary versus voluntary autobiographical memories on a daily basis. In this study, involuntary retrievals of past events happened three times more frequently than their voluntary counterparts, consistent with the view that involuntary memories are basic.

Memory system

The claim that involuntary autobiographical memories operate on the same episodic memory system as voluntary autobiographical memories is contrary to prominent clinical theories assuming the existence of two parallel memory systems – one that can be accessed only involuntarily through situational cues, and one that can be accessed in a voluntary and goal directed fashion (e.g., Brewin *et al.*, 1996; Brewin, Gregory, Lipton, *et al.*, 2010). In these theories, the involuntary memory system encodes detailed sensory and perceptual information, whereas the voluntary system retains more abstract, conceptual, and contextualized information. In response to highly negative events (e.g., traumas), the involuntary system predominates during encoding, for which reason central aspects of the trauma may be inaccessible to subsequent voluntary recall, but persistently come to mind in the form of involuntary (intrusive) memories.

In contrast with this view, I propose a single episodic memory system that supports both voluntary and involuntary recall. The two types of recall differ with regard to the way in which retrieval is initiated and monitored. But they are affected in similar ways by basic encoding factors. Thus, emotion and novelty associated with the event at the time of encoding will enhance subsequent access for both types of recall. Below, I review two sets of findings supporting this view. One is the distribution of involuntary and voluntary memories across the life span, and the other is experimental studies of the effects of emotion at encoding for involuntary and voluntary recall.

Distribution across the life span   The claim that involuntary autobiographical memories derive from the same memory system as their voluntary counterparts is consistent with the fact that they show the same distinctive distribution across the life span as do voluntary memories. First, when adults are asked to recollect their earliest memories, very few – if any – memories are seen from the first 3 years of life, followed by a steep increase in memories up to age 7, at which point the curve levels out (e.g., Rubin, 2000). This phenomenon, known as childhood amnesia, is also found for involuntary memories recorded in diary studies (Berntsen, 2009).

Second, when middle-aged and older adults are asked to recollect their past, they report disproportionally more memories from the second and third decades of life, compared to the surrounding periods. This phenomenon is known as the reminiscence bump (Rubin, Wetzler, and Nebes, 1986) and is also found for involuntary autobiographical memories both when examined in diary studies (Schlagman *et al.*, 2007) and in survey studies (Berntsen and Rubin, 2002) involving older participants.

Third, involuntary memories show the standard forgetting curve that was originally pointed out by Ebbinghaus (1885/1964) in his studies of memory for nonsense syllables and has been replicated numerous times (see Rubin and Wenzel, 1996, for an overview). The decrease in retention is steep in the beginning of the retention period, after which the curve evens out. Research shows that the forgetting curves for the involuntary memories and their voluntary counterpart are highly similar (when the latter is triggered through word cues). Both distributions are best described in terms of a power function (e.g., Berntsen, 1998, 2009).

Encoding Following well-established principles of attention, learning, and memory, novelty and emotion are major decisive factors for how well an event is encoded. The importance of novelty is well described in relation to attention (Berlyne, 1966), associative learning (Rescorla and Holland, 1982), and long-term memory (Hunt and Worthen, 2006). The importance of emotion in relation to encoding and maintenance is likewise well established (e.g., McGaugh, 2003, 2004). Both novelty and emotion are associated with increased visceral arousal and often involve discrepancies with expectations or interruptions of ongoing activity (Mandler, 1985). Consequently, to the extent that involuntary and voluntary remembering derive from the same memory system, they should show similar effects of emotion and novelty during encoding.

Very few studies have systematically examined the relationship between emotion as measured at encoding and subsequent involuntary and voluntary remembering. Hall and Berntsen (2008) conducted a study in which participants recorded their emotional reactions while watching 20 upsetting negative pictures. After the participants had seen the pictures and recorded their reactions, they took part in a diary study of involuntary and voluntary memories. On each of five consecutive days, they were to record one voluntary picture memory and the first involuntary picture memory that might occur on that day. The participants wrote brief keyword phrases of the memory content so that it was possible to identify which pictures they had recorded as voluntary versus involuntary memories in the diary. For both kinds of memory, a clear effect of emotion was found: pictures the participants remembered during the diary had been rated as more upsetting and more emotionally intense during encoding than pictures they did not record in the diary study. This effect was equally strong for voluntary and involuntary memories. Using emotional versus neutral films, Ferree and Cahill (2009) replicated the symmetrical effects of emotion on involuntary and voluntary recall.

These findings go against the widespread belief that involuntary remembering has privileged access to negative/stressful material (e.g., Brewin *et al.*, 1996; Brewin and Holmes, 2003; Ehlers and Clark, 2002; Horowitz, 1975, 1986). They are consistent with findings from diary studies showing no differences between the emotional valence of involuntary versus voluntary memories. Instead both types of memories show a pronounced dominance of emotionally positive events (see Berntsen, 2009, for an overview). The findings from Hall and Berntsen (2008) and Ferree and Cahill (2009) are also consistent with a study by Rubin *et al.* (2008), in which participants with high versus low levels of PTSD symptoms participated in a diary study of involuntary and voluntary autobiographical memories. Not surprisingly, the high-PTSD symptom group recorded more trauma-related memories than the low-symptom group. However, they did so to the same extent for both involuntary and voluntary recall, in contrast to the idea that involuntary remembering more easily accesses traumatic/negative material. These findings were recently replicated with clinically diagnosed PTSD patients (Rubin, Dennis, and Beckham, 2011).

In sum, involuntary autobiographical memories show the same distinctive distribution across the life span as do voluntary memories – that is, they show childhood amnesia, the reminiscence bump, and the retention function. The two types of recall are similarly affected by emotion at the time of encoding, consistent with the claim that they are supported by the same episodic system. We shall now turn to the differences between the two types of autobiographical remembering.

Different retrieval processes   The retrieval of involuntary autobiographical memories is often examined through diary studies in which the participants make records of the memory and the retrieval context immediately when they have become aware of having an involuntary memory. In order to reduce retrospection, the recording is divided into two steps. First, each participant carries a small notebook with a short list of key words and rating scales, to which he or she responds immediately when an involuntary memory occurs. Second, later on the same day, the subject answers a more comprehensive questionnaire about each memory, assisted by the notebook. The participant usually retrieves a voluntary (word-cued) memory for each involuntary memory as part of the same diary, in order to allow comparison between the two types of recall (e.g., Berntsen and Hall, 2004, for details).

Diary studies conducted in different laboratories yield consistent findings regarding the retrieval of involuntary autobiographical memories (see Berntsen, 2009, for an overview). First, the great majority of the memories have identifiable cues in the retrieval situation in terms of some overlapping features between the retrieval situation and the memory. Second, when participants are asked to classify the cues as external (present in the physical surroundings), internal (only present in thoughts), or mixed (a combination of external and internal features), external cues are generally more frequent than internal cues (see Berntsen, 2009, for review). Thus, specific features of the environment are more frequently experienced as triggers for involuntary autobiographical memories than are features of thoughts and emotions. Third, the cue is often peripheral to the ongoing activity in the retrieval situation (e.g., a song played on the radio while the person is studying) but central to the content of the memory (e.g., a school performance in the music class involving this particular song). Fourth, involuntary autobiographical memories most frequently arise when the person is not concentrated and engaged in a particular task. One possible explanation is that focusing attention on a specific task may interfere with the automatic associative processes that lead to the formation of an involuntary memory (Mandler, 1994, 2007; McVay and Kane, 2010). Fifth, a study using positron emission tomography (PET) recording of neural activity has shown that both involuntary and voluntary recall activate brain areas associated with retrieval success (the medial temporal lobes, the precuneus, and the posterior cingulate gyrus), whereas voluntary compared to involuntary recall shows enhanced activity in areas in the right prefrontal cortex that are known to be involved in strategic retrieval (Hall, Gjedde, and Kupers, 2008). Similarly, using Functional magnetic resonance imaging (fMRI) and event-related potentials (ERP) recordings of brain activity, Kompus, Eichele, Hugdahl, *et al.* (2011) found that voluntary compared to involuntary retrieval was associated with increased activation in the dorsolateral prefrontal cortex, whereas retrieval success was associated with increased activation in the same areas for both conditions (the hippocampus, precuneus, and ventrolateral prefrontal cortex). These findings agree with the idea that voluntary recall is a goal-directed process that requires executive control to initiate and monitor the search process, whereas involuntary recall is an associative process that takes place with little executive control and therefore relies less on frontal lobe structures in comparison with the voluntary mode. The assumption that involuntary retrieval requires little cognitive effort is also supported by markedly shorter retrieval times for involuntary than voluntary episodic memories (Berntsen, Staugaard, and Sørensen, in press; Schlagman and Kvavilashvili, 2008; but see Kompus *et al.*, 2011).

These findings suggest that involuntary autobiographical memories represent an associative, context-sensitive, and presumably evolutionarily older mode of remembering – a mode that is dependent on salient characteristics of the environment and the links they have formed to memory through the previous activities of the individual, rather than on internal control and top-down search. This raises the important question as to how exactly it is possible to recollect a past event with no deliberate monitoring of the search process. The relevance of this question is underscored by the fact that theories of episodic memory generally consider the retrieval of discrete memories to be a cognitively highly advanced process that requires sophisticated search-and-control processes, often considered to be unique to humans (Suddendorf and Corballis, 2007; Tulving, 2002).

Many theorists have invoked the notion of encoding specificity in order to explain the activation of involuntary episodic memories (see Berntsen, 2009, for a review). According to this principle, the probability of successfully retrieving a memory increases by increasing overlap between the information present at retrieval (i.e., the cue) and the information stored in memory (Tulving and Thomson, 1973). For example, in a revision of his theory of direct (involuntary) retrieval, Conway (2005) emphasizes the central role of encoding specificity, stating that "the term 'direct retrieval' is simply a convenient synonym for encoding specificity" (p. 619).

Although intuitively meaningful, the adherence to the encoding–retrieval match leaves several questions of involuntary episodic memories unresolved. First, assuming that features in the retrieval context overlap with the content of several past events, why does one of these memories (but not the others) become activated? Second, explanations based on the encoding–retrieval match fail to explain why we are not constantly flooded by involuntary episodic memories. Any moment in our lives seems to include an almost endless number of potential memory cues in terms of features that were also part of our past experiences, such as the computer I am sitting at, or the neighboring building which I am looking at. When we dwell upon such features in an ongoing situation, we are able to voluntarily generate memories in response to many of them, as demonstrated in experiments conducted by Galton (1907) and replicated and extended by Berntsen and Hall (2004). Thus, if having involuntary autobiographical memories were simply a matter of an encoding–retrieval match, it seems that we should be flooded by such memories throughout our waking life (Berntsen, 2009). Why aren't we?

In order to resolve this problem, the encoding-specificity principle has to be supplemented by the principle of cue overload: "The probability of recalling an item declines with the number of items subsumed by its functional retrieval cue" (Watkins and Watkins, 1975, p. 442). In other words, the likelihood of a cue providing access to a given target memory depends on the extent to which this cue is uniquely associated with the target. Its strength declines to the extent it is associated with other memories as well. Thus, if you have been driving through a particular landscape only once before, this occasion is likely to come to mind when you drive through the same landscape again. However, if you have driven through this particular landscape many times, driving through it once more is less likely to spontaneously activate specific memories of earlier trips.

Building upon the notion of cue overload, Rubin (1995) introduces the notion of cue-item discriminiability. He describes it as "how easily a given cue isolates an item . . . Simply put, a word is likely to be recalled if, on the basis of the cues available at the time, it can be discriminated from all else in memory" (p. 146). In the present context, the notion captures the important idea that in order to spontaneously activate an autobiographical memory, a cue is needed that is sufficiently distinct to discriminate a past event from alternatives through spreading activation in an associative network. In other words, the cue (or cues) has to be able to activate event-relevant units, or nodes, in the network, and deactivate irrelevant units that would otherwise interfere with the construction of the memory (Berntsen, 2009; Rubin, 1995).

In a naturalistic context, there are several ways in which a sufficiently high level of cue-item discriminability may accidentally occur (see Berntsen, 2009, for details). For example, multiple cues may work together to activate a memory. Although they may all be frequently encountered features when viewed in isolation, their specific combination in the retrieval situation may be sufficiently unique to discriminate a past event from alternatives. In the example in the beginning of the chapter, there are several overlapping features between the remembered event and the ongoing situation: in both situations, the person is running for exercise and the weather is frosty. Although we are not explicitly told, the narrator is most likely wearing her running outfit and running shoes, and has very similar bodily sensations and sensory impressions in both situations. In addition to this, she encounters ice on the trail in both situations. This unique combination of features provides a distinct link to the past event, for which reason the current situation (considered as a cue) is capable of discriminating the remembered episode from alternatives.

Obviously, the notion of cue-item discriminability as used here implies an informational overlap between the cue and the event, just like the notion of encoding specificity. However, unlike the encoding specificity principle, it is the uniqueness, not the size, of this overlap that matters. If a cue matches a number of past events equally well, it is unlikely to be an efficient cue for any of them (assuming that other things are equal), no matter how big this overlap is. However, if a cue matches a distinctive feature of just one past event, this event is likely to be brought to mind because it can be discriminated from alternatives by this cue. Therefore, although our environment is filled with features that were also present in past activities and thus can be considered as potential memory cues, these features do not constantly bring memories to mind, because they overlap with too many past events to be able to discriminate any of them from alternatives. In addition to cue-item discriminability, the activation of one event over others also depends, of course, on its recency, emotionality, relevance to current concerns, and other factors known to influence the general accessibility of memories for both voluntary and involuntary recall. Ongoing experiments in our laboratory provide evidence that the uniqueness of the associative link between the cue and the target (memory) is decisive for the activation of involuntary memories (Berntsen *et al.*, in press).

Cue-item discriminability thus explains two things: (1) how episodic memories can be retrieved with no deliberate search and conscious monitoring of the retrieval process, and, just as importantly, (2) why we are not constantly flooded by involuntary memories, although our environment is filled with potential cues. Next I shall argue that this principle also helps to explain some of the differences that are seen concerning the characteristics of involuntary versus voluntary autobiographical memories.

Differences in content and qualities   Since variations in the temporal distance, emotionality, and novelty of past events render some past events more accessible for recall than others, irrespectively of whether recall is involuntary or voluntary (as pointed out earlier in this chapter), differences in the characteristics of the two types of memory are limited to relatively few dimensions – namely, dimensions that vary as a function of the retrieval process.

A key difference between voluntary and involuntary remembering is that voluntary remembering involves search descriptions generated from schematized autobiographical knowledge and elaborated throughout the retrieval process (e.g., Conway and Pleydell-Pearce, 2000; Norman and Bobrow, 1979), whereas involuntary remembering is an automatic, associative process, initiated by a situational cue and involving no conscious monitoring of the retrieval process. Instead the process is contingent upon the cue providing an informational overlap with a past event that is sufficiently distinct to discriminate this event from alternatives through association. As a consequence, the two types of remembering sample somewhat different autobiographical memories.

A number of studies have shown that involuntary autobiographical memories, more frequently than voluntary (word-cued) memories, refer to specific episodes – that is, events that happened on a specific day in the past, such as a particular trip to the beach (Williams, 1996). Compared to voluntary memories, they therefore deal less frequently with general event representations – that is, memory representations that, instead of representing a specific episode, provide an extraction of common characteristics of many similar events, such as a general representation of going to the beach (Berntsen, 1998; Berntsen and Hall, 2004; Berntsen and Jacobsen, 2008; Johannessen and Berntsen, 2010; Mace, 2006; Schlagman, Kliegel, Schulz, *et al.*, 2009; Schlagman and Kvavilashvili, 2008). The only exceptions to this pattern are two studies in which the participants were explicitly instructed to record only specific events (Rubin *et al.*, 2008; Rubin *et al.*, 2011).

This difference regarding level of specificity is likely to be partly due to the principle of cue-item discriminability logically favoring memories with distinctive (nonrepeated) features. Distinctive features are more likely to be maintained in memories of specific events than in general event representations, because the latter focus on conceptual similarities across several events and represent a more semantic level of autobiographical knowledge (e.g., Conway and Pleydell-Pearce, 2000). In addition, involuntary recall is less tied to generic autobiographical knowledge, because this type of recall involves no search description generated from higher-order autobiographical memory. As a result, involuntary autobiographical memories deal more frequently with specific episodes than do their voluntary counterparts.

Further support for this explanation comes from a diary study of involuntary and voluntary autobiographical memory in relation to aging (Schlagman *et al.*, 2009). When measured through voluntary recall, old people recall fewer specific events than do young people. This is assumed to reflect an age-related deficit in the executive control processes that normally monitor retrieval (Levine, Svoboda, Hay, *et al.*, 2002). Schlagman *et al.* (2009) compared involuntary and voluntary memories among old and young participants and showed that the young participants, as expected, recorded more specific episodes in voluntary recall. However, this difference was absent for the involuntary memories, for which the old and the young participants recorded an equal number of specific events. This suggests that involuntary remembering accesses specific episodes through processes that require little executive control.

Involuntary memories also tend to be less relevant to the life story and identity than voluntary memories (Johannessen and Berntsen, 2010; Rubin *et al.*, 2008). Again this is likely to reflect the effects of associative retrieval versus a voluntary top-down search, since the latter is more likely to be biased toward knowledge that has self- and life-story relevance because it is governed by schema-based search descriptions.

Involuntary recall not only brings back memories of specific events. Such recollections are often accompanied by a noticeable mood change or reaction. Anecdotal accounts provide examples of intense happiness accompanying involuntary recollections (e.g., Proust, 1927/1949). In the clinical literature, on the other hand, fear responses or other powerful negative emotional reactions are reported in relation to involuntary (intrusive) memories of traumatic events. These observations agree with a number of studies showing that involuntary memories involve more mood impact and physical reaction at the time of recall than voluntary memories (e.g., Berntsen and Hall, 2004; Johannessen and Berntsen, 2010; Rubin et al., 2008, 2011). These characteristics appear to be unrelated to the fact that involuntary memories are more specific (Berntsen and Hall, 2004). One possible explanation as to why involuntary memories are more frequently accompanied by an emotional reaction is that their sudden and spontaneous nature allows little time for antecedent emotion regulation (Gross, 2001). One important function of antecedent emotion regulation is to re-evaluate (or reappraise) a potentially emotional situation in such a way that it is less likely to influence us. Such re-evaluations are unlikely to precede involuntary memories, because they are unexpected, whereas voluntary retrieval may involve antecedent-focused emotion regulation through the construction of the search description guiding the retrieval process. Additional explanations involve the idea of multiple levels of emotion activation (e.g., LeDoux, 1996), according to which emotions can be activated associatively with no preceding cognitive evaluation, as in fear conditioning, as well as follow more elaborate cognitive processes.

In sum, compared to their voluntary counterparts, involuntary autobiographical memories more frequently refer to specific episodes, they are seen as less relevant to life story and identity, and they are accompanied by more emotional impact at the time of retrieval. These differences are most likely a byproduct of the disparate retrieval processes that characterize the two types of autobiographical memories. This claim is further supported by the fact that similar differences concerning specificity and emotional impact are found in studies contrasting voluntarily and involuntarily generated images of possible future events (Berntsen and Jacobsen, 2008).

Evolution and function

It is hard to imagine how survival in complex spatial and social environments would be possible without the ability to remember past episodes. It therefore seems unlikely that episodic memory would be limited to humans, as sometimes claimed (Suddendorf and Corballis, 2007; Tulving, 2002). Observations on nonhuman animals suggest than many of them have the ability to remember past events (e.g., Clayton and Dickinson, 1998; Donald, 1991; Olton, 1984; Tomasello and Call, 1997).

Episodic memory in nonhuman animals may reflect the effects of the involuntary mode, and not (or at least rarely) the cognitively much more demanding voluntary retrieval mode (Clayton, Bussey, Emery, et al., 2003). This position is expressed most clearly by Donald (1991;

also see Donald, this volume). According to Donald, only humans are capable of voluntary recall, which he calls autocuing and considers as a pivotal ability in relation to the development of human culture, since it allows humans to rehearse and improve skills and knowledge in a conscious and goal-directed fashion. Donald (1991) grants that nonhuman animals have episodic memory – but only in an involuntary form.

If this view is correct, we should expect involuntary episodic remembering to be central to the regulation of behavior, as well as to maintaining and updating environmentally relevant knowledge in many species. Moreover, such basic functions would still be lingering on in the involuntary autobiographical memory processes of humans, although for humans such processes would interact with our ability to also conduct goal-directed voluntary retrieval (Rasmussen and Berntsen, 2009).

The claim that involuntary memories are functional does not imply that every individual involuntary recollection has a distinct and identifiable function for our well-being and survival. Rather, it means that involuntary remembering operates overall in ways that optimize the likelihood of the recollections being relevant to the situation in which they occur. At a more specific level, the utility of involuntary memories can be described in terms of three levels that vary with regard to the time windows in with they operate. These levels should not be viewed as an exhaustive description of possible functions of involuntary recollections, but as a useful division for the present purpose. These levels will be labeled as *knowledge transfer*, *selective rehearsal*, and *enlarged temporal horizon*.

Knowledge transfer Involuntary memories assist knowledge transfer from a past to a present situation (i.e., from the remembered event to the situation in which the memory arises). The unique informational overlap that allows the memory to come to mind in this particular situation (cf. the principle of cue-item discriminability) optimizes the probability that the remembered information is of relevance to the current situation. Sometimes this relevance may be as simple as helping the person to recognize and contextualize the memory cue. At other times, it may assist the person in better orienting in his or her physical and social environment, and becoming aware of changes and potential dangers (see the example at the beginning of this chapter), and it may support analogical reasoning.

In a social context, an involuntary memory may move the person to tell other people about the remembered event and thereby facilitate entertainment and social bonding (Bluck, Alea, Habermas, *et al.*, 2005; Pillemer and Kuwabara, this volume). At times, an involuntary memory may instigate a direct change in an ongoing activity or suggest a solution to a problem and thus hold a directive function (see Pillemer, 2003; Pillemer and Kuwabara, this volume; Rasmussen and Berntsen, 2009). For instance, in the example quoted in the beginning of this chapter, the memory may have helped the person to be more alert to the ice on the trail. The motivational force of such embedded functions is enhanced by the fact that involuntary memories are accompanied by more emotional impact than their voluntary counterparts.

Selective rehearsal   Rehearsal is a major factor in the extent to which memories are maintained over time (e.g., Ebbinghaus, 1885/1964). One important role of involuntary autobiographical remembering is to provide an automatic rehearsal of certain past events rather than others. Through such selective rehearsal, involuntary remembering contributes to the development of a structured autobiographical knowledge base, including the formation of personal scripts (e.g., summarized events), "turning points" and "anchoring events" (e.g., Conway, 2005; Pillemer, 1998). Obviously, the mechanisms that cause the activation of involuntary memories also determine which past events are more likely to be rehearsed involuntarily over time. Events favored by involuntary rehearsal are past events with a distinct feature overlap with the current situation. With repeated rehearsal in similar contexts, this informational overlap may lead to the extraction of rules and the formation of personal scripts (Schank, 1982, 1999). In addition, involuntary (as well as voluntary) remembering favors past events that were emotional or novel when they took place, thus giving such memories a more prominent role in the knowledge base, as, for example, by forming turning points or landmark events (Pillemer, 1998). The selective involuntary rehearsal contributes to the formation (and continuous revision) of a mental model of the individual's physical and social environment at the same time. However, the selective rehearsal (as I shall point out shortly) may have maladaptive consequences after traumatic events.

Enlarged temporal horizon   A very simple function of involuntary memories is to prevent us from living in the present, as we would probably do to a much greater extent if all recollections had to be initiated in a voluntary, goal-directed fashion. Being able to abstract from the present reality and mentally situate oneself in a possible future or past reality is called mental time travel and is considered to be a major evolutionary advantage (Suddendorf, 2006; Tulving, 2002). Among other things, traveling mentally in time enables the individual to plan the future in the light of past experiences. Thus, it renders behavior flexible. Involuntary autobiographical remembering constitutes an important mechanism for "escaping the present." It is especially useful because it requires little cognitive effort and typically happens in non-attention-demanding situations, as pointed out earlier. It thus helps us to maintain a wider time horizon with low cognitive costs (Berntsen, 2009).

These basic functions of involuntary episodic memories are unlikely to be limited to humans. However, in humans, involuntary remembering takes on another quality, in part because involuntary remembering can be supplemented and elaborated by voluntary recall (Moscovitch, 1995), and in part because culturally transmitted schemata and time technologies (e.g., clocks, calendars) help to enlarge the temporal horizon of humans compared to those of other species (e.g., Roberts, 2002). Thus, we are capable of remembering temporally more remote past events and imagining temporally more distant future events, compared to other species, both voluntarily and involuntarily (e.g., Berntsen, 2009). Culturally transmitted schemata for spatial and social relationships likewise add to the complexity of involuntary autobiographical memories in humans (see Berntsen and Rubin, this volume, for a more extended discussion).

Dysfunctions   All three types of functions described above can become dysfunctional when applied to extreme situations. Although normally adaptive, involuntary autobiographical remembering can be a source of distress. This is most clearly observed in relation to PTSD. In PTSD, the traumatic event is "persistently re-experienced" in terms of, among other things, "recurrent and intrusive distressing recollections of the event" (American Psychiatric Association, 2000).

In the clinical field, there is a long tradition for accounting for such intrusive recollections in terms of mechanisms that apply specifically to traumas and in terms of a dissociation between involuntary and voluntary recall (Brewin *et al.*, 1996, 2010; Ehlers and Clark, 2000; Horowitz, 1986). However, an accumulating amount of evidence suggests that involuntary, intrusive recollections after traumatic events are more adequately explained in terms of the same mechanisms that characterize involuntary episodic remembering in healthy individuals (e.g., Berntsen and Rubin, 2008; Berntsen, 2009; Rubin *et al.*, 2008, 2011).

Following this view, the basic functions described above may have maladaptive consequences after traumatic events. Due to the extreme emotion and novelty that (by definition) are associated with traumatic experiences during the time of encoding, the accessibility of such events is enhanced in memory compared to the accessibility of more mundane events. This enhancement is present for both involuntary and voluntary recall (Ferree and Cahill, 2009; Hall and Berntsen, 2008; Rubin *et al.*, 2008, 2011); however, the enhanced availability is likely to be particularly bothersome in relation to involuntary recall, because this type of retrieval is uncontrolled and is accompanied by more emotional impact and physical reaction. Furthermore, as a result of its extraordinary accessibility, the traumatic memory may come to mind even in response to nondistinctive cues (that is, features that also overlap with other events), consistent with the "persistent" nature of such memories, as described in the diagnosis of PTSD (American Psychiatric Association, 2000).

The ensuing repeated involuntary recall of the trauma further increases the accessibility of this event in memory as compared to other autobiographical memories. Through the repeated activation, the trauma memory may form multiple links to other events in the autobiographical knowledge base. Thus, the traumatic memory may become a central component of personal identity, a turning point in the life story, and a reference point for everyday inferences. Research has shown that such centrality is robustly related to PTSD and depression (Berntsen and Rubin, 2007). The interaction between involuntary and voluntary remembering that normally takes place in healthy cognition – with voluntary remembering supplementing and elaborating the involuntary memories – may in such situations have maladaptive consequences in terms of rumination (e.g., Nolen-Hoeksema, Wisco, and Lyubomirsky, 2008). Furthermore, the normally adaptive mechanisms of knowledge transfer from a past to a present situation, via involuntary memories, may often have maladaptive consequences after traumatic events in terms of exaggerated emotional responses in relatively neutral situations, consistent with the notion of traumatic flashbacks, i.e., "acting or feeling as if the traumatic event was recurring" (American Psychiatric Association, 2000, p. 468).

In short, according to the present view, no trauma-specific mechanisms may be needed to explain maladaptive intrusive memories after traumatic events, contrary to prominent clinical theories. It appears that most, if not all, of their characteristics can be derived from the ways in which involuntary autobiographical memories normally operate (for more evidence on this claim, see Berntsen, 2009; Berntsen and Rubin, 2008; Rubin *et al.*, 2008, 2011).

Summary

I have presented a framework suggesting that involuntary autobiographical memories are a basic mode of remembering. This mode operates on the same episodic memory system as voluntary (strategic) remembering, but accesses this memory system through different mechanisms of retrieval. Whereas voluntary recall involves a top-down, schema-based search, the activation of involuntary memories depends on cue-item discriminability – that is, the ability of a situational cue to associatively discriminate a past event from alternatives. Because involuntary remembering represents a less controlled, more associative, context-sensitive, and presumably evolutionarily earlier way of accessing memories, this mode samples autobiographical events with somewhat different properties than voluntary memories. Involuntary memories are more specific and involve more emotional reaction at the time of recall. Involuntary intrusive memories in PTSD and other affective disorders can be understood as dysfunctional side effects of the normally adaptive mechanisms underlying involuntary autobiographical remembering.

Acknowledgements

The author thanks the Danish National Research Foundation and the Danish Council for Independent Research: Humanities for funding. Thanks to Merlin Donald and David C. Rubin for comments.

References

American Psychiatric Association (2000). *Diagnostic and statistical manual of mental disorders* (4th edn.) (DSM-IV-TR). Washington, DC: American Psychiatric Association.

Ball, C. T. and Little, J. R. (2006). A comparison of involuntary autobioigraphical memory retrievals. *Applied Cognitive Psychology*, **20**, 1167–1179.

Berlyne, D. E. (1966). Curiosity and exploration. *Science*, **153**, 25–33.

Berntsen, D. (1996). Involuntary autobiographical memories. *Applied Cognitive Psychology*, **10**, 435–454.

  (1998). Voluntary and involuntary access to autobiographical memory. *Memory*, **6**, 113–141.

  (2007). Involuntary autobiographical memories: speculations, findings and an attempt to integrate them. In John H. Mace (ed.), *Involuntary memory* (pp. 20–49). Malden, MA: Blackwell.

  (2009). *Involuntary autobiographical memories: an introduction to the unbidden past.* Cambridge University Press.

Berntsen, D. and Hall, N. M. (2004). The episodic nature of involuntary autobiographical memories. *Memory & Cognition*, **32**, 789–803.

Berntsen, D. and Jacobsen, A. S. (2008). Involuntary (spontaneous) mental time travel into the past and future. *Consciousness and Cognition*, **17**, 1093–1104.

Berntsen, D. and Rubin, D. C. (2002). Emotionally charged autobiographical memories across the lifespan: the recall of happy, sad, traumatic, and involuntary memories. *Psychology and Aging*, **17**, 636–652.

  (2007). When a trauma becomes a key to identity: enhanced integration of trauma memories predicts posttraumatic stress disorder symptoms. *Applied Cognitive Psychology*, **21**, 417–431.

(2008). The reappearance hypothesis revisited: recurrent involuntary memories after traumatic events and in everyday life. *Memory & Cognition*, **36**, 449–460.

Berntsen, D., Staugaard, S. R., and Sørensen, M. L. (in press). Why am I remembering this now? Predicting the occurrence of involuntary (spontaneous) episodic memories. *Journal of Experimental Psychology: General*.

Bluck, S., Alea, N., Habermas, T., and Rubin, D. (2005). A tale of three functions: the self-reported uses of autobiographical memory. *Social Cognition*, **23**(1), 91–117.

Brewin, C. R., Dalgleish, T., and Joseph, S. (1996). A dual representation theory of posttraumatic stress disorder. *Psychological Review*, **103**, 670–686.

Brewin, C. R., Gregory, J. D., Lipton, M., and Burgess, N. (2010). Intrusive images and memories in psychological disorders: characteristics, neural basis, and treatment implications. *Psychological Review*, **117**, 210–232.

Brewin, C. R. and Holmes, E. A. (2003). Psychological theories of posttraumatic stress disorder. *Clinical Psychology Review*, **23**, 339–376.

Clayton, N. S., Bussey, T. J., Emery, N. J., and Dickinson, A. (2003). Prometheus to Proust: the case for behavioural criteria for "mental time travel." *Trends in Cognitive Sciences*, 7, 436–437.

Clayton, N. S. and Dickinson, A. (1998). Episodic-like memories during cache recovery by scrub jays. *Nature*, **395**, 272–274.

Conway, M. A. (2005). Memory and the self. *Journal of Memory and Language*, **53**, 594–628.

Conway, M. A. and Pleydell-Pearce, C. W. (2000). The construction of autobiographical memory in the self-memory system. *Psychological Review*, **107**, 261–288.

Davachi, L. and Dobbins, I. G. (2008). Declarative memory. *Current Directions in Psychological Science*, **17**, 112–118.

Donald, M. (1991). *Origins of the modern mind: three stages in the evolution of culture and cognition*. Cambridge, MA: Harvard University Press.

Ebbinghaus, H. (1885/1964). *Memory: a contribution to experimental psychology*. New York: Dover Publications.

Ehlers, A. and Clark, D. M. (2000). A cognitive model of posttraumatic stress disorder. *Behaviour Research and Therapy*, **38**, 319–345.

Ehlers, A., Hackmann, A., and Michael, T. (2004). Intrusive re-experiencing in post-traumatic stress disorder: phenomenology, theory, and therapy. *Memory*, **12**, 403–415.

Ferree, N. K. and Cahill, L. (2009). Post-event spontaneous intrusive recollections and strength of memory for emotional events in men and women. *Consciousness and Cognition*, **18**, 126–134.

Galton, F. (1907). *Inquiries into human faculty and its development*. London: J. M. Dent & Sons.

Gross, J. J. (2001). Emotion regulation in adulthood: timing is everything. *Current Directions in Psychological Science*, **10**, 214–219.

Hall, N. M. and Berntsen, D. (2008). The effect of emotional stress on involuntary and voluntary conscious memories. *Memory*, **16**, 48–57.

Hall, N. M., Gjedde, A., and Kupers, R. (2008). Neural mechanism of voluntary and involuntary recall. *Behavioural Brain Research*, **186**, 261–272.

Hintzman, D. L. (2011). Research strategy in the study of memory: fads, fallacies, and the search for the "coordinates of truth." *Perspectives on Psychological Science*, **6**, 253–271.

Horowitz, M. J. (1975). Intrusive and repetitive thought after experimental stress. *Archives of General Psychiatry*, **32**, 1457–1463.

(1986). *Stress response syndromes* (2nd edn.). Northvale, NJ: Jason Aronson.

Hunt, R. R. and Worthen, J. B. (eds.) (2006). *Distinctiveness and memory*. New York: Oxford University Press.

James, W. (1890). *The principles of psychology*, vol. I. New York: Henry Holt & Co.

Johannessen, K. B. and Berntsen, D. (2010). Current concerns in involuntary and voluntary autobiographical memories. *Consciousness and Cognition*, **19**, 847–860.

Klinger, E. (1975). Consequences of commitment to and disengagement from incentives. *Psychological Review*, **82**, 1–25.

Kompus, K., Eichele, T., Hugdahl, K., and Nyberg, L. (2011). Multimodal imaging of incidental retrieval: the low route to memory. *Journal of Cognitive Neuroscience*, **23**, 947–960.

Kvavilashvili, L. and Mandler, G. (2004). Out of one's mind: a study of involuntary semantic memories. *Cognitive Psychology*, **48**, 47–94.

LeDoux, J. E. (1996). *The emotional brain: the mysterious underpinnings of emotional life*. New York: Simon & Schuster.

Levine, B., Svoboda, E., Hay, J. F., Winocur, G., and Moscovitch, M. (2002). Aging and autobiographical memory: Dissociating episodic from semantic retrieval. *Psychology and Aging*, **17**, 677–689.

Mace, J. H. (2004). Involuntary autobiographical memories are highly dependent on abstract cuing: the Proustian view is incorrect. *Applied Cognitive Psychology*, **18**, 893–899.

(2005). Priming involuntary autobiographical memories. *Memory*, **13**, 874–884.

(2006). Episodic remembering creates access to involuntary conscious memory: demonstrating involuntary recall on a voluntary recall task. *Memory*, **14**, 217–224.

(ed.) (2007). *Involuntary memory*. Malden, MA: Blackwell.

Mandler, G. (1985). *Cognitive psychology: an essay in cognitive science*. Hillsdale, NJ: Lawrence Erlbaum Associates.

(1994). Hypermnesia, incubation, and mind-popping: on remembering without really trying. In C. Umilta and M. Moscovitch (eds.), *Attention and performance: conscious and unconscious information processing* (pp. 3–33). Cambridge, MA: MIT Press.

(2007). Involuntary memory: variations on the unexpected. In Mace (ed.), *Involuntary memory* (pp. 208–223).

McGaugh, J. L. (2003). *Memory and emotion: the making of lasting memories*. New York: Columbia University Press.

(2004). The amygdala modulates the consolidation of memories of emotionally arousing experiences. *Annual Review of Neuroscience*, **27**, 1–28.

McVay, J. C. and Kane, M. J. (2010). Does mind wandering reflect executive function or executive failure? Comment on Smallwood and Schooler (2006) and Watkins (2008). *Psychological Bulletin*, **136**, 188–197.

Moscovitch, M. (1995). Recovered consciousness: a hypothesis concerning modularity and episodic memory. *Journal of Clinical and Experimental Neuropsychology*, **17**, 276–290.

Nairne, J. S. (2002). The myth of the encoding-retrieval match. *Memory*, **10**, 389–395.

Nolen-Hoeksema, S., Wisco, B., and Lyubomirsky, S. (2008). Rethinking rumination. *Perspectives on Psychological Science*, **3**, 400–424.

Norman, D. A. and Bobrow, D. G. (1979). Descriptions: an intermediate stage in memory retrieval. *Cognitive Psychology*, **11**, 107–123.

Olton, D. S. (1984). Comparative analysis of episodic memory. *Behavioral and Brain Sciences*, **7**, 250–251.

Pillemer, D. B. (1998). *Momentous events, vivid memories*. Cambridge, MA: Harvard University Press.

(2003). Directive functions or autobiographical memory: the guiding power of the specific episode. *Memory*, **11**, 193–202.

Proust, M. (1927/1949). *Time regained*. In *Remembrance of things past*, vol. XII. Stephen Hudson (trans.). London: Chatto & Windus.

Rasmussen, A. S. and Berntsen, D. (2009). The possible functions of involuntary autobiographical memories. *Applied Cognitive Psychology*, **23**, 1137–1152.

(2011). The unpredictable past: spontaneous autobiographical memories outnumber memories retrieved strategically. *Consciousness and Cognition*, **20**, 1842–1846.

Rescorla, R. A. and Holland, P. C. (1982). Behavioral studies of associative learning in animals. *Annual Review of Psychology*, **33**, 265–308.

Roberts, W. A. (2002). Are animals stuck in time? *Psychological Bulletin*, **128**, 473–489.

Rubin, D. C. (1995). *Memory in oral traditions: the cognitive psychology of epic, ballads, and counting-out rhymes*. New York: Oxford University Press.

(2000). The distribution of early childhood memories. *Memory*, **8**, 265–269.

Rubin, D. C. and Berntsen, D. (2009). The frequency of voluntary and involuntary autobiographical memory across the life span. *Memory & Cognition*, **37**, 679–688.

Rubin, D. C., Boals, A., and Berntsen, D. (2008). Memory in posttraumatic stress disorder: properties of voluntary and involuntary, traumatic and non-traumatic autobiographical memories in people with and without PTSD symptoms. *Journal of Experimental Psychology: General*, **137**, 591–614.

Rubin, D. C., Dennis, M. F., and Beckham, J. C. (2011). Autobiographical memory for stressful events: the role of autobiographical memory in posttraumatic stress disorder. *Consciousness and Cognition*, **20**, 840–856.

Rubin, D. C. and Wenzel, A. E. (1996). One hundred years of forgetting: a quantitative description of retention. *Psychological Review*, **103**, 734–760.

Rubin, D. C., Wetzler, S. E., and Nebes, R. D. (1986). Autobiographical memory across the adult lifespan. In D. C. Rubin (ed.), *Autobiographical memory* (pp. 202–221). New York: Cambridge University Press.

Schank, R. C. (1982). *Dynamic memory*. New York: Cambridge University Press.
(1999). *Dynamic memory revisited*. New York: Cambridge University Press.

Schlagman, S., Kliegel, M., Schulz, J., and Kvavilashvili, L. (2009). Effects of age on involuntary and voluntary autobiographical memory. *Psychology and Aging*, **24**, 397–411.

Schlagman, S. and Kvavilashvili, L. (2008). Involuntary autobiographical memories in and outside the laboratory: how different are they from voluntary autobiographical memories? *Memory & Cognition*, **36**, 920–932.

Schlagman, S., Kvavilashvili, L., and Schulz, J. (2007). Effects of age on involuntary autobiographical memories. In Mace (ed.), *Involuntary memory* (pp. 87–112).

Suddendorf, T. (2006). Foresight and the evolution of the human mind. *Science*, **312**, 1006–1007.

Suddendorf, T. and Corballis, M. C. (2007). The evolution of foresight: what is mental time travel and is it unique to humans? *Behavioral and Brain Sciences*, **30**, 299–313.

Tomasello, M. and Call, J. (1997). *Primate cognition*. New York: Oxford University Press.

Tulving, E. (1983). *Elements of episodic memory*. New York: Oxford University Press.
(2002). Episodic memory: from mind to brain. *Annual Review of Psychology*, **53**, 1–25.

Tulving, E. and Thomson, D. M. (1973). Encoding specificity and retrieval processes in episodic memory. *Psychological Review*, **80**(5), 352–373.

Watkins, O. C. and Watkins, M. J. (1975). Build up of proactive inhibition as a cue-overload effect. *Journal of Experimental Psychology: Human Learning and Memory*, **1**, 442–452.

Williams, J. M. G. (1996). Depression and the specificity of autobiographical memory. In D. C. Rubin (ed.), *Remembering our past: studies in autobiographical memory* (pp. 244–267). Cambridge University Press.

16   Autobiographical memory and future thinking

Arnaud D'Argembeau

From the moment we wake up to the moment we fall asleep, we spend much time thinking about all sorts of events and situations that are yet to happen – an errand to run this afternoon, an appointment at the dentist tomorrow, the next lab meeting, a romantic dinner tonight, plans for the weekend, a job interview next month, to give just a few examples. Young adults may experience, on average, around sixty thoughts about the future during a typical day (i.e., one future thought every 16 minutes), and much of these thoughts probably serve important functions, such as planning and decision making (D'Argembeau, Renaud, and Van der Linden, 2011). The ability to imagine and plan for the future (here referred to as "future thinking") is thus clearly a prominent feature of the human mind.

How do we mentally represent future events? What are our thoughts and mental images of the future made of? How are they constructed? The purpose of this chapter is to explore these issues. The first section reviews recent research that has revealed that the capacity to imagine future events is closely related to the capacity to remember past events. Next, I dig further into the nature of this relationship and consider the possible contribution of different kinds of autobiographical knowledge structures to the representation of future events. Finally, recent findings about the component processes underlying future thinking are presented and discussed.

Relationship between remembering and future thinking

Human beings have for a long time had the intuition that the awareness of the past and future are intimately related. This is well illustrated in Roman mythology by Janus, one of the earliest gods of Rome. According to legend, Janus had received the gift to see both the past and the future, as symbolized by his two heads facing opposite directions, one oriented

Arnaud D'Argembeau is supported by the Fund for Scientific Research (F.R.S.-FNRS), Belgium.

311

toward the past and the other toward the future (Berens, 1894/2010). This idea that remembering and future thinking are somehow related has recently received increasing support in various areas of research in psychology and neuroscience.

Evidence from patients with memory deficits

Perhaps the most compelling evidence for the relationship between remembering and future thinking comes from the study of patients with memory deficits. There is evidence that patients with amnesia are not only incapable of consciously remembering specific past events but also present with difficulties in imagining specific situations that might happen in their personal future. Tulving (1985) was one of the first to note this relationship, in a severely amnesic patient who later became known as K.C. As a result of a traumatic brain injury, K.C. became unable to consciously represent any specific episodes from his personal past or future. When asked to imagine what he would be doing tomorrow, for example, K.C. replied that he did not know. When asked to describe his state of mind when trying to think about his personal future, K.C. said it is "blank," the "same kind of blankness" he experienced when trying to remember past events (Tulving, 1985). A parallel deficit in representing events from one's personal past and future has been documented in another amnesic patient, D.B. (Klein, Loftus, and Kihlstrom, 2002).

Confabulation (a memory disorder characterized by the production of false memories) provides another case for the relationship between remembering and future thinking. Dalla Barba, Cappelletti, Signorini, et al. (1997) have reported the case of patient G.A., who confabulated not only when remembering past events but also when planning future events. For example, when questioned about what she would be doing tomorrow, G.A. replied that she would go shopping alone by car, despite the fact that she had never done so since her disease and certainly would not do so on the following day given her medical condition. Unlike amnesic patients, confabulating patients are still able to consciously represent specific episodes from their personal past or future, but they make errors in this process. Most frequently, confabulation consists either of true episodes misplaced in time and place or of personal habits and routines that are mistaken by the patients as specific past or future episodes (Dalla Barba and Boissé, 2010).

A relationship between memory impairments and future thinking abilities has also been observed in Alzheimer's disease (AD). Addis, Sacchetti, Ally, et al. (2009) asked AD patients and age-matched, healthy, elderly controls to recall specific past events and to imagine specific future events in as much detail as possible. They found that AD patients produced fewer details than controls for both types of events. Moreover, across participants, there was a positive correlation between the number of details reported for past events and the number of details reported for future events, providing further evidence for the close linkage between the ability to remember past events and the ability to imagine future events.

Parallel impairments in remembering and future thinking have also been evidenced in some psychopathological conditions. Williams, Ellis, Tyers, *et al.* (1996) asked suicidal patients to remember specific past events and to imagine specific future events in response to cue sentences (e.g., "try to imagine a future situation in which you feel successful"). The results showed that suicidal patients were less able than controls to report specific events (i.e., unique situations that happen in a particular place and time and last no longer than a day), for both the past and the future. Individuals with schizophrenia also present with difficulty in both remembering specific past events and imagining specific future events, and the two deficits are positively correlated (D'Argembeau, Raffard, and Van der Linden, 2008).

Recent findings suggest that, for some patients at least, deficits in representing specific episodes may not be confined to the past and future, but may instead reflect a more general deficit in constructing detailed representations of complex events or narratives. Hassabis, Kumaran, Vann, *et al.* (2007) found that patients with bilateral hippocampal damage are impaired not only at envisioning possible future events but also at imagining new fictitious experiences that do not explicitly refer to the past or future (e.g., imagining lying on a white, sandy beach in a beautiful tropical bay). When asked to imagine such situations in as much detail as possible, amnesic patients reported fewer details than control participants, and their imagined experiences lacked spatial coherence, consisting instead of fragmented images. Rosenbaum, Gilboa, Levine, *et al.* (2009) recently reported that patient K.C. (described above) is also impaired in constructing detailed nonpersonal semantic narratives (i.e., fairy tales and Bible stories) that were learned many years prior to his injury. Finally, it has been shown that individuals with schizophrenia construct less detailed and more fragmented representations not only when they imagine future events but also when they imagine new fictitious experiences that are not explicitly related to any time period (Raffard, D'Argembeau, Bayard, *et al.*, 2010).

Taken together, these findings suggest that difficulty in representing specific past and future events may reflect, at least for some patients, a more general deficit in generating and binding details to construct representations of complex events (Hassabis and Maguire, 2007). Of course, this does not exclude the possibility that processes other than binding and constructive processes also contribute to autobiographical remembering and future thinking (see the later section on the component processes involved in future thinking for further discussion of this issue).

Evidence from cognitive studies

The relationship between remembering and future thinking has also been demonstrated in healthy individuals by showing that a number of factors have similar effects on the construction and representation of past and future events. Williams *et al.* (1996) have shown that manipulating "retrieval style" influences not only memories for past events but also the imagination of future events. In one experiment, retrieval style was manipulated by asking some participants to retrieve specific events from their personal past (i.e., events that happened at a particular time and place), whereas other participants were asked to retrieve generic information (i.e., repeated events, such as "the types of events that make you unhappy"). Both groups of participants were then asked to generate future events in response to cue sentences. The results showed that participants who had previously retrieved specific events from their personal past generated more specific future thoughts than participants who had previously retrieved generic information. In a subsequent experiment, Williams *et al.* manipulated retrieval style by a different procedure (i.e., varying the imageability of cues used to retrieve past events) and observed similar effects. These findings thus show that the experimental induction of particular retrieval styles affects the specificity of not only memories but also future thoughts.

Specific events can be remembered or imagined with more or less detail. Sometimes we remember or imagine an event with considerable detail – for example, "seeing" in our mind's eye the location where the event takes place and the persons and objects that are involved. At other times, we simply represent the gist of past and future events and experience few, if any, sensory and contextual details. The number of details with which events are represented depends on various factors, and there is evidence that these factors influence past and future event representations in similar ways. D'Argembeau and Van der Linden (2004) investigated the influence of temporal distance and affective valence. Participants were asked to remember positive and negative events from the recent or distant past (i.e., from the last year versus the past 5–10 years) and to imagine positive and negative events that might happen in the near or far future (i.e., within the next year versus the next 5–10 years). They were instructed to remember or imagine each event in as much detail as possible, and then to rate their representation of the event on various dimensions (e.g., the number of sensory details, clarity of contextual details, and feeling of "experiencing" the event). The results showed that temporally close events were associated with more sensory details, clearer contextual information, and a stronger feeling of experiencing than were temporally distant events, and this influence of temporal distance was similar for past and future events (see also Berntsen and Bohn, 2010). Moreover, positive events were associated with more sensory details and a stronger feeling of experiencing than negative events, again for both the past and the future. These findings thus demonstrate that temporal distance and affective valence influence phenomenological characteristics in parallel ways for past and future events.

There is also evidence that the voluntary versus involuntary nature of event construction has largely similar effects on past and future event representations. Berntsen and Jacobsen (2008) asked participants to record past and future events that came spontaneously to mind during their everyday activities, and also to generate past and future events voluntarily in response to cue words. Each event was then rated on various dimensions (e.g., specificity, vividness, valence, and mood impact). The results showed that involuntary representations were more specific, more vivid, and less positive, and had more negative mood impact than voluntary representations, both for past events and for future events. The findings further revealed that involuntary future representations came to mind under conditions that were highly similar to ones characterizing the occurrence of involuntary memories (for further discussion of spontaneous recollections, see Berntsen, this volume).

Another study has shown that the phenomenological characteristics of future event representations depend on the quality of the memorial information used to construct the future images (Szpunar and McDermott, 2008). Szpunar and McDermott found that people construct representations of future events that include more sensory details, a higher clarity of context, and a greater feeling of "pre-experiencing" when the events are imagined in familiar settings (e.g., a friend's apartment) than in unfamiliar settings (e.g., the jungle). Moreover, future images that are cued by recently experienced settings (e.g., university campus) are rated as containing more sensory details, a higher clarity of context, and a greater feeling of pre-experiencing than future images cued with remote settings (e.g., high school). Insofar as familiar and recently experienced settings are represented more clearly in memory than unfamiliar and remotely experienced settings, these findings thus demonstrate that the quality of future event representations depends on the quality of the memorial information used in the construction process.

There is also evidence that past and future event representations are similarly affected by certain individual differences. For example, D'Argembeau and Van der Linden (2006) found that individual differences in visual imagery, a key dimension of autobiographical memories (Brewer, 1996; Conway and Pleydell-Pearce, 2000; Greenberg and Rubin, 2003), showed similar correlations with the phenomenological characteristics of past and future event representations – people with better visual imagery capacities experienced more visual and other sensory details, both when remembering past events and when imagining future events. Some personality traits and emotion-regulation strategies also seem to have similar effects on past and future event representations. For example, it has been found that people who score high on the trait of conscientiousness construct more detailed representations of both past and future events (Quoidbach, Hansenne, and Mottet, 2008). On the other hand, individuals who tend to habitually suppress their emotions construct less detailed representations of personal events, for both the past and the future (D'Argembeau and Van der Linden, 2006).

Finally, the temporal distributions of past and future events also show remarkable similarities. Spreng and Levine (2006) asked participants to generate personal past events and probable future events in response to cue words, and then to record the temporal distance of each event. They found that the temporal distribution of future events followed the same power function as the temporal distribution of past events (showing in both cases the greatest frequency of events near the present, and a decline in frequency as a function of temporal distance), although the slope of the future event distribution was somewhat steeper (indicating a greater number of events occurring near the present). Furthermore, the past and future data sets were highly correlated, demonstrating a remarkable concordance in the frequency and recency of past and future thoughts.

Evidence from developmental studies

Further evidence for the relationship between remembering and future thinking has been provided by developmental research. Several studies suggest that the capacity to remember specific past events and the ability to imagine specific future events emerge at the same time, approximately between 3 and 5 years of age (for further discussion of autobiographical memory development, see Bauer and Fivush, this volume). Suddendorf and colleagues (Suddendorf, 2010; Suddendorf and Busby, 2005) asked preschoolers to report something they did yesterday and something they were going to do tomorrow, and their answers were then evaluated by their parents as either likely or unlikely to be correct. The results showed that most 3-year-olds were unable to provide likely correct responses to both questions. There was an increase of performance for both the past and the future questions at 4 years old, and there was a positive correlation between producing a likely correct response to the two questions. The relationship between remembering and future thinking capacities remained significant when controlling for divergent thinking perform- ance, suggesting that this link cannot be explained by verbal response generativity alone (Suddendorf, 2010). These findings thus suggest that rudiments of episodic remembering and future thinking can be detected at 3 years of age, and that the two capacities increase in parallel in older children. Several other studies found that the capacity to project oneself into the future emerges between 3 and 5 years of age (e.g., Atance and Jackson, 2009; Atance and Meltzoff, 2005), but these studies did not directly assess relationships with memory capacity.

The question of whether the ability to engage in future imagining can develop normally in the absence of episodic memory has been recently addressed in studies of developmental amnesia. Kwan, Carson, Addis, *et al.* (2010) examined the ability to imagine the future and to remember the past in patient H.C., a woman who was born prematurely and experienced reduced hippocampal development, resulting in a bilateral volume reduction of approximately 50 percent relative to healthy con- trols. These authors found that H.C. generated fewer episodic details both when remembering past events and when imagining future events in response to cue words, with past and future thinking being impaired to a similar degree. This finding suggests that the development of the two abilities is intertwined, with both depending on intact hippocampal function. However, another recent study described a patient with devel- opmental amnesia (also with 50 percent volume loss in his hippocampi) who was able to richly imagine future experiences in a comparable manner to control participants (Maguire, Vargha-Khadem, and Hassabis, 2010). Additional work is therefore needed before any firm conclusion can be made about the development of future thinking in the absence of episodic memory.

The relationship between the capacity to remember past events and capacity to imagine future events has also been documented in normal aging. Addis, Wong, and Schacter (2008) asked healthy young and older adults to recall specific past events and to imagine specific future events in as much detail as possible. They found that older adults produced fewer episodic details than young adults both when remembering past events and when imagining future events. Furthermore, there was a positive correlation between the number of episodic details reported for past events and the number of episodic details reported for future events.

Addis, Musicaro, Pan, *et al*. (2010) investigated further the nature of older adults' difficulties in imagining specific future events. It could be argued that the observed relationship between the capacity to remember past events and capacity to imagine future events is simply due to younger and older adults' "recasting" entire memories of past events into the future (i.e., remembering a past event and then projecting this event into the future). To address this issue, Addis *et al*. (2010) used a new experimental recombination paradigm that required the generation of novel events on the basis of details extracted from separate past episodes. The results showed that older adults produced fewer episodic details than younger adults, and again there was a positive correlation between the number of details produced for past and future events. These findings thus confirm the existence of a close link between the ability to remember past events and the ability to imagine future events, even under conditions that preclude recasting of remembered events as imagined events.

Evidence from functional neuroimaging

A growing number of functional neuroimaging studies provide evidence that the imagination of future events relies largely on the same set of brain regions as the retrieval of past events (for a review of functional neuroimaging studies of autobiographical memory, see St. Jacques, this volume). In one of the first neuroimaging studies focusing on future thinking, participants were asked to talk freely about their personal past or future while their brain activity was measured by positron emission tomography (Okuda, Fujii, Ohtake, *et al*., 2003). The results showed that, compared to a control semantic task, the past and future thinking tasks were associated with common activations in the medial temporal lobe and the medial and lateral prefrontal cortex.

Although the study by Okuda *et al*. demonstrates common activations when thinking about the past and future, it is unknown whether participants thought about specific events in the scanner or whether they brought to mind more general (semantic) information about their personal past and future. This issue was addressed by Addis *et al*. (2007) in a functional magnetic resonance imaging (fMRI) study. Participants were asked to remember specific past events and to imagine specific future events in response to cue words. On each trial, participants were first instructed to bring a past or future event to mind (construction phase), and then to retrieve as much detail as possible about the event (elaboration phase). The results showed that past and future event construction commonly engaged a number of brain regions (including the left hippocampus, right inferior parietal lobule, and occipital areas) compared to semantic retrieval and visual imagery control tasks. Furthermore, past and future event elaboration was associated with common activations in several brain regions as well, including the medial and lateral prefrontal cortex, medial and lateral temporal lobe, medial posterior regions, inferior parietal cortex, and cerebellum.

In another fMRI study, Szpunar, Watson, and McDermott (2007) asked participants to envision themselves in specific past and future events, and to imagine Bill Clinton in similar events. A number of brain regions (including the medial prefrontal cortex, medial temporal lobe, posterior cingulate cortex, occipital cortex, and cerebellum) were found to be more activated both when remembering past personal events and when envisioning future personal events compared to imagining Bill Clinton. A common pattern of brain activations when remembering past events and imagining future events has been observed in several other fMRI studies, in both young adults (e.g., Botzung, Denkova, and Manning, 2008; Spreng and Grady, 2010; Weiler, Suchan, and Daum, 2010) and healthy older adults (Viard Chetelat, Lebreton, *et al.*, 2011), thus providing further evidence that remembering and future thinking rely on largely similar neural substrates.

Conclusion

Converging evidence from neuropsychology, psychopathology, cognitive psychology, developmental research, and functional neuroimaging indicates that remembering and future thinking are closely related mental faculties. It should be noted, however, that there are also clear differences between remembering the past and imagining the future. Memories refer to events that have been previously experienced, whereas future thoughts represent events that have yet to take place and that are, by definition, imbued with uncertainty. These differences are in part reflected in the phenomenology of past and future event representations. Indeed, representations of past events typically contain more sensory and contextual details than representations of future events (Berntsen and Bohn, 2010; D'Argembeau and Van der Linden, 2004, 2006). On the other hand, representations of future events tend to be more positive and idyllic (Berntsen and Bohn, 2010; Berntsen and Jacobsen, 2008; D'Argembeau and Van der Linden, 2006), perhaps because they are less constrained by reality considerations than are memories of past events (Van Boven, Kane, and McGraw, 2009). There is also evidence that certain aspects of remembering and future thinking develop at different rates; for example, children seem to discriminate between the times of past events before they can do so for future events (Busby-Grant and

Suddendorf, 2009). Finally, neuroimaging studies also point to some differences in the neural substrates of remembering and future thinking (Addis, Pan, Vu, *et al.*, 2009; Weiler *et al.*, 2010).

In spite of these differences, the bulk of evidence clearly shows that remembering the past and imagining the future are intimately related. This linkage may be due to at least two factors. First, past and future event representations may draw upon the same information stored in memory. Second, the construction of both kinds of representation may rely on the same component processes. These two issues are addressed in the next sections.

Knowledge structures involved in future thinking

The first reason why remembering and future thinking are closely related mental faculties is that both may draw upon the same information stored in memory. It has been proposed, in particular, that episodic memory not only allows the recollection of past experiences but also provides the "vocabulary" or source of details for future event construction – in order to imagine future events, we would use details extracted from our past experiences, such as details about previously encountered objects, people, and locations (Schacter and Addis, 2007; Schacter, Addis, and Buckner, 2008; Suddendorf and Corballis, 1997, 2007). It is likely that the construction of mental representations of future events does not solely involve episodic memory, however. In this section, I speculate that the selection of episodic details for constructing episodic future thoughts is not random, but rather is guided by more general knowledge structures. Specifically, people may hold conceptual knowledge about their personal future which provides a context or frame for retrieving, assembling, and interpreting relevant episodic details from memory. Before considering this possibility in more detail, I first specify further what I mean by episodic details.

In line with others (Schacter and Addis, 2007; Suddendorf and Corballis, 2007), I endorse the view that episodic memories and episodic future thoughts are, at least in part, built from a common pool of episodic details. The question of exactly what these episodic details may consist of is a complex and still largely underexplored issue, however. Generally speaking, episodic details (also referred to as "event-specific knowledge"; Conway and Pleydell-Pearce, 2000) may be conceived as components of experience (i.e., sensory-perceptual-conceptual-affective details; Conway, 2009) that are represented as simulations in the brain's modality-specific systems for perception, action, emotion, and introspection (Barsalou, 2008; Rubin, 2006). They may consist either of elements that have been extracted from a single past event that can be specifically located in space and time (Addis, Pan, *et al.*, 2009; e.g., a visual image that represents the appearance of my friend Steve when I saw him this morning) or of elements that are more generic (in the sense that they summarize multiple past experiences) and yet "experience-near" (Conway, 2009; e.g., a visual image that represents what my friend Steve typically looks like); of course, these two possibilities are not mutually exclusive. Note also that the details used to mentally represent possible future events might consist not only of elements that have been extracted from first-hand, personal experiences (e.g., the representation of a known location) but also of information gleaned more indirectly – for example, through the media (e.g., television, magazines, and so on). Thus, for example, even if a person has never been to India, she may still be able to imagine visiting a particular location in India by using details extracted from photographs or movies she has previously seen about that country.

Whatever the precise nature of its constituents, the same pool (or at least partly the same pool) of episodic details might be used when remembering past events and when constructing episodic future thoughts (and also when constructing episodic-like mental representations that are not specifically located in time; Hassabis, Kumaran, and Maguire, 2007). Still, we do not usually confuse the past and future status of represented events (although note that children before 6 years of age often do; Friedman, 2005), so the question that arises is, how do we differentiate between the two kinds of events? One possibility is that conceptual autobiographical knowledge locates episodic details in distinct temporal contexts. Conway (2001, 2009; Conway and Pleydell-Pearce, 2000; see also Conway, this volume) has put forward the idea that autobiographical memories include not only episodic details but also more general contextualizing knowledge that locates specific episodes within the individual's personal history. This conceptual autobiographical knowledge consists of knowledge about significant others, common locations, and goals that characterize broad lifetime periods (e.g., "when I was in primary school"), as well as summary representations of repeated events (e.g., "Sundays at Grandma's house") or events extended in time (e.g., "our vacation in France last summer"), collectively referred to as general events. In the same vein, people may hold conceptual autobiographical knowledge about their personal future, including knowledge about goals (e.g., "I would like to become an architect"), anticipated lifetime periods (e.g., "when I'll be married"), and general events (e.g., "my trip to India next summer"). There is indeed evidence that a substantial amount of future thoughts that people experience in daily life consist of abstract representations that do not necessarily refer to a specific event (D'Argembeau *et al.*, 2011). Furthermore, when people are instructed to complete sentence stems with reference to their personal future (e.g., "Next year I ..."), they spontaneously report general information (i.e., future thoughts relating to extended future life periods or personal semantic information) more frequently than specific events (Anderson and Dewhurst, 2009).

This kind of conceptual knowledge about one's personal future could play an important role in the construction of episodic future thoughts – it might guide the selection of relevant episodic details and provide a context or frame for integrating and interpreting those details. When attempting to imagine a specific and plausible future event, an individual might first access general knowledge about her personal future (e.g., she might think about the fact that she would like to go to India next summer) and then construct specific moments of experience by retrieving relevant episodic details (e.g., she might imagine a specific place she would like to visit and picture herself asking directions of an Indian guide). Recent data from our laboratory suggest that this is how people typically proceed when attempting to imagine future events in response to cue words (D'Argembeau and Mathy, 2011).

Although this issue remains to be investigated in detail, it might be that an individual's conceptual knowledge about the future is mainly structured around his or her personal goals (i.e., internal representations of future states that the individual strives to attain or avoid; Austin and Vancouver, 1996). Episodic future thoughts may thus be primarily governed by personal goals, their main function being to allow the representation of specific events that incarnate and exemplify personal goals (e.g., possible selves; Markus and Nurius, 1986) and the construction of scenarios that implement efficient ways to achieve goals (Taylor, Pham, Rivkin, et al., 1998). There is indeed evidence that cuing people with personal goals facilitates the construction of episodic future thoughts (D'Argembeau and Mathy, 2011). Some of these goals may be transmitted culturally through "cultural life scripts" (i.e., culturally shared expectations about the order and timing of major life events, such as graduation, marriage, and childbirth; Berntsen and Jacobsen, 2008; Berntsen and Rubin, 2004), whereas others may be more idiosyncratic (e.g., studying abroad, buying a sports car, taking golf lessons), and recent findings suggest that both kinds of goals can guide the construction of episodic future thoughts (D'Argembeau and Mathy, 2011).

In summary, the construction of episodic future thoughts may draw, at least in part, on the same pool of episodic details as autobiographical memories but may involve distinct pieces of conceptual knowledge that place those details in novel temporal contexts. Abstract representations of the personal future, which might be mainly organized in terms of personal goals and associated time periods, might provide a context or frame for retrieving, integrating, and interpreting episodic details.

Component processes underlying future thinking

The second reason why remembering and future thinking are related is that they may rely, at least in part, on the same component processes (for a detailed account of the different systems and processes involved in auto-biographical memory, see Rubin, 2006, this volume). Tulving (1985, 2005) is one of the first to have called attention to such commonalities, noting that "mental time travel" into the past and into the future involves a notion of self and the capacity to become aware of the temporal dimension of one's own existence. Suddendorf and Corballis (1997, 2007) have further argued that remembering and future thinking both require a processing space where information is temporarily maintained and manipulated (working memory); processes that initiate, organize, and monitor the retrieval of relevant elements from long-term memory (executive processes); and processes that flexibly combine and integrate retrieved elements into a coherent representation (recursive and relational processes). Schacter and Addis (2007) have emphasized the importance of constructive and relational processes, arguing that the constructive nature of episodic memory allows the flexible recombination of bits and pieces of information extracted from past episodes in order to create coherent simulations of novel events (the "constructive episodic simulation hypothesis"). Hassabis and Maguire (2007) have made a related proposal and have put special emphasis on visual-spatial processing, maintaining that "scene construction" (i.e., the construction of a complex scene by retrieving relevant information and its integration into a coherent spatial context) is a key component process in both remembering and future thinking. Finally, Buckner and Carroll (2007) have called attention to "self-projection" processes, which enable the temporary withdrawal of attention from the immediate environment in order to mentally explore alternative perspectives.

The ability to mentally represent future events might therefore rely on multiple component processes, most of which are also involved in remembering past episodes. We recently investigated this question and examined whether different component processes support distinct aspects of future thinking (D'Argembeau, Ortoleva, Jumentier, et al., 2010). To do so, we had participants complete a series of tasks and questionnaires measuring various component processes thought to underlie remembering and future thinking (i.e., working memory, executive functioning, visual-spatial processing, relational memory processing, self-consciousness, and future time perspective), as well as several tasks assessing different aspects of past and future event representation (i.e., fluency in generating events, capacity to represent specific episodes, number of episodic details generated, and phenomenological characteristics). We found that measures of executive processes involved in the organization and monitoring of retrieval (i.e., verbal fluency tasks) correlated with various autobiographical measures (i.e., event fluency, number of episodic details), for both past events and future events. This finding suggests that executive processes mediate access to information about both the past and the future, at different levels of specificity (e.g., general events, episodic details), at least when there is a willful attempt to bring past and future events to mind (see Berntsen and Jacobsen, 2008, however, for evidence that both autobiographical memories and representations of future events can be formed spontaneously, and thus presumably with little involvement of executive processes).

The results further showed that the capacity to construct truly episodic future thoughts (i.e., representations of specific events that contain many sensory details) was predicted not only by executive processes but also by measures of visual-spatial constructive abilities and future time perspective. On the other hand, the role of visual-spatial constructive abilities was less evident for past events. This suggests that constructive processes are recruited more intensively for imagining future events than for remembering past events, perhaps because one has to flexibly recombine multiple details (e.g., details about objects, people, locations) to generate a novel episode that has not been experienced as such in the past (Schacter and Addis, 2007). Finally, we also found that individual differences in self-consciousness (more specifically, the general tendency to think about the self and to focus attention on one's inner experience) specifically predicted the subjective feeling of "pre-experiencing" imagined future events. Overall, these findings show that multiple component processes are involved in future thinking (most of which are also involved in remembering), and that different processes support distinct aspects of future-event representation.

As mentioned earlier, functional neuroimaging studies have shown that remembering past events and imagining future events recruit a common set of brain regions, which provides further evidence that both mental activities rely on the same neurocognitive processes. Interestingly, the same brain regions have been associated with other tasks as well, for example imagining new fictitious experiences that are not explicitly temporal in nature (Hassabis, Kumaran, and Maguire, 2007), imagining events that might have occurred in the past but actually did not happen (Addis, Pan, et al., 2009) or inferring the mental states of other persons (Spreng and Grady, 2010; see also the meta-analysis of Spreng, Mar, and

Kim, 2009). These findings suggest that a core network of brain regions supports processes that are involved in, but not specific to, autobiographical remembering and future thinking. The precise nature of these processes is still debated, however. Buckner and Carroll (2007) have proposed that the core network supports self-projection (i.e., the ability to shift perspective from the immediate present to mentally explore alternative perspectives), whereas Hassabis and Maguire (2007) have argued that scene construction (i.e., the process of mentally generating and maintaining the representation of a complex scene or event) is better able to account for the commonalities in the brain areas engaged in the different tasks mentioned above. Although this issue requires further investigation, it is likely that distinct subregions within the core network support different processes (Andrews-Hanna, Reidler, Sepulcre, et al., 2010). For example, there is evidence that the medial temporal lobe may support relational and constructive processes (Buckner, 2010; Schacter and Addis, 2009), while the medial prefrontal cortex may participate in evaluating the personal significance of constructed events (Andrews-Hanna et al., 2010; D'Argembeau, Stawarczyk, Majerus, et al., 2010), and the left lateral parietal cortex may mediate the consciousness of subjective time (Nyberg, Kim, Habib, et al., 2010).

In summary, multiple component processes seem to be involved in future thinking, most of which are also involved in autobiographical remembering as well as in other cognitive functions. Different component processes may support different aspects of future-event representation. Executive processes may support the strategic aspects of retrieval (e.g., establishing retrieval goals, initiating and guiding search, monitoring and selecting retrieved information), which may play a general role in accessing information about past and future events at different levels of specificity. The capacity to generate representations of future events that are infused with sensory details may further depend on visual-spatial constructive abilities, and perhaps also on future time perspective. Self-processes may be involved in imbuing constructed representations with the subjective feeling of "traveling through time" to pre-experience one's personal future. This multiplicity of component processes is mirrored in the multiple brain regions that have been associated with the imagination of future events, with different component processes being likely subserved by distinct brain areas.

General conclusion and future directions

Although human beings have for a long time had the intuition that the awareness of the past and that of the future are intimately related, it has only been recently that scientific evidence for this relationship has been gathered. Findings from various areas of research in psychology and neuroscience converge to show that remembering and future thinking do indeed have much in common, although some differences have also been noted. Memories and future thoughts may be generated from largely the same pool of episodic details, and their construction may involve similar component processes. The constructed events may acquire their past or future status only when linked with more general knowledge structures that place episodic details in different temporal contexts. Abstract representations of the personal future, which might be mainly organized in terms of personal goals and associated time periods, may thus be an integral part of an individual's autobiographical knowledge that complements knowledge of the personal past and provides a context or frame for retrieving, integrating, and interpreting episodic details.

An important question that deserves further investigation concerns the functions of future thinking. The capacity to imagine and plan for the future has clearly provided the human species with important advantages (Suddendorf and Corballis, 1997, 2007; Tulving, 2005). Our actions are not irremediably tied to our immediate environment; we can anticipate and explore mentally a wide range of possible futures, allowing us to make better decisions and plan actions in more effective ways. Most future thoughts that people experience in daily life seem to serve such a directive function (D'Argembeau *et al.*, 2011; for a detailed account of the functions of autobiographical memory, see Pillemer and Kuwabare, this volume). However, not all future thoughts are useful (e.g., constantly worrying about future situations that are unlikely to ever materialize), and the precise conditions under which future thinking actually provides advantages have to be investigated further. Finally, it is likely that the future events we anticipate are important constituents of our sense of self and identity. This identity function of future thinking also merits further attention.

References

Addis, D. R., Musicaro, R., Pan, L., and Schacter, D. L. (2010). Episodic simulation of past and future events in older adults: evidence from an experimental recombination task. *Psychology and Aging*, **25**, 369–376.

Addis, D. R., Pan, L., Vu, M. A., Laiser, N., and Schacter, D. L. (2009). Constructive episodic simulation of the future and the past: distinct subsystems of a core brain network mediate imagining and remembering. *Neuropsychologia*, **47**, 2222–2238.

Addis, D. R., Sacchetti, D. C., Ally, B. A., Budson, A. E., and Schacter, D. L. (2009). Episodic simulation of future events is impaired in mild Alzheimer's disease. *Neuropsychologia*, **47**, 2660–2671.

Addis, D. R., Wong, A. T., and Schacter, D. L. (2007). Remembering the past and imagining the future: common and distinct neural substrates during event construction and elaboration. *Neuropsychologia*, **45**, 1363–1377.

(2008). Age-related changes in the episodic simulation of future events. *Psychological Science*, **19**, 33–41.

Anderson, R. J. and Dewhurst, S. A. (2009). Remembering the past and imagining the future: differences in event specificity of spontaneously generated thought. *Memory*, **17**, 367–373.

Andrews-Hanna, J. R., Reidler, J. S., Sepulcre, J., Poulin, R., and Buckner, R. L. (2010). Functional-anatomic fractionation of the brain's default network. *Neuron*, **65**, 550–562.

Atance, C. M. and Jackson, L. K. (2009). The development and coherence of future-oriented behaviors during the preschool years. *Journal of Experimental Child Psychology*, **102**, 379–391.

Atance, C. M. and Meltzoff, A. N. (2005). My future self: young children's ability to anticipate and explain future states. *Cognitive Development*, **20**, 341–361.

Atance, C. M. and O'Neill, D. K. (2001). Episodic future thinking. *Trends in Cognitive Sciences*, **5**, 533–539.

Austin, J. T. and Vancouver, J. B. (1996). Goal constructs in psychology: structure, process, and content. *Psychological Bulletin*, **120**, 338–375.

Barsalou, L. W. (2008). Grounded cognition. *Annual Review of Psychology*, **59**, 617–645.

Berens, E. M. (1894/2010). *The myths and legends of ancient Greece and Rome: a handbook of mythology*. Bremen: Europäischer Hochschulverlag.

Berntsen, D. and Bohn, A. (2010). Remembering and forecasting: the relation between autobiographical memory and episodic future thinking. *Memory & Cognition*, **38**, 265–278.

Berntsen, D. and Jacobsen, A. S. (2008). Involuntary (spontaneous) mental time travel into the past and future. *Consciousness and Cognition*, **17**, 1093–1104.

Berntsen, D. and Rubin, D. C. (2004). Cultural life scripts structure recall from autobiographical memory. *Memory & Cognition*, **32**, 427–442.

Botzung, A., Denkova, E., and Manning, L. (2008). Experiencing past and future personal events: functional neuroimaging evidence on the neural bases of mental time travel. *Brain and Cognition*, **66**, 202–212.

Brewer, W. F. (1996). What is recollective memory? In D. C. Rubin (ed.), *Remembering our past: studies in autobiographical memory* (pp. 19–66). Cambridge University Press.

Buckner, R. L. (2010). The role of the hippocampus in prediction and imagination. *Annual Review of Psychology*, **61**, 27–48.

Buckner, R. L. and Carroll, D. C. (2007). Self-projection and the brain. *Trends in Cognitive Sciences*, **11**, 49–57.

Busby-Grant, J. and Suddendorf, T. (2009). Preschoolers begin to differentiate the times of events from throughout the lifespan. *European Journal of Developmental Psychology*, **6**, 746–762.

Conway, M. A. (2001). Sensory-perceptual episodic memory and its context: autobiographical memory. *Philosophical Transactions of the Royal Society of London. Series B, Biological Sciences*, **356**, 1375–1384.

(2005). Memory and the self. *Journal of Memory and Language*, **53**, 594–628.

(2009). Episodic memories. *Neuropsychologia*, **47**, 2305–2313.

Conway, M. A. and Pleydell-Pearce, C. W. (2000). The construction of autobiographical memories in the self-memory system. *Psychological Review*, **107**, 261–288.

Dalla Barba, G. and Boissé, M.-F. (2010). Temporal consciousness and confabulation: is the medial temporal lobe "temporal"? *Cognitive Neuropsychiatry*, **15**, 95–117.

Dalla Barba, G., Cappelletti, Y. J., Signorini, M., and Denes, G. (1997). Confabulation: remembering "another" past, planning "another" future. *Neurocase*, **3**, 425–436.

D'Argembeau, A. and Mathy, A. (2011). Tracking the construction of episodic future thoughts. *Journal of Experimental Psychology: General*, **140**, 258–271.

D'Argembeau, A., Ortoleva, C., Jumentier, S., and Van der Linden, M. (2010). Component processes underlying future thinking. *Memory & Cognition*, **38**, 809–819.

D'Argembeau, A., Raffard, S., and Van der Linden, M. (2008). Remembering the past and imagining the future in schizophrenia. *Journal of Abnormal Psychology*, **117**, 247–251.

D'Argembeau, A., Renaud, O., and Van der Linden, M. (2011). Frequency, characteristics, and functions of future-oriented thoughts in daily life. *Applied Cognitive Psychology*, **25**, 96–103.

D'Argembeau, A., Stawarczyk, D., Majerus, S., Collette, F., Van der Linden, M., Feyers, D., *et al.* (2010). The neural basis of personal goal processing when envisioning future events. *Journal of Cognitive Neuroscience*, **22**, 1701–1713.

D'Argembeau, A. and Van der Linden, M. (2004). Phenomenal characteristics associated with projecting oneself back into the past and forward into the future: influence of valence and temporal distance. *Consciousness and Cognition*, **13**, 844–858.

(2006). Individual differences in the phenomenology of mental time travel: the effect of vivid visual imagery and emotion regulation strategies. *Consciousness and Cognition*, **15**, 342–350.

Friedman, W. J. (2005). Developmental and cognitive perspectives on humans' sense of the times of past and future events. *Learning and Motivation*, **36**, 145–158.

Greenberg, D. L. and Rubin, D. C. (2003). The neuropsychology of autobiographical memory. *Cortex*, **39**, 687–728.

Hassabis, D., Kumaran, D., and Maguire, E. A. (2007). Using imagination to understand the neural basis of episodic memory. *Journal of Neuroscience*, **27**, 14365–14374.

Hassabis, D., Kumaran, D., Vann, S. D., and Maguire, E. A. (2007). Patients with hippocampal amnesia cannot imagine new experiences. *Proceedings of the National Academy of Sciences of the United States of America*, **104**, 1726–1731.

Hassabis, D. and Maguire, E. A. (2007). Deconstructing episodic memory with construction. *Trends in Cognitive Sciences*, **11**, 299–306.

Klein, S. B., Loftus, J., and Kihlstrom, J. F. (2002). Memory and temporal experience: the effects of episodic memory loss on an amnesic patient's ability to remember the past and imagine the future. *Social Cognition*, **20**, 353–379.

Kwan, D., Carson, N., Addis, D. R., and Rosenbaum, R. S. (2010). Deficits in past remembering extend to future imagining in a case of developmental amnesia. *Neuropsychologia*, **48**, 3179–3186.

Maguire, E. A., Vargha-Khadem, F., and Hassabis, D. (2010). Imagining fictitious and future experiences: evidence from developmental amnesia. *Neuropsychologia*, **48**, 3187–3192.

Markus, H. and Nurius, P. (1986). Possible selves. *American Psychologist*, **41**, 954–969.

Nyberg, L., Kim, A. S., Habib, R., Levine, B., and Tulving, E. (2010). Consciousness of subjective time in the brain. *Proceedings of the National Academy of Sciences of the United States of America*, **107**, 22356–22359.

Okuda, J., Fujii, T., Ohtake, H., Tsukiura, T., Tanji, K., Suzuki, K., *et al.* (2003). Thinking of the future and past: the roles of the frontal pole and the medial temporal lobes. *NeuroImage*, **19**, 1369–1380.

Quoidbach, J., Hansenne, M., and Mottet, C. (2008). Personality and mental time travel: a differential approach to autonoetic consciousness. *Consciousness and Cognition*, **17**, 1082–1092.

Raffard, S., D'Argembeau, A., Bayard, S., Boulenger, J. P., and Van der Linden, M. (2010). Scene construction in schizophrenia. *Neuropsychology*, **24**, 608–615.

Rosenbaum, R. S., Gilboa, A., Levine, B., Winocur, G., and Moscovitch, M. (2009). Amnesia as an impairment of detail generation and binding: evidence from personal, fictional, and semantic narratives in K.C. *Neuropsychologia*, **47**, 2181–2187.

Rubin, D. C. (2006). The basic-systems model of episodic memory. *Perspectives on Psychological Science*, **1**, 277–311.

Schacter, D. L. and Addis, D. R. (2007). The cognitive neuroscience of constructive memory: remembering the past and imagining the future. *Philosophical Transactions of the Royal Society of London. Series B, Biological Sciences*, **362**, 773–786.

(2009). On the nature of medial temporal lobe contributions to the constructive simulation of future events. *Philosophical Transactions of the Royal Society of London. Series B, Biological Sciences*, **364**, 1245–1253.

Schacter, D. L., Addis, D. R., and Buckner, R. L. (2008). Episodic simulation of future events: concepts, data, and applications. *Annals of the New York Academy of Sciences*, **1124**, 39–60.

Spreng, R. N. and Grady, C. I. (2010). Patterns of brain activity supporting autobiographical memory, prospection, and theory-of-mind and their relationship to the default mode network. *Journal of Cognitive Neuroscience*, **22**, 1112–1123.

Spreng, R. N. and Levine, B. (2006). The temporal distribution of past and future autobiographical events across the lifespan. *Memory & Cognition*, **34**, 1644–1651.

Spreng, R. N., Mar, R. A., and Kim, A. S. N. (2009). The common neural basis of autobiographical memory, prospection, navigation, theory of mind, and the default mode: a quantitative meta-analysis. *Journal of Cognitive Neuroscience*, **21**, 489–510.

Suddendorf, T. (2010). Linking yesterday and tomorrow: preschoolers' ability to report temporally displaced events. *British Journal of Developmental Psychology*, **28**, 491–498.

Suddendorf, T. and Busby, J. (2005). Making decisions with the future in mind: developmental and comparative identification of mental time travel. *Learning and Motivation*, **36**, 110–125.

Suddendorf, T. and Corballis, M. C. (1997). Mental time travel and the evolution of the human mind. *Genetic, Social, and General Psychology Monographs*, **123**, 133–167.

(2007). The evolution of foresight: what is mental time travel and is it unique to humans? *Behavioral and Brain Sciences*, **30**, 299–351.

Szpunar, K. K. and McDermott, K. B. (2008). Episodic future thought and its relation to remembering: evidence from ratings of subjective experience. *Consciousness and Cognition*, **17**, 330–334.

Szpunar, K. K., Watson, J. M., and McDermott, K. B. (2007). Neural substrates of envisioning the future. *Proceedings of the National Academy of Sciences of the United States of America*, **104**, 642–647.

Taylor, S. E., Pham, L. B., Rivkin, I. D., and Armor, D. A. (1998). Harnessing the imagination: mental simulation, self-regulation, and coping. *American Psychologist*, **53**, 429–439.

Tulving, E. (1985). Memory and consciousness. *Canadian Psychologist*, **26**, 1–12.

(2005). Episodic memory and autonoesis: uniquely human? In H. S. Terrace and J. Metcalfe (eds.), *The missing link in cognition: origins of self-reflective consciousness* (pp. 3–56). Oxford University Press.

Van Boven, L., Kane, J. M., and McGraw, A. P. (2009). Temporally asymmetric constraints on mental simulation: retrospection is more constrained than prospection. In K. D. Markman, W. M. P. Klein, and J. A. Suhr (eds.), *Handbook of imagination and mental simulation* (pp. 131–147). New York: Psychology Press.

Viard, A., Chetelat, G., Lebreton, K., Desgranges, B., Landeau, B., de La Sayette, V., et al. (2011). Mental time travel into the past and the future in healthy aged adults: an fMRI study. *Brain and Cognition*, **75**, 1–9.

Weiler, J. A., Suchan, B., and Daum, I. (2010). When the future becomes the past: differences in brain activation patterns for episodic memory and episodic future thinking. *Behavioural Brain Research*, **212**, 196–203.

Williams, J. M. G., Ellis, N. C., Tyers, C., Healy, H., Rose, G., and MacLeod, A. K. (1996). The specificity of autobiographical memory and imageability of the future. *Memory & Cognition*, **24**, 116–125.

Part VI

Discussion

There is one chapter in this part. In this final chapter, the editors attempt to integrate the preceding contributions to this book into a coherent ecological theory of autobiographical memory.

17 Understanding autobiographical memory: an ecological theory

Dorthe Berntsen and David C. Rubin

> If we are in search of the self, we can look either inward or outward. To look inward is to focus on mental representations, on the self-concept or inner experience. To look outward is to see the self as embedded in its environment, ecologically and socially situated in relation to other objects and persons.   (Neisser, 1994, p. 392)

It is appropriate to begin this chapter by quoting one of the most influential pioneers of cognitive psychology (Neisser, 1967) and autobiographical memory research (Neisser, 1986, 1988, 1994). The position expressed by Neisser is not just relevant in relation to understanding the self. In this chapter we will propose a similar ecological approach to the understanding of autobiographical memory.

According to most definitions, autobiographical memory is the ability to consciously remember personal events. However, personal events are not unchanging, ontological entities. They are constructions that vary substantially with regard to their temporal, spatial, and social complexity. Some event constructions are simple – e.g., eating a sandwich in a cafe – whereas others are more complicated – e.g., eating a sandwich in a cafe while attending a conference on autobiographical memory and discussing shared past experiences with colleagues. In the latter example, the event (eating the sandwich) embeds other personal events (the shared past experiences being discussed over the meal) and is itself embedded in the overarching event of participating in the conference. It involves complex social knowledge, including knowledge of conferences and knowledge of the other persons who take part in the event, such as their roles, expertise, and mutual relations.

Some scholars have suggested a distinction between episodic and autobiographical memory and proposed that the term "autobiographical memory" should be reserved to relatively comprehensive events with some significance for our life stories (e.g., Nelson, 1993). Rather than

We thank the Danish National Research Foundation and the Danish Council for Independent Research: Humanities for funding.

operating with such a dichotomy, we here use the term "autobiographical" for both simpler and more complex event constructions since both are about happenings in an individual's life and thus describe aspects of this individual's past (see Rubin, this volume). We believe that simpler event constructions can be found in many nonhuman species, whereas autobiographical memory in more complex forms may be specific to humans.

In our view, it is the complicated social organization of human life that is mainly responsible for this complexity. The coordination of activities in extended societal co-operation has come along with multiple types of schemata for time (e.g., week schemata, day schemata) and time technologies (the clock, calendar time), which are largely culturally transmitted and which enable the individual to construct representations of autobiographical events shaped by such structures (e.g., Friedman, 2005). Likewise any human being's life is characterized by a complicated set of social roles in relation to both work life and family life. Such roles are generally culturally defined with regard to their expected content as well as time of transition from one role to another (Settersten and Hägestad, 1996a, 1996b). Knowledge of social roles and stereotypes shapes the individual's interpretations of his or her own behavior as well as that of others and thereby influences the construction of personal events.

In humans a major function of autobiographical memory is likely to enable individuals to orient themselves and participate in such complex social environments. For some animals living in socially less complicated environments, orienting spatially may be a much more dominant memory function. The pervasive social function of human autobiographical memory, on the other hand, manifests itself in several ways. One important function is to remember our past history with other individuals, in order to build upon this knowledge in present interactions and in the planning of future interactions (see Pillemer and Kuwabara, this volume, for a discussion of such directive functions). Another function is to share our memories with other individuals in order to arrive at some consensus, or shared interpretation of past events that will enhance social cohesion (Hirst, Cuc, and Wohl, this volume). In general, autobiographical memory can be viewed as an event-simulation system (Rubin, this volume). Not just past events are being constructed from autobiographical memory. As reviewed and discussed by D'Argembeau (this volume), autobiographical memory plays a key role in generating representations of possible events in the future.

Although autobiographical memory as a general event-simulation system is most likely also found in some nonhuman animals (see Donald, this volume), the cultural structuring of time, space, and social relations,

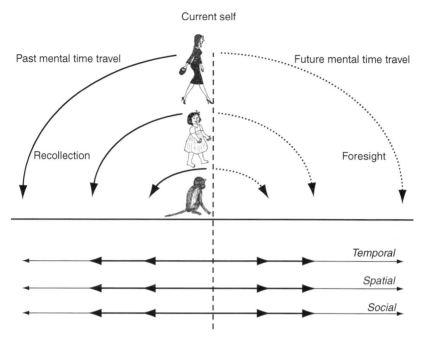

Figure 17.1. Autobiographical remembering and episodic future thinking taking place along culturally structured dimensions for time, space, and social relations, and varying in range and complexity between human adults, children, and nonhuman animals. Autobiographical remembering and episodic future thinking can be both voluntary (strategic) and involuntary (spontaneous). Adapted from Berntsen, 2009, Figure 8.1.

which is acquired through childhood, allows the adult human to have more comprehensive and multilevel autobiographical memory representations. In addition, as we shall clarify later, the ability of nonhuman animals to retrieve autobiographical events may be limited to involuntary, associative retrieval (see Berntsen, this volume; Donald, this volume). Figure 17.1 illustrates our position. The adult human, the human child, and the nonhuman animal all have some ability to remember past events and envision possible events in the future. However, the temporal, spatial, and social knowledge that goes into these event constructions is dramatically more complex in the case of the adult human, primarily due to the cultural transmission of knowledge structures for time, space, and social relations. For example, only adult humans are capable of combining personal events into temporally, causally, and thematically coherent life stories, building upon such knowledge (Habermas and Bluck, 2000).

Figure 17.1 is an elaboration of a previous figure by Berntsen (2009, Figure 8.1), in which only the relative enlargement of the temporal dimension in humans was emphasized. However, although the temporal dimension presumably involves more complex constructions (Brewer, 1996; Friedman, 2005), similar extensions of the social and spatial dimension are likely, due to cultural transmissions of relevant knowledge structures also for these domains.

According to the present view and unlike most definitions of episodic memory (e.g., Tulving, 2002; Wheeler, Stuss, and Tulving, 1997), autobiographical memory is not considered as a unified memory system. Constructing an autobiographical event or a life story draws upon many different sources of knowledge, of which only some derive specifically from the individual's personal life. Most of the knowledge that goes into the formation of personal memories (or future projections) is culturally shared, "semantic" knowledge (e.g., event scripts, cultural life scripts, knowledge of temporal structures, spatial maps, stereotypes, schemata for public places, and so forth). Therefore, it does not make sense to speak of autobiographical memory as a unified memory system distinct from semantic memory (see Moscovitch, this volume; Rubin, this volume).

From this starting point, we shall now discuss autobiographical memory in relation to its organization, retrieval processes, existence in nonhuman animals, ontogenetic development, and the self.

Organization

Theories of autobiographical memory have often been concerned with identifying the key cognitive structures that are supposed to organize autobiographical memory. Generally these structures are assumed to arise from subjectively experienced regularities, changes, and overarching themes in the individual life. Identifying such structures was a frequent aim in early theoretical developments of autobiographical memory (Barsalou, 1988; Linton, 1986; Neisser, 1986; Robinson, 1992). Conway and colleagues extended and refined this line of theorizing in a comprehensive model of multiple nested structures and retrieval processes constrained by the goals of the self (e.g., Conway, 2005; Conway and Jobson, this volume; Conway and Pleydell-Pearce, 2000; Conway and Rubin, 1993).

We will here take a different approach. We propose that there is no stable organization of autobiographical memory in terms of a fixed hierarchical system. Rather, there are different levels of autobiographical knowledge with some being more abstract (or schematic) and others being more concrete (or specific). For example, it is meaningful to distinguish between lifetime periods and specific events and to consider them as referring to different levels of abstraction. However, our position differs from nested (hierarchical) models in two ways. First, the concrete nesting of these different forms of knowledge is not a stable one. It varies as a function of situational demands, notably as a function of the retrieval process and its context, including the goals and concerns of the individual. Second, we identify at least three dimensions along which autobiographical knowledge can be abstracted: temporal, spatial, and social. These dimensions vary with regard to how central a role they play in the organization of our past. Sometimes the temporal dimension is in the foreground as the major structuring principle; sometimes the spatial dimension is in the foreground; and sometimes, as in response to loss and relationship crises, the social dimension predominates (e.g., Horowitz, 1988). In our view, the simplicity that characterizes current models of nested autobiographical memory structures derives from the fact that such models have focused mostly on abstractions along the temporal dimension. In contrast, the intersection of the temporal, spatial, and social dimensions, which we propose, yields multiple ways in which autobiographical memory can be nested. Therefore, any diagrammatic description of nested structures is bound to be a snapshot of a complex system at work, not a general description of stable structures in a stable autobiographical memory system.

It might be argued that autobiographical knowledge can be abstracted along many other dimensions than the ones we focus on here. While this is true, it nonetheless seems justified to regard space, time, and social relationships as the major components of autobiographical events. Time and space are usually considered as key dimensions in definitions of events, and multilevel social relations (changing and unfolding over time) can be seen as the major constituents of human environments (Bronfenbrenner, 1979). In the following discussion, we provide a more detailed account of the three dimensions.

The temporal dimension

Autobiographical memory is often described in terms of different levels of abstraction that vary along a dimension of event specificity (e.g., Bluck and Habermas, 2001; Conway, 2005; Conway and Pleydell-Pearce, 2000; Levine, Svoboda, Hay, et al., 2002). Some components include mostly schematic information. This is information that is not specific to a particular episode but applies to a variety of past experiences and summarizes characteristics that are shared by several events, such as thematic and temporal similarities. A relevant example is general event representations, summarizing shared characteristics of recurrent episodes (i.e., going by train to work in X-town) and thus abstracting from specific incidents of this category of events. The opposite end of the specificity continuum is information that pertains to particular episodes and helps to discriminate each unique episode from similar occurrences (i.e., the day the train was canceled because of a strike).

According to this view, specificity is to a large extent a matter of the time span covered by the information in question. A memory of a specific moment is considered as more specific than a memory of a more extended course of episodes (e.g., a particular day), which in turn is more specific than an event that took place over several days (such as a vacation), and so forth. Indeed, a "specific episode" is usually operationalized exclusively with reference to temporal duration – i.e., something that lasted a day or less (e.g., Williams, Barnhofer, Crane, *et al.*, 2007). It is meaningful to think of specificity as varying along a dimension of temporal duration. However, this is not the only relevant dimension along which autobiographical knowledge is abstracted. At least two other dimensions are needed in order to begin to complete the picture, one is a spatial dimension and the other is a social dimension.

The spatial dimension

Spatial specificity is inversely related to the extension of the location, just as temporal specificity is inversely related to the duration of the experience (Trope and Lieberman, 2003). A memory of an event located to a particular spot in a wood is spatially more specific than an event located to having taken place "in the wood." This is independent of its temporal duration. An autobiographical event can be temporally nonspecific, while at the same time being highly specific with regard to spatial location. Imagine two lovers secretly meeting evening after evening by a particular tree in the wood. Their memory of these meetings is likely to be temporally nonspecific in summarizing shared characteristics of many similar meetings. However, the memory will be highly specific with regard to spatial information (e.g., we used to meet at the old oak tree by the river).

Obviously, spatial specificity is extremely important for our ability to orient ourselves in our physical environment. In addition, memories for specific locations are often associated with strong emotion and high levels of personal significance, as observed in homesickness (Fisher, 1989; Salaman, 1982). Thus, memory for locations plays an important role in structuring our past and in the way we ascribe meaning to past events. Schematized knowledge in the spatial domain includes schemata for common places, such as offices or classrooms (Brewer and Treyens, 1981), and cognitive maps, representing routes or locations in a particular environment (e.g., my way to school). Cognitive maps are present in many nonhuman species, such as rats (Tolman, 1951) and birds (see Gould, 1982, for review). Although spatial knowledge is central and needs to be maintained probably by most animals, culturally transmitted technologies, such as maps and GPS, help to improve human spatial knowledge compared to those of other species. However, even without such technologies, remarkable spatial abilities are observed in nonhuman animals (e.g., Gould, 1982).

The social dimension

Often overlooked in cognitive approaches, but emphasized in the psycho-dynamic tradition (e.g., Habermas, this volume), are socially derived structures of autobiographical memory. Retaining precise information about our relationship with particular others is important in order to orient ourselves in complex social communities, collaborate, keep track of kinship, and predict the behavior of others and adjust our own accord-ingly. But it is also important to extract rules of conduct, probabilities of reactions that apply broadly across individuals. Thus, again, it is mean-ingful to speak about variations along a continuum of specificity and schematization, with some aspects being distinct for our relationship with particular individuals and others applying more broadly. Social stereotypes are a key example of abstract social representations. By a common definition, stereotypes are "beliefs about the characteristics, attributes and behaviors of members of certain groups" (Hilton and Van Hippel, 1996, p. 240). Thus, such schematized knowledge helps us to differentiate between groups at the cost of individual differences (within group variations). It is therefore one form in which social knowledge can be abstract. There is evidence that social stereotypes affect memory. In relation to homogeneous groups, stereotype-inconsistent information often is better retained, whereas the reverse tends to be true for more heterogeneous groups (Hilton and Van Hippel, 1996). More broadly, social stereotypes have large effects on how we perceive and classify others and their roles, and thus on how we construct social aspects of events.

Whereas social stereotypes can be conceived as schemata that apply broadly across individuals and across settings (i.e., Danes are happy), psychodynamic theories (e.g., Horowitz, 1988) have been concerned with the kinds of schemata we develop for relationships with concrete individuals, a topic closely associated with attachment. Horowitz (1988) introduced the notion of person schemata, which depict individual relationships with significant others including anticipations for these relationships in the future. The schemata "summarize past interpersonal experience into integrated, generalized, and modular forms against which incoming information is measured and reorganized for 'goodness-of-fit'" (Horowitz, 1988, p. 13). Following early observations on autobiographical memory (Linton, 1986), some memories may contain information that is highly indicative of our relationship with particular others. Linton (1986) observed that "Sometimes my whole relationship with people spanning years or decades seems encapsulated in a series of such fragments" (p. 53). Such memories are specific in the sense that they represent qualities of our relationship with particular people, but abstract in the sense that they represent rules and general characteristics of these unique relationships. At the same time, they may be indistinct with regard to temporal and spatial information.

The social dimension includes not just knowledge of others but also knowledge of oneself, which likewise can be considered as varying on levels of abstraction. At the abstract level, our personal identity integrates knowledge of our past behavior, social roles, skills, and attitudes as abstracted across many different domains and situations in order to provide a general sense of who we are (Conway and Jobson, this volume). Social stereotypes influence how we view ourselves as a function of group membership, a phenomenon known as self-stereotyping (Sinclair, Hardin, and Lowery, 2006). More specific personal knowledge pertains to our relationship with concrete individuals or particular activities, such as being especially good (or bad) at playing tennis. The cultural life script (Berntsen and Rubin, 2004) is an example of a higher-order structure which combines the temporal and social dimension by dealing with social roles and their expected transition times in the life course (e.g., when to become a parent, when to retire). We will address the emergence of a sense of self later in this chapter.

Emotion further adds to the complexity of the social domain. Self-knowledge is positively biased (in nondepressed individuals). Thus, we have a tendency to view ourselves and our accomplishments through rose-colored glasses (e.g., Taylor and Brown, 1988; Wilson and Ross, 2003). In general, autobiographical memory is biased toward emotionally positive events in the sense that positive events are more often and more easily recalled than emotionally negative events (Walker, Skowronski, and Thompson, 2003). Also, when cued by a request for emotional events, positive events show a reminiscence bump in young adulthood, whereas negative events generally do not (Berntsen and Rubin, 2002). This may in part be because positive memories help to maintain a positive image of oneself and others, which is important for our ability to participate in social relationships.

Pleasantness versus unpleasantness is a basic distinction (e.g., Holland and Kensinger, 2010), associated with approach and avoidance (e.g., Cacioppo and Berntson, 1999, for a review), and exceedingly important for survival. It is also at the core of the idea of defense mechanisms as observed in psychodynamic theories (e.g., Freud, 1920/1943; Horowitz, 1986; see Habermas, this volume). For autobiographical memory, there is evidence that people often sort by emotional content when asked to freely categorize previously sampled personal memories (Larsen and Berntsen, 2000). For instance, when asked to categorize her memories, a young female subject put all her memories about her father in one pile, except for one memory. When confronted with this deviation, she explained: "Yes, I have a whole group of memories about my dad, but this one did not fit into it, because it refers to a good experience, whereas the other memories about my dad are associated with some negative emotions" (Larsen and Berntsen, 2000, p. 111). In extreme cases, a division into positive (good) and negative (bad) is known as splitting in the psychodynamic literature (Habermas, this volume); this is a primitive defense mechanism that may obscure more coherent (or mature) constructions and integrations of autobiographical knowledge along the temporal, spatial, and social dimensions (e.g., Jørgensen, 2006).

Cultural transmission versus experience-derived structures

The schemata for the temporal, spatial, and social domains can derive in two ways. First, the structures can be culturally transmitted, meaning that they exist independently of the individual's life experiences, are usually learned in childhood, and are superimposed in a top-down fashion as a standard way of making sense of individual experiences. Second, structures can derive from subjectively experienced regularities (and their exceptions) in the life of the individual, and thus evolve from each person's life experiences in a bottom-up fashion. Culturally transmitted structures ensure social and cultural coherency. Experience-derived structures provide individual variability. The top-down structuring relies on a vast number of culturally transmitted knowledge structures, such as temporal schemata and time technologies (e.g., Friedman, 2005; Thompson, Skowronski, Larsen, et al., 1996); cultural life scripts (Berntsen and Rubin, 2004); scripts for recurrent events (Schank and Abelson, 1977); schemata for people, such as social stereotypes (Hilton and von Hippel, 1996) and shared expectations to social roles (Settersten and Hägestad, 1996a, 1996b); schemata for places (Brewer and Treyens,

1981); and culturally transmitted knowledge of spatial structures such as maps. The experience-derived organization is discussed by Brown, Hansen, Lee, *et al.* (this volume). The structures in their model consist of intersections of temporal, spatial, and social autobiographical knowledge. New *event components* are assumed to occur when "fabric of daily life" is changed. The "the fabric of daily life" metaphor connotes all three dimensions described here (in addition to "things" and "activities").

Obviously the two types of structuring interact with one another. The experienced-derived structures are to some extent shaped by culturally transmitted schemes, although deviations may be seen. Likewise the understanding and use of cultural schemes may to some extent be modified by personal experience (see Fitzgerald and Broadbridge, this volume, for more reflections on this interaction viewed in a life-span perspective; see also Conway and Jobson, this volume).

The top-down structuring through culturally transmitted schemata and technologies is important for understanding why human autobiographical memory is more advanced than that of nonhuman species as well as for understanding the ontogenetic development of autobiographical memory. But before we address these topics, we will discuss how memories of autobiographical events are constructed during retrieval.

Retrieval

Retrieval is a constructive process, in which spatial, temporal, and social information is combined together with information derived from individual senses, such as vision (Rubin, this volume; St. Jacques, this volume). Following the present view, the spatial, social, and temporal information that is integrated during retrieval to form an autobiographical event can be more or less specific (i.e., less or more schematized) on all three dimensions. Some of the combination during retrieval is automatic and simply derives from contiguity associations – that is, things that were experienced together also tend to be remembered together (Warren, 1916). The development of schemata for all three dimensions allows increasingly complex event constructions to be formed. Similar constructive processes are involved with imagining possible future events (D'Argembeau, this volume), although, for the latter, nonspecific, schema-derived knowledge generally plays a more dominant role (e.g., Berntsen and Bohn, 2010).

Retrieval of autobiographical memories can take place in two ways. One is voluntary in the sense that it is consciously initiated and goal-directed. The other is involuntary in the sense that the memory is formed with no preceding conscious retrieval attempt (see Berntsen, this volume). Voluntary recall is assumed to begin with the development of a search description that is modified throughout the search process until the search is completed or abandoned (Norman and Bobrow, 1979). Voluntary retrieval therefore requires substantial executive control to monitor the process, including inhibiting irrelevant associations. Involuntary retrieval, on the other hand, is situation dependent in that it occurs as the result of an associative connection between features of the current situation and features of a past event. Previous research reviewed by Berntsen (this volume) has consistently shown that involuntary recall more frequently than voluntary recall leads to the construction of memories of specific episodes, using the standard operationalization of this notion (i.e., memories of particular occurrences that lasted no longer than a day). The reason may be that such unique information is more likely than abstract information to provide associative links that are sufficiently distinct to discriminate a memory from alternatives (Watkins and Watkins, 1975). Although this has not yet been examined empirically, it is likely that a similar specificity effect can be observed along the spatial and social dimensions, so that involuntary memories also contain more specific information about distinct places and distinct people than voluntary recollections. In contrast, voluntary retrieval is likely to favor more abstract, schematic information on all three dimensions relative to what is the case for involuntary retrieval because the voluntary retrieval process is based on search descriptions generated from such abstract information. This claim is supported by the fact that voluntary recollections are less specific and tend to be seen as more relevant to the person's life story (see Berntsen, 2009, for a review).

Conway and colleagues have made a related, but conceptually different, distinction between generative (strategic) and direct (associative, spontaneous) retrieval. As with the voluntary versus involuntary distinction used here, the key difference between generative and direct retrieval is that the former is modulated by control processes whereas the latter is dependent on a distinct associative match. In addition, however, a number of conceptual differences are seen between the two distinctions. Most importantly, the distinction between generative and direct retrieval implies a view of autobiographical memory as a stable hierarchical system. Direct retrieval takes place when this hierarchical system is activated from the bottom up; that is, by a distinct match between a situational feature and an aspect of event-specific knowledge. In contrast to this, generative retrieval accesses the system at higher levels of abstraction and works itself down the levels (Conway and Pleydell-Pearce, 2000). Both types of retrieval may lead to the conscious activation of a specific episode, but from two different routes. The distinction between generative and direct retrieval therefore implies a stable nested system upon which these retrieval processes operate (e.g., from the bottom versus from the top). The distinction between involuntary and voluntary remembering, on the other hand, is neutral with regard to the underlying organization of autobiographical memory. As we shall discuss shortly, the involuntary, associative retrieval of past events may be found (in species-specific forms) in many animals species, whereas the voluntary, schema-driven search may be specific to humans, as suggested by Donald (1991, this volume) and Berntsen (2009, this volume). Also, this type of recall is likely to be present earlier in life than voluntary recall, a point we shall return to later.

As pointed out by Conway and colleagues (e.g., Conway, 2005; Conway and Jobson, this volume; Conway and Pleydell-Pearce, 2000), motivational factors, such as goals, play an important role in the relative salience of autobiographical information and thus in how easily events are constructed. There is substantial evidence that goal-consistent information is more accessible than goal-inconsistent information (see Conway and Pleydell-Pearce, 2000, for an overview).

The notion of current concerns introduced by Klinger (1975) offers an operationalization of goals and how they relate to cognitive processes. Current concerns are defined as "the state of the organism between the time of commitment and the time of consummation or disengagement" from a certain goal (p. 3). Current concerns lead to an increased sensitivity to cues related to the desired goal (Klinger and Cox, 2004). Klinger and his collaborators have found support for the influence of current concerns in a number of areas, such as memories for stories, contents of thoughts, and dreams (see Johannessen and Berntsen, 2010, for a review). Current concerns also affect the accessibility and quality of autobiographical memories (e.g., Johannessen and Berntsen, 2010). The fact that autobiographical memories are influenced by goals further speaks to the directive functions of such memories (see Pillemer and Kuwabara, this volume).

Autobiographical memory in nonhuman animals

Consistent with the evolutionary thesis of Donald (this volume), most of the neural structures involved in constructing autobiographical memories (Moscovitch, this volume; Rubin, this volume; St. Jacques, this volume) are well developed in other species. Thus, it is not surprising that several lines of research suggest that the ability to remember past events is not specific to humans. For example, primates live in complex social environments that demand sophisticated social cognition. According to Tomasello and Call (1997, p. 193), this involves the ability (1) to recognize other individuals in their group, (2) to understand and predict at least some of their behavior, (3) to remember prior interactions with other group members in order to form relationships to them, and (4) to remember some of the interactions that other individuals have had with one another, in order to understand their relationship to one another. At least some of these skills involve memory of past events. Similarly, many animals live in environments that require complex foraging behavior, which involves remembering where and when certain food objects can be found.

Following the theoretical definitions of episodic memory, the ability to remember past events can be operationalized in at least two ways. One way is in terms of content – that is, the ability to remember events located in time and space (Tulving, 1972). The other is in terms of subjective quality – that is, the experience of mentally reliving the past event in consciousness (Tulving, 1985, 2000). With regard to animals, the operationalization in terms of mental quality works poorly in that it is virtually impossible to show that animals have, or do not have, conscious reliving in association with retrieving information about past experiences. Therefore, most researchers rely on a content-based definition. Clayton and Dickenson (1998) coined the term "episodic-like memories" in their studies of western scrub jays to indicate an ability to remember when an event took place, what happened, and where it happened. In a series of experiments, they have shown that scrub jays can remember where and when two different types of food objects were cached. The scrub jays prefer wax worms to peanuts when both food items are fresh. However, the worms decay more quickly than the peanuts, and the birds prefer the peanuts to the decayed worms. In the initial experiment, the scrub jays cached worms and peanuts at two different locations and two different times. One group of birds first cached peanuts and 5 days later worms. The other groups first cached worms and 5 days later peanuts. Four hours after caching the last food items, the birds were given the opportunity to recover the cached food (with the food being removed). The jays whose worms had been decaying for 5 days searched more for peanuts, whereas the other group whose worms had been cached only 4 hours earlier showed a preference for the worms. These preferences suggest that the birds were capable of remembering both the what (peanuts versus worms), the where (which tray), and the when (5 days or 4 hours earlier) of the preceding caching event. It has also been shown that scrub jays are sensitive to the social context of the original events – that is, whether co-species were present during food cashing (Dally, Emery, and Clayton, 2006; Toomey, Bowman, and Woolfenden, 2007) – and this shows that the birds also remember information pertaining to the social dimension of past events. A similar ability to remember the what, the where, and the when of previous experiences has been reported for other birds (see Salwiczek, Watanabe, and Clayton, 2010, for review) rats (Crystal, 2010), and apes (Martin-Ordas, Haun, Colmenares, *et al.*, 2010).

Thus, episodic-like memories present in other animal species also seem to combine temporal, spatial, and (at least sometimes) social information. An important difference between episodic-like memories present in other animal species and autobiographical memories in humans is that, for the former, very little top-down structuring takes place in terms of culturally transmitted schemata and technologies. This means that higher-order structures (e.g., spatial schemata) develop largely in a bottom-up fashion, through the interactions between an animal and its environment, and not through cultural transmission (Tomasello, 1999). The schemata/rules developed are therefore considerably less sophisticated than the ones humans acquire and integrate with their own autobiographical experiences. In part due to culturally transmitted time technologies (e.g., clocks, calendars) and culturally transmitted schemata for the accepted age-segmentation of the life course within a given culture (e.g., cultural life scripts) as well as other types of culturally transmitted knowledge, the temporal horizon of human episodic memory is considerable enlarged compared to those of other species (e.g., Roberts, 2002). Thus, we are able to remember temporally more distant past events and imagine temporally more distant future events than other species in part due to such cultural structuring of time (e.g., Friedman, Reese, and Dai, 2011). A similar enlargement most likely characterizes the spatial and social dimensions (see Figure 17.1). This allows more sophisticated attributions of causality and thematic reasoning and thus facilitates the ability to think of one's life in terms of a life story (Habermas and Bluck, 2000).

Unlike humans, nonhuman animals are likely to be highly (and perhaps solely) dependent on involuntary retrieval (e.g., Donald, this volume), which is a context-sensitive, situation-dependent – and therefore quite inflexible – retrieval form. In contrast, human autobiographical memory does not operate solely through involuntary, situational cuing. Humans have the ability to voluntarily search their memory for particular events. This ability is what Donald (1991, this volume) calls autocuing and considers as a pivotal ability in relation to the development of human culture, since it allows humans to rehearse and improve skills and knowledge in a conscious and goal-directed fashion. Voluntary recall most likely also allows the construction of substantially more complex, multilayered autobiographical events, as compared to what can be derived through purely associative mechanisms.

Development of autobiographical memory in humans

According to the current view, two achievements appear central for autobiographical memory development. One is the acquisition of still more sophisticated schemata for time, space, and social relationships and the mastering of cultural technologies for time and space. The other is an increasing ability to combine temporal, social, and spatial information in the construction of autobiographical events, leading to increasing levels of coherence in autobiographical memory narratives. Although memory for simple events appears to be present at an early age, information regarding what, where, who, and when often goes unspecified in young children's memory narratives, seemingly because the child lacks the skills and knowledge required to make such integration (Bauer, this volume).

These two aspects of development interact with one another. For example, the acquisition of schemata for weekdays or knowledge of the clock enables the child to date and order events in more coherent ways than would otherwise be possible. Friedman and colleagues have shown that time from a psychological point of view consists of many different structures. Knowledge of short time scales is developed earlier than knowledge of long time scales, with the consequence that children are better at judging when an event took place in terms of time of the day than time of the year (see Friedman, 2005, for a review). Friedman *et al.* (2011) showed that children who had acquired conventional knowledge of time gave more accurate time estimates for their own events on long time scales, even when age and general cognitive skills were controlled for. Similarly, children who have acquired knowledge of culturally defined social roles and their expected transition points in the prototypical life course (e.g., cultural life scripts; Berntsen and Rubin, 2004) tell more coherent life stories than children who have not (Bohn and Berntsen, 2008). Thus, the cultural transmission of schematized knowledge for the spatial, temporal, and social domains enables the child to have more coherent and more comprehensive autobiographical memories. The acquisition of such knowledge structures takes place throughout childhood. Even at age 14, children's cultural life scripts are less conventional than the ones of adults (Bohn and Berntsen, 2008; Habermas and Bluck, 2000).

The present view is consistent with central tenets of the sociocultural theory of autobiographical memory development (Nelson and Fivush, 2004), according to which autobiographical memory emerges gradually over the preschool years in close relation to the development of other cognitive skills and the acquisition of culturally shared knowledge structures. Especially in early childhood (i.e., the preschool years) the acquisition of such structures and the ensuing ability to combine episodic elements into increasingly complex narratives of events (and series of events) seems to depend very much upon conversations between the child and a caregiver (Fivush, Haden, and Adam, 1995). During such conversations, the child's narratives are structured (or scaffolded) by the adult, and the child fills in his or her accessible memory details. Hereby the child learns which elements are expected to be included in stories, and how they should be interpreted and placed into a greater social, spatial, and temporal context. Narratives, according to Fivush and colleagues, are sociocultural tools for expressing, sharing, and representing personal experiences (see Fivush, this volume). The impact of culture is also reflected in important cultural differences in early autobiographical memories (e.g., Wang, 2006; see also Conway and Jobson, this volume).

Later in the child's life, much of this structuring would happen outside caregiver–child interactions, such as in school settings and through popular culture. Narrative structures and normative schemes are conveyed in many ways. Fairy tales, folktales, songs, popular music, movies, games, and so on are powerful instruments of socialization, consistent with the universal nature of oral traditions (Rubin, 1995). Cultural norms and ideals are ubiquitous and seep in through various media. In Nelson's (2003) model of the cultural self, the absorption of cultural myths and representative stories is included as part of the developmental process.

Understanding what forms a good autobiographical narrative is likely to also influence how experiences are segmented into meaningful event units during encoding (Zacks and Swallow, 2007). Surprisingly little is known about how the ability to segment the flow of experience into meaningful event units develops in childhood. While infants' abilities regarding object segregation (Needham, Baillargeon, and Kaufman, 1997), object individuation (Krøjgaard, 2004), and event categorization (Baillargeon and Wang, 2002) have been studied thoroughly, event segmentation has remained almost unexplored in infancy and early childhood, and little is known as to how this ability and other aspects of event and object perception relate to the development of autobiographical memory.

According to the present view, involuntary remembering is an earlier ontogenetic development than voluntary remembering, in part because it involves less executive control processes and thus is less dependent on the development of frontal lobe structures (Hall, Gjedde, and Kupers, 2008). Similarly, voluntary retrieval is dependent on the acquisition and development of schematized knowledge to allow a more free combination of elements in a process of goal-directed event construction. Involuntary recall, on the other hand, relies on associative processes that can operate at a very early age. However, so far, no systematic studies have been conducted of involuntary memories among children. Only anecdotal evidence exists. For example, Fivush (1997) reports a 34-month-old girl who called out "pumpkins, pumpkins" when the family drove past a field where they had gotten Halloween pumpkins 8 months previously. This involuntary memory has many of the characteristics of adults' involuntary autobiographical memories: it is about a unique and distinct event. The memory is activated by a particular spatial location that is also part of the memory content. Similar observations of preschool children's involuntary memories were reported by Morton (1990).

Some of the memory tests that are administered to young children may in fact probe involuntary remembering, although this has been little discussed. Studies with infants show the memory-enhancing effects of exposure to nonverbal reminders of an event (Rovee-Collier, 1999), but it is not clear whether this effect might involve some involuntary event memories (or event memory fragments) that are conscious to the child, or whether it is an unconscious reinstatement effect. Deferred imitation is usually assumed to probe conscious episodic memories of past events (Bauer, 2007). In deferred imitation, the child is shown the props that go into the construction of a certain toy, such as a gong, which the child has seen demonstrated on an earlier occasion. Because of this extensive feature-overlap, it is possible that the props function as retrieval cues for the memory and that the retrieval process is largely one of spontaneous, involuntary recollection.

There is evidence that the forgetting rate of younger children is faster than that of older children, even when the initial level of learning is held constant (Bauer, this volume). According to Bauer, this suggests that younger children have more fragile memory traces than older children, possibly reflecting poorer consolidation and reconsolidation (see Bauer, this volume, for evidence on two different types of consolidation in childhood and their relevance to childhood amnesia). However, speculatively, this may reflect the fact that younger children to a great extent rely on involuntary remembering, whereas older children are capable of rehearsing their memories in a more strategic manner. As proposed by Berntsen (this volume), involuntary remembering is an important form of rehearsal that is likely to support the long-term maintenance of autobiographical memories. However, it is also an uncontrollable and context sensitive type of recall that favors events with distinct episodic overlaps with the current situation. This type of rehearsal is therefore likely to lead to a different, and probably more fragile, type of consolidation of past events, as compared to voluntary, strategic recall. Or, put differently, the ability to remember/rehearse past events in a voluntary, and thus selective, fashion allows the child to better integrate the events into the overall network of autobiographical knowledge. More robust memories may be the result.

The self

According to the present view, the self is an inherent part of any autobiographical event (Conway and Jobson, this volume, and the self-reference section in St. Jacques, this volume), meaning that variations in the complexities of the event constructions will lead to variations in the complexities of self-constructions. Thus, for some animals with very simple event perceptions/constructions, a sense of self may be limited to the self as perceived in relation to an immediate physical activity and spatial location. Neisser (1988) called this kind of self-knowledge "the ecological self." This was one of five different kinds of self-knowledge, varying in content and complexity. The other four were the interpersonal self (the self perceived as an agent in an immediate, ongoing social exchange), the extended self (the self as remembered over time), the private self (knowing that you alone are conscious of your own experiences), and the conceptual self (seeing yourself through the conceptual lenses of the culture – that is, the self as formed by knowledge about one's social roles, values, traits, importance to other people, self-stereotyping, etc.). Following this view, increasingly complex kinds of self-knowledge emerge from the ability to construe increasingly complex autobiographical events, both developmentally and evolutionarily. This variation also takes place within individuals. In situations with very simple goals or strong emotion, our conceptions of both ourselves and the event may be much more simplistic (black and white) than during moments of tranquil contemplation and theorizing. This, of course, also means that the self is not a stable pattern or entity. It varies as a function of the events we construct, both momentarily and retrospectively through our autobiographical memories.

References

Baillargeon, R. and Wang, S. (2002). Event categorization in infancy. *Trends in Cognitive Sciences*, **6**, 85–93.

Barsalou, L. W. (1988). The content and organisation of autobiographical memories. In U. Neisser and E. Winograd (eds.), *Remembering reconsidered: ecological and traditional approaches to the study of memory* (pp. 193–243). New York: Cambridge University Press.

Bauer, P. J. (2007). *Remembering the times of our lives: memory in infancy and beyond.* Mahwah, NJ: Lawrence Erlbaum Associates.

Berntsen, D. (1996). Involuntary autobiographical memories. *Applied Cognitive Psychology*, **10**, 435–454.

(2009). *Involuntary autobiographical memories: an introduction to the unbidden past.* Cambridge University Press.

Berntsen, D. and Bohn, A. (2010). Remembering and forecasting: the relation between autobiographical memory and episodic future thinking. *Memory & Cognition*, **38**, 265–278.

Berntsen, D. and Rubin, D. C. (2002). Emotionally charged autobiographical memories across the lifespan: the recall of happy, sad, traumatic, and involuntary memories. *Psychology and Aging*, **17**, 636–652.

(2004). Cultural life scripts structure recall from autobiographical memory. *Memory & Cognition*, **32**, 427–442.

Bluck, S. and Habermas, T. (2001). Extending the study of autobiographical memory: thinking back about life across the life span. *Review of General Psychology*, **5**, 135–147.

Bohn, A. and Berntsen, D. (2008). Life story development in childhood: the development of life story abilities, and the acquisition of cultural life scripts from late middle childhood to adolescence. *Developmental Psychology*, **44**, 1135–1147.

Brewer, W. F. (1996). What is recollective memory? In D. C. Rubin (ed.), *Remembering our past: studies in autobiographical memory* (pp. 19–66). Cambridge University Press.

Brewer, W. F. and Treyens, J. C. (1981). Role of schemata in memory for places. *Cognitive Psychology*, **13**, 207–213.

Bronfenbrenner, U. (1979). *The ecology of human development: experiments by nature and design*. Cambridge, MA: Harvard University Press.

Cacioppo, J. T. and Berntson, G. G. (1999). The affect system: architecture and operating characteristics. *Current Directions in Psychological Science*, **8**, 133–137.

Clayton, N. S., Bussey, T. J., Emery, N. J., and Dickinson, A. (2003). Prometheus to Proust: the case for behavioural criteria for "mental time travel." *Trends in Cognitive Sciences*, **7**, 436–437.

Clayton, N. S. and Dickinson, A. (1998). Episodic-like memories during cache recovery by scrub jays. *Nature*, **395**, 272–274.

Conway, M. A. (2005). Memory and the self. *Journal of Memory and Language*, **53**, 594–628.

Conway, M. A. and Pleydell-Pearce, C. W. (2000). The construction of autobiographical memory in the self-memory system. *Psychological Review*, **107**, 261–288.

Conway, M. A. and Rubin, D. C. (1993). The structure of autobiographical memory. In A. C. Collins, S. E. Gathercole, M. A. Conway, and P. E. M. Morris (eds.), *Theories of memory* (pp. 103–137). Hove: Lawrence Erlbaum Associates.

Crystal, J. D. (2010). Episodic-like memory in animals. *Behavioural Brain Research*, **215**, 235–243.

Dally, J. M., Emery, N. J., and Clayton, N. S. (2006). Food-caching western scrub-jays keep track of who was watching when. *Science*, **312**, 1662–1665.

Donald, M. (1991). *Origins of the modern mind: three stages in the evolution of culture and cognition*. Cambridge, MA: Harvard University Press.

Fisher, S. (1989). *Homesickness, cognition and health*. Hove: Lawrence Erlbaum Associates.

Fivush, R. (1997). Event memory in early childhood. In N. Cowan and C. Hume (eds.), *The development of memory in childhood* (pp. 139–162). Hove: Psychology Press.

Fivush, R., Haden, C., and Adam, S. (1995). Structure and coherence of preschoolers' personal narratives over time: implications for childhood amnesia. *Journal of Experimental Cognitive Psychology*, **60**, 32–50.

Freud, S. (1920/1943). *A general introduction to psychoanalysis*. New York: Garden City Publishing Company.

Friedman, W. J. (2005). Developmental and cognitive perspectives on humans' sense of the times of past and future events. *Learning and Motivation*, **36**, 145–158.

Friedman, W. J., Reese, E., and Dai, X. (2011). Children's memory for the times of events from the past years. *Applied Cognitive Psychology*, **25**, 156–165.

Gould, J. L. (1982). *Ethology: the mechanisms and evolution of behavior*. New York: W. W. Norton.

Habermas, T. and Bluck, S. (2000). Getting a life: the emergence of the life story in adolescence. *Psychological Bulletin*, **126**, 748–769.

Hall, N. M., Gjedde, A., and Kupers, R. (2008). Neural mechanism of voluntary and involuntary recall. *Behavioural Brain Research*, **25**, 261–272.

Hilton, J. J. and von Hippel, W. (1996). Stereotypes. *Annual Review of Psychology*, **47**, 237–271.

Holland, A. C. and Kensinger, E. A. (2010). Emotion and autobiographical memory. *Physics of Life Reviews*, **7**, 88–131.

Horowitz, M. J. (1986). *Stress response syndromes* (2nd edn.). Northvale, NJ: Jason Aronson.

(1988). Person schemas. In M. J. Horowitz (ed.), *Person schemas and maladaptive interpersonal patterns* (pp. 13–31). University of Chicago Press.

Johannessen, K. B. and Berntsen, D. (2010). Current concerns in involuntary and voluntary autobiographical memories. *Consciousness and Cognition*, **19**, 847–860.

Jørgensen, C. R. (2006). Disturbed sense of identity in borderline personality disorder. *Journal of Personality Disorders*, **20**, 618–644.

Klinger, E. (1975). Consequences of commitment to and disengagement from incentives. *Psychological Review*, **82**, 1–25.

Klinger, E. and Cox, W. M. (2004). Motivation and the theory of current concerns. In W. M. Cox and E. Klinger (eds.), *Handbook of motivational counseling: concepts, approaches and assessment* (pp. 3–27). Chichester: Wiley.

Krøjgaard, P. (2004). A review of object individuation in infancy. *British Journal of Developmental Psychology*, **22**, 159–183.

Larsen, S. F. and Berntsen, D. (2000). Bartlett's trilogy of memory: reconstructing the concept of attitude. In A. Saito (ed.), *Beyond Bartlett: interface of cognitive and sociocultural science* (pp. 90–114). London: Psychology Press.

Levine, B., Svoboda, E., Hay, J. F., Winocur, G., and Moscovitch, M. (2002). Aging and autobiographical memory: dissociating episodic from semantic retrieval. *Psychology and Aging*, **17**, 677–689.

Linton, M. (1986). Ways of searching and the content of memory. In D. C. Rubin (ed.), *Autobiographical memory* (pp. 50–67). New York: Cambridge University Press.

Martin-Ordas, G., Haun, D. B. M., Colmenares, F., and Call, J. (2010). Keeping track of time: evidence for episodic-like memory in great apes. *Animal Cognition*, **13**, 331–340.

Morton, J. (1990). The development of event memory. *The Psychologist*, **1**, 3–10.

Needham, A., Baillargeon, R., and Kaufman, L. (1997). Object segregation in infancy. In C. Rovee-Collier and L. Lipsitt (eds.), *Advances in infancy research*, vol. XI (pp. 11–44). Norwood, NJ: Ablex.

Neisser, U. (1967). *Cognitive psychology*. East Norwalk, CT: Appleton-Century-Crofts.

(1986). Nested structure in autobiographical memory. In D. C. Rubin (ed.), *Autobiographical memory* (pp. 71–82). Cambridge University Press.

(1988). Five kinds of self-knowledge. *Philosophical Psychology*, **1**, 35–59.

(1994). Self-perception and self-knowledge. *Psyke & logos*, **15**, 392–407.

Nelson, K. (1993). Explaining the emergence of autobiographical memory in early childhood. In A. C. Collins, S. E. Gathercole, M. A. Conway, and P. E. M. Morris (eds.), *Theories of memory* (pp. 355–387). Hove: Lawrence Erlbaum Associates.

(2003). Narrative and self, myth and memory: emergence of the cultural self. In R. Fivush and C. A. Haden (eds.), *Autobiographical memory and the construction of a narrative self: developmental and cultural perspectives* (pp. 3–28). Mahwah, NJ: Lawrence Erlbaum Associates.

Nelson, K. and Fivush, R. (2004). The emergence of autobiographical memory: a social cultural developmental theory. *Psychological Review*, **111**(2), 486–511.

Neugarten, B. L., Moore, J. W., and Lowe, J. C. (1965). Age norms, age constraints, and adult socialization. *American Journal of Sociology*, **70**, 710–717.

Norman, D. A. and Bobrow, D. G. (1979). Descriptions: an intermediate stage in memory retrieval. *Cognitive Psychology*, **11**, 107–123.

Pillemer, D. B. (2003). Directive functions or autobiographical memory: the guiding power of the specific episode. *Memory*, **11**, 193–202.

Roberts, W. A. (2002). Are animals stuck in time? *Psychological Bulletin*, **128**, 473–489.

Robinson, J. A. (1992). First experience memories: context and functions in personal histories. In M. A. Conway, D. C. Rubin, H. Spinnler, and W. A. Wagenaar (eds.), *Theoretical perspectives on autobiographical memory* (pp. 223–239). Dordrecht: Kluwer Academic.

Rovee-Collier, C. (1999). The development of infant memory. *Current Directions in Psychological Science*, **8**, 80–85.

Rubin, D. C. (1995). *Memory in oral traditions: the cognitive psychology of epic, ballads, and counting-out rhymes*. New York: Oxford University Press.

Salaman, E. (1982). A collection of moments. In U. Neisser (ed.), *Memory observed: remembering in natural contexts* (pp. 49–63). San Francisco, CA: Freeman.

Salwiczek, L. H., Watanabe, A., and Clayton, N. S. (2010). Ten years of research into avian models of episodic-like memory and its implications for developmental and comparative cognition. *Behavioural Brain Research*, **251**, 221–234.

Schank, R. C. and Abelson, R. P. (1977). Scripts, plan, and knowledge. In P. N. Johnson-Laird and P. C. Wason (eds.), *Thinking: Readings in cognitive science* (pp. 421–435). Cambridge University Press.

Settersten, R. A. and Hägestad, G. O. (1996a). What's the latest? Cultural age deadlines for family transitions. *The Gerontologist*, **36**, 178–188.

(1996b). What's the latest? II. Cultural age deadlines for educational and work transitions. *The Gerontologist*, **36**, 602–613.

Sinclair, S., Hardin, C. D., and Lowery, B. S. (2006). Self-stereotyping in the context of multiple social identities. *Journal of Personality and Social Psychology*, **90**, 529–542.

Taylor, S. E. and Brown, J. D. (1988). Illusion and well-being: a social psychological perspective on mental health. *Psychological Bulletin*, **103**, 193–210.

Thompson, C. P., Skowronski, J. S., Larsen, S. F., and Betz, A. L. (1996). *Autobiographical memory: remembering what and remembering when.* Hillsdale, NJ: Lawrence Erlbaum Associates.

Tolman, E. C. (1951). *Purposive behavior in animals and men.* Berkeley and Los Angeles, CA: University of California Press.

Tomasello, M. (1999). *The cultural origins of human cognition.* Cambridge, MA: Harvard University Press.

Tomasello, M. and Call, J. (1997). *Primate cognition.* New York: Oxford University Press.

Toomey, M. B., Bowman, R., and Woolfenden, G. E. (2007). The effects of social context on the food-caching behavior of Florida scrub-jays (*Aphelocoma coerulescens*). *Ethology*, **113**, 521–527.

Trope, Y. and Liberman, N. (2003). Temporal construal. *Psychological Review*, **110**, 403–421.

Tulving, E. (1972). Episodic and semantic memory. In E. Tulving and W. Donaldson (eds.), *Organisation of memory* (pp. 382–403). London: Academic Press.

(1985). Memory and consciousness. *Canadien Psychology*, **26**, 1–26.

(2002). Episodic memory: from mind to brain. *Annual Review of Psychology*, **53**, 1–25.

Walker, W. R., Skowronski, J. J., and Thompson, C. P. (2003). Life is pleasant – and memory helps to keep it that way! *Review of General Psychology*, **7**, 203–210.

Wang, Q. (2006). Earliest recollections of self and others in European American and Taiwanese young adults. *Psychological Science*, **17**, 708–714.

Warren, H. C. (1916). Mental association from Plato to Hume. *Psychological Review*, **23**, 208–230.

Watkins, O. C. and Watkins, M. J. (1975). Build up of proactive inhibition as a cue-overload effect. *Journal of Experimental Psychology: Human Learning and Memory*, **1**, 442–452.

Wheeler, M. A., Stuss, D. T., and Tulving, E. (1997). Toward a theory of episodic memory: the frontal lobes and autonoetic consciousness. *Psychological Bulletin*, **121**, 331–354.

Williams, J. M. G., Barnhofer, T., Crane, C., Hermans, D., Raes, F., Watkins, E., *et al.* (2007). Autobiographical memory specificity and emotional disorder. *Psychological Bulletin*, **113**, 122–148.

Wilson, A. E. and Ross, M. (2003). The identity function of autobiographical memory: time is on our side. *Memory*, **11**, 137–149.

Zacks, J. M. and Swallow, K. M. (2007). Event segmentation. *Current Directions in Psychological Science*, **16**, 80–84.

Index

Printed in Great Britain
by Amazon.co.uk, Ltd.,
Marston Gate.